DIPLOMACY AND THE FUTURE OF WORLD ORDER

Diplomacy

AND THE FUTURE
OF WORLD ORDER

CHESTER A. CROCKER,
FEN OSLER HAMPSON,
AND PAMELA AALL, EDITORS

GEORGETOWN UNIVERSITY PRESS / WASHINGTON, DC

The publisher is not responsible for third-party websites or their content. URL links were active at time of publication.

Library of Congress Cataloging-in-Publication Data

Names: Crocker, Chester A., editor. | Hampson, Fen Osler, editor. | Aall, Pamela R., editor.
Title: Diplomacy and the future of world order / Chester A. Crocker, Fen Osler Hampson, and Pamela Aall, editors.
Description: Washington, DC : Georgetown University Press, 2021. | Includes bibliographical references and index.
Identifiers: LCCN 2020035282 | ISBN 9781647120931 (hardcover) | ISBN 9781647120948 (paperback) | ISBN 9781647120955 (ebook)
Subjects: LCSH: Diplomacy. | Conflict management. | Peace-building.
Classification: LCC JZ1305 .D54414 2021 | DDC 327.2—dc23
LC record available at https://lccn.loc.gov/2020035282

22 21   9 8 7 6 5 4 3 2   First printing

Printed in the United States of America

CONTENTS

ILLUSTRATIONS

FIGURES

TABLES

FOREWORD

This is a timely and important book about the diplomacy of conflict management and peacemaking. The editors use the term *peace and conflict diplomacy* to describe managing others' conflicts, coping with major power competition in third areas, and dealing with threats to the state system itself. By structuring their discussion around key actors, regions, and functional issues, they illustrate the varied roles that this kind of diplomacy may play in alternative futures for world order—and underscore its significance for the years ahead. Because we do not yet know how events will unfold or how leaders will behave, the book challenges us to imagine a range of possibilities, to grasp the importance of state and regional interactions, and to appreciate the critical role of leaders and leadership.

There are nineteen contributors to this provocative work; thankfully, they do not agree about everything. They note that regions may differ in the way they experience—and shape—the scenarios of world order considered here. But there is a broad consensus on two points: the centrality of human agency, and the role of major states in determining which scenario is realized. These factors will determine the "space" available for the important contributions to peacemaking by international and regional bodies and medium-sized to small states, as well as by civil society and nongovernmental organizations.

Too often, public commentary on world affairs and foreign policy occurs in an all-American echo chamber. Pundits opine on the ups and downs of the United States' global leadership as if there were a widespread if not universal view of it. Commentary tends to oversimplify future global scenarios as the result of US decisions. But this book is different. It posits three potential scenarios for world order, and it evaluates them through the prism of nine regional or bilateral perspectives and four functional ones. Regional perspectives are provided by contributors from those global regions—a welcome feature of this analysis, and one that we at the Carnegie Endowment find very compatible with our own way of doing things.

Today's diplomatic in-box is bursting with both challenges at our doorstep and others just over the horizon—which most diplomats and their bosses would prefer not to think about yet. In recent years, some of these challenges—from the maintenance of alliances to the strengthening of the global arms control regime—have been sadly and dangerously neglected. Others, like multilateral engagement with international institutions, have become a political football in the United States, as other powers leap at the leadership roles that have long been the hallmark of American influence.

Evidently, diplomatic action is needed on many fronts—from coping with the human and economic fallout of the COVID-19 pandemic, to working with partners to address climate change, to countering terrorism. Many of the most difficult and urgent diplomatic challenges occur in conflict environments, as the editors and contributors to this book rightly recognize.

Some have argued that political-military conflicts are yesterday's story, that our "better angels" are winning the struggle for the human soul, and that—in any case—the United States is overcommitted and should refrain from engaging in conflict management. However, my view of history is different. Although diplomatic intervention in conflicts can be sobering and sometimes futile, the costs of disengagement and retrenchment are likewise high. The arguments and analyses assembled by Crocker, Hampson, and Aall find a central place for peace and conflict diplomacy in each of the scenarios examined, even if the outcomes differ sharply. As the contributors lay out clearly in this thoughtful volume, much will depend on whether major powers—including but not limited to the United States—renew habits of diplomatic collaboration, despite their intense competition in many areas, to shape a new and more effective multilateralism in the deeply contested era unfolding before us.

Ambassador William J. Burns
President, Carnegie Endowment for International Peace

ACKNOWLEDGMENTS

Planning for this project began in the fall of 2016, and there are many people to thank for their contributions and advice as we developed the themes and worked with our contributors, many of whom were present for the planning phase. We begin by recognizing the institutions that have supported our work: the Centre for International Governance Innovation (CIGI), Georgetown University, and the US Institute of Peace.

Three workshops played an important role in shaping our thought process throughout the project, and we offer our thanks to the participants in them, some of whom also contributed chapters to the volume. An initial workshop in Washington in June 2017 included Hans Binnendijk, Charles Call, Elizabeth Cousens, David Cunningham, Ashe Jain, Bruce Jones, Oliver Kaplan, Lauren Van Metre, George Moose, Deepa Ollapally, Simon Palamar, Tom Scherer, Jonathan Wilkenfeld, and William Zartman. A second workshop was convened by CIGI in Addis Ababa in February 2018, and we would like to thank the following African and Canadian participants: Yonas Adaye, Lloyd Axworthy, Abdeta Beyene, Solomon Dersso, Alfred Dube, Bushra Ebadi, Mulugeta Gebrehiwot, Mesfin Gebremichael, Paul and Yasemin Heinbecker, Kidane Kiros, Barouk Mesfin, Abdul Mohamed, Sunday Okello Angoma, Tigist Yeshiwas, and Fana WeldeSenbet.

In May 2019, with CIGI's support, we convened a workshop in Middleburg, Virginia, to review first drafts of chapters and a number of authors joined in person. We wish to thank the following individuals who also joined this meeting and offered important comments and suggestions: Bathsheba Crocker, Len Edwards, Patricia Kim, Alvaro de Soto, and Paul Stronski.

We are also indebted to the support of research assistance from graduate students Christopher Anthony, Rami Ayyub, Miriam Frost, and Simon Palamar, who played multiple roles in the process. Carol Bonnett, Brenda Woods, and Simon Palamar provided invaluable administrative and research support.

We are especially indebted to Don Jacobs of Georgetown University Press for his consistently candid and constructive feedback and encouragement of the project, and to the press's staff members for their excellent work.

PART I

Peace and Conflict Diplomacy in the Current International Environment

CHAPTER 1

A Challenging Time for Peace
and Conflict Diplomacy

Chester A. Crocker, Fen Osler Hampson, and Pamela Aall

We believe in disarmament but must arm to the teeth in order to discourage others from taking advantage of us. We wish to see disputes settled in a legal and orderly way, but we confront forces that want not to change the existing law but to substitute an entirely different legal and political order. We want to use our national and economic resources constructively, but must expend them prodigally on a technical race of essentially military hardware. . . . In the main, it is no wonder that people both at home and abroad are confused about American motives and American actions. (Bloomfield 1959, 3–4)

As Lincoln Bloomfield observed sixty years ago, the practice of peace and conflict diplomacy has long been a complex activity. Although diplomacy is often seen as fluid and adaptable, changing to address evolving circumstances, there have been rules and expectations that governed diplomacy in the past. Diplomacy took place between countries or other official bodies and engaged the elite. With few exceptions, envoys in a conflict situation were granted immunity and offered protection by the belligerents, valued by all sides for their ability to gather intelligence and pass messages. Much diplomacy was bilateral and involved the envoy of one ruler visiting the ruler(s) of the opposing side (Meerts 2015). At other times, however, a number of rulers joined together in larger diplomatic undertakings to form alliances, end wars, or agree on new rules that led to systemic change, as the European states did in 1648 with the treaties enshrined in the Peace of Westphalia. Implementation in this case was guaranteed by implied threat—a country that did not honor the agreement was liable to retaliation by an alliance of countries on the other side. The Peace of Westphalia, of course, was an elite agreement. The obligation to consult stakeholders in these reorganizations was not considered a priority—or, perhaps more accurately, was not considered at all.

Peace and conflict diplomacy retains some of the features of traditional diplomacy. It is, for instance, often conducted by elites in closed settings. However, it has also expanded to meet changing needs, particularly in the area of mediation, a type of third-party-assisted negotiations to resolve conflicts. Today, peace and conflict diplomacy takes many forms—bilateral diplomacy, multilateral negotiations, public diplomacy, facilitation, mediation, and other activities. It has expanded beyond the realm of governments and official bodies to include people-to-people programs and cultural exchange. Nongovernmental and civil society organizations are also late-twentieth-century and early-twenty-first-century elements of the current diplomatic sphere, both as participants in peace processes and as advocates for change.

WHAT IS PEACE AND CONFLICT DIPLOMACY?

We use the term *peace and conflict diplomacy* as an overarching phrase, shorthand for a number of activities that states, international organizations, and civil society groups employ to make peace and manage conflict. These activities range from negotiation, mediation, and facilitation to peacekeeping and humanitarian intervention and, though related, are different from each other in their objectives and in their implementation. The term highlights the fact that diplomacy in the twenty-first century is not simply what one observer has referred to as "the art of high-level engagement across national bodies, i.e., government to government," but also a process characterized by the involvement of intergovernmental, nonstate, civil society actors who are key players in the management and resolution of conflict (Schomerus 2017). There are three dimensions of peace and conflict diplomacy:

- Diplomatic strategies to cope with / manage other people's conflicts—for example, in Cyprus, South Sudan, Colombia, and Kashmir.
- Strategies for dealing with and regulating the actual or potential conflicts of interests among major powers themselves in third areas, such as North Korea, Ukraine, Syria, and the South China Sea.
- Strategies for coping with challenges to the governance of existing states and societies of the international system and from transnational threats such as piracy and terrorism.

Peace and conflict diplomacy is about the capacity of states and institutions to maintain stability in turbulent zones and order among themselves while working together to stem challenges to the wider global community. The practice of peace and conflict diplomacy includes negotiation, mediation, coercive diplomacy (i.e., sanctions and deterrence), intervention, peacekeeping, peacebuilding, and building capacity for resolving differences through discussion and political action rather than violence. Too often, these individual approaches are framed as being mutually exclusive, especially in debates between realist and liberal scholars about the relationship between force and diplomacy. As experience shows, however, both kinds of statecraft or diplomacy are required and the real challenge is to develop and employ them in a structure of pragmatic principles tailored to the situation at hand.

Diplomacy vis-à-vis peace and conflict management has changed in response to its environment. Toward the end of the Cold War and for some months thereafter, lessened contention between the United States and the USSR led to cooperative engagement in winding down regional conflicts—Afghanistan, Angola / South Africa / Namibia, El Salvador, and Cambodia. In the early 1990s, the outbreak or expansion of civil wars in Africa, Central America, Southeast Asia, and other places led to a dramatic increase in the number of UN-led efforts to end violence and mediate a negotiated settlement to civil wars. But UN reverses in Somalia, Rwanda, and Bosnia led to a phase of sober reflection about military intervention. Then the cycle turned again, as seen in the uptick in robust action in East Timor, Kosovo, and the Democratic Republic of Congo. Negotiation and mediation produced impressive results due to increased cooperation and engagement in ending conflicts in Peru/Ecuador, Bosnia, Northern Ireland, Burundi, Liberia, and Sierra Leone.

During this period, peace and conflict diplomacy was often used in conjunction with military intervention. Diplomatic engagement to end conflict—efforts to tamp down the violence, get to the table, find negotiable issues, define an area for mutual agreement—rarely worked without the threat or use of force. However, peace and conflict diplomacy has also advanced its knowledge about sources of soft power leverage to aid in peaceful settlements of conflict, as the global community refined its sanctions policies and learned to work together to put pressure on conflict parties.

A CHANGING PRACTICE

A snapshot of the current environment presents a different picture, and a challenging one for peace and conflict diplomacy. International polarization on critical issues regarding human rights, state sovereignty, and the appropriate role of the international community presents serious obstacles to peace and conflict diplomacy. Tensions between Russia, China, and the West are high, and the consequences of this polarization have played out both on the ground in Syria and at the United Nations.

Competing national priorities also affect the types of diplomacy in which states are willing to engage. For example, military campaigns to counter violent extremism and radicalization in conflicts such as those in Iraq, Syria, Libya, and Afghanistan have overshadowed diplomatic efforts to help warring parties reach negotiated settlements over their differences.

The transnational threat posed by al-Qaeda and the Islamic State in Iraq and the Levant (ISIS) network, and the ability of these groups to launch terrorist attacks far from their bases of power, introduced a model of conflict different from the one we have dealt with over the past forty years. Another challenge is the proliferation of NSAs as negotiating parties. The NSAs may share a common goal but have very different negotiating positions and experience a good deal of hostility toward each other. The opposition parties in Syria shared the goal of overthrowing Syrian president Bashir Assad but could not agree on much else. The challenges of developing a negotiable agenda have always been difficult, with much time spent on deciding what is on and off the agenda. In these new circumstances, setting a negotiating agenda has been beyond the reach of all involved in the process. How does diplomacy have to change in order to engage effectively with these nonstate actors, including those cases where the NSAs are identified as terrorists by the United Nations, the United States, or other powerful entities?

Another challenge for current diplomacy is to make room for diverse voices while promoting a sense of unity and common purpose for the effort. International donors and peacemakers increasingly recognize that inclusion is critical to enduring settlements and have made efforts to bring in previously underrepresented groups, including women and young people, into peace negotiations. In addition, civil society has become a more active participant in peace and conflict work over the past thirty years. International nongovernmental organizations and local civil society organizations participate both as independent entities promoting political, social, and economic development and as implementing partners for outside donor programs. Another change in the conflict environment has been the development of new media. Social media and the twenty-four-hour news cycle allow people who are directly affected by the negotiations to voice their support or opposition; they also allow pressure groups and interested parties from outside the affected sphere to try to shape the negotiations (Fletcher 2016).

Dealmaking in private between world leaders may still be an option in closed systems; but in open or partially open societies, peace and conflict diplomacy is subject to domestic and international scrutiny. Although the representation of diverse points of view is very important to the outcome of any agreement, the proliferation of voices makes developing a unified negotiating position difficult for the dealmakers—that is, for the governments and institutions that purport to represent those diverse points of view. In addition, the inconsistency of domestic support for global engagement and the rise in populism make long-term commitments to mediation much more difficult in democratic states, as other national priorities take precedence over third-party work in faraway lands.

Diplomacy vis-à-vis conflict has usually been associated with peace talks and negotiation for conflict prevention or resolution, but diplomacy is also part of the conflict itself. As is often the case, antagonists fight and talk at the same time. For instance, in the civil war in Sudan, negotiations between the north and the south continued throughout many decades of violent conflict, as each party tried to gain the upper hand both through fighting and through talking.

The habitual targeting of civilians in current conflicts and the resulting floods of refugees have also led to the development of humanitarian diplomacy, because organizations such as the International Committee of the Red Cross are required to negotiate for humanitarian access with governments as well as to negotiate the rules of the road and bargain over resources with other humanitarians and with official donors. Humanitarian diplomacy contains elements of traditional diplomacy and advocacy but differs from both in its desire to balance "impartial and neutral humanitarian operations on the ground with equally neutral, impartial, and effective humanitarian advocacy in the corridors of power and on the global street" (Slim 2019, 67).

FRAMING THE QUESTIONS

Is the space for peace and conflict diplomacy shrinking in this environment? There is some evidence that it is not, particularly in the increasing activity of regional organizations in this space; cooperation to combat global pandemics such as SARS, Ebola, and COVID-19; and also increased attention to mediation at the United Nations. However, the evidence that the space is shrinking is compelling, as seen by the retreat or retrenchment of great powers from peacemaking, attacks on elements of the liberal rules-based order, the increased reliance on military solutions, and the challenges facing

UN peacekeeping and growing polarization of the UN Security Council. A "sovereign backlash" in Russia, Poland, Hungary, Italy, and Austria, and the rise of nationalist parties in Brazil, the Philippines, India, and other parts of the world, have also placed limits on third-party initiatives.

Is peace and conflict diplomacy effective? Here, the picture is more balanced. There have been a number of successes: for instance, the Joint Comprehensive Plan of Action for Iran, the Paris climate accord, the Colombia peace process, and the European Union's management of the Kosovo/Serbia split. Resurgent sovereignty, however, has swept away commitments to joint international action, big states increasingly assert their right to do as they like, and successful peacekeeping or military victories often lack a political context and do not often lead to durable political outcomes. In the Middle East, problem-solving diplomacy is easily eclipsed by the instinct to polarize relationships along national or confessional lines. More generally, relations between states and their societies are under stress in both the Global South and Global North.

Major states and institutions involved in peace and conflict diplomacy have grown wary of military intervention using force—particularly boots on the ground—in support of the effort. Can international actors develop means to persuade or pressure parties to sign a peace settlement without resorting to force, and if so, what are those means? Perhaps more important, can international and regional actors improve their competence in making connections between the application of military power and the quest for legitimate political solutions? The case of Libya bears eloquent testimony to this issue.

A consensus on the aims of peace and conflict diplomacy has broken down. If in the current climate, nation building is off the menu, there is little accord on what should replace it. Consequently, conflict zones are hosts to many different kinds of programs—for instance, countering violent extremism, ensuring stability, building local capacity and resilience—without an overarching framework to give these activities definition and direction. Although there is considerable lip service paid to the issue of governance, the ways that local conflict management and resolution mechanisms can be nurtured to promote pluralism, inclusivity, and tolerance in nondemocratic societies are less well understood. What options are available to diplomats and conflict management practitioners to build collaboration among third-party actors in order to bring coherence to peace and conflict negotiations? How can collective conflict management emerge out of the discordant international environment?

Finally, there is little agreement on who should be the main agents of peace and conflict diplomacy. Diplomacy, once the purview of major states and the United Nations, has been delegated to others and distributed around the international system. Regional organizations, civil society organizations, and private peacemaking efforts have taken up the challenge and become much more active in the peace and diplomacy arena. At times, local or regional organizations are the first responders in a crisis situation, with outside actors engaging only when invited by the local or regional body. How does the presence of multiple actors affect peace and conflict diplomacy? What are the consequences of gatekeepers guarding access to the conflict, especially if they have their own agendas or if their lack of capacity to be coherent and competent may in fact exacerbate the problem?

FOCUS OF THE BOOK

The aim of this book is to develop thinking about these questions; as a consequence, its potential scope is very wide. Chapters 1 through 3, which constitute part I of the book, give an overview of the current international environment for peace and conflict diplomacy and define the scope. However, in an effort to narrow the book's focus and to encourage a comparative aspect among the chapters, we asked the authors to give us their thoughts on three possible scenarios for the future. Scenario 1 captures a return to a world of geopolitical contestation at the global and regional levels, in which each sovereign state would look only to protecting its own interests. Scenario 2 envisions a return to a liberal international order, in which the welfare of individual states and organizations would be defined in terms of larger common interests and goals. And scenario 3 describes a world of ad hoc, outcome-oriented temporary arrangements between states and organizations, concentrating on solving problems but not on changing the international order.

Chapter 2 recognizes that all three scenarios may operate with differing degrees of salience at the same time globally and/or regionally. It also recognizes that though many believe that the period of liberal international order was open, democratic, and characterized by a general respect for a rules-based approach, major powers continued to dominate and to act in their own interests when it suited them rather than subordinating themselves to the interests of the global community. Even in this period, peace and conflict diplomacy furthered the agenda of the most powerful players because the world did not operate entirely on the basis of either realist or liberal principles.

Jean-Marie Guéhenno reflects on this idea in chapter 3 on international organization perspectives on the instruments of diplomacy and conflict management. The chapter examines the effect of the decline of international cooperation and the rise of nationalism on international organizations' capacity to play a productive role in peace and conflict diplomacy. Many observers believe these factors have marginalized international organizations, especially the United Nations, as the world returns to a Cold War–like order. Guéhenno points out, however, that the current environment differs significantly from the bipolar Cold War, particularly in the growth of multipolarity, as Russia, China, the United States, and Europe follow different and often opposing paths, and regional powers strengthen their own positions through alliances or through regional institutions. This multipolarity makes the world more complex, but it also opens up space for other players, including international and regional organizations, to continue to have significant roles in regional or global security.

Regional Perspectives

In designing this book, we thought it essential to review the major questions and potential answers from the perspective of various regions. Part II of the book, which comprises chapters 4 through 12, captures views from the United States, South and Central America, Russia, Europe, South Asia, Southeast Asia, China, Africa, and the Middle East.

Chapter 4, by Hans Binnendijk, on US peace and conflict diplomacy in a state-centric world, examines the abiding role of states in shaping peace and conflict activity. He reviews ten cases of international peacebuilding from 1993 to 2018, and finds that in most examples, the United States and other states retained their central role and were critical to the successful termination of conflict or settlement of differences. Interestingly, international organizations, though not central players in conflict termination, played significant roles in facilitating the negotiation and implementation of agreements that followed the cease-fires. Binnendijk also looks ahead to the types of issues that will challenge global peace and security, and he concludes that US leadership is essential to their resolution. Without renewed American commitment to resolving international security problems, he fears that the "concert of nation-states" that might arise in its stead will fall prey to interstate squabbling and lose direction and the will to act. However, he argues that "with strong global leadership, the United States and its democratic allies can still rescue the opportunity to collaborate on the management of these problems."

A central theme is the importance of decisions made by powerful nations. In chapter 7, Marco Tourinho notes, for instance, that the ongoing antagonism between the United States and Venezuela has affected Latin America's network of conflict management institutions, causing competition between the Organization of American States (which includes the United States as a member) and the Union of South American Nations (which does not). In chapter 9, Shadi Hamid also zeroes in on the American role in shaping events in the Middle East. He remarks that the decline of US peace and conflict diplomacy in the region and increase in the politicization of US policies fuels regional polarization. If, as he suggests, steady engagement is vital for helping countries in conflict overcome their differences and engage in political dialogue, the inconsistency of US engagement in the Middle East can only hurt the process.

Turning to Europe, in chapter 5 Ana Palacio notes that the perceived Russian threat to that continent both animates the European Union's peace and conflict diplomacy efforts and reveals its weaknesses. The European Union's overtures to Ukraine in 2014 represented a clear attempt to bring Ukraine into the European family of nations, broadening the gap between Russia and its former satellite. The Russians reacted by annexing Crimea; and despite outcries against the behavior, the European Union has been able to do little to counter this action. Palacio reiterates, however, that the paralysis in this situation should be juxtaposed with the achievements in peace and conflict diplomacy that Europe has made: over fifty years of peace in Europe's heartland, a strong drive toward democracy in Southern Europe, and a powerful force in Eastern Europe's peaceful transitions since the end of the Cold War. The European Union offered a living laboratory for liberal democracy to develop in the more permissive post–Cold War period. However, times have changed. In order to remain relevant to peace and conflict diplomacy in the new international environment, Palacio concludes that "it must recognize its limitations and play to its strengths," including providing regional security through its role in development and governance.

Stability in South Asia, particularly in the conflict between India and Pakistan, depends on great power engagement, according to chapter 10, by Kanti Bajpai: "Given the deep differences in South Asia, periodic extremist attacks on India by groups based in Pakistan, and the presence of nuclear weapons, great power efforts to manage deterrence and crises and to get Pakistan to curb violent Islamists are the most viable diplomatic interventions." However, this would require a careful balancing act on the part of the great powers in order to avoid taking sides and to encourage the two parties to settle differences diplomatically. It is an area where the United States and China share an interest in tamping down conflict; perhaps this shared goal would be enough to effect a pragmatic cooperation over the conflict in Kashmir and lessen the possibility of a nuclear conflagration between India and Pakistan. If this were to happen, it would provide an example of interest-based cooperation between the United States and China in one sphere (India-Pakistan) while tensions continue at a high level in others.

Increasing polarization and antagonism between and among major powers cast shadows over other regions. In chapter 11 See Seng Tan cites many instances in which tensions between the United States and China affected negotiations within the Association of Southeast Asian Nations (ASEAN) Regional Forum as well as efforts between ASEAN and China to develop a "code of conduct" to guide actions in the South China Sea. Tan focuses on the institutional capacity of the Southeast Asia region to achieve conflict prevention, one of its primary goals, an activity led by ASEAN and its partners in the ASEAN Defense Ministers Plus grouping. He concludes that "absent ASEAN, it is questionable that any Asia-Pacific arrangement comanaged by the great powers would automatically fare better than an ASEAN-led one, especially in the present era of great power rivalry and discord."

In chapter 8 on Africa, Solomon Ayele Dersso also reflects a concern about great power polarization playing out on the continent, especially as China and Russia expand their economic interests and engage on a continent-wide basis on topics related to peace and conflict. However, also worrisome for Africa is the opposite reaction—the global indifference and disengagement that the continent experienced in the immediate post–Cold War period. Countering the effects of the withdrawal of outside engagement was a motivating factor in the strengthening of the African peace and security architecture since the 1990s. It has also shored up ties with external players—largely the United Nations and the European Union—in a symbiotic relationship. As Dersso remarks, these ties reflect "that the international order cannot on its own and without support from regional mechanisms effectively address peace and security challenges, [and] they are also predicated on the recognition of the APSA [African Peace and Security Architecture] as a regional arrangement anchored in and complementary to the international collective security order."

Chapters 6 and 12, which attempt to explain what lies behind the polarization between China and the United States, and between Russia and the West present quite different scenarios. In chapter 12 Chas Freeman describes China's challenge to the United States as largely economic in origin but stresses that a poorly executed US response will expand the arena in which the two countries vie for global predominance. Russia's much smaller economy does not present a direct threat to US economic interests, but its ability to "disrupt," in Dmitri Trenin's word in chapter 6, makes it into a powerful rival.

Both countries challenge the American preeminence that emerged after the end of the Cold War, but through different means. China has taken a strong interest in UN peacekeeping, as Lise Howard's documents in chapter 13, and its other multilateral connections are growing stronger. Russia, conversely, is becoming more isolated. In Trenin's words, "One of the most popular quotations in today's Russia is that the country 'has only two friends in the world, its army and its navy.'"

Nevertheless, there are similarities. Both countries are strong defenders of state sovereignty. Trenin notes that sovereignty "tops the list of state values." Freeman's discussion of Taiwan emphasizes the high stakes at play for China (and the United States) in a peaceful resolution of this issue, pointing out that "the People's Republic is the only nuclear-armed power whose frontiers are challenged by the United States." The primacy of sovereignty as a political value translates into a reluctance to interfere in the internal matters of other states, and this of course has had a significant impact on the peace and conflict diplomacy of all international bodies. Both Trenin and Freeman emphasize differences in perceptions between the United States, Russia, and China. The United States considers the Chinese political system as illegitimate; the Chinese view the United States as ineffective. The United States considers Russian activities over Crimea to be offensive, while Russia considers them a defensive move against Western expansion into its former spheres of influence. These two factors—a difference over core values and a difference in perception—underscore what Freeman terms a lack of empathy between the United States and its two rivals. Without this empathy, the hostility between these powerful nations will continue to undermine peace and conflict diplomacy around the world.

Functional Perspectives

In this review, certain functional issues merited a closer look, not because they were front-page news but because they each had a strong potential to explode into conflict. In part III of the book, which comprises chapters 13 through 16, we focus on the challenges for peacekeeping, nuclear nonproliferation, the struggle for digital dominance, and terrorism. These functional chapters reflect the effects of global discord and polarization but also uncover a few areas where collaboration continues to occur, particularly in the areas of peacekeeping, nonproliferation, and fighting terrorism.

In chapter 13 Lise Morjé Howard reminds us that the international community has collaborated over peacekeeping for decades, even as relationships in other arenas have broken down. Recent studies have confirmed peacekeeping's contribution to peace and security. Despite its successes, however, peacekeeping has been hampered by a lack of resources behind ambitious mandates and by a hint of colonial residue between developing and developed countries, as the donors have shown a reluctance to provide troops, leaving that dangerous work to poorer countries. In recent years, there has been a change in this picture, as China has increased its efforts in the peacekeeping area, providing both funding and personnel. This positive outcome may have consequences for the transition to more free and open societies. As Howard notes, under Chinese leadership, UN peacekeeping will be strengthened "as long as everyone else is willing to go along with Chinese terms" or, in other words, a tendency to privilege sovereignty and stability over the introduction of liberal values.

In chapter 15, Stacie Hoffmann, Samantha Bradshaw, and Emily Taylor explore a different functional area in which the US-Chinese relationship affects global security. The chapter provides an illustration of how changes in technological advances—in this case cyberspace—could threaten peace and security and open up new battlefields among the powerful states. The authors point out that the struggle to control the development of 5G is not just over corporate profit. It is also about national security, power, control, and sovereignty, and is complicated by the fact that this conflict is taking place at a moment when the rules of the road in the area are just being or not yet written. The irony is that this technology, which contributes to faster communication and better connectivity and should be facilitating global understanding among all parts of the world, is now a hot-button issue in the deteriorating relationship between the United States and China. Lowering the levels of international tension over this sector will require the development of new norms and principles of behavior among the community of nations.

Nuclear diplomacy has had a robust history of collaboration in the post–World War II period, as the United States and the then Soviet Union worked together to create, in Toby Dalton's words in chapter 14, a nuclear order—"an arrangement of states and institutions in the international system based on beliefs about the relationship between nuclear technology and international political power." That order is now fraying, and Dalton identifies a number of trends that may threaten it, including relations between the United States, China, and Russia as well as relations between the United States and its key allies. He also notes changes in institutional capacity that will have an impact, including shifts in the governance procedures of the multilateral nonproliferation institutions and the rise of Russian and Chinese state-owned enterprises' engagement in nuclear technology. Another set of problems is the lowering barriers to entry into the nuclear enrichment field as the technology becomes more common and norms against nuclear proliferation weaken. Finally, he remarks on the on-again/off-again impact that civil society has had on shaping public attitudes and governmental policies toward nuclear issues. His recommendations for strengthening nuclear diplomacy include considering whether the "consensus principle that beleaguers diplomacy in several institutional contexts" could be relaxed, and for greater participation of civil society in supporting the nonproliferation order and its norms.

In chapter 16 Daniel Benjamin tackles transnational terrorism, the final issue of the book. He identifies several factors that make this chronic problem increasingly global in its expression: bad governance, repressive societies, economic stagnation, state weakness, intercommunal tension, and resource scarcity. However, he also points out that the response to terrorism since the terrorist attacks of September 11, 2001, has been notable for its strong international cooperation and for its accomplishments. The model has combined elements of collaboration that were seen as a characteristic of the liberal world order and interest-based cooperation. He believes that this cooperation will continue to exist in the future, whether it features strengthened states or a more ad hoc joining together of forces, because "counterterrorism cooperation is insulated in a way few other forms of multilateral cooperation are—a reflection of the unusual nature of the international counterterrorism architecture."

Conclusion

This book features multiple forward-looking scenarios and explores their diplomatic implications in the context of multiple regions and a range of cross-cutting issue areas. As we note in concluding chapter 17, these authors do not necessarily agree on the extent to which scenario trends will be synchronized across regions and issues, and they emphasize that our scenarios will spill into each other at various times and places. In Kanti Bajpai's words, "International order is unlikely to be a flat, homogeneous space but rather an undulating one, varying by the mix of realism, liberalism, and functionalism across space, time, and issue area." Many contributions to this volume remind us that the current international order is characterized by contradictory trends, with clear signs of continued capacity for collaborative peace and conflict diplomacy mixing with the reassertion of state sovereignty. This resurgent sovereignty is in some ways more virulent than in the last century, when states were prepared to negotiate and limit the significance of sovereign boundaries. The "new" sovereignty is defensive, nationalistic, and driven by populism. It is generally resistant to various forms of interstate cooperation, especially in multilateral institutions, and it is able to circumscribe the activities of nonstate actors that are engaged in peace and conflict diplomacy.

Counteracting the deleterious effects of this new sovereignty will require that international institutions, individual states, and civil society develop new ways of resolving problems together. As we argue, if it is to be effective, the diplomacy of conflict management will need to be pragmatic and driven less by ideology or the cardinal tenets of some predesigned "grand strategy" but instead by the art and science of what the political scientist Charles Lindblom called "muddling through." Muddling through, however, should not be mistaken for stumbling or bumbling along. Rather, as we explain in greater detail in chapter 2, it is a brand of diplomacy that is informed by a heightened awareness of political uncertainty and a clear recognition that international cooperation with the like-minded—and sometimes the un-like-minded— may be required to develop innovative solutions to new problems.

In other words, in today's world, we do not always have the luxury of choosing who our fellow travelers will be when it comes to addressing major global security and diplomatic challenges. We will need to look to improvised solutions and make frequent midcourse corrections as we adapt our strategies and approaches to addressing problems in a shifting geopolitical landscape, especially when new problems and challenges are thrust upon us. This new kind of diplomacy also requires major state leaders to invest heavily in their diplomatic relationships and political systems to generate leaders with the ability and vision to do so.

CHAPTER 2

Grasping Global Problems
by Root or by Branch

Chester A. Crocker, Fen Osler Hampson,
and Pamela Aall

Diplomacy in pursuit of peace and security is under pressure from a number of corners. We may emerge from this period with strengthened sovereign states or strengthened global institutions or somewhere in between. In this chapter, we explore the potential for and constraints on "peace and conflict diplomacy" as we approach the third decade of the twenty-first century in a system marked by increasing turbulence at the interstate level and within states.

DIFFERENT SCENARIOS

It is clear that some international relations scholars have become futurologists as they offer their prognosis about the nature of international politics and the direction in which systemic change is headed. We join them in this chapter, describing three possible scenarios for the global environment that will shape peace and conflict diplomacy in the future. These contending views about the future are based on different theoretical assumptions about the nature of the international system and its evolutionary path. In presenting these alternative scenarios about the future, we aim not so much to rehash these existing theories or perspectives on the evolving international order as to tease out what each set of predictions would mean for the future and for the practice of peace and conflict diplomacy.

Scenario 1: A Realist's View—A More Dangerous World of Nationalistic and Assertive States

The world may be dominated by nationalistic sovereign states, raising the possibility of more competition and discord in international relations as they try to maximize their own gains. In this "discord" scenario, there is growing potential for interstate conflict and competitive interstate relations with changing power balances in the international system.

A powerful statement of hegemonic war theory, or "offensive realism," is Graham Allison's book *Destined for War* (Allison 2017).[1] Allison argues that the rise of China, coupled with the relative decline of the United States, is increasing the risks of direct military confrontation between the two powers. According to Allison, the pattern we see today of growing great power competition during a period of hegemonic transition is a familiar one, going back centuries to the days of Athenian rule in the eastern Mediterranean. Although hegemonic war theory or offensive realism has strong deterministic overtones, war is not "inevitable" if states act prudently and exercise what Henry Kissinger once called "the necessity for choice" (Kissinger 1984).

Offensive realists typically focus on the strategic diplomatic challenges of deterrence and compellence. These challenges revolve around how to calibrate the instruments of coercion, which include the use of sanctions and military force, to deter an adversary from doing something it might want to do, but also to force an adversary to give up or relinquish something it has already done (e.g., China's assertion of territorial claims in the South China Sea by building military bases on coral reefs and islands) (Lewis and Litai 2016). Compellence, as noted by Thomas Schelling many years ago, is the much tougher of the two because the action in question has already taken place, but that does not mean deterrence itself is easy (Schelling 1966). Offensive realists worry about the dangers of not being tough enough with clever adversaries, like Chamberlain with Hitler at Munich, who can dupe a more conciliatory (or naive) adversary (Mearsheimer 2014; Kaplan 2012).

However, there is an active debate between offensive realists as to whether Russia or China poses the greatest threat to global stability. For Allison, it is China, which is a rising power economically and politically, a country whose actions in the South China Sea, for example, bespeak its growing military and economic power and assertiveness under the leadership of President Xi Jinping. For power cycle theorists, like Charles Doran (2012), declining hegemons, like Russia, are more the dangerous adversary. This is evidenced in Russian incursions into Eastern Ukraine, the seizure of the Crimea, continuous probes along the northern flanks of NATO and in the Arctic, meddling in elections and sophisticated propaganda and dis-information campaigns, the poisoning of foreign spies and dissidents, and growing influence in the Middle East, where it has backed Assad's brutal and murderous regime in Syria with its air power and other forms of support. All point to a Russia that is asserting its power and influence beyond its borders.

For classical realists, who assert the primacy of national interest over ide-ology or "values," political strategy during periods of hegemonic transition requires not just the maintenance of robust military and deterrent capabil-ities but also the proper care and feeding of alliance partners so that they remain strong and durable and do not invite predatory behavior by rival powers that will try to wean those partners away or (less subtly) threaten them into submission (Morgenthau 1951; Lebow 2003).

One of the important lessons in Thucydides' account of the Pelopon-nesian wars is that Athens' clear failure to properly manage its diplomatic rela-tions with its alliance partners as well as its relations with smaller, independent states exacerbated its demise (Waelchli and Shah 1994). Athens' bullying tac-tics—for example, against small states like Melos—undermined not only its own soft power democratic credentials but also the strength and legitimacy of its own alliance. One of the main tenets of offensive realism in today's world is that going it alone is not a viable, long-term strategy for great powers because they need to maintain strong alliances and healthy relations with other pivotal states vis-à-vis their great power competitors (Lynch 2018a).

Defensive realism, the other main variant of realist theory, points to another set of growing risks in the international system (Glaser 2010, 2011). In nationalist sovereign states led by strong executives, the main motivations for defensive realism are self-preservation and protection. Defensive realists believe that states generally seek to conserve and preserve their power. In a defensive realist frame of reference, though states should recognize that all states have national survival instincts, they should commit themselves to maintaining the balance-of-power status quo and not go out of their way to provoke rivals by taking preemptive military action (Van Evera 1999).

Defensive realists typically view situations of strategic rivalry in terms of reassurance and tempering the insecurities arising from misperception and security dilemmas, where actions ostensibly taken for defensive purposes are mistaken by adversaries as being offensive in nature (Jervis 1976, 1978). For defensive realists, the Anglo-German arms race that preceded World War I or Japan's fears in the 1930s that its economy would be strangled by an oil embargo are historical examples of the dangers of provocation. Some defensive realists stress the importance of developing confidence-building measures and other institutional innovations to foster dialogue, communication, and trust between strategic rivals. Others point to the use of controlled strategies of "offshore balancing," selective engagement, or "soft balancing" as the path to conserving state power and securing global stability (Layne 1997; Art 2013; Paul 2005). These are not necessarily mutually exclusive options, however.

Elites play a critical role in some defensive realist theory and can be driven to make imprudent choices either by exaggerating external threats and promoting expansionist policies or retracting state power by focusing inordinately on domestic concerns (Christensen 1996; Schweller 2006). In other words, defensive realists worry about the growing dangers of strategic miscalculation in a world where domestic, populist pressures and nationalism are in the ascendancy. These include both democratic and authoritarian states where new social and economic pressures threaten to challenge the primacy of ruling elites unless they exert strong social and political control by appealing to atavistic, nationalist sentiments (Judis 2016; Clover 2017; Gries 2005).

Defensive realists do not see periods of hegemonic transition as inevitably leading to conflict to the same degree as offensive realists. But they do point to the dangers of populist pressures that can drive elites to exaggerate external threats or, the opposite, to understate the risks of diplomatic and military withdrawal or retrenchment, especially when a state is experiencing relative decline vis-à-vis other powers in the international system (Layne 2006a, 2006b).

Some defensive realists look askance at the populism-driven policies of the Trump administration, though not all defensive realists agree (Rogin 2018; Walt 2018; Schweller 2018). By seeking to avoid foreign entanglements and withdrawing US troops, particularly in the Middle East and Afghanistan, Trump is hunkering down and retracting US power and influence. However, because of the United States' abstention from strategic commitments that require common and/or cooperative action, defensive realists foresee dangers of political exploitation and manipulation by America's strategic rivals, notably Russia and China (Pillsbury 2015).

Similarly, Trump's efforts to engage North Korea through his highly personalized and idiosyncratic diplomacy may also be laying the seeds for greater confusion and strategic miscalculation as North Korea and the United States blow hot and cold about a peace process that has raised unrealistic expectations on both sides about the timetable for a denuclearized Korean Peninsula or eventual US military withdrawal (Wright 2019).

Defensive realists also point to the growing dangers of strategic miscalculation in regional dyadic rivalries, notably those between India and Pakistan,

Israel and Iran, and Saudi Arabia and Iran (Motwani 2018; Yusuf 2018; Tre-viño 2013; Mabon 2018; Lacey 2010). These risks may be compounded by a combination of great power withdrawal and manipulation of these conflicts by external powers that are seeking to project their power globally.

For defensive realists, the path to securing global stability lies in a dual policy of credible deterrence that is coupled with the effective diplomacy of reassurance, especially in the policies of great powers. However, defensive realists are less sanguine about the ability of political elites to maintain this equilibrium in the current political environment, when populism and nationalism are the main drivers of foreign and security policy.

Scenario 2: Liberal Internationalism—Strengthened Global Institutions

According to liberal international relations scholars, the postwar liberal international order that was spun out of the Bretton Woods institutions and the United Nations has fundamentally tempered the dangerous pathologies of an anarchical international system of sovereign states (Deudney and Ikenberry 1999). Scenario 2 posits that this state of affairs will continue into the future.

Liberals believe that the presence of global institutions in a complex, interdependent world will likely mean continued collaboration among states, even with the weakening of US hegemony (Ikenberry 2018). However, this collaboration scenario can take a variety of different forms. It may see a countervailing resurgence of liberal internationalism in the form of global liberal social networks, which go beyond the nation-state (Adler 1997, 2004; Ikenberry 2009; Nye 2017; Richmond 2012). Alternatively, it might see a world dominated by liberal democratic states that act together more cohesively than they do now (Daalder and Lindsay 2007; Ikenberry and Slaughter 2006; Kagan 2008; Archibugi 2008).

Regional institutions provide further cement for the foundations of the liberal international order. Notwithstanding some of its current Brexit and other difficulties, the European Union is one of the noblest experiments in promoting economic and political cooperation, democracy, and integration among its members (Drozdiak 2017; Piris 2011). In Latin America and Africa, regional organizations have also played an important role in preventing or managing threats to regional stability (Wallensteen 2014). There has also been a corresponding effort by leading members of these institutions to strengthen the norms, rules, and responsibilities under which these institutions operate and function.

Although we are still a long way from having a Kantian-style world league of democratic states, Kant's proposition that democratic states are less likely to go to war against each other when they have conflicts of interest nonetheless holds true for liberal internationalists.[2] Since the overthrow of Portugal's dictatorial regime in April 1974, the number of democracies in the world has multiplied dramatically, from roughly 40 countries to 122 electoral democracies (roughly 60 percent). To be sure, there are wide variations in the nature (and depth) of democracy in these countries, and the dangers of recidivism loom large, as Freedom House (2018) warns in its annual democracy index. However, liberals like to remind us that if we take the long view, "the share of the world population living in democracies [has] increased continuously [since the nineteenth century;] . . . [today] more than every second person in the world lives in a democracy" (Roser 2013).

Liberal scholars also view the globalization of trade and investment as a generally positive force for peace. When the British economist and Nobel laureate Norman Angell forecast in his book *The Great Illusion* that the forces of globalization would inevitably create a more peaceful world, he was not wrong, just perhaps fifty or sixty years too early with his forecast. "Commercial development," he wrote, "is broadly illustrating one profound truth: that the real basis of social morality is self-interest. If the subject of rivalry between nations is business, the code which has come to dominate business must necessarily come to dominate the conduct of governments" (Crocker, Hampson, and Aall 2013, 7). The system of rules, institutions, and procedures to regulate the international monetary system at Bretton Woods, and the reduction of tariff barriers, quantitative restrictions, and subsidies on trade through the General Agreement on Tariffs and Trade and World Trade Organization have obviously played a key role in promoting postwar economic prosperity and stability.

This is surely the story of the transatlantic region, but it is also true of much of the Asia-Pacific region, where many countries have until recently enjoyed some of the highest economic growth rates in the world and the bonds of economic interdependence have deepened enormously. It is surely no accident that this region has gone from being one of the most violent to one of the most peaceful. As a recent RAND study notes, "In broad terms, the incidence of armed conflict has declined in both number and intensity since the end of the Cold War, with particularly sharp declines in interstate and higher-intensity conflicts; . . . future projections of the key drivers of conflict suggest these trends are likely to continue over the long term. There has been an uptick in some forms of intrastate conflict in 2012–2015, but . . . the current spike in armed conflict is likely to prove relatively short-lived" (Watts et al. 2017, xvii).

To summarize, the evolution of the liberal international order could take one of two generic forms: (1) a system comprising a collection of states, reinforced by transnational civil society, that share liberal values and promote these values through, for example, existing or strengthened instruments of collective security and cooperation at the global and/or regional levels; or (2) a system led by a *minilateral* group of leading democratic states that promotes (or "imposes") liberal internationalism. In both, the space for civil society organizations, activists, and technology-empowered "bottom-up" actors continues to strengthen.

Scenario 3: Pragmatic Cooperation

The British historian E. H. Carr once wrote that "international government is, in effect, government by the state [or states] which supplies [supply] the power necessary for the purpose of governing." Or as Raymond Aron put it, "The structure of the international system is always oligopolistic. In each period the principal actors have determined the system more than they have been determined by it" (Gilpin 1981, 29). The structure of the international system generally follows from one of three canonical types: imperial or hegemonic; bipolar, in which two powerful states dominate the system; or multipolar, in which three or more states manage the system through diplomacy, shifting alliances, and even "managed" conflict. Over the past fifty or so years, we have gone from a bipolar to a unipolar system, in which the United States is the predominant power, but one that has played a critical role in managing and maintaining the current international order.

We are now entering a third, hybrid phase of "weakened" or "soft" hegemony, coupled with "aspiring multipolarity," as the great powers of Asia, China, and India, in particular, begin to assert themselves on the world stage. Europe is also part of this new multipolar equation. This scenario 3 would see a period of pragmatic and selective cooperation in a kind of new "concert of nations" (Hampson and Heinbecker 2013). In this scenario, the major powers would not interfere to any great degree in other countries' domestic situations but would uphold common principles of dispute resolution and intermittently cooperate in order to solve common pool resource problems, such as climate change and humanitarian crises.

Aspiring multipolarity does not pose a threat to world order if the great powers in the system continue to believe that stability serves their core national interests, especially their own economic and political survival. As the nineteenth century illustrates, however, stability is not automatic. A twenty-first-century concert scenario puts a premium on leadership, personal relations, and deft diplomacy to manage relationships and the latent rivalries that come with the assertion of great power status (Mitzen 2013).

Scenario 3 is not confined to aspiring multipolarity among states. It also captures a world where a multiplicity of institutions play roles in an expanded version of diplomacy. Nongovernmental organizations, business associations, corporations, and civil society have taken on roles in a variety of activities: building constituencies for peace, providing the social glue that holds together societies under stress, pressuring their governments to pursue peace or war, and developing transnational relationships that can support, challenge, and sometimes contravene their governments' policies. Finally, in this scenario the reach of social media has an unpredictable but powerful influence on peace and conflict diplomacy, as private citizens have a direct impact on decision-makers in foreign capitals.

In this world of multipolarity and a proliferation of influences, states will band together in ad hoc and temporary coalitions to protect their interests, which may at times include the resolution of international or intrastate conflict. These coalitions may endure over time, but they will not be formal institutions or even alliances. They will instead serve the interests of a concert of nations and other actors to achieve limited goals.

What probabilities should be attached to these different scenarios? Will we see two or three great powers compete for primacy over a number of spheres, or will we see a return to a liberal, rules-based order that many say reigned supreme in the post–World War II era? Or will it be a period of unstructured, ad hoc collaboration among states and other entities to solve common problems? In order to fully understand these questions, it may be helpful to examine more carefully the assumption that the world has enjoyed a truly liberal, rules-based order (LRBO) over the past sixty years. We suggest that the prevailing character of this period has actually combined elements of the realist and internationalist worlds. We also suggest that in this time of shifting sands, it is prudent to plan for scenario 3—a world of mutable and temporary collaboration among states and other entities.

IS THE LIBERAL, RULES-BASED INTERNATIONAL ORDER REALLY DEAD—OR DYING?

It is now widely accepted among many experts that current political developments have undermined the liberal, rules-based order. Opinions differ on whether the LRBO lost a battle with its opposite ("bipolar disorder"), died naturally from old age, or was euthanized by cynical leaders and angry publics (Heisbourg 2018). Commentators give less attention, however, to defining the LRBO and coming to an agreed-on analysis of its origins. These are important issues if we are to imagine possible scenarios for the future of world order or attach probabilities to potential outcomes for the international system as we approach the third decade of this century.

A major reason for LRBO nostalgia is that global politics has become uglier and the international system seems to behave in less systematic ways, raising the question of whether any set of rules and rule-enforcers still exists. If this is an age of disruption, it is important to know how much is being disrupted and what—apart from the law of the jungle—might come next. Before succumbing to an excess of nostalgia, it is useful to remind ourselves of what has *not* been disrupted. In fact, a great deal has not been disrupted. Writing about the challenge of conflict prevention just five years ago, the conflict scholar I. William Zartman (2015, 5–6) argues: "For those who would question the existence of a World Order and mistake exceptions and imperfections for normalcy, the widespread practice of prevention should be recognized as pervasive patterns consensually followed to maintain basic, regular responses to deviant challenges. Were it not so, international politics would indeed be total anarchy, wasting all time and energy in unregulated conflict and unprevented violence."

It is also useful, however, to remind ourselves of the likelihood that the world order of our memories never really existed in quite the way we imagine it. Dating it is not as easy as is often described in standard accounts pointing to the immediate post–World War II and Cold War eras. One account finds its roots in the seventeenth-century Peace of Westphalia, where the statist norms enshrined in the UN Charter are clearly reflected (Deudney and Ikenberry 2018).

In this view, the liberal order is both old and inexorably ever-renewed because, as Deudney and Ikenberry argue, "As long as interdependence— economic, security-related and environmental—continues to grow, peoples and governments everywhere will be compelled to work together to solve problems or suffer grievous harm. By necessity, these efforts will build on and strengthen the institutions of the liberal order" (Ikenberry 2018). Other accounts find the LRBO's genesis in more specific periods, such as the twentieth-century's interwar era, with the Washington Naval Treaty, the 1929 effort to build upon the pre–World War I Hague Conventions on the treatment of combatants in wartime and the 1928 Kellogg-Briand Pact on the elimination of war as an instrument of national policy (Hathaway and Shapiro 2017).

Robert Kagan emphasizes the history of pre–Cold War allied diplomacy in 1944–45 that built the consensus for the institutions that would guide international politics, through, for instance, the UN Charter and the global free trading system through the Bretton Woods system (Kagan 2018). In his view, this was a realist order centered on American power and will, aimed at checking nationalist aggression, protectionism, and autarky, and thereby creating the opportunity and space for a liberal order to emerge and thrive after the horrors of pre-1945 world history.

In contrast to Kagan's appeal to sustain the Western-led, post–Cold War liberal hegemony, there are the scathing critics who dismiss the LRBO as an illusion. To Graham Allison, the LRBO is a "myth," and its proponents offer little except "conceptual Jell-O" (Allison 2018). That is because the UN Security Council's five permanent members do not respect it, including the United States, which proposes rules for others but has often behaved without reference to any rules, international or domestic. Instead, American leaders should accept that "other countries have contrary views about governance and seek to establish their own international orders governed by their own rules." Accordingly, Allison appeals for "a minimal order that can accommodate that diversity."

The British scholar Patrick Porter (2018) categorically rejects the notion that there is or was an LRBO: "Under America's aegis, there were islands of liberty where prosperous markets and democracies grew. US internationalism rebuilt Western Europe and East Asia and successfully contained Soviet communism. The central issue is whether this created a wider 'liberal' system, and whether the actual historic process of world ordering can even be achieved by liberal means. The answer, in both cases, is no."

As these examples suggest, the turbulence of geopolitics and domestic politics has spawned a conceptual ferment reflecting a simple reality: there is very little agreement on either the drivers or the outcomes of the post-1945 international system. Many elements of an order (however labeled) appear likely to survive today's turbulence, because many important states and groupings of states wish it to survive, reflecting an alliance between realists and internationalists.

Moreover, as scenario 3 suggests, there are interesting examples of states joining ad hoc coalitions for jointly managing conflict outside or alongside formal institutions (Crocker, Hampson, and Aall 2011a). In such cases, order flows from the efforts of a "neighborhood watch" mechanism with all the efficiency benefits and vigilante risks associated with them. Moreover, it is possible, as Jake Sullivan observes, for states to participate in programs and projects in a wide range of functional fields through variable geometry without the need for a formal, rules-based institutional focus. The search for an acceptable history of the LRBO—to say nothing of its definition—is somewhat eased by his argument that the order has always been an uneasy blend of state sovereignty principles and the liberalizing thrust derived from American and British legal norms and political cultures (Sullivan 2018).

In sum, we are in a time of transitions once again, not agreeing on what the LRBO really is but knowing it when we see it. Still less do we have clarity on the road ahead. François Heisbourg suggests that the most likely next phase of order would look like what he terms bipolar disorder at the same time, conceding that there might be a chance to build a multipolar concert of powers provided a climate of carefulness and strategic due diligence can be cultivated (Heisbourg 2018). This second possibility may be the best bet for champions of peace and conflict diplomacy. It could offer the chance for states, regional and international institutions, and civil society groups to feel their way cautiously forward in addressing those conflicts they can agree on, debating which norms should be applied and to whom, while agreeing to disagree when compromises are out of reach.

"ROOT" VERSUS "BRANCH" PEACE AND CONFLICT DIPLOMACY: MANAGING OR MUDDLING?

As mentioned in chapter 1, the Yale political scientist Charles Lindblom once drew an important distinction between two kinds of policymaking, which, we believe, are relevant to the contemporary challenges of peace and conflict diplomacy (Lindblom 1959, 1979). He distinguished between "root-based," or strategic, decision-making based on a comprehensive consideration of different options (where you assume perfect or near-perfect information) and the "branch method," where decisions are made on a step-by-step incremental way to deal with very complex problems under high levels of uncertainty (feeling your way through the fog until the mist clears). According to Lindblom, the latter approach—which he referred to as the "science of muddling through"—was the only effective way to deal with highly complex public policy problems.

Lindblom also stressed the importance of negotiation processes to the branch method of decision-making. As Allison and Saint-Martin explain, "Policy-making is not a hierarchical and centrally controlled process, but rather involves 'partisan mutual adjustment', i.e., a process of negotiation and bargaining where decision-makers make compromises and adjust to one another . . .

[and] for coordinating policy-making within a fragmented political system with diverging interests. Punctuated equilibrium theory proposes an alternative but related view on 'mutual adjustment,' by assuming that a policy image shared by a majority of actors within a subsystem contributes to policy stability and phases of incremental change" (Allison and Saint-Martin 2011).

Like Lindblom, we are tempted to conclude that peace and conflict diplomacy increasingly will become an exercise in creative "muddling through," navigating complexity via negotiated arrangements and the formation of ad hoc coalitions where parties have mutual and divergent interests. Despite their differences, they are nonetheless prepared to compromise and work together to promote collective action in specific situations where their interests converge (e.g., on the issue of piracy) and/or their economic or political well-being is threatened (Crocker, Hampson, and Aall 2011a, 2011b). This is certainly a possibility in a world where states are reasserting themselves as dominant actors, alliances are shifting, and international and intergovernmental institutions are hobbled by profound disagreements among their core members. If this is the case, the future of peace and conflict diplomacy is not indeed as dim as some conclude, and neither are the prospects for active external engagement in conflict management and peacebuilding in troubled zones.

As suggested in the discussion of scenario 3, states and other international actors will need to protect their interests in fields and sectors that impose themselves on their agenda. Coping with the challenges posed by cybercrime, terrorist attacks, catastrophic climate events, health pandemics, and maritime and aviation disasters—to name examples—can trigger effective ad hoc collaborative responses. As the example of nonproliferation and counterterrorism strategies illustrates, concerted action is sometimes the indispensable response to protect states and societies, no matter how different their domestic systems and values. An ad hoc, modernized concert could evolve to mitigate risks and maintain minimal international order in relevant fields, some of which could otherwise trigger conflict.

Whatever the prevalence of our three scenarios in various times and places, powerful states and global institutions will not be alone. They will be accompanied by regional and nongovernmental organizations—newer participants in peace and conflict diplomacy—either as partners or rivals.

Regional organizations are on the rise, due in part to the same trends that have produced the fractures in the liberal, rules-based order. Apart from exceptional circumstances, regional organizations are not going to be able to fully fill the vacuum left by the withdrawal of powerful states and global institutions in the peace and conflict diplomacy arena. But their increasing activism points to a new model of cooperation between global and local actors.

This cooperation may be ad hoc and mission-specific, or it might develop its own rules of the road. The African model is based on the principle of subsidiarity—meaning that the subregional organization responds to a conflict first, and then invites the African Union to become involved (Bellamy, Williams, and Griffin 2010). In similar fashion, the larger powers (e.g., the US or UN) would wait for (or quietly stimulate) an invitation from the African Union before it engaged. In this way, regional organizations act as gatekeepers in the security realm and set the agenda for the external response. Of course, this principle is often ignored in practice—the Economic Community of West African States went directly to France for help with the Côte d'Ivoire conflict in 2011—and even in cases where it is observed, the capacity of the regional organizations to act consistently over long periods of time is limited due to a lack of resources and the same kind of internal disputes that plague the UN (Aall and Crocker 2018). Despite these drawbacks, regional organizations are more engaged and empowered than they were in the Cold War and its aftermath. Supporting this development and taking advantage of their willingness to step up to the plate could be a central element of a reformulated peace and conflict diplomacy portfolio.

The other important set of participants in peace and conflict diplomacy is not part of the official process. International nongovernmental organizations and local civil society play critical roles in preventing and resolving conflict and building the foundations for peace, both on the ground and in partnership with donor countries and international organizations. In so doing, they directly advance the cause of peace, but they also augment the peace and conflict diplomacy efforts of others. Traditional views of diplomacy did not have room for these voices, but current practice—except in the most authoritarian states—looks to support and cooperation from these citizen groups.

Local civil society in particular is vital to the effort to bring as many people into the process as possible. Much has been written on the importance of inclusion in resolving conflicts—the importance of reaching out to marginalized and otherwise ignored groups such as women, youth, and minority groups, and bringing their voices into the decision-making mix. The effort requires a different kind of diplomacy, one that engages on the ground and in the streets, that cultivates but does not impose ideas, that supports but does not manipulate. This kind of engagement has not been the forte of foreign service officers or foreign ministry officials in the past, but they are learning to extend their diplomatic hand to civil society in order to strengthen the impact on peace and conflict.

Muddling through does not sound like much of a policy prescription; nor is it meant to be an alternative to a grand strategy in situation when such a strategy is possible. But in these uncertain times, its step-by-step adaptive approach—anchored in negotiation and compromise, engaging a diverse group of actors—may be the best mechanism for successful peace and conflict diplomacy in the complex international environment we live in.

NOTES

1. See, e.g., Gilpin (1981).
2. The classic study on this matter is by Doyle (1983).

CHAPTER 3

International Organizations— Down but Not Out

Jean-Marie Guéhenno

Can international institutions play a useful role in peace and conflict diplomacy at a time when international cooperation is in decline, nationalism is on the rise, and nonstate actors are playing, for better and worse, an increasingly central role? International organizations are always a reflection of the power dynamics that drive relations between their member states. During the Cold War, the United Nations did not play much of a role in regulating the central conflict between the Soviet Union and the United States. Progress was made through direct arms control negotiations between the two superpowers. But peacekeeping operations contributed to stability by preventing some localized conflicts from escalating to the critical east-west conflict. In the immediate aftermath of the end of the Cold War, the dominance of the United States allowed the West to define the agenda of international organizations. Many conflicts came to an end, in Central America, in Asia, and in Africa. There were variations in the model of conflict resolution due to local circumstances, but there were shared characteristics: limited interference of external actors (except in the Democratic Republic of Congo), efforts to develop an inclusive process, and internationally supervised elections. Meanwhile, regional organizations played only a secondary role, except for NATO and for the European Union, which had the resources to fund the peacebuilding work of the United Nations. Catastrophic failures occurred—in Somalia, Rwanda, and Bosnia— which had tragic humanitarian consequences, but they were of little strategic importance, because a US-led West still dominated the international narrative.

This chapter argues that the immediate aftermath of the Cold War was an exception, and that the role played by international institutions in peacemaking during that period is unlikely to continue. At the same time, it would be wrong to draw the conclusion that we are returning to the period of the Cold War. We are actually entering a new phase, as different from the post–Cold War period as from the Cold War itself. International organizations will play a more limited role but will not become irrelevant.

THE POST–COLD WAR PERIOD IS OVER

The self-confidence and optimism that characterized the period after the end of the Cold War are gone. The world today is a long way from where it was in January 1992, when UN secretary-general Boutros Ghali issued his "Agenda for Peace." Who today can credibly assert that "authoritarian regimes have given way to more democratic forces and responsive governments." Who can say with confidence that "the manifest desire of the membership [of the Security Council] to work together is a new source of strength in our common endeavour." While in 1992 Boutros Ghali could contrast with satisfaction the absence of a veto since May 1990 with the 279 vetoes cast during the Cold War, the statistics today are far less encouraging: since 1993, some 40 draft resolutions have been vetoed, including 9 in the last 24 months. The Security Council has not heeded the appeal made to it by the secretary-general of the UN: "Never again must the Security Council lose the collegiality that is essential to its proper functioning." Today, there is little collegiality in the Security Council, and that absence of collegiality greatly exacerbates the inability of the United Nations to effectively support peacemaking efforts.

The Syrian conflict is the most glaring illustration of the paralysis that is affecting the UN Security Council. When, in 2012, Kofi Annan was appointed joint special envoy of the United Nations and the Arab League for Syria, the expectation was that he would approach this conflict with the experience and authority gained as secretary-general of the UN. And he did, but to no avail. His strategy was to work first with Russia and the United States, to build a joint understanding between the two global powers of a possible solution. This would lay the groundwork for successful peacemaking: the two global powers would use their influence on regional powers (essentially Iran, Saudi Arabia, and Turkey), so that they in turn would put sufficient pressure on local Syrian actors to agree to a negotiated resolution. That strategy failed, because no shared understanding of the solution could be reached between Moscow and Washington. At the Geneva meeting in June 2012, the constructive ambiguity of the communiqué—which described a process for a "transition" in Syria—was quickly destroyed when Secretary of State Hillary Clinton stressed in a press conference that President Assad would not pass the "mutual consent test," while Minister Sergey Lavrov pointed out that there was no mention in the communiqué of Assad. In the absence of agreement at the global level, regional rivalries took precedence, and regional powers have since fed the conflict instead of stopping it. As the number of victims grew and the destruction spread, it became increasingly clear that the approach that had been favored by Kofi Annan and his successors—to start from the outer circle of global powers—was not going to work.

In this new context, the United Nations has seen its role diminished. In the case of Syria, the UN-led peace process, rather than a genuine collective effort, has looked more and more like a diversion, which has allowed the UN Security Council to maintain the pretense that it was interested in ending the war. All actors have showed more interest in creating facts on the ground than looking for a compromise. Such dynamics have exposed the asymmetries of interests and capabilities among outside powers, giving the advantage to those actors that have the most at stake and are prepared to escalate accordingly. For Turkey, the future of Syria was a secondary consideration, but the Kurdish question was a critical national security issue. For Iran, Syria was a key battleground, all the more important because Hezbollah— essential to Iran as an offensive deterrent against Israel—would be strengthened or weakened, depending on the outcome of the war. For Russia, the Middle East is its immediate neighborhood, and the nature of the regimes in the region has a direct impact on its security. Saudi Arabia, as a regional power, which considers Iran a strategic threat, also has had a direct interest in Syria, but it never had the operational capacity to create facts on the ground as Russia and Iran have. Meanwhile, neither the United States nor the Europeans showed any willingness to fill this gap: their interest in Syria was not comparable to that of Iran and Russia, and they were therefore unwilling to raise the stakes and escalate. The United States never had a strategic interest in Syria, and when the threat of terrorism and flows of refugees began to change the domestic political dynamics of Europe, and to create a strategic threat for the Europeans, it was too late, and the Europeans did not have the capacity to act decisively without American engagement.

Russia understood earlier than the Western powers that the evolution of the situation on the ground mattered more than negotiations to which key actors were only halfheartedly committed. It has acted accordingly, and would now like to convert its military success into a diplomatic victory. The so-called Astana process, launched by the three outside powers with direct influence and clear interests—Russia, Iran, and Turkey—has helped manage a gradual deescalation of violence, accompanying the shifting balance of power, for the benefit of the Syrian government. What it has not achieved are the conditions for a longer-term recovery of Syria. That would require significant money, which needs to come from other powers.

Russia may therefore have an interest in bringing back the UN umbrella, although international dynamics have changed since the Kosovo war, or even the Iraq war. In both cases, the war was not sanctioned by the United Nations, but the UN helped the Security Council regain its unity after the war. In the case of Kosovo, the UN played a substantive role, assuming unprecedented executive responsibilities as the de jure trustee of Kosovo. In the case of Iraq, the UN was more a fig leaf than a real player, and the real power rested with the United States. Considering the present state of relations in the UN Security Council, and the situation on the ground, the UN would be unlikely to play a central role in Syria, including in a postwar peacebuilding phase. But it could again be a useful fig leaf if Russia wanted to wrap its diplomatic victory in the UN flag, in the same way the United States did in Iraq. It is, however, doubtful that this would lead to a significant flow of Western money—American and European—into Syria, absent a genuine political process (Barnes-Darcey 2019). The polarization that has made conflict resolution in Syria so difficult is likely to also affect peacebuilding efforts.

The situation today is different from the one that prevailed twenty years ago. The "unipolar" moment, if ever there was one, is gone, and Western countries are rediscovering that interventionist policies carry a price. There is no shared understanding of the circumstances that could justify foreign interventions. On the contrary, Russia and China want to roll back the new norms surrounding the responsibility to protect and humanitarian intervention, which they consider a convenient pretext to infringe on the principle of sovereignty, and their position is supported by many countries that find that principle to be the only effective equalizer in a world of enormous imbalances of power. Moreover, Russia has regained enough capacity to project power to raise the price of intervention for the West.

This has strategic consequences: the ambitious agendas that were promoted during the last two decades are unlikely to be pursued, and we are entering a period of strategic retrenchment, which reflects both the greater resistance to intervention and globalism, and the exhaustion and skepticism of the interventionists themselves. Interfering in the lives of other countries has proven to be more costly, more dangerous, and more difficult than initially anticipated. Both the UN under the leadership of Kofi Annan and the United States under the leadership of President George W. Bush embarked in interventions that would be unthinkable today. There is today a much greater awareness of the complexity of peacemaking, and little political support in liberal democracies for costly engagements. The United Nations is aware of this diminishing support, which is a greater challenge than ideological hostility because it is likely to last. In this new context, it becomes much harder for international institutions to take the initiative and lead, and there are no agreed-on principles around which to rally.

THERE IS NO RETURN TO THE COLD WAR, AND THE PRESENT SITUATION IS UNPRECEDENTED

The Syria case is a stark illustration of the impact on the United Nations of the discord between the permanent members of the UN Security Council when their interests are directly engaged. It may bring the United Nations back to the role it had during the Cold War, as an actor that plays a role at the margins of more strategic confrontations on which it has no influence. The present situation is, however, quite different from the Cold War, and the analogies that are often made are misleading. Although the competition between the United States, Russia, and China has indeed intensified, and an increasing number of situations play out like a zero-sum game, the world of 2020 has little in common with the world of the 1960s.

The first and major difference is that it is not a bipolar world. It is a genuinely multipolar world, in which the interests of China and Russia, even if they are allies, do not coincide. Nor, for that matter, can one speak of a Western camp under the leadership of President Trump. This creates a much more flexible, and possibly unstable, international system. And this fluidity is further increased by the absence of deep ideological confrontation. Even though one can still categorize the world according to the nature of the regimes, there are no longer blocs, and the pillars of this new multipolar world actively trade with each other, even if Russia remains under Western sanctions. The various systems are not locked in a competition to impose their own systems. This makes it much less difficult to switch allegiances, or to have multiple conflicting allegiances. Countries can be allies on one issue and opponents on another. Turkey is a good example of this increased complexity (de Waal 2016). It is at once a NATO member, but for the moment a friend of Russia. Another consequence of multipolarity is that it empowers regional actors: they can play global powers against each other.

This leads to a much more bottom-up world in which major powers lose their capacity to control smaller powers. Not only are the relations between major powers more complex, but new regional dynamics also assert themselves, for better and worse. For instance, the divisions that afflict the Horn of Africa are further deepened by the divisions between Gulf countries, divisions that themselves are not a consequence of the competition between global powers but can actually feed on them. In Somalia, the federal government received support from Qatar and Turkey, while the federated entities are backed by the United Arab Emirates. Each of these external actors pursues its own national agenda, irrespective of the agenda of the United States, which is an ally of them all and would rather see the Gulf countries reconcile. Regional powers as well as subnational actors are thus empowered, turning on its head the traditional approach to conflict resolution. This happens at a time when the powers in North America and Europe that have traditionally been at the forefront of interventionist policies are entertaining doubts on the wisdom of foreign interventions, which have proven to be costlier and more challenging than initially anticipated. The overall trend is toward retrenchment, as a pervasive sense of loss of control pushes countries to focus on their domestic priorities and scale down their international ambitions. National security tends to be defined in increasingly narrow terms, leaving the world with less engaged global actors and more activist regional players.

The multipolarity makes the new emerging international system more complex: the diffusion of power among nations reverberates on state and nonstate actors, also changing the dynamics between a global organization like the United Nations and regional organizations. The greater political and economic space that the end of bipolar confrontation has created is being quickly occupied by emerging regional powers, which in some cases have a national interest in bolstering regional organizations on which they hope to have more influence than they can ever have on the United Nations.

This is particularly true in Africa, where regional powers are investing political capital in subregional and regional organizations. Ethiopia with the Intergovernmental Authority on Development, Nigeria with the Economic Community of West African States (ECOWAS), and South Africa with the Southern African Development Community combine critical influence in their respective subregional organizations with efforts to boost the international clout and influence of the African Union (AU). This has led to mixed results when the international engagement includes a peacekeeping operation.

In Côte d'Ivoire during the crisis with President Gbagbo in the 2000s, the various organizations involved (United Nations, AU, and ECOWAS) were clearly canceling each other out. The AU, under the influence of then President Mbeki, was close to President Gbagbo, while the United Nations and ECOWAS were willing to increase the pressure on the president to hold elections. At the time, the AU was less influential than it is now, and the UN/ECOWAS line eventually prevailed, including by enforcing, with the military help of France the result of the elections.

In Darfur, the United Nations and the AU decided to join their efforts in a so-called hybrid peacekeeping mission, with dual reporting lines to the AU and the UN—known as the United Nations–African Union Mission in Darfur, or UNAMID. This formula was chosen under pressure from the government of Sudan, which had rejected a UN peacekeeping mission, and rightly assumed that it would have more leverage and influence on the AU than on the United Nations. (For a detailed analysis of the origins of UNAMID, see Guéhenno 2015.) The hybrid format was chosen not to combine the clout of two organizations but rather to weaken the mission. And it did. The United Nations still has a much stronger headquarters structure than the AU, and the operational day-to-day conduct of the mission stayed with the UN department of peacekeeping operations. But at the strategic level, and for key decisions such as the appointment of heads of mission and other senior personnel, the influence of the AU has been considerable, and the result has been a dilution of responsibilities that has been damaging to both organizations. The hybrid mission has not had the clarity of purpose and decisiveness of command that are essential ingredients of success in a complex and difficult situation like Darfur. Although UNAMID has made a contribution to the stabilization of Darfur, and has helped reduce the level of violence there, it has not played a decisive role.

In Somalia, the peacekeeping operation has been entrusted to the AU, while the United Nations provides logistical support and keeps a political role. This distribution of roles is partly the result of history. The United Nations, after the disasters of the 1990s and considering the lack of clarity on the operational goals of a peace operation in Somalia, successfully resisted pressure—for full disclosure, in part because of my advice—from its member states to deploy an operation, while neighboring states, Ethiopia and Kenya, had a national interest in containing the Somali situation. Deploying an AU mission (African Union Mission in Somalia, AMISOM) became a way for the UN Security Council to reconcile such national interests with a broader strategy of the international community. It had the advantage of solving the troop-generation challenge, which was particularly difficult to address in a country where the previous UN deployment had ended in disaster. But it has shown its limitations: neighboring countries contributing troops have a greater tolerance for risk because their national interest is engaged, but the same does not apply to other troop contributors, and the unity of purpose of the mission is further undermined by weak command

and control. Meanwhile, the interests of financial contributors (the European Union, which pays the troops, and the UN, which funds and manages the logistical support) are not aligned with those of troop contributors. More importantly, both the UN, through a special representative of the secretary-general, and the AU, through the head of the peacekeeping operation, have a political role in supporting the process; but they inevitably have very different perspectives, as the AU chief is responsible for troops engaged in fighting antigovernment groups, while the UN representative has no such constraints and can be more open to political engagement with rebel groups. Political divergence compounds the risks of bureaucratic rivalries. After more than ten years of deployment, the mission suffers from the same ills that have affected UN missions that have been deployed for a long time. The host country is relieved of its obligation to take charge for its own security, while at the same time it resents the foreign presence. The troops settle in an increasingly static posture. In the end, pulling out the troops is dangerous because there is no substitute in place, but there is also no incentive to build that substitute. The peacekeeping trap has closed on the peacekeepers, with the added complication, in a hybrid mission, that there is a disconnect between the financial concerns of the organizations that pay for the deployment and the financial interest of the organization that deploys the troops. When compared with the hybrid model of UNAMID, the AMISOM model has different, but equally serious, drawbacks.

More recently, at the initiative of France, another model is being tried in the Sahel ("Finding the Right Role" 2017). It is an effort to address the characteristics of contemporary conflict: no longer confined to a single country, they involve a whole region; they require a mix of peacekeeping and war-fighting capabilities; they include asymmetric threats that can only be addressed by dedicated high-quality forces; military activities need to be complemented by civilian development activities, to beef up government presence in remote areas and ensure service delivery. In the Sahel, this means the combination of three categories of forces: the national forces of the countries concerned; the peacekeeping mission already deployed in one country, Mali; and national forces from external actors—in particular France—deployed to fight terrorist groups. To ensure effective coordination of the national forces involved and good cooperation with the external forces and the UN mission, and to integrate the military strategy in a broader development effort, an institutional framework, the "G5 Sahel," has been created. The result has been disappointing, and some observations can already be made. First—and this is indicative of the retreat of multilateral solutions—the proposal for multilateral funding on assessed contributions of the integrated framework has been rejected by the United States, which gives absolute priority, in the Sahel as in Somalia, to bilateral support. Second, an addition of weak forces does not create a strong force, and international efforts to build more capable national forces have so far largely failed: the situation in the region is deteriorating rather than improving. Third, the peacekeeping mission in Mali is overwhelmed, as reflected in the record number of casualties; while focused on peacekeeping/stabilization duties, it is also expected to provide support to the G5 Sahel, and is increasingly exposed to terrorist attacks. Fourth, the integration of the political, developmental, and military strategies is very weak, as it has become clear that there is no genuine unity of purpose among so many actors, who pursue different, and sometimes conflicting, agendas.

These different models are in part a reflection of the increasing influence of regional powers and regional organizations, in part a reflection of the interests of global powers that leverage their influence through regional actors. That is the case of France in the Sahel, or of the United States with several African countries (for which the relationship with the United States is the most important relationship) that allow Washington to influence through them the AU: in so doing, global powers face less difficulties than they would in the UN, where they can be blocked in the Security Council.

This diffusion of power is further complicated by the changing nature of conflict in a world that is no longer shaped by a global confrontation between two ideologies. Civil wars used to be about control of power, and it was assumed that all protagonists shared at least one goal: the termination of conflict. This assumption is no longer valid, because protracted conflicts create an economy of conflict in which some protagonists, both external and internal, have no interest in ending conflict (Cockayne 2020). States that are close to a conflict area increasingly reach the conclusion that a permanent weakness of their neighbor contributes to their own security. They do not want chaos that could spill over their borders, but low-intensity conflict and a weak neighboring state may suit them. This may apply to several frozen conflicts of the former Soviet Union, and it has applied to the Democratic Republic of Congo for many years. Such situations of fragility are, however, intrinsically unstable, and external actors may eventually agree that peace is a better option. But that does not apply to internal criminal actors that pursue a criminal agenda. They have no interest in full stabilization that would strengthen the state and threaten their dominant position in a criminal economy. They have developed a symbiotic relationship with conflict, in which conflict makes their criminal activities possible, and their criminal activities feed conflict. Libya is a case in point. Its oil wealth is captured by a number of actors that have no interest in the full restoration of the authority of the state, and it funds various militias that compete with and undermine a weak state's security sector. Likewise, in the Sahel, various kinds of trafficking (drugs, human beings, weapons) support state and nonstate actors, which have an equal and shared interest in maintaining the state in a permanent condition of weakness that benefits their criminal activities. The distinction between criminal and political actors, and criminal and political agendas, is blurred, complicating peace negotiations and putting international organizations, which are organizations of states, in a difficult position.

This is all the more significant as the international impact of nonstate actors grows. Although nonstate actors are not a new feature of conflict, the expanding nature of their agendas is. Groups using terrorist tactics like al-Qaeda and the Islamic State have emerged, which claim to have a transnational agenda. This, combined with attempts to hit distant enemies—9/11 being the most spectacular illustration of that tactic—has a transformative impact on conflict. Asymmetric warfare is as old as warfare, but the use of asymmetric tactics to pursue transnational goals is unprecedented and reflects a connected world in which, through the instant dissemination made possible by modern media, local events can quickly become national and even global events, irrespective of the number of casualties. Both local tactics—including for peacekeepers— and international politics have to adjust. The 9/11 attack triggered a chain of events—through the so-called global war on terrorism—which has blurred the distinction between war and peace, and whose end is still not in sight. Likewise, terrorist attacks in France have contributed to solidifying military engagements in the Sahel, which, although considerably smaller than was the massive US engagement in Afghanistan and Iraq, represent a heavy burden for a midsized country like France. Such protracted military engagements raise new and difficult political questions, as groups employing terrorist tactics often mix militants pursuing a transnational agenda with fighters motivated by local grievances or criminal interests. How to fight one category without abandoning political efforts with another is a difficult and yet unresolved challenge. The time frame and objectives are not the same. Although there is little to negotiate with the first category, a political solution may sometimes be reached with the second. In the first case, the time frame for a military solution may be elusive, and that in turn may put at risk the outcome of a peace process with those groups that pursue an agenda with a geographically defined agenda. Agreeing on an end-state is difficult when some of the actors are determined to undermine it. The difficulty is compounded by the fact that there is no clear and stable separation between the various categories and the borders between them are porous.

This confusion is a characteristic of our time, when concepts that have structured international relations lose their clarity. In the preceding period, after the end of the Cold War, there was hope that the legal framework established by the UN Charter would be complemented by emerging norms such as the responsibility to protect and new enforcing institutions such as the International Criminal Court. A political agreement was reached at a UN summit in 2005 on the response to war crimes and crimes against humanity. Today, the erosion of the international consensus and the evolution of warfare conspire to blur the distinction between war and peace, the conditions under which force can be used, and the principles that should underpin a peace agreement. The international community—if that misleading expression can be used—seems to be moving backward rather than forward. The controversy over the use of force to achieve humanitarian goals, as in Libya, may have been overtaken by events, as the aftermath of the fall of Qaddafi is likely to discourage other interventions of that type, including by those powers that participated in the operation. But the war on terrorism—with no end in sight, as noted above—has set in motion a reinterpretation of international law that may have more far-reaching consequences. Rather than let the UN Security Council decide on matters that directly affect their national security, the members of the Security Council have agreed de facto to a considerable extension of self-defense: it is now used to justify the use of force in countries that have not agreed to it on their territory, and this legal extension is in some cases facilitated by the evolution of technology. The use of drones eliminates the risk of pilots being taken prisoners, and facilitates offensive covert operations. Cyber warfare is even more consequential, as it allows for a wide range of offensive actions that cannot be attributed with certainty, and the nature of the technology is such that it needs to be continuously tested through real, small-scale offensive actions to ensure the effectiveness of a major attack. The clarity of the concept of aggression—well understood in 1945, when the memory of Nazi troops crossing the Polish border was fresh—is now lost, whether a drone strike hits a remote village, an anonymous cyberattack is launched, or a government-supported militia takes control of a region.

Whether it is criminal violence reaching levels that challenge the authority of states, low-intensity conflicts wittingly encouraged by states benefiting from them, or offensive actions that are not decisively attributable, ambiguity has become a feature and even a strategy for some actors. This applies to a wide range of actors, from major powers like Russia to nonstate actors. In a multipolar, more bottom-up, and increasingly contentious world, the distinction between war and peace has lost its clarity in many situations, and there is now often a continuum between war and peace, which should force a rethinking of peacemaking strategies.

RETHINKING PEACEMAKING

International relations are always characterized by a mix of competition and cooperation. The specificity of the present period is that not only is competition—even confrontation—between global powers again growing quickly after the ebb of the post–Cold War moment, but this increased competition is happening in a more complex environment whose features are not yet fully understood, let alone agreed on by major powers. What are the implications for international institutions, and in particular the United Nations, in discharging their peacemaking responsibilities?

As noted above, the international system today is much more complex than it was even twenty years ago, when the only model of cooperation considered was cooperation between the UN and NATO, as happened in Kosovo and Afghanistan (initially a US-led coalition): the UN took the political lead, while the United States and/or NATO provided the military muscle. That was a reflection of the overwhelming dominance of the West at the time. That benign environment played a big part in the success of several peacekeeping operations. The mission in Cambodia would not have succeeded if the peace conference that preceded it had not produced a convergence not just between Cambodians but also between the major powers, including China and the United States, while other regional powers like Australia and Indonesia were supporting the effort. In the case of Mozambique, Namibia, and El Salvador, success was facilitated not so much by the active convergence of the major powers as by the absence of powerful spoilers. Likewise, in Côte d'Ivoire, the absence of serious opposition to the strong involvement of France was critical.

The situation today is different and, as noted above, regional organizations are now playing an increasingly important role, and conflict resolution needs to reflect this complexity, and become, like the conflict itself, multilayered. In many situations, several countries and organizations—subregional, regional, and global—may be involved. The United Nations today cannot ignore their role and it must work with them, so that parallel efforts can be combined and not subtracted. This now happens more often in Africa than on any other continent, but it remains difficult. For instance, in the case of the elections that took place in the Democratic Republic of Congo in 2018, the chairpersons of the AU (Kagame) and of the Peace and Security Commission (Faki) took the political lead in requesting a recount of the vote, but when the Congolese authorities did not budge and proclaimed results widely seen as flawed, several African heads of state congratulated the winner, and the AU, as an institution, was not prepared to follow the lead of its chairpersons, who had not acted through its formal bodies. As for the United Nations, it was in no position to take a more assertive line. In that particular case, the United Nations was clearly not in the driver's seat, but African divisions were also exposed.

That example is important because it is taken from a country that still hosts the biggest UN peacekeeping operation: the political marginalization of the UN, even when it has a major operation deployed, suggests that the United Nations peacekeeping role in the new context is likely to be scaled down as a key instrument of peacemaking in the coming period. It confirms that with a divided UN Security Council, in which there are widely diverging views on what "peace" really means—a government capable of enforcing stability or institutions robust enough to manage dissent, new ambitious multidimensional peace operations are unlikely to be deployed. To be successful, they would require a unity of purpose and strategic persistence that is not attainable in the absence of a dominant power and in a context of retrenchment. Neither the political will nor the resources are available to underwrite complex operations that require the cooperation of multiple actors. This does not mean that UN peace operations will come to an end, but they are likely to be more limited in scope and to complement other international deployments. In some situations, high-intensity counterterrorist operations will coexist with more traditional peacekeeping operations. In a fragmented and multipolar international scene, situations in which the United Nations is the only or the main actor will be increasingly rare. International organizations have to learn to work with each other. At the same time, the ambition to have a clear and stable distribution of roles is unrealistic. Roles will depend on circumstances, and specific balance-of-power considerations will determine the configuration. Each case is likely to be unique, and it would be naive to hope for a general agreement on who does what. In each situation, relevant powers will determine whether it is in their interest to give a preeminent role to a particular organization.

Regional organizations are likely to see their role increase, but the influence of regional actors—regional powers as well as regional organizations—will vary considerably from one region to the other. And they will face their own challenges. As the African precedent shows, regional organizations are not immune to the influence of competing regional powers, and a regional consensus can be as difficult to produce as a global one. In Europe, the impotence of the Organization for Security and Cooperation in Europe over "frozen conflicts" and in Latin America, the deep divisions over the Venezuelan crisis, are cases in point. Meanwhile, in the Middle East, the League of Arab States is not in a position to address the conflicts of the region, even within its own member states. And a Middle Eastern regional organization that would include Iran, Israel, and Turkey could only be the product of a successful peace process, not its instrument. In eastern Asia, the strategic dominance of China will probably block any attempt to create an effective regional structure, and the same applies to South Asia with respect to India. In many situations, regional or subregional organizations, rather than being peacemakers, can become a tool in the hands of a dominant regional power; they can also more easily be manipulated by global powers than the United Nations. However, in some situations, the competition between global powers may open a space for regional powers: Indonesia and a subregional organization like the Association of Southeast Asian Nations are cases in point. In the end, regional organizations and regional powers will not replace global powers in conflict management and conflict resolution. They will often be used by them, while at the same time carving out for themselves a political space of which they are unable to fully take advantage.

In this new context, the role of the United Nations will need to evolve, adapting to a world that is shaped neither by a dominant power nor by a dominant confrontation. Its role is likely to be mainly political, even if situations may present themselves—the monitoring of a cease-fire and redeployment in Hodeida, for instance—where a military contribution of the United Nations is needed. In most cases, what will be expected from the UN is quiet, high-level diplomacy that will allow reaching understandings that direct engagement between global powers would not.

Even if raw balance-of-power dynamics reassert themselves at global, regional, and local levels, and powers try to create facts on the ground, there remain issues on which some convergence of interest exists and can lead to cooperation. In this vein, much has been made of the fight against terrorism. There may be some exaggeration and excessive expectations on the cooperation that can be generated by shared concerns over terrorism. Many governments conveniently label as terrorists their opponents, and the member states of the United Nations have been unable to reach an agreement on a definition of terrorism. Moreover, different countries have different views on how to fight terrorism and put sharply different priorities on political and military means. There may, however, be situations where a limited convergence of interests will make the United Nations an indispensable partner of states. In an overall trend toward less international engagement, powers that are eager to scale down their international engagements—notably the United States—want to limit the risk of opening up space to terrorist groups looking for safe havens, and the UN can help.

Afghanistan is a case in point. The United States is actively engaged in negotiations with the Taliban as it withdraws from the country. The level of military pressure it can apply is diminishing, and is known to be diminishing.

It needs to be complemented by political pressure, both direct and indirect—through Pakistan—that only China can provide. And this is just a particular illustration of a broader point. The long-term stability of Afghanistan will not be assured unless and until a set of powers, both global and regional (the United States, Russia, China, Pakistan, Iran, Saudi Arabia, and the EU countries) agree to it and support it. There are today too many tensions and enmities between those powers for the United States alone to be able to bring them together. This is typically a situation where UN facilitation, closely coordinated with the United States and Afghanistan as principal players, could help find a sufficiently comprehensive agreement. Yemen, Libya, and even Syria are other examples where the United Nations may eventually have to play a role in finding a solution.

More generally, in a world where an increasing number of actors—both state and nonstate—consider talking with each other to be an unacceptable concession, the United Nations should continue to provide the venue where engagement is not considered legitimation. This will be particularly necessary in those parts of the world where, for specific reasons, no regional or subregional organization can provide an alternative forum. The Middle East and Asia are two continents where, in many situations, there will not be an alternative to a UN role.

Finally, UN political facilitation may be valuable in those situations where there is no direct geopolitical competition between the major powers, even if a major power has significant interests. Colombia is a case in point, where the UN has played an important role, even though the United States, with its extensive antidrug program and extensive role in the country, was involved. Only the UN—able to speak to the Armed Forces of Colombia–People's Army (Fuerzas Armadas Revolucionarias de Colombia) and to Cuba—could, in a low-key manner, steer the process toward a peaceful conclusion.

In an era of increased strategic competition and aggressive nationalism, international organizations, and the United Nations at the center of them, will not be the architects of an international order structured by universally agreed-on principles. But they can continue to play an essential role by allowing ad hoc practical, peaceful solutions to prevail. This recalibration of ambitions will be the condition for more modest, less visible success. But such discrete efforts, by preventing local conflicts from further poisoning relations between the major powers, may become critical contributions to global peace.

PART II

Regional Perspectives on Discord and Collaboration

In this part, each author is asked to comment on the general implications for future diplomacy and conflict management flowing from our three scenarios.

CHAPTER 4

US Peace and Conflict Diplomacy in a State-Centric World

Hans Binnendijk

This chapter assesses peace and conflict diplomacy through the lens of a more state-centric world. For decades, the post-Westphalian international system had been eroding as international organizations stripped authority from states at the global level and nongovernmental organizations gained influence at the substate level.

That diffusion of power is changing, for better or worse. The Westphalian system is coming back. Power is being transferred back to nation-states. The United Nations still has many noble missions; for example, it is leading negotiations on a settlement of the civil war in Yemen. But with Chinese and Russian vetoes in the Security Council, the UN's ability to consolidate authority and conduct vigorous diplomacy is waning. Supranational regional organizations like the European Union are still major players, but the EU itself is suffering from centrifugal pressures that are tearing it apart.

Populism—driven by a reaction against centralized authority, the 2008 global recession, the COVID-19 pandemic, and migration crises in Europe and the United States—is stoking a nativist brand of nationalism and the return to a more state-centric system, and is thus stressing a return to the prominence of national sovereignty. Often, democratic systems are becoming more illiberal in the process. This phenomenon, in turn, is challenging the liberal international order created after World War II by the United States and its allies.

Populism is a global phenomenon. In different forms, it is evident in Putin's Russia; in Xi's China; in Britain's vote on Brexit; in the actions of Central European governments like those of Poland, Hungary, Austria, and the Czech Republic; in Mediterranean countries like Turkey and Italy; and in the Philippines, Venezuela, and Brazil—just to name a few. Even Western European states, the bastion of democracy, have strong domestic populist movements such as those of Le Pen in France, the Alternative fur Deutschland in Germany, and Wilders in the Netherlands.

Populism has also infected the United States. A state-centric, more nationalistic world is being embraced by the administration of President Donald Trump, which is accelerating the pace and magnifying the process. In his 2018 speech at the United Nations, Trump said: "America is governed by Americans. We reject the ideology of globalism, and we embrace the doctrine of patriotism. Around the world, responsible nations must defend against threats to sovereignty not just from global governance but also from other, new forms of coercion and domination."

The Trump administration's disdain for most international bodies extends to organizations, treaties, and agreements. On December 4, 2018, Secretary of State Mike Pompeo criticized an array of international organizations—including the United Nations, the European Union, the Organization of American States, the African Union, the International Criminal Court, the World Bank, the International Monetary Fund, and the World Trade Organization. He only listed three institutions as serving American interests: NATO, the Proliferation Security Initiative, and the Society for Worldwide Interbank Financial Telecommunications (SWIFT) (Harris 2018). The Trump administration has also walked away from the Paris Agreement on Climate Change, the World Health Organization, the Iran nuclear agreement, the Intermediate-Range Nuclear Forces Treaty, and the Open Skies Treaty.

This assessment therefore takes into account not only the impact of a more state-centric system but also one where existing international treaties and agreements, some based on previous peace and conflict diplomacy, are being adjusted or dismantled.

The chapter begins with two historical sections. The first section looks at seven different international systems that have prevailed since the 1815 Conference of Vienna to ascertain what happened to previous state-centric international systems. It compares those historical systems with the three scenarios discussed in chapter 2. The second section analyzes the characteristics of ten selected efforts at peace and conflict diplomacy that have been made since the end of the Cold War and suggests lessons for the future.

In the third section, the chapter assesses the emerging world order and its impact on future peace and conflict diplomacy. Which of the three alternative scenarios introduced in chapter 2 is most likely to emerge? This section introduces seven key global trends that will shape this order. It reviews several major emerging state-against-state rivalries. And it evaluates the decline of the liberal international order that will have a further impact on peace and conflict diplomacy.

The United States has played a critical role in most efforts at peace and conflict diplomacy since the end of the Cold War. So future American strategic direction will shape the future of state-centric diplomacy. This chapter's fourth section introduces three alternative American strategic approaches to the emerging world order and their possible impact on future diplomacy. It also reviews the path chosen by the current American presidential administration, which may or may not set the tone for the decades to come.

The chapter's fifth section provides an evaluation of what may be the new agenda for peace and conflict diplomacy in a state-centric world. It evaluates the concerns that are shaping the future agenda. It also previews several conflicts that may require diplomatic solutions during the next decade. It evaluates who might take the lead to seek solutions to those possible conflicts.

BACK TO THE FUTURE

The modern state system was born in 1648 with the Peace of Westphalia. A series of treaties ended the Thirty Years' War, in which religious conflict turned to anarchy and took 8 million lives, primarily in Central Europe. The emerging Westphalian system was based on the inviolability of borders and noninterference in the domestic affairs of the sovereign state. Writing at this time of religious warfare, the English philosopher Thomas Hobbes suggested the need for a social contract between the people and an absolute sovereign to avoid the brutal anarchy of the "state of nature" (Hobbes 2010). Over a century later, the German philosopher Emanuel Kant took a different approach during the Age of Enlightenment, which, though still primarily state-centric, envisioned greater democracy, more limited state power, and peace through international cooperation (Kant 2016). The shifting balance between a Hobbesian and Kantian state system has tended to define international affairs since then.

A review of two centuries of history since the 1815 Congress of Vienna (see table 4.1) demonstrates, in the first instance, that a purely state-centric system can deliver peace or war depending upon the relations among the sovereign nations. Drawing upon the three alternative future scenarios discussed in chapter 2—discord, collaboration, concert of nations—one can conclude that a "concert of nations," with Britain holding the balance of power, was able to keep the peace between 1815 and the outbreak of the Crimean War in 1853. That concert broke down with the Crimean War and

Table 4.1 The History of State-Centric International Systems

Period	International System	State-Centric?	Scenario	Outcome
1815–53	Balance of power	State	3	40 years of peace
1856–1914	Rise of Germany	State	1	Discord / World War I
1918–39	Competing alliances	State	1	Discord / World War II
1945–91	Bipolar	Hybrid	1 and 2	Soviet Union falls
1991–2001	Unipolar	Global	2	Democratization
2001–14	War on terrorism	Concert	1 and 3	Fragmentation
2014–	Back to bipolarity?	Mostly state	1 or 3	Disruption

Note: Scenario 1 = discord; Scenario 2 = collaboration; Scenario 3 = concert of nations.

the subsequent rise of German nationalism under Otto von Bismarck and his wars to unite Germany. Bismarck was skilled enough to use flexible alliances to manage "discord" among nations. But after he lost power, alliances began to be cemented, and the growing discord needed only a spark at Sarajevo to trigger World War I. The failure of the League of Nations, an imbalanced Versailles Peace Treaty, and the Great Depression created further state-centric discord with the rise of Adolf Hitler and World War II.

The Western victors in World War II recognized that to maintain the peace, the state-centric system needed a series on international institutions and agreements to reduce tensions, distribute global power, promote security, manage political differences through the rule of law, deal with financial crises, and promote economic development. The liberal international order was born. But this order existed initially in an ideologically divided, bipolar world where these institutions were primarily used by the democratic nations to strengthen one another. The communist nations created other institutions on their side of the bipolar divide. Collaboration coexisted in two separate worlds, with discord between those two worlds. Peace was maintained through balanced military forces and nuclear deterrence.

The George H. W. Bush administration oversaw the end of the Cold War with astute diplomacy and the use of military power: unifying Germany; establishing, with Operation Desert Storm, that the United States would resist naked aggression; and peacefully managing the collapse of the Soviet Union. Together, these events constituted a masterpiece of peace and conflict diplomacy. The decade after the end of the Cold War was the "golden age" of globalization and collaboration. With the collapse of the Soviet Union, the international system was described as unipolar. International relations became even more interdependent, and political scientists predicted that the use of force and coercive power would decline. The Western institutions created during the Cold War thrived. The number of democratic states increased dramatically (Huntington 1991; Roser 2020). The European Union was created. The Clinton administration continued many of the foreign policies of George H. W. Bush and adopted a strategy of "enlargement" as democracy and defensive alliances such as NATO expanded.

But this golden age did not last long. The September 11, 2001, terrorist attacks on the United States triggered a dramatic and flawed response from the George W. Bush administration. The adversary was not a nation-state but organized international groups of armed radical Islamists. Though most US allies supported and participated in the Afghanistan War, there was sharp dissent when it came to the US invasion of Iraq. The global consensus of the 1990s began to fragment. The Obama administration sought to reverse many aspects of the more unilaterally assertive George W. Bush administration's policies by developing approaches closer to those of the Clinton administration. Some argue that it overreacted to George W. Bush's policies and further undermined the global system by retrenching too far. During this 2001–14 period, there were significant signs of discord developing again in the international system, and often coalitions of the willing, aka a "concert of nations," were used to implement peace and conflict diplomacy.

By 2014, the collaborative global system was in retreat. Putin's remilitarized Russia had invaded parts of Georgia and Ukraine, and it was practicing constant low-level or "hybrid" warfare against the West. China emerged as a potentially dangerous economic and military rival to the United States. And democracy in many states became illiberal. As noted, the Trump administration appeared to join Russia and China in challenging the very system that the United States had built after World War II. A more state-centric international system was back.

The conclusions of this brief review are that state-centric systems have tended to dominate since the Peace of Westphalia, whether they are Hobbesian or Kantian in nature. They have not always led to discord and conflict, but often they have. Periods of true global collaboration with more limited national sovereignty have been infrequent. Wars have tended to result when discord has not been balanced by collaboration or a concert of power. Today, the world is embarking on a more state-centric and possibly more dangerous path, on which nations will need to manage growing discord. This will be a time when peace and conflict diplomacy is badly needed but will be difficult to implement.

THE RECENT RECORD OF PEACE
AND CONFLICT DIPLOMACY

If peace and conflict diplomacy will be critical to the emerging state-centric world order, learning from the recent past may provide insights into how these efforts might be useful in the future. Ten selected examples since the end of the Cold War were reviewed for this assessment.[1] They are of course not complete or all inclusive, but they do represent a good sample across time and geography. These cases include:

- *The 1993 Oslo Accords* were initiated by a Norwegian nongovernmental institute, which began a process that led to a more autonomous Palestinian Authority, mutual security arrangements, and greater economic cooperation. The Oslo Accords stalled with the assassination of Prime Minister Yitzhak Rabin ("The Oslo Accords" n.d.).
- *The 1994 Agreed Framework* was negotiated by the US State Department and North Korean officials, with the intervention of former president Jimmy Carter. It froze North Korea's plutonium programs and placed about 8,000 fuel rods under inspection by the International Atomic Energy Agency (IAEA), in exchange for American-financed fuel oil and the construction of two light water nuclear reactors. Construction of the reactors was delayed, and North Korea was caught developing a uranium enrichment capacity. The Bush administration abrogated the Agreed Framework, and the subsequent Six-Party Talks failed ("The US–North Korean Agreed Framework" 2018).
- *The 1995 Dayton General Framework Agreement* ended the Bosnian War after NATO air strikes on Serb targets determined the military outcome. Six nations and the EU negotiated with Bosnian and Serbian leaders. The subsequent UN Security Council Resolution 1088 created the Stabilization Force to enforce the peace, which continues to hold today (Clinton 2019).
- *The 1998 Good Friday Agreement* created new power-sharing arrangements in Northern Ireland and ended the insurgency by the Irish Republican Army (IRA). Brokered in part by the American envoy George Mitchell, the deal was overwhelmingly supported in a referendum, and despite some implementation difficulties in 2002, it has continued to keep the peace in Northern Ireland ("What Was the Good Friday Agreement?" 2018).
- *The 1999 Plan Colombia*, in which the United States provided over $10 billion to Colombia over sixteen years to counter narcotics

production and end the insurrection by the Revolutionary Armed Forces of Colombia–People's Army (Fuerzas Armadas Revolucionarias de Colombia, FARC). The funding tripled the Colombian defense budget. In 2017, the Colombian government and FARC negotiated a peace agreement (Shifter 2012).

- *The 2002 creation of the International Security Assistance Force (ISAF) for Afghanistan* was an American led, UN-supported, and NATO-operated effort to bring stability to Afghanistan. At its peak, it included about 130,000 soldiers from 51 nations ("ISAF's Mission In Afghanistan" 2015).

- *The 2005 Sudan Comprehensive Peace* created a referendum on the creation of a new nation called the Republic of Southern Sudan, which was held in 2011. Civil war broke out in the new republic in 2013, and this war ended in September 2018. Various international actors participated in the long process, including an East African bloc called the Inter-Governmental Authority on Development, and Western powers including the United States, Italy, Norway, and Britain. The UN Mission in Sudan, created in 2005, was unable to contain the violence (Maasho 2018).

- *The 2014 Minsk Protocol*, using the so-called Normandy Format (Ukraine, Russia, Germany, and France), with monitors from the Organization for Security and Cooperation in Europe (OSCE), sought to terminate a conflict in Ukraine's Donbas area and remove Russian forces from that area of Ukraine. Minsk 2 reached an agreement, and some prisoners and hostages were exchanged. But the agreement has failed to remove Russian troops from the Donbas ("The *Economist* Explains" 2016).

- *The 2015 Joint Comprehensive Plan of Action* effectively halted Iran's nuclear program in exchange for lifting US, EU, and UN sanctions. The deal was negotiated between the so-called P5+1—the United States, Russia, China, Britain, France, and Germany—and Iran, with EU participation and IAEA verification. The Trump administration withdrew from the deal, despite the fact that Iran remained in compliance ("Joint Comprehensive Plan of Action" n.d.).

- *The 2018 North Korean denuclearization effort* is an ongoing initiative by the United States to negotiate directly at the head-of-state level. The United States consults closely with South Korea, which conducts its own efforts to reduce North/South tensions. The United States also pressures China and others to impose sanctions on North Korea. Despite three summits, there are no signs that North Korea is willing to truly denuclearize.

Table 4.2 presents fourteen characteristics of peace and conflict diplomacy and highlights which of these characteristics were present in each case.

Despite the fact that half or more of these cases took place during the "golden age of globalization," all but one of the ten cases reviewed were driven at the outset by nation-states or groups of nation-states rather than international organizations. The one exception was the Oslo Accords, which eventually did become state-centric.[2] This indicates that in a more state-centric world, peace and conflict diplomacy can flourish if the conditions are right.

In seven of the ten cases, the United States played a principal role in setting the stage for negotiations and leading the negotiating process. This is in part a function of America's global interests, power, and responsibilities. The United States controls a mix of instruments that can expedite peace and conflict diplomacy. But other nations or groups have stepped up when the United States has not led. One recent example is the so-called Normandy Format, in which France and Germany led the process that created the Minsk II Agreements on the Donbas. Another example is the Sudan Comprehensive Peace case, in which local African nations eventually drove much of the process with Western support.

Based on these ten cases, multinational coalitions and regional organizations appear to be more prevalent in the negotiations than international organizations. The United Nations featured prominently in only two of these cases (Dayton and ISAF), and then they were used to support US policies. In contrast, six of the cases involved other nation-states working primarily in concert with the United States or with one another to direct the diplomacy. Several cases involved regional organizations such as NATO or the EU working alongside nation-states.

The purpose of peace and conflict diplomacy during the past two and a half decades, judging by these ten cases, appear to be primarily twofold: conflict termination and nonproliferation. Conflict termination efforts were generally designed to end civil wars in countries as diverse as Britain, Colombia, Afghanistan, Bosnia, and Sudan. The Oslo Accords were an extension, without much US involvement, of the US-led Middle East diplomacy started by Henry Kissinger. And efforts to end Russia's incursion into Ukraine's Donbas region were also European led.

Nonproliferation diplomacy was dominated by the United States in the case of both North Korea and Iran. American interests in not becoming the target of a nuclear attack generated by a so-called rogue state drove American policy. But in both cases, the United States brought in other nation-states to strengthen their negotiation position. These ten cases are also instructive in terms analyzing the various instruments used to conduct peace and conflict

Table 4.2 Peace and Conflict Diplomacy since 1991

Characteristic	1993 Oslo Accords	1994 Agreed Framework Korea	1995 Dayton Accords	1998 Good Friday Agreement	1999 Plan Colombia	2002 ISAF	2005 Sudan CPA	2014 Minsk Protocol	2015 JCPOA	2018 US–North Korea summits
Participant										
State-centric		✓	✓	✓	✓	✓	✓	✓	✓	✓
US led	✓	✓	✓	✓	✓	✓	✓		✓	✓
IO in negotiation			✓			✓				
Regional/NGOs	✓	✓	✓			✓	✓			
Multinational	✓	✓	✓			✓	✓	✓	✓	✓
Purpose										
End conflict	✓		✓	✓	✓	✓	✓	✓		
Counterproliferation		✓							✓	✓
Instruments										
Use/threat of US force		✓	✓		✓	✓			✓	✓
Coercion/sanctions		✓			✓	✓	✓	✓	✓	✓
Economic/political incentives	✓	✓		✓	✓	✓	✓	✓	✓	✓
IO in implementation		✓	✓			✓	✓	✓	✓	
Stabilization force	✓	✓	✓	✓		✓	✓	✓		
Formal agreement	✓		✓	✓	✓	✓	✓	✓	✓	
Success/in force			✓	✓	✓	✓	✓	?	?	

Note: CPA = Comprehensive Peace Agreement in Sudan; IO = international organization; ISAF = International Security Assistance Force, Afghanistan; JCPOA = Joint Comprehensive Plan of Action (Iran); NGO = nongovernmental organization.

diplomacy. Carrots and sticks were often effective when used together. In seven of the ten cases, efforts were made to compel parties to negotiate:

- In the case of the 1994 Agreed Framework, the United States had imposed sanctions on North Korea and was threatening to use force to destroy nuclear facilities if North Korea did not comply.
- In Bosnia, the United States led an air campaign that destroyed Serbian positions and shifted the local balance of forces.
- Plan Colombia was a US effort to both eradicate drugs and compel the FARC to negotiate, primarily by providing military assistance and support to Colombia's military forces.
- The US effort to construct a NATO-led coalition of the willing in Afghanistan was designed to put maximum military and political pressure on Taliban fighters' inertia to terminate the Afghan civil war.
- In the case of the Minsk Agreement, compellence was limited to Western economic sanctions on Russia and provision of defensive military assistance to Ukraine.
- In the case of Iran, international sanctions were the principal tool to compel that nation to the negotiating table, although the threat of US-led military action was also clear.
- Finally, in the case of President Trump's effort to denuclearize North Korea, the campaign opened with American threats of "fire and fury" if North Korea continued on its path.

In most of the cases reviewed, economic incentives or other carrots played a crucial role in final negotiations. In some cases, it was simply the promise of better economic conditions in a postwar environment. That postwar economic situation was sometimes sweetened, as in the case of Oslo and Dayton, with the promise of new postwar economic cooperation between the parties. In the case of Sudan, it was distribution of oil revenue. But in many cases—such as North Korea, Iran, and Minsk—it was the promise of sanctions relief that provided useful carrots at the negotiations. In the cases of Plan Colombia and Afghanistan, US economic and military assistance to an ally was an integral part of the plan to bring the adversary to the negotiating table. And in the case of the 1994 Agreed Framework, assistance to support North Korean energy needs was a critical component of the final deal.

Although these cases did not feature many international organizations as principal drivers of the negotiations, in a majority of the cases, they were critical to implementation of the final agreement. Without those capabilities, the agreements may not have been reached, let alone implemented. In nonproliferation cases such as the 1994 Agreed Framework and the Joint Comprehensive Plan of Action, the IAEA's verification procedures were integral to the final agreement. In the case of Minsk II, the OSCE Special Monitoring Mission was designed to oversee implementation of the agreement. In the Sudan case, the UN Mission in the Sudan was established to monitor the peace. In these last two cases, however, the monitoring missions were weak and ineffective. In the case of the Dayton Accords and the establishment of the ISAF mission, the implementation forces were authorized by the UN but operated by NATO. They were relatively strong and effective. Although implementation of an agreement by an international organization does not guarantee success, a state-only system trying to negotiate peace and conflict diplomacy without them would be at a great disadvantage.

All the cases reviewed except the last, which is still ongoing, produced written agreements that laid out the terms in detail. This raises the issue of the senior diplomat's role in successful negotiations. In some cases, the negotiations were carried out by senior career diplomats, but in other difficult cases it took someone with more international clout to carry the ball. In the case of the 1994 Agreed Framework, it took Jimmy Carter's informal presence in Pyongyang to stimulate an agreement. In the Oslo case, Johan Holst, the former Norwegian defense minister, had the international gravitas to bring the sides together. Former Senate majority leader George Mitchell helped broker the Good Friday Agreement by presenting a draft agreement at a critical moment in the talks. And American diplomat, Richard Holbrooke, had enough bravado and political clout in Washington, Europe, and the Balkans to engineer the Dayton Accords. In the current negotiations with North Korea, Secretary of State Mike Pompeo is the lead US diplomat.

A final look at these cases indicates the need for continued persistence to sustain agreements that have been reached. Two of the agreements have failed. The Oslo Accords have been overtaken by continued Israeli and Palestinian confrontation. The 1994 Framework Agreement failed because North Korea was caught cheating and the George W. Bush administration was not creative enough to sustain what was important—plutonium that was under IAEA safeguards, which now sits in North Korean nuclear weapons.

Four agreements have fallen on hard times. The ISAF operation and its 2015 successor Resolute Support Mission have continued to provide military assistance for the Afghan government, but the civil war continues despite renewed negotiations. The 2005 Sudan Comprehensive Peace led to creation of a new nation in 2013 and to five years of civil war; it remains to be seen if the new peace agreement will hold. The Minsk II Protocol has not stopped the fighting in Ukraine's Donbas area. And the Iran Joint Comprehensive

Plan of Action agreement has been abandoned by the Trump administration but may survive with European support.

Only three of these agreements appear to be on fairly solid ground, but even they require continued maintenance. The Good Friday Agreement stopped the IRA's terrorist attacks and must now survive Brexit. The Dayton Agreement stopped the killing in Bosnia, but Bosnia remains essentially two states with limited internal cooperation. And Plan Colombia led to the 2017 agreement with FARC, but agreement with the National Liberation Army (Ejército de Liberación Nacional) is less certain; some former rebel fighters are reportedly retuning to the mountains, and the Colombian military has suggested the need to respond more vigorously.

The seven major conclusions to emerge from this review of past cases are:

- The two principal purposes of peace and conflict diplomacy during this period have been to end conflict (often civil wars) and to halt efforts at nuclear proliferation.
- Even in a more global international system, states and multinational groups of states have been the principal drivers of peace and conflict diplomacy.
- US leadership has been central to most recent peace and conflict diplomacy.
- International organizations have not led most peace and conflict negotiations, but they have nonetheless been critical to the implementation of agreements through their ability to monitor and verify, and when necessary to provide troops for stabilization efforts.
- Diplomats need an array of sticks and carrots to conduct successful negotiations, including the possible use of armed force, sanctions and other forms of coercion, and economic incentives (Gompert and Binnendijk 2016).
- Diplomats with global credibility can make a major difference in delivering positive outcomes.
- Agreements once reached need continued nurturing to remain in effect.

THE NEW STRATEGIC ENVIRONMENT: DISCORD, COLLABORATION, OR CONCERT?

This section analyzes the evolving strategic environment to assess which of the future scenarios discussed in chapter 2—discord, collaboration, or concert—is most likely to become a reality in a more state-centric system. To do this, it reviews seven global trends to see in which direction these trends may carry the strategic environment:

Global trend	Consequence
Autocratic regimes and populism on the rise	Probable discord
State versus state rivalries on the rise	Probable discord
Climate change and humanitarian crises on the rise	Further discord, need collaboration
Emerging weapons technology spreading	Further discord, need collaboration
Further economic shocks a continuing risk	Further discord, need collaboration
Expect more strategic surprises	Further discord, need collaboration
Liberal international order challenged	Is concert the default?

The first two trends are related and together portend greater global discord. Russian and China are two major autocratic regimes that are gaining power, and they are working more closely together to challenge and divide the current liberal international order. They offer social contracts in which their citizens give up freedoms in exchange for either security (Russia) or economic growth (China). They are having some new success in selling these authoritarian models to other nations. Russian in particular tends to promote division and populism in democratic states.

The rise of populism globally generally undercuts democratic values and creates more extreme positions on issues of sovereignty as states respond to more narrow nationalistic positions pressed by their constituents. A comparison with the periods of unconstrained nationalism (discussed in the first section above, from 1856 to 1945) reminds us that extreme nationalism has yielded a series of costly wars.

Freedom House has recorded the results of more than a decade of declining freedom around the globe. In its 2018 report, it concluded: "Democracy faced its most serious crisis in decades in 2017 as its basic tenets—including guarantees of free and fair elections, the rights of minorities, freedom of the press, and the rule of law—came under attack around the world. . . . Over the period since the 12-year global slide began in 2006, 113 countries have seen a net decline, and only 62 have experienced a net improvement" ("Freedom in the World" 2018). Nonetheless, despite this backsliding, some 4 billion of the world's 7 billion inhabitants now live in some form of democracy.

This decline of democracy has been coupled with a rise in state sovereignty. This combination has been driven in part by populism and has created increased competition and potential conflict among nation-states. This is evident in the 2018 US National Defense Strategy, which says: "We are facing increased global disorder, characterized by decline in the long-standing rules-based international order—creating a security environment more complex and volatile than any we have experienced in recent memory. Interstate strategic competition, not terrorism, is now the primary concern in US national security. . . . America's military has no preordained right to victory on the battlefield."

Table 4.3 lists nine state rivalries and their motivations. For example, Russia's desire to regain control over its "near abroad" and to protect the rights of Russian-speaking peoples has led to armed attacks on Georgia and Ukraine. Similarly, Chinese nationalism has contributed to its so-called nine-dash-line claim over and militarization of the South China Sea. This in turn has created additional tensions between these two countries and the United States as the United States seeks to protect its partners and international law.

Tensions between the United States and two nations that have sought to acquire nuclear weapons, North Korea and Iran, have become more intense since the United States has walked away from both the 1994 Agreed Framework with North Korea and the Joint Comprehensive Plan of Action with Iran. Armed conflict between the United States and any of these four nation-states (Russia, China, North Korea, Iran) is within the realm of the possible during the coming decade.

Tensions among other major powers are also on the rise. India and China, for example, are both rising powers who together house 35 percent of the world's population, are affected by populism, and live in the same neighborhood. Blood has been shed in the Himalayas as Chinese and Indian troops jockey for position on the Siachen Glacier. A summary of a recent book edited by T. V. Paul assesses this relationship:

India and China's relationship faces a number of challenges, including multiple border disputes that periodically flare up, division over the status of Tibet and the Dalai Lama, the strategic challenge to India posed by China's close relationship with Pakistan, the Chinese navy's greater presence in the Indian Ocean, and the two states' competition for natural resources. Despite these irritants, however, both countries agree on issues such as global financial reforms and climate change and have much to gain from increasing trade and investment, so there are reasons for optimism as well as pessimism. (Paul 2018)

Table 4.3 Nine Major State Rivalries

Rivals	Motive/Cause	Peace and Conflict Diplomacy Goal
NATO-Russia	Russian Illiberal Democracy	Avoid miscalculation/escalation
US–North Korea	DPRK Nuclear Program	DPRK denuclearization
US-Iran	Iranian regional behavior	Avoid a nuclear Iran
Ukraine-Russia	Crimea and Donbas	Russian withdrawal from Ukraine
China-ASEAN	Chinese regional hegemony	Settle South China Sea claims
India-China	Contending regional powers	Settle border disputes, nuclear balance
Iran–Saudi Arabia	Sunni/Shia and Arab/Persian	Halt fighting in Yemen and Syria
Israel-Palestine	Who controls territory	Two state solution
Colombia-Venezuela	Ideological Divide	Reform in Venezuela

Note: ASEAN = Association of Southeast Asian Nations; DPRK = Democratic People's Republic of Korea (North Korea).

In the Middle East, the Iran-Saudi confrontation has both religious and ethnic elements, with Iran's Shia/Persian and Saudi's Sunni/Arab composition driving the rivalry. The two nations are on opposite sides of confrontation in Syria, Yemen, and Lebanon. Russia tends to support Iran, while the United States has supported Saudi Arabia. Israeli-Palestinian conflict continues to flare despite efforts by every American administration to broker a peace settlement.

And new leaders in Colombia and Venezuela have led to the risk of military conflict between these two Latin American neighbors. Colombia's Ivan Duque Marquez has called for increased sanctions against Venezuela as Venezuela's Nicolás Maduro has moved troops to the Colombian border. The United States supports Colombia while Russia supports Maduro.

Four other global trends tend to exacerbate the movement towards discord set by the first two trends. But these trends also threaten to disrupt all nations. In addition to the risk of further discord, these trends should create incentives for global collaboration to alleviate their impact:

- Global warming in the US alone could cut GDP by 10 percent by 2100; increase premature deaths, mosquito borne diseases, and wildfires; cost $1 trillion in lost coastal real-estate and threaten dependable water and energy supplies (Christensen and Nedelman 2018). The social and political consequences may be extreme. Collaborative responses stronger than the recent UN COP-24 Agreement may be needed to halt negative trends.

- Emerging weapons technologies—including nuclear, cyber, biological, and biochemical methods, drones and autonomous weapons, nano-technology, additive manufacturing, wearable devices, and artificial intelligence—will make smaller adversaries and terrorist groups more formidable. It threatens most nation-states and will take international collaboration to limit and control these technologies (Kaspersen 2015).
- The combination of growing income inequality in most countries and the risk of another financial meltdown due to unregulated global debt creates the prospect of further economic, social, and political upheaval. International financial institutions must collaborate to pre-pare ("World Inequality Report" 2018; Inman 2018).
- The volume, velocity, and variety of information in the international system creates the risk of more strategic surprises that require rapid decision-making. This limits the time available for international con-sultation and collaboration (Gewirtz 2018; Yost 2018).

These trends have contributed to the increase of conflict around the globe since 2010. The data of Uppsala University's Department of Peace and Conflict Research shows a sharp increase in fatalities from conflict beginning about 2013–14, with about 100,000 people dying annually from conflict during those years. The growth area in these conflicts is "internationalized intrastate conflict," that is, civil wars with intervention by external states (Uppsala Conflict Data Program n.d.). The World Bank's project on fragility, conflict, and violence demonstrates further the negative impact of state fra-gility, which when combined with the growth of state-against-state confron-tation explains the growth of internationalized intrastate conflict ("Fragility, Conflict & Violence" 2020).

These global trends can lead to even greater international discord unless nations in the international system establish diplomatic mechanisms to man-age them. But the so-called liberal international order, created after World War II, is eroding, making it more difficult to manage these disruptive trends. Table 4.4 records the changes that have taken place in the past twenty years. As noted, major power confrontation is back, and democracy is in decline. The United Nations is no longer used to legitimize the use of force. Inter-national effort to promote the rule of law, such as the US Convention on the Law of the Sea and the International Criminal Court, have not been ratified by the United States. The Russians are cheating, and United States is abrogating key arms control agreements. Regional organizations such as

Table 4.4 Erosion of the Liberal International Order, 1990s–2020

Characteristic	1990s	2020
Major powers	Cooperation	Confrontation
Democracy	Third wave	Illiberal democracy
United Nations	Cooperation	Security Council dysfunctional
UN / Use of force	Bosnia	Iraq/Libya/Georgia/Ukraine/Yemen
Rule of law	UNCLOS/ICC	US not ratified either agreement
Arms control	START agreed	Abrogate ABM, INF, JCPOA, Open Skies
Regional	Creation of EU	Brexit / Eastern revolt / Southern debt
Trade	NAFTA	USMCA agreed on; TPP/TTIP dropped
Climate change	Kyoto Protocol	US leaves Paris Agreement

Note: ABM = Anti-Ballistic Missile Treaty; INF = Intermediate Nuclear Forces; JCPOA = Joint Comprehensive Plan of Action (Iran); NAFTA = North American Free Trade Agreement; START = Strategic Arms Reduction Treaty; TPP = Trans-Pacific Partnership; TTIP = Transatlantic Trade and Investment Partnership; UNCLOS = United Nations Convention on the Law of the Sea; USMCA = United States–Mexico–Canada Agreement. See also Haass 2019.

the European Union are in danger of fragmenting. Trade wars have replaced trade agreements. And though the international community is seeking to address climate change, the efforts are weak, and the United States has for now abandoned even those weak efforts.

Putin's Russia has actively sought to destroy the US-built international order. Moscow harbors grievances related to NATO's enlargement, US-led military engagements undertaken without UN Security Council authorization, the colored revolutions that overthrew pro-Moscow leaders in Ukraine and Serbia, and Western efforts to bolster democracy in Russia. Russian efforts have included use of social media to divide Western nations and undermine the democratic process, financial support for populist leaders, military invasion of neighbors, and support for authoritarian rulers in places like Syria. China, by contrast, has sought to adapt the international order to serve its own purposes by creating institutions like the Asian Infrastructure Investment Bank. Ironically, President Trump's efforts sometimes appear to be supportive of the Russian and Chinese efforts to undermine the system.

What does this assessment of the future international environment mean for peace and conflict diplomacy? Several conclusions might be drawn:

- Populism and greater state-against-state conflict appear to be driving the world in the general direction of greater discord. This discord will be amplified by other dominant trends like global warming, emerging weapons technology, possible future economic crises, and more strategic surprises hampered by ponderous decision-making. This discord will create a rich menu for future peace and conflict diplomacy, but it will also make future diplomacy more difficult if discord becomes complex and threatens many countries.

- There may be a countertrend as states realize that they cannot manage most of these global threats alone and that they need to collaborate.
- Many of the instruments of peace and conflict diplomacy are embedded in the current liberal international order and its institutions; and to the extent that this order is eroded, the instruments of diplomacy will be diminished.
- If widespread international collaboration becomes difficult to orchestrate because of these trends, then a concert of nation-states might form issue by issue to protect their interests. But they will need to operate on an ad hoc basis and may not carry the degree of international legitimacy that is needed to be successful.
- These trends are not all irreversible. With strong global leadership, the United States and its democratic allies can still rescue the opportunity to collaborate on the management of these problems.

WHERE IS THE UNITED STATES HEADED?

President Trump's America First policy toward the international system in general and peace and conflict diplomacy in particular is a distinct change from what in retrospect is remarkable continuity over seven decades of American national security leadership. This list records the characteristics of the foreign policy elements of America First:

- Focus on:
  - Economic over security interests
  - Bilateral over multilateral relations
  - Interests over values like human rights
  - Short term economic interests over climate change
- Decision-making
  - Transactional
  - Erratic and abrupt
  - Intuition over analysis and intelligence
- Diplomatic style
  - Insult, disrupt, reconcile, hype results
  - Discount value of alliances and partners

    – Ambiguity towards adversaries
    – Spending on defense over diplomacy
- Limited interest in peace and conflict diplomacy

American leaders have traditionally placed international security policy above economic policy in the pecking order of issues. Trump has reversed that, declaring trade wars on allies and placing NATO burden sharing above the credibility of NATO's Article 5 commitment. American leaders have traditionally sought multilateral solutions to problems and to balance American interests and values. Trump approaches issues bilaterally, generally using multilateral formats like the Group of Seven to disrupt. He places American interests, usually narrowly defined, above American values.

Trump's foreign policy decision-making style is transactional, erratic, and abrupt; he usually places his "gut" instincts above facts drawn from intelligence agencies and careful analysis. His diplomatic style is to insult, disrupt, reconcile, and then hype any accomplishments. Unlike all his postwar predecessors, he discounts the value of America's alliances. He has increased defense spending but disparaged military leaders and proposed drastic cuts on the instruments of diplomacy. For example, his 2019 budget would reduce the State Department's diplomatic budget by 18 percent while foreign aid would be cut by about 30 percent (Epstein, Gill, and Lawson 2019). He has certainly not placed a priority on peace and conflict diplomacy as traditionally practiced.

That does not mean Trump has failed in every instance. This effort to renegotiate the North American Free Trade Agreement was somewhat successful, although the improvements in the United States–Mexico–Canada Agreement were modest and the collateral damage to America's relations with its neighbors was great. Trump's high stakes negotiations with Pyongyang are, to say the least, unconventional; although the "insult, disrupt, reconcile, hype" negotiating style has at least yielded summit meetings if not denuclearization.

Trump's style and policies have created an overwhelming lack of confidence abroad in American leadership. During the Cold War, the United States' military strength and democratic values made it the unquestioned leader of the West. There were often differences, such as over the Vietnam and Iraq wars, but not much happened in NATO, the United Nations, or other international institutions without US leadership and approval.

Today America's leadership role is in rapid decline. Global public opinion is divided over how powerful a role the United States will play in future global affairs. According to a recent Pew poll, "A global median of 35 percent say the country is as important on the world stage as before, while 31 percent say it plays a more important role and 25 percent say it plays a less important role. But lack of confidence in US foreign policy has shifted dramatically." The Pew poll concluded: "Of the 25 countries surveyed, a median of 70 percent lack confidence in Trump to do the right thing regarding world affairs" (Bialik 2014). That is a dramatic fall in the global confidence compared with the Obama years.

American attitudes are also shifting. Five years ago, roughly half the Americans polled felt that the wars in Iraq and Afghanistan had failed or were a mistake (Drake 2014; Newport 2014). They were more inclined to support a restrained American foreign policy. Today, the public attitude is more positive toward American engagement abroad. For example:

- 70 percent of Americans favor the US taking an active part in world affairs
- 75 percent favor maintaining or increasing the US commitment to NATO
- 91 percent say it is more effective for the US to work with allies
- 57 percent say the US is losing allies
- 66 percent say they are more willing to make decisions in the UN
- 68 percent support the Paris climate agreement
- 66 percent support the Iran nuclear agreement (Smeltz et al. 2018)

With this shift, it is fair to ask which direction US foreign policy might take under the Biden Administration, and what that might mean for peace and conflict diplomacy. Three alternative approaches and their characteristics have been posited by me (Binnendijk 2016):

1. Assertiveness (Iraq invasion 2003)
   - Values based
   - Interventions alone or in small coalitions
   - Partners and alliances secondary
   - Avoid international organizations
   - Confront adversaries
   - High defense budget
   - Low diplomatic and aid budgets
   - Peace and conflict diplomacy is a low priority
   - Limit: US overstretch
2. Collaborative engagement (Desert Storm, Kosovo)
   - Pragmatic
   - Lead military and diplomatic coalitions

- Partnerships and alliances are critical
- Use international organizations
- Confront and compromise with adversaries
- Moderate defense budgets
- High diplomatic and aid budgets
- Peace and conflict diplomacy is a high priority
- Limit: high reliance on partners

3. Retrenchment (rapid withdrawal from Iraq and Afghanistan)
   - Narrow interest based
   - Limit military intervention
   - Seek greater burden sharing from partners
   - Use international organization when possible
   - Negotiate with adversaries when possible
   - Lower defense budget
   - Moderate diplomatic and aid budgets
   - Peace and conflict diplomacy is a moderate priority
   - Limit: partners vulnerable

The first potential US strategic direction might be called "assertiveness." The model is US policy under the George W. Bush administration when the United States acted boldly to execute a global war against terrorism, including the invasion of two countries. The policy was sold as value based because the goal was to democratize the Middle East and make it more peaceful. It had limited international appeal, and the United States had to operate with a small coalition of the willing with regard to Iraq. Under an assertive US strategy, peace and conflict diplomacy might have a relatively low priority because the United States would seek more unilateral and military solutions. It would likely be a more state-centric approach.

The second potential strategic direction might be called "collaboration." The model is George H. W. Bush's global coalition for Desert Storm or Bill Clinton's coalition to fight the Bosnia and Kosovo wars. In the Desert Storm and Bosnia cases, significant efforts were made to seek UN authority for military intervention. The Clinton administration was also more inclined to negotiate international agreement to deal with conflict resolution and arms control issues. This strategy would be most inclined to pursue peace and conflict diplomacy and use the international institutions of the liberal international order to accomplish the mission.

The third potential strategic direction might be called "retrenchment." The model here is the Obama administration's policy for the Middle East, where it sought to draw down the costly trillion dollar wars in Iraq and Afghanistan.

But Trump's foreign policy has even stronger elements of retrenchment as he seeks to remove nearly all US troops from the Middle East and presses for greater international burden sharing to relieve the United States of what he considers to be excessive commitments. This strategy would highlight diplomacy over military solutions, but the degree to which the United States sought to engage in the disputes of others might be limited.

It is of course difficult to predict the future, but some signposts do exist. The assertive strategy of 2001–8 is generally considered to have created American overextension and global criticism of American policies. Many believe that the Obama administration overreacted to George W. Bush's policies and that its retrenchment policies further weakened the United States. There is also likely to be an effort by the Biden Administration to reclaim America's lost leadership position in global affairs. As this pendulum has swung and given US public willingness to engage more in foreign affairs, there may be a return to some form of collaboration after Trump leaves office. But that collaboration may be tempered by a demand for greater global burden sharing to relieve the high bill that the United States has paid over seven decades.[3]

Several conclusions might be drawn from this section:

- Although the United States has for seven decades been instrumental to the practice of peace and conflict diplomacy, during the Trump administration it dramatically reversed course and rejected the use of international institutions for this purpose.
- Global public opinion has little confidence in this approach.
- US public opinion, reacting to Trump's policies, now seems more willing to engage globally with international institutions.
- After the Trump administration leaves office, there are several alternative strategies to shape American foreign policy. They vary with regard to how integral peace and conflict diplomacy will be to the United States.
- If the demand for peace and conflict diplomacy increases, as the review of the changing strategic environment suggests, then even a return to a US policy of collaboration will probably include a greater demand for global burden sharing. Other nations may need to pick up the slack.

A NEW AGENDA WITH NEW ACTORS?

This final section explores areas where peace and conflict diplomacy may be needed in the next decade and who might lead these efforts. Two different documents reviewed together may shed light on future peace and conflict diplomacy requirements. The first document presents a summary of a US Council on Foreign Relations survey of about five hundred US foreign policy experts (Stares 2019):

- Tier One
  - A highly disruptive cyberattack
  - Renewed tensions on the Korean Peninsula
  - Armed confrontation between Iran and the United States
  - Armed confrontation in the South China Sea
  - Mass casualty terrorist attack
  - Heightened tensions among external parties to Syria conflict
  - Violent civil unrest in Venezuela
  - Worsening of the humanitarian crisis in Yemen
  - Increased instability in Afghanistan
- Tier Two
  - Military confrontation between Russia and NATO members
  - Crisis between the United States and China over Taiwan
  - Intensified clashes between Israel and Iranian-backed forces
  - Intensification of organized-crime-related violence in Mexico
  - Increasing political instability in Iraq
  - Increased fighting in eastern Ukraine
  - Heightened tensions between Israelis and Palestinians
  - Political instability in Nicaragua worsening the migration crisis
  - Escalation of violence between Turkey and various Kurdish armed groups

These potential crises that may need preventive action are presented from an American point of view. Tier One cases are those deemed to be at least moderately likely with high impact on the United States. Tier Two cases are either less likely or have less impact on the United States than Tier One cases.

The top five Tier One cases deal with China, two proliferation risks, and major cyberattacks or terrorist attacks. The last four are regional contingencies. The first two Tier Two cases deal with major powers, but the rest focus on various regional issues.

The second document is the 2018 NATO Summit Declaration, which views future trouble spots through a more European lens but there are many similarities:[4]

1. Strategic environment, "We face a dangerous, unpredictable and fluid environment" ("Brussels Summit Declaration" 2018, paragraph 2)

2. "Russia, 'Russia has breached values, principles and commitments'" ("Brussels Summit Declaration" 2018, paragraph 4)
3. Deterrence, "Respond . . . by enhancing our deterrence and defense" ("Brussels Summit Declaration" 2018, paragraph 5)
4. Russian Occupation, "Call on Russia to withdraw" ("Brussels Summit Declaration" 2018, paragraph 7)
5. Counterterrorism, "Integral part of the Alliance's 360 degree approach" ("Brussels Summit Declaration" 2018, paragraph 10)
6. Cyber Security, "Cyber security is part of NATO's core task" ("Brussels Summit Declaration" 2018, paragraph 20)
7. Hybrid Warfare, "Assist an Ally in any stage of a hybrid campaign" ("Brussels Summit Declaration" 2018, paragraph 21)
8. Middle East Stability, "Through regional partnerships and capacity building" ("Brussels Summit Declaration" 2018, paragraph 27)
9. Nuclear Use, "Would fundamentally alter the nature of conflict" ("Brussels Summit Declaration" 2018, paragraph 36)
10. Nuclear Proliferation, "Growing threat to our populations" ("Brussels Summit Declaration" 2018, paragraph 43)
11. Southern/immigration, "Regional hub will improve ability to anticipate, respond" ("Brussels Summit Declaration" 2018, paragraph 55)
12. Libya, "Support for Libyan-led and Libyan-owned process" ("Brussels Summit Declaration" 2018, paragraph 58)
13. Balkans, "Fully committed to stability and security of Western Balkans" ("Brussels Summit Declaration" 2018, paragraph 59)
14. Energy Security, "Ensure allies not vulnerable to coercive manipulation" ("Brussels Summit Declaration" 2018, paragraph 78)

Major power confrontation is front and center, followed by nuclear and nuclear proliferation risks. High on both lists are cyberattacks and terrorist attacks. NATO's regional concerns are limited to the Balkans and the Middle East. But three new concepts are introduced here: immigration, energy security, and hybrid warfare.

For analytical purposes, these two sets of potential peace and conflict diplomacy issues can be catalogued in the following baskets:[5]

- Major power confrontation
- Proliferation risks
- Regional conflict involving US troops
- Regional conflict not involving US troops
- Cyberattacks and terrorist attacks

- Hybrid attacks including energy intimidation
- Mass migration

Comparing this with the focus of peace and conflict diplomacy practiced since the end of the Cold War, which dealt with regional conflict and non-proliferation, it is clear that the scope has expanded. The future peace and conflict diplomacy agenda may now include efforts to manage major power confrontation, cyberattacks and terrorist attacks, and hybrid attacks.

Hybrid warfare in particular could become an important part of the new peace and conflict diplomacy agenda. This refers to methods now being used primarily by Russia to influence political decision-making in democratic societies. It includes use of social media to divide societies and alliances, and the use of energy dependencies to intimidate other nations.

If the United States emerges from the Trump period in a state-centric world with a greater willingness to be collaborative but also with a greater emphasis on global burden sharing, then it might be useful to posit a new division of labor to manage the expanded peace and conflict diplomacy agenda, such as these:

- Probable US lead
  - Major power confrontation
  - Proliferation risk
  - Regional conflict involving US troops
  - Mass migration into US
- Collaborative efforts required
  - Cyberattacks and terrorist attacks
  - Hybrid war and energy intimidation
  - Climate change and resource scarcity
- Areas where others might lead
  - Regional conflict not involving US troops
  - Mass migration into Europe

The United States would probably take the lead in four sets of cases: major power confrontation, nuclear proliferation risk, regional conflicts involving US troops, and mass migration into the United States. Although collaboration would be useful in these cases, a concert or coalition of the willing led by the United States would probably suffice. Three areas where global collaboration would be important, given that the nature of the threat are (1) cyberattacks and terrorist attacks, (2) hybrid war and energy security, and (3) climate change and resource scarcity. One category in which other nations or groups of nations might take a greater leading role is regional conflicts where the United States is not involved.

NATO is a good example of a regional defense alliance that could help lift the burden from a more engaged United States. NATO can be seen as part of a state-centric system because its key commitment under Article 5 of the Washington Treaty declares that each individual state shall act "individually and in concert" to meet the common threat. NATO pursues these tasks as an alliance or increasingly using so-called lead nation operations in which one NATO member leads with the support of other allies.

NATO is organizing itself as an alliance to not only deter a newly aggressive Russia but also, as the Brussels Summit declaration suggests, to deal with cyberattacks, terror strikes, hybrid warfare, energy intimidation, and uncontrolled immigration. More recently, NATO has also been focusing on the challenges in Europe from China. This NATO effort involves military operations and deterrent efforts. For example, NATO is building a new cyber operations center and is patrolling the Aegean and Mediterranean Seas to deal with immigration. Part of these efforts should also involve using diplomacy to find nonmilitary solutions to these problems. For example, negotiating agreed-on rules to stop hybrid attacks or setting up mechanisms for North African countries to better control immigrant departures.

NATO's lead nation approach could also be used to enhance peace and conflict diplomacy. For example, France is leading operations in several African countries with the support of other allies. Italy has the lead in Libya. Turkey is taking the lead in Syria. These nations might also increase their peace and conflict diplomacy efforts to seek negotiated solutions to end civil wars and regional conflict.

This section thus concludes that

- the agenda for peace and conflict diplomacy is expanding significantly from the post–Cold War focus on regional conflict and nonproliferation, and
- other nations and regional organizations like NATO will need to play a larger role in leading peace and conflict diplomacy efforts to relieve the burden that the United States has carried in the past.

GENERAL CONCLUSIONS

The first section indicates that state-centric systems have tended to dominate international affairs since the 1648 Peace of Westphalia. History demonstrates that state-centric systems can be stable or unstable. Much depends on power balances and the degree of collaboration or competition within the international system. Periods of true global collaboration with more limited national sovereignty have been infrequent. A "golden age" of international collaboration was the ten-year period after the end of the Cold War. Today, the world is moving from a more globalized international order back to a more state-centric one. This is the result of populist, nativist, and nationalist movements caused by a reaction to globalization, centralized government, the 2008 recession, the CIOVID pandemic and mass migration. It stresses a return to the prominence of national sovereignty and distrust for international organizations and agreements. This movement has not been caused by President Trump, but he is accelerating it.

A review in the second section of ten cases of peace and conflict diplomacy since the end of the Cold War indicates that even in a period when there was considerable global collaboration, most negotiations were driven by nation-states. US leadership was generally critical. The two principal purposes of peace and conflict diplomacy during this period have been to end conflict (often civil wars) and to halt efforts at nuclear proliferation. International organizations have nonetheless been critical to the successful implementation of peace and conflict diplomacy through their ability to monitor and verify agreements, and when necessary to provide troops for stabilization efforts. The review also shows that diplomats usually need an array of sticks and carrots to conduct successful negotiations, including the possible use of armed force, sanctions and other forms of coercion, and economic incentives. Agreements once reached need continued nurturing to remain in effect (Gompert and Binnendijk 2016).

The third section highlights that populism and greater state-versus-state conflict appear to be driving the world in the general direction of greater discord. That discord will be amplified by other dominant trends like global warming, emerging weapons technology, possible future economic crises, and more strategic surprises hampered by ponderous decision-making. This discord will create a rich menu for future peace and conflict diplomacy, but it will also make future diplomacy more difficult if discord becomes complex and threatens many countries. Many of the instruments of peace and conflict diplomacy are embedded in the current liberal international order and its institutions. This order is being eroded, and to the extent that this continues, the instruments of diplomacy will also be diminished. If widespread international collaboration becomes difficult to orchestrate because of these trends, then a concert of nation-states might form issue by issue to protect their interests. But they will need to operate on an ad hoc basis and may not carry the degree of international legitimacy that is needed to be successful. These trends are not all irreversible. With strong global leadership, the United States and its democratic allies can still rescue the opportunity to collaborate on the management of these problems.

The fourth section explores whether the United States can indeed lead the world out of a period that appears headed for greater discord. Although the United States has for seven decades been instrumental to the practice of peace and conflict diplomacy, during the Trump administration it has dramatically reversed course and rejected the use of international institutions for this purpose. America's allies and partners have little confidence in Trump's approach. US public opinion, reacting to Trump's policies, now seems more willing to engage globally with international institutions. After the Trump administration leaves office, there are several alternative strategies to shape American foreign policy. They vary with regard to how integral peace and conflict diplomacy will be to future US strategies. If the demand for peace and conflict diplomacy increases, as the review of the changing strategic environment suggests, then even a return to a US policy of collaboration will probably include a greater demand for global burden sharing.

Finally, the fifth section reviews the possible agenda for future peace and conflict diplomacy. It suggests that the pervious agenda, which focused on regional crises and nonproliferation, will be expanded to include major power confrontation, cyberattacks and terrorist attacks, hybrid attacks including energy intimidation, and mass migration. Even if the United States emerges from the Trump period with renewed energy and the will to reengage in collaborative diplomacy, other nations and regional organizations like NATO will need to increase not just their financial burden sharing but also their willingness to lead.

NOTES

1. These ten cases were chosen as examples across the twenty-five-year period and in all geographic regions. Three deal with peace and conflict diplomacy in the Greater Middle East, three are in Europe, two are in Asia, and one each are in Africa and Latin America. Though it is impossible to prevent some selection bias, hopefully these ten cases represent an adequate cross sample of cases to draw reasonable conclusions about the recent nature of peace and conflict diplomacy.
2. More recently, the UN efforts to bring peace to Yemen would be a second example.
3. Only about half of America's NATO allies are likely to meet the agreed-on defense spending goal of 2 percent of GDP by 2024.
4. The Washington Treaty creating the NATO Alliance was signed on April 4, 1949. Article 5 of the Washington Treaty states: "The Parties agree that an armed attack against one

or more of them in Europe or North America shall be considered an attack against them all and consequently they agree that, if such an armed attack occurs, each of them, in exercise of the right of individual or collective self-defense recognized by Article 51 of the Charter of the United Nations, will assist the Party or Parties so attacked by taking forthwith, individually and in concert with the other Parties, such action as it deems necessary, including the use of armed force, to restore and maintain the security of the North Atlantic area. Any such armed attack and all measures taken as a result thereof shall immediately be reported to the Security Council. Such measures shall be terminated when the Security Council has taken the measures necessary to restore and maintain international peace and security."

5. In both cases, these documents tend to focus on potential confrontation and not on longer-term issues like global warming and resource scarcity.

CHAPTER 5

Europe's Persistent Gap between Rhetoric and Reality

Ana Palacio

Jean Monnet, one of the founding fathers of the European Project, famously said: "Europe will be forged in crises, and will be the sum of the solutions adopted for those crises" (Monnet 1979). In the last decade Europe has seen no shortage of crises in which to forge itself. There have been the Great Financial Crisis, the migration crisis, the Ukraine crisis, chaos in Libya, Brexit—the list goes on and on. During this time of upheaval, Monnet's quotation has frequently been turned to for succor. But for a forge to function, it requires fire, and frequently that fire has been absent. The solutions adopted for these crises have been much more along the lines of muddling through than the assertive problem solving to which Monnet seemed to be alluding.

Today, in the face of the global COVID-19 pandemic that simultaneously and fundamentally is challenging economic, social, and political models, to say nothing of global order, Europe, like most of the rest of the world, is facing its most profound crisis since World War II.

Too often in the recent past, crisis response has brought out familiar patterns in Europe: division between member states, half-measures, and most of all a gap between soaring rhetoric and actual results. These trends and in particular the tendency to overpromise and underdeliver are highlighted in this chapter. If there was ever a time for Europe to rise above itself, to steel itself, to find the better angels of its nature, it is now.

There is some reason for optimism. The outbreak of COVID-19 has come at a transitional moment for the European Union. The EU has a new Commission, a new Parliament, and a new president of the European Council. On January 31, 2020, the United Kingdom formally left the EU, putting an end to an extended period of uncertainty and ambiguity that had consumed much-needed energy and bandwidth on both sides of the English Channel for years. There is also the growing realization and acceptance within the EU that the world is changing around it, allies are no longer as dependable, and foes are growing bolder, which necessitates changes in standard operating procedures.

This window of change is important. For Europe must get out of its rut, both for its own sake and the world's.

In considering peacebuilding and conflict diplomacy, the topic of this book, there is no greater example than Europe. Wracked by conflict for centuries, burdened by history, destroyed by war, the Europe that has emerged in the last sixty years, more accurately the Europe that has been constructed, has made a return to arms unthinkable.

The European Union represents the pinnacle of what might be achieved in peacebuilding. The EU is not just a monument to the end of Franco-German enmity; it has entrenched democracy in Southern Europe, healed the wounds of a divided continent after the Cold War, and brought forth the peaceful transition of former communist states in Central and Eastern Europe. Over a period of decades, Europe has delivered.

With this success and status comes a certain aura. This sense has been both a blessing and a curse for Europe. In a stable world, the European Union embodied its role as an engine for peace and the deepening of values. It has been a symbol for good. It must continue to be so. But in a shifting, contentious world where hard power is again ascendant, Europe has had trouble finding its place. Where Europe has erred, as is outlined in this short chapter, is when it has strayed from a realistic vision of itself and what it can achieve. For Europe to be a relevant actor in the years to come and to contribute to peacebuilding and diplomacy, it must recognize its limitations and play to its strengths. This is truer than ever in the uncertain and turbulent times we all face ahead.

WHAT IS EUROPE? THE RISE AND FALL OF ENLARGEMENT

This chapter is about "Europe," but really it is focused on the European Union and its member states. As such, it contributes to a broader problem of identity that the European construction suffers, and that is today coming to a head, with implications for how the EU projects itself abroad.

For the better part of the last quarter century, Europe and the European Union have been synonymous. But they are not the same, and never have been. This is not just a question of shorthand; it is a mentality that has been adopted by the EU itself. At its best, it is an aspirational position that provides legitimacy and soft power. More often, however, it represents a lack of clarity in vision or, worse, a gap between rhetoric and reality that leads to outsized expectations and underwhelming results.

Since its inception, the European Project has assumed a calling beyond the geographical boundaries of its member states. In 1950, French foreign minister Robert Schuman launched the endeavor, calling for the creation of the first community project, the European Coal and Steel Community (ECSC). Though it encompassed only six countries—France, West Germany, Italy, Belgium, the Netherlands, and Luxembourg—and was restricted to a narrow area of economic activity, the ECSC's purpose was much broader. Schuman famously declared "Europe will not be made all at once" ("The Schuman Declaration" 1950). It was a construction meant to be continental in scale though without any precise idea of what that meant.

This lack of certainty is evident in the EU's founding documents. Article 98 of the Treaty of Paris establishing the ECSC states that "any European state" could apply to join the organization ("Treaty Establishing . . . the ECSC" 1951). It was language used six years later, when the original six ECSC members came together to sign the Treaty of Rome establishing the European Community. It was repeated again in the 1992 Maastricht Treaty establishing the European Union ("Treaty on European Union" 1992). And it still remains the geographical qualifier for membership in the European Treaty today ("Treaty of Lisbon" 2007). Yet no one has ever defined what "European state" actually means. It is a vague term with purposely blurry boundaries.

There is some limit to what could be considered "European." In 1987, Morocco's application to join the European Community was rejected for failing to meet the "European state" criterion (Teasdale and Bainbridge 2012). But knowing what it is not is not the same as knowing what it is. That ambiguity, the amorphous notion of "Europe," has allowed the EU to take on a personality that goes beyond itself.

This mixing of Europe and European Union has been fed by the process of enlargement. The original six members became nine in the 1970s, with the entrance of Denmark, Ireland, and the United Kingdom. In the 1980s the accession of former dictatorships in Southern Europe—Greece, Spain, and Portugal—raised the number to twelve. The 1990s brought in Austria, Finland, and Sweden. Finally, in the early 2000s—with postunification Germany's desire to solidify its environs, along with a US push for a Europe whole, free, and at peace—the EU undertook its largest and most ambitious enlargement yet to include the former communist states in Central, Eastern, and Southeastern Europe—a process that pushed membership to a robust twenty-eight.

The EU's enlargement, particularly after the end of the Cold War, increasingly became the central narrative and driving force for Europe and its external relations. The dramatic expansion created a sense of inevitability. There was a feeling of a certain European manifest destiny. With it came self-confidence and an idea that Europe was a singular player to be reckoned with in global affairs—its own pole.

Today this inevitability has vanished. The dual economic and migration crises that have beset Europe for the last decade are certainly the core exacerbating factors here. The former cut away at the legitimating narrative of prosperity that the European Project had built for itself, while the latter has propelled centrifugal forces that erode the idea of a transnational endeavor. The weaknesses of the EU have been laid bare, though it continues to limp ahead, albeit at a much slower pace.

The efforts to address these challenges, which are particularly evident in relation to the financial crisis, have responded to immediate emergencies but have failed to implement the full structural reforms necessary to prevent future crises. The European Central Bank under outgoing President Mario Draghi and his famous pledge to "do whatever it takes" has taken bold steps to institute so-called outright monetary transactions and quantitative easing, despite misgivings in some member states ("Speech by Mario Draghi" 2012). This has stabilized things, and yet these acts have not been met by commensurate structural changes. Eleven years after the monetary crisis, the European Banking Union, which was supposed to be a bulwark to prevent the next shock, remains incomplete. The deep divisions and uncertainty that marked the early attempts to respond to the economic impact of COVID-19 are the evidence. The same could be said with regard to migration, where results have been limited short-term deals with transit states, the foremost one being Turkey, rather than actual reform of the European asylum system or, more deeply, addressing the push factors in neighboring regions.

The consequences of these half measures and the scars of these underlying challenges are seen nearly everywhere, from the return of nationalist populism and the fracturing of the electorate to persistent sluggish economic growth and weak institutional reform.

More centrally, in these difficult years, cracks have begun to form in the artifice of EU-European synonymy. The idea of the natural expansion of the EU and its values throughout Europe now seems fanciful.

Perhaps no development captures this crisis of identity more than Brexit. Yes, the United Kingdom has always held itself apart from the rest of Europe.

Yes, the UK has often been a thorn in the side of efforts to build community responses. And yes, the UK has long touted its transatlantic special relationship at the expense of its transchannel one. Despite all this, the departure of the United Kingdom from the EU is an earthquake. For the first time, Greenland's 1985 departure from the European Community is more factoid than precedent—the European Union will shrink. It will not comprise more of Europe, but less of it. This is a tangible, physical reality check. Beyond the loss of Britain's capabilities—the nuclear deterrent, permanent seat on the UN Security Council, professional armed forces, experienced and able diplomatic corps—the EU is losing a part of itself. The European construction no longer moves in one direction. This is supremely unsettling.

Equally dislocating, however, has been the loss of the impulse to enlarge the EU. Enlargement provided a raison d'être for the European Union. It validated the project, and in many ways it was the central policy defining and encompassing its external projection. But it has now hit rocky waters.

The former communist states that entered the EU during the fifth enlargement and thereafter have proven exceedingly difficult as member states, blocking common approaches to migration and flouting core values. Hungarian president Victor Orban has become the poster child of so-called illiberal democracy, while attacks on press freedom, the separation of powers, and anticorruption institutions have been pervasive. Formal proceedings under Article 7 of the EU Treaty have been brought against Poland and Hungary, the only two times the procedure has ever been activated, in response to their serious breach of fundamental EU values.

The result has been a great unsettling of the idea of the EU as an inevitably expanding European entity. The 2014 announcement by the then-incoming Juncker Commission that the EU had no intentions of pursuing further enlargement during the forthcoming Commission mandate was an incredible sign of the EU's uncertainty in its own model and its place in Europe ("The Juncker Commission" 2014). Recent plans to pursue enlargement in Southeastern Europe are a tentative move back, but the vehicle that has driven Europe's external projection has been disabled. Indeed, even these small steps—the opening of a number of chapters for accession negotiations with Serbia and Montenegro in the last few years—have been doused with cold water by member states, particularly France and Germany, which are concerned about providing further ammunition to Euroskeptics. The idea of widening, which has for so long provided an impulse to the EU, is now all but gone. This has left the project adrift, searching for a new role to play.

As we look ahead, at how Europe might act in a changing world, the EU is today at a profound moment of disorientation. The myths it has built for itself and its identity are melting away. Combining this with the profound challenges to the European social model that will play out in the aftermath of COVID-19 is deeply unsettling. Europe is therefore in need of reorientation and clarity.

EUROPE ADRIFT: ATTEMPTS AT REGIONAL AND GLOBAL LEADERSHIP

The problem is that clear-eyed self-awareness does not come naturally to Europe, particularly in foreign affairs and conflict diplomacy. The history of the European Project since it moved from Community to Union in the 1990s is one of either vast overreach, though often solely rhetorical, or utter non-performance. The areas in which the EU and its members have been successful have been when there is an appreciation and understanding of Europe's relative position. As Europe moves ahead to a postenlargement moment, its limitations as a regional and global actor loom large.

The EU's long and troubled role in the Balkans offers a telling example of both success and failure. With the breakup of Yugoslavia, there was an expectation, promoted by Europe itself, that the deteriorating situation was a regional problem that would be solved regionally. After the end of the Cold War, Europe, which for five decades had been dependent on the United States to guarantee security on the continent, was ready to take on responsibility for itself. Only it was not. With the crisis spiraling out of control, European states showed both a lack of unity of purpose and material capacity to stem violence and humanitarian suffering. The United States once again had to step in, with Europe playing a supporting role. On peacebuilding, however, particularly in the context of Kosovo, where the European Union Rule of Law Mission in Kosovo continues to serve an important purpose, the EU has performed a stronger and more constructive part. Likewise, this has been true diplomatically, where Catherine Ashton, the first EU high representative for foreign affairs and security policy, negotiated a landmark agreement between Serbia and Kosovo in 2013, in which the EU used the carrot of possible accession as a sweetener ("First Agreement" 2013). The effort was importantly backed by support from member states, particularly by Germany, and has produced a common approach. It shows what Europe can do if it acts within itself to attain concrete and achievable results with the proper authorities.

But there have been setbacks. In 2014, the people of Ukraine took to the streets of Kiev to protest President Viktor Yanukovych's decision to withdraw from a proposed EU-Ukraine association agreement in favor of closer ties to Moscow. The protesters, many waving EU flags, braved sniper fire, physical attacks, and freezing temperatures, ultimately ousting Yanukovych. It was a demonstration of how powerful the European Union could be as a symbol and magnet for all of Europe. Five years later, however, Russia's continued destabilizing presence in the country, its efforts to cut off Ukraine from gas routes through the construction of the Nord Stream II pipeline into Germany, and its annexation of Crimea, the first forcible seizure of territory in Europe since World War II, are constant reminders of the limits of the EU and its member states in Europe.

The disastrous 2011 Libya intervention epitomizes the failures of Europe's foray into regional affairs. Launched without proper preparation or a true sense of capabilities, European states pushed headlong into an intervention for which they were ill prepared. Once again Europe, lacking basic logistical and supply capacities, had to turn to the United States to bail it out. Worse, the absence of postintervention planning or a willingness to engage in difficult and dangerous reconstruction efforts created a governance and security black hole in the Southern Mediterranean. The whole episode underlined European weakness. More damagingly, it dealt a fatal blow to the concept of responsibility to protect while confirming Russian and Chinese arguments that the West's rhetoric about values was nothing more than a pretext for messy regime change. It was a costly experiment in failed leadership.

So also was the European attempt to lead on climate action. Europe has always seen itself as a leader on environmental issues. The 2009 UN Climate Change Conference in Copenhagen was to be the centerpiece of Europe's global leadership on the issue, setting the world on the path to long-overdue legally binding emissions caps. The plan was simple; Europe would lead by example, announcing unilateral commitments to cut emissions. The thought was that if Europe took the first step, the rest of the world would follow. But the Europeans made two fatal mistakes. First, they did not put in the requisite effort to build a critical mass of support behind their approach. Emulation alone, particularly when the issue is perceived as counter to short-term interests, is not enough. This was precisely the type of matter in which months of legwork—lobbying, trading favors, and applying pressure where necessary—was needed. It did not occur. More crucially, however, Europe misread the will, and relative weight, of the powers that be. China and the United States (and also India) were simply not on board. Europe, especially without mustering the support of other states, did not weigh enough to push through an agreement on its own.

In a sharp rebuke to European pretensions, nobody followed. Instead, the United States, China, India, Brazil, and South Africa brokered their own separate, watered-down agreement as European plans fell apart (Vidal, Stratton, and Goldenberg 2009). There was not even a European face to be seen in the final photo-op.

Six years later in Paris, Europeans had adjusted learning from past mistakes. Rather than stepping far out in front, the EU and its member states, crucially the host France, worked as facilitators, shoring up support at the retail level and crucially bringing along other powers with it. The outcome was not only a European success but also a global one. In the years since Paris, difficulties in implementing the agreement and creating a common rulebook have shown the limits of European influence, particularly in the absence of an American presence; but the model remains a window into what Europe can achieve as a scene setter.

Europe's relationship with Africa, particularly in the area of peace and security, provides a different angle from which to observe both its potential and its limits as a regional and global actor. There, Europe has rested largely on its power as a donor to try to influence policy development. Since 2004, the EU has provided more than €2 billion to the African Peace Facility, which supports African-led peace and security operations. Such assistance has contributed to a remarkable increase in capacity and the positioning of the African Union and other subregional organizations as viable partners ("Time to Reset" 2017). At the same time, resting on the power of the purse has created a damaging donor-recipient dynamic, itself clouded by historical memory, that created friction and undermined cooperation. Mindful of this development, the EU and African Union have in recent years made "partnership" core to messaging about the relationship—emphasizing trade and investment instead of aid and ownership rather than dependency. The results of this repositioning of the relationship away from paternalism and toward partnership are pending. And indeed, the Africa Strategy launched by the new Commission just ahead of the pandemic was sorely lacking in substantive detail ("Joint Communication" 2020). However, it shows at the very least a mindfulness of the need to use financial resource sensitively and smartly.

Europe has much to contribute as an institution builder, norm generator, and, yes, a source of funding. Its expertise and resources can be marshaled to great effect. But they can also narrow Europe's profile, reducing it to simply being a cash dispenser. Recognizing this fact is key to allowing Europe to maximize this strength.

Europe can be a convener and an engine for cooperation. To succeed, it simply must become conscious of its limitations.

EUROPE AT AN INTERGOVERNMENTAL MOMENT: THE EXTERNAL PROJECTION OF INTERNAL POLICIES AND POLITICS

Europe has found more success in recent years when efforts are led by a single member state acting under the banner of European action rather than communitarized European action per se. Here, French-led deployments in Africa, notably the Central African Republic and Mali, stand out. They have brought tangible stability and reconstruction. But these accomplishments themselves are telling of the current state of the EU.

This is a profoundly intergovernmental moment. The implications are significant. The reality is that it is not the EU's common institutions but its member states, and really only its most powerful member states, that determine its direction. It was a dynamic that came to the fore a decade ago in the midst of the euro crisis. It was not to then–European Commission president Jose Manuel Barroso that Europeans looked but to the president of the European Council, Herman Van Rompuy, and most of all to German chancellor Angela Merkel. It was a testament to where the real power in Europe lay. It also produced policy responses that reflected at least as much about what was best from a domestic political perspective in key member states as what was best from a policy perspective for the EU. The religious application on austerity during the depths of the crisis, even as the United States was demonstrating the importance of ensuring liquidity, is a testament to this.

With Jean Claude Juncker's assumption of the European Commission presidency in September 2014, there was some thought that supranationalism was making a comeback. There was a promising sense of urgency, and all the right things were said about streamlining and effectiveness. This was to be "the last chance Commission" ("Time for Action" 2014). However, this, like much in Brussels, proved to be more bark than bite. The five years of the Juncker Commission only saw a deepening of intergovernmentalism, as Europe has struggled to construct European solutions to challenges.

Here, and in particular at a moment when enlargement is on life support and the Common Foreign and Security Policy has yet to get off the ground, it is important to consider the external project of internal policies as exemplars.

In 2013, Italy unilaterally launched Operation Mare Nostrum, a sea and air deployment patrolling the Mediterranean to combat irregular migration.

The operation was successful, but expensive (Taylor 2015). After a year, the Italians went to Brussels and asked that Mare Nostrum be transitioned into an EU operation with costs and operations shared. Non-Mediterranean EU members, in particular Germany, saw no need to contribute to such an operation and rebuffed Italy's request. Forced to continue alone, amid an economic crisis, Italy halted its patrols. Shortly thereafter, mass irregular migration across the Mediterranean began initiating a crisis that has engulfed Europe ever since. In 2015, in response to the growing humanitarian tragedy in the Mediterranean, Angela Merkel announced that Germany would begin an open-door policy for refugees seeking asylum. It was a unilateral decision, not vetted or discussed with either the EU institutions or other member states.

Though it was a German decision, the impact was felt throughout Europe, with swelling numbers of migrants trying to reach Germany through other member states. When the EU tried to act to alleviate the pressure on frontline states, particularly Italy and Greece, by introducing obligations to engage in burden sharing, it was denied by member states, particularly the four countries comprising the Visegrad Group—Poland, Hungary, Slovakia, and the Czech Republic. And so the problem grew, with Mediterranean states under increasing pressure and, as migrants arrived in numbers in Germany, with Merkel herself facing political blowback. Under threat, she pushed in a new policy direction, brokering an agreement with Turkey, whereby the EU would provide funding (€3 billion) in exchange for Turkish support in combating irregular migration. It was a fraught deal, with serious questions raised regarding its humanitarian impact and effectiveness. Moreover, it was an agreement of questionable legality under EU rules, which necessitated a certain terminological fudging. Rather than being called an agreement, the deal was termed a "statement and action plan" ("EU-Turkey Joint Action Plan" 2015). But despite all this, it was what was needed in Germany at that moment. And so it became EU policy. It is not direction by community method or partnership, but by diktat. Where power fundamentally lies in the hands of the member states, as in migration, policy is bound to be weak. And indeed, Turkey's unilateral abrogation of the deal in February 2020 underlined this weakness.

This type of policymaking is not rare in today's European Union. Russia's 2014 annexation of Crimea and destabilization of Eastern Ukraine were deeply unsettling events for a Europe that had grown accustomed to peace in its eastern neighborhood. Suddenly, European vulnerabilities to Russian pressure became a focus. Central to these discussions was Europe's dependence on Russian energy.

In 2015, driven by this concern, the Energy Union was launched with great fanfare. The goal was to create an open and efficient internal energy market that would enhance European production, reduce external dependence, and allow the free flow of energy within the EU. Innumerable speeches were made calling for increased energy interconnections between European countries, reform of market regulators, and, of course, hitting out on dependence on Russian gas supplies. It all sounded very reasonable and important. The EU even created a separate commissioner for energy union with the status of commission vice president alongside the existing commissioner for energy and climate action. This was to be a priority, a sign that the EU could act as one to address a serious challenge and build a path forward together.

And then, less than six months after the launch of the Energy Union, a European consortium announced that it had signed an agreement with the Russian energy company Gazprom to build new pipelines to bring Russian gas directly into Germany via the Baltic Sea, in a project known as Nord Stream II. Suddenly, the narrative changed. Dependence on foreign energy sources was downplayed, as was the importance of increasing interconnections within Europe. Now establishing a modern electricity grid that would connect cheap German electricity production (fueled by Russian-gas-powered plants and renewables) with European consumers became the focus. That the most powerful do as they want and the weak do what they can is no surprise. But in Europe, what is in the national interest of the strong is often framed as what is in the interest of the community as a whole. Understanding this dynamic is key to charting what course Europe may take.

Recently, there has been a great deal of focus on building European defense capacity. Russian revanchism, chaos in Europe's southern neighborhood, and above all the presidency of Donald Trump have shaken Europeans into realizing that change is needed. Europe's dependence on America as a guarantor of security cannot be overstated. The United States remains the dominant European power, while NATO is the central framework for defense. The mold-breaking administration currently in Washington therefore does more than roil; it petrifies.

Europeans facing a world in which the United States is more distant, the Russian threat is more real, and China is more present have begun to act. Small policy steps, though touted as major advancements by Brussels, have started to appear. The first such moves have been seen through efforts to build cohesiveness within Europe's notoriously inefficient and redundant defense industry. An initial tranche of common projects was launched under Permanent Structured Cooperation and plans to establish the European Defense Fund, amounting to €13 billion under the 2021–27 EU budget, to support joint industrial projects in defense were put in place ("Our Current Priorities" n.d.). Even these modest plans, however, have come under question given the budget crunch created by COVID-19.

Moreover, these limited efforts have been framed by much more ambitious rhetoric. There is talk about Europeans building their own strategic autonomy, though there is little agreement on what this autonomy would entail. Indeed, there remains a significant gap in perceptions of the threats that Europe faces with the specter of Russia looming large in the east and in the Baltics, but largely shrugged off in the south. The converse is the case in relation to destabilization in Europe's southern neighborhood. All threats are local. From a practical perspective, Europe remains decades away from developing the capacity to fully defend itself and project power. Despite this, an increasingly common refrain is the call to establish a European army, with Juncker, Merkel, and French president Emanuel Macron each publicly lending support to the idea. It is all enough for one to think that despite it all, Europe may actually begin to focus on a common approach to defense and move closer to becoming a unitary actor in global and regional affairs. New European Commission president Ursula von der Leyen's claims of establishing a "geopolitical Commission" certainly raised hopes in that regard.

And yet, even in the midst of European awakening, the reality of the EU's intergovernmentalism peeks through. In 1963, French president Charles de Gaulle and German chancellor Konrad Adenauer signed the so-called Élysée Treaty establishing the framework for Franco-German cooperation that would serve as the driving force behind the European construction for the next five decades ("Treaty Between Germany and France" 1963).

In January 2019, Merkel and Macron, the modern-day keepers of the European flame, met in the border city of Aachen to sign the Élysée 2.0 Treaty ("Treaty Between Germany and France" 2019). The agreement symbolized the reaffirmation of French-German partnership and joint commitment to Europe. It is a document of soaring language and less substance. One element, however, was exceedingly telling of where Europe is. In the run-up to the agreement and in light of Brexit, there had been talk, including from some in Germany, of converting France's permanent UN Security Council membership to a common European seat. Such a move appears nowhere in the agreement. Instead, the parties agreed to support Germany's efforts to gain a permanent UN Security Council seat, not as a European seat but as a German one. For all the discussion about more Europe and a closer EU, the prerogatives of the core member states remain central.

Where the EU has been most successful is where it acts as Europe. It is no coincidence that these successes are in areas where legal authority lies not in the capitals of member states but in Brussels. Here the two clearest examples are competition policy and particularly trade, where Europe truly does speak with one voice. In the area of competition, Europe's effectiveness is clear, but is has not had a strategic perspective. Indeed, the February 2019 decision by the European Commission to block the proposed merger of Siemens Mobility and Alstom, which purportedly would have protected European industry from Chinese competition, raised questions about the lack of strategic vision in EU competition policy ("Summary of Commission Decision" 2019). The March 2020 release of a new European Industrial Strategy by the Commission has answered some of these questions. Meanwhile, in the field of trade, these doubts do not arise.

Combining the power of the European market, the EU is the top trading partner for eighty countries globally, with a strategic approach. It is not surprising that it is in trade where Europe is a global leader and trendsetter. At a time of national retrenchment, Europe has pushed forward an aggressive trade agenda, completing next-generation trade agreements with Canada and Japan, even as the United States pulls back or settles for limited, traditional trade deals focused on tariff reduction. In this, we have a glimpse of what Europe could be as an actor building on its strengths and combining its voices into a focused direction.

LOOKING AHEAD: EUROPE AND THE VARYING SCENARIOS OF A CHANGING WORLD

And this is where Europe finds itself: at a moment of uncertainty about its identity, with a tradition of overpromising and underperforming, and driven by the interests of its member states rather than the Union as a whole. This is an uncertain moment for the West generally. But for a Europe that is aging, whose social model is increasingly under strain, and whose history is rapidly coming back to meet it, this is a time of turbulence. Add in the period of greatest doubt about the transatlantic alliance since World War II, domestic upheaval, Russian interference, terrorism, the broader breakdown of the rules-based international order, and the impact of an unprecedented global pandemic that will play out for years to come. It is not a pretty picture.

So what does this mean for the scenarios outlined in this book? A mix between hope, fear, and just getting by.

First, hope. Clearly the collaboration scenario is the most comfortable and is ideal for Europe. For the six decades after World War II, Europe lived in a world that looked ever more like it: open, rules-based, respectful of human rights, and predictable. The European Union was the product and a propellant of this world order. Where Europe has recently excelled has been precisely as a cog in multilateral efforts—facilitating agreement, generating funds, and building and disseminating knowledge. It minimizes the danger of overreach and maximizes the opportunity to contribute. Europe does not have the commonality of vision or purpose to lead, but it can co-lead or be a partner of first resort. This scenario offers Europe the luxury of acting within itself and its capabilities.

Second is fear. This manifests in the discord scenario. Europe is not ready to go it alone in a world of great power competition. Its vulnerabilities are great, and its resources are not efficiently deployed. Preparing Europe to exist in such a world will be a long and slow process, which will only deepen its disadvantageous position. This reality will likely force EU member states to make increasingly individualistic decisions, hindering the EU's capacity to gird itself for a hostile new world. Indeed, fault lines between member states in the initial phases of the COVID-19 pandemic pointed to such behavior. Under this scenario, it is not altogether out of the question to imagine the dissolution of the European Union or its reduction to a rump core.

Finally, and most likely, Europe will find itself in a world where it does just enough to get by in the pragmatic cooperation scenario. Muddling through is a particular European vocation, and this would be in full effect in such a scenario. Here, the intergovernmental impulses that already predominate will be heightened. As such, a few core states, or most likely simply Germany, will act out of their own pragmatic interest, but in the name of Europe. In this, it is not much different than the Europe we have seen in recent years, though with ever-less pretext. The EU will continue along legitimating action, but its agenda will be driven increasingly by forces outside Brussels. In such a world, the question will be whether enough of the EU's élan can survive to rebuild itself, if and when the world returns to a more cooperative and positive period.

We should hope so. For all its warts and weaknesses, the European Project has unquestionably been a force for good in Europe and the world. It symbolizes the ideals of liberalism and the enlightenment. It solidifies the importance of rules and institutions. And it has brought peace and prosperity.

The world ahead needs more, not less, cooperation. It needs institutions, rules, and structure. These are characteristics that Europe can bring. The crippling or end of the European Project would be a tragedy at the worst time.

This chapter has provided an admittedly stark view of the reality of where Europe is as a foreign policy actor—what its limitations are, and where it has gone wrong. But all that being said, if Europe can get its act together; if it can learn to enhance its strengths and minimize its weaknesses; and if it breaks free from certain damaging behavior, it can be a force regardless of the scenario.

The EU is the second-largest economy in the world, both in real terms and in terms of purchasing power parity. It is the largest global trading bloc. It is the world's leading source and destination for foreign direct investment. This gives Europe a voice in setting the terms for regulation, trade, and corporate governance. We see evidence of this still, in regulating privacy and wielding the sword of competition and in pushing for cutting edge agreements in trade at a time when the global trade agenda has stalled.

Europe has a complicated history, but a rich one, that provides legitimation and unique connections with virtually the entire world. In this, the diversity of its membership can be a strength. It can be the basis for partnership and influence—and hints of this approach are emerging in Africa, where the EU is trying to turn the corner on a vital, but difficult relationship. If Europe can truly begin building defense capacity and if it embraces a realistic vision of strategic autonomy that extends to influencing events in its immediate neighborhood, it can create a platform for broader action.

This puts forth the potential for a selective, but effective actor. Able to weigh in globally in areas of strength—trade, regulation—while maintaining the regional stability necessary to maintain these advantages. It is a rosy outcome, but not one totally beyond Europe's grasp.

At a moment when global power is turning away from liberal institutionalism and faces the abyss of an unprecedented pandemic, Europe should be a force to keep the flame of values and rights lit. Let us hope this is just a low ebb. To make it so, however, there is much work to be done.

CHAPTER 6

A View from Russia on Diplomacy and Conflict Management

Dmitri Trenin

The three scenarios laid out at the beginning of this volume roughly represent, respectively, the present (scenario 1, strengthened states), the recent past (scenario 2, strengthened global institutions), and a possible future (scenario 3, pragmatic cooperation). For now, Russia is heavily involved in scenario 1; it has had little role in developing and implementing scenario 2, which is unlikely to be realized in the future; and it would be best served if scenario 3 becomes a reality.

MANAGING GREAT POWER RIVALRY

The scenario of strengthened states is already in full swing. It is essentially a product of the failure of liberalism-inspired global institutions to work to the satisfaction of some of the bigger states.

The return of great power rivalry in the 2010s has been a result of the inability, since the end of the Cold War, to build an inclusive global system capable of accommodating all major players. This, alas, is a historically typical phenomenon. When in 1818, three years after Napoleon's final defeat, Russian emperor Alexander I invited France to join the Concert of Europe, nearly forty years of European peace followed.[1] Alternatively, when in 1919 after the end of World War I the victorious allies imposed a new European and world order at Versailles, that system pointedly excluded both the defeated Germany and the rogue Communist Russia. With the United States opting out of the system that its president, Woodrow Wilson, had conceived, the three most consequential states of the first half of the twentieth century found themselves outside the postwar arrangement. This—within two decades—paved the way for World War II.

In 1991, the victorious West essentially came to believe that "history was over." Not only did intense ideological strife subside, but neoliberal capitalism also triumphed as the universal economic model. In geopolitical terms, the entire world was for the first time ever dominated by a single power, the United States of America—the global leader, flanked by dozens of allies and admired or feared by the rest. The title of the sole superpower was deemed too lowly for the United States' new condition. Hyperpuissance and Ueberpower were suggested as more fitting.[2] Yet, two decades later, Russia—the rump of the defeated Soviet Union, by then variously dismissed as "last year's snow," a "gas station masquerading as a country" ("John McCain" 2014), or, with a bit more dignity, a mere "regional power" (Holland and Mason 2014)—was back on its feet, smaller but alive, and increasingly kicking. Thus, Russia, through its forceful interventions in Ukraine (2014) and in Syria (2015), and its interference in the US elections (2016), became the first disruptor of the post–Cold War order.

Even if a more inclusive security system, with Russia part of it on mutually acceptable terms, might have been conceivable for the Euro-Atlantic area, little thought was given to accommodating China within the global system. There were ideas of China as a "responsible stakeholder" (Zoellick 2005) and a Group of Two member—alongside the United States, but clearly in a more junior capacity.[3] The belief, widely shared, was that eventually capitalism will democratize Chinese society and policy, and Beijing will find it in its interest to follow the general guidance and lead of Washington. By the mid-2010s, China's spectacular economic rise—accompanied, however, by Beijing's even stronger adherence to its authoritarian political system—reached the point where it overtook the United States in terms of gross domestic product (measured on a purchasing power parity basis), and began threatening to undercut America's technological superiority. Clearly, China has by now turned into a much bigger disruptor of the system than Russia.

Paradoxically, the United States' reaction to Russia's breakout and China's rise has contributed to the global disruption. Even under President Barack Obama, Washington became conscious of the rising cost of maintaining the United States' global dominance and set about to strengthen its home base.

Under President Donald Trump, this trend became much more pronounced. Trump's "Make America Great Again" slogan essentially put the American national interest—as understood by Trump and his supporters—above the interests of the US-led global system. It also meant remodeling relations with Washington's longtime allies, making sure, for example, that they pay in full for the protection offered by the United States. The United States officially identified China as its prime all-round challenger, and Russia as a military and political adversary (White House 2017; US Department of Defense 2018a, 2018b). The sea change in Washington's foreign policy—away from emphasizing global institutions, from trading systems such as the Trans-Pacific Partnership and the Transatlantic Trade and Investment Partnership to security and politico-economic arrangements like NATO and the EU to new global norms as the Paris Climate Accord or the Joint Comprehensive Plan of Action, also known as the Iran nuclear deal—has become the most effective factor to date disrupting the global system.

The resumption of major power rivalry is not only the result of the dominant power not being able or willing to accommodate its defeated rivals and new powerful competitors. It also flows out of the domestic trend observable on a global scale: the resurgence of nationalism within a large number of countries. This resurgence appears to be a pushback against globalization, driven by those who see themselves as losers in the process. Here again, America's nationalism—supported, on one hand, by those who feel their individual position at risk, and, on the other hand, by those who feel America's global standing to be threatened—has the most impact, due to the United States' position in the global system. This nationalism already has made significant inroads into the post–World War II US foreign policy of internationalism and global institution building. Other major powers do not have such a tradition. China, from Mao Zedong to Xi Jinping, has always been nationalist. Post-imperial Russia, having shed its communist version of globalism, has come back as a polity that has the interest of the state—that is, those that own and control it—at its center. Even when the Trump presidency is over, the United States is unlikely to revert to the strategies of global institution building. Washington will remain America-centric.

For Russia, the confrontation with the United States that started over Ukraine in 2014 is suboptimal and clearly damaging, though competition and occasionally rivalry with the United States are a normal condition. Psychologically, the Russian elites are prepared by their collective historical experience for standing up to formidable rivals. Indeed, most history-conscious Russians regard great power competition as a natural modus operandi of global politics. Competition with the United States is often seen in Russia as a continuation of the Great Game that Saint Petersburg waged against London throughout the nineteenth century. It is historical experience rather than abstract intellectual exercises that has formed a worldview here that is dominated by great power thinking. A country can be either a hammer or an anvil. To Russia's leaders, for the country to exist as an independent player, it must be a great power. "The weak get beaten," in Putin's memorable phrase ("Address by President Vladimir Putin" 2004). Sovereignty tops the list of state values, and state values rank highest in elite thinking. One of the most popular quotations in today's Russia is that the country "has only two friends in the world, its army and its navy."[4]

The main idea is not that international discord is good, or that it particularly benefits Russia. Indeed, in the twentieth century Russia suffered much more than virtually any other country from the two world wars and several smaller ones (Davis 2015). Rather, it is that power politics is endemic to international relations, not to be wished away. It cannot be stopped but can be only managed, on the basis of superior or at least adequate strength. From the Russian perspective, the best model for managing power rivalries is some sort of a global Concert of Powers, modeled on the nineteenth-century Concert of Europe. The twentieth-century Yalta system of the US-Soviet bipolar hegemony in Europe and then in the wider world was a reductionist modification of this. A great power consensus is also the idea embodied in the UN Security Council, with its five veto-wielding permanent members jointly constituting a form of world government. This idea, first advanced by US president Franklin D. Roosevelt, has always found strong advocates in Russia. Moscow's support for the United Nations is due, overwhelmingly, to Russia's elevated status at the UN Security Council.

This traditional and again dominant thinking briefly lost ground in the final years of the Soviet Union and then in the early 1990s. Many Russians hoped then that their country and the West may have ended their historical rivalries once and for all. The part of the Russian elites that emerged on top after the fall of communism believed that Russia itself would become part of an expanded and peaceful Western family. This integration, however, was not to be. Between 1991 and 2011, several attempts at "docking" Russia with the Euro-American community came to naught, essentially over Russia's insistence on its co-deciding role in the new arrangement, and its rejection of US leadership. Needless to say, the United States never fancied giving Russia a coequal role with itself in running the Western world.

Parallel Russian efforts to reintegrate the countries of the former Soviet Union were generally unsuccessful. The Commonwealth of Independent States turned out to be more of a vehicle for orderly dismantlement of the Soviet Union state rather than a tool for creating a new association in its place. The Collective Security Treaty Organization and the Eurasian Economic Union, which bring together roughly half the commonwealth members, are rather modest multilateral organizations. Due to its size, Russia dominates both, but Moscow increasingly has to take account of its partners' special interests. For all post-Soviet states, independence still means, first and foremost, independence from Moscow.

Current Russian official nationalism—despite all the phraseology of the "Russian world" as it applies to Ukraine, Belarus, and the Russian-speaking communities in the Baltic states and elsewhere—is characteristically state-centered and nonethnic. This is a natural stage in society's exit from the empire and its abandonment of the former internationalist ideology of communism. It underlay attempts to strengthen the Russian state after a period of extreme weakness ushered in by the collapse of the Soviet Union. The resurgence of the Russian state under Vladimir Putin starting in the 2000s followed the traditional model of restoring effective authoritarian rule at home in place of the semichaos that prevailed under the veneer of post-Soviet democracy, and regaining respect—however grudging and involuntary—for Russia and its interests abroad. A stronger Russian state with its revived great power ambitions, however, soon came into conflict with the US-upheld and -dominated post–Cold War order.

From 2014 on, Russia's foreign policy has changed fundamentally from the pattern it had followed in the preceding quarter century. After the Ukraine crisis, attempts at integration into an expanded West and a parallel effort to integrate the former Soviet borderlands into a Russia-led power center in northern Eurasia had to be abandoned. As of now, Russia is alone but is politically, militarily, and financially sovereign; it is recognized or reviled as a great power, despite its obvious drawbacks, including its relatively small and undiversified economy; and it is again able to operate globally, though on a far smaller scale than in Soviet times.

President Putin and his associates pursue a policy built on traditional Realist precepts. Moscow's realism comes in several varieties. Closer to home, it is defensive in strategic terms, though offensive tactically. The Russian intervention in Ukraine aimed at pushing back the expansion of Western geopolitical and strategic influence into Russia's strategic buffer. The specter of a Ukraine in NATO, hosting US military bases, worked in the Kremlin as a stimulus for preventive military action. As in Georgia in 2008, Russia reacted forcefully to the West and its local surrogates trespassing across the red lines set by Moscow.

Elsewhere, Russian realism turned offensive. The main reason for the Russian military campaign in Syria, started in 2015, was to win back recognition—not least from the United States—of Russia as a great power, beyond its post-Soviet periphery. This has paid off, in terms of Russia now playing a significant role in an important region, and being recognized by the United States, alongside China, as a major power rival. The Syria operation also had a defensive element: seeking to eliminate or at least seriously reduce the terrorist/extremist threat to Russia itself, given the fact that thousands of Islamic State fighters had come from the Russian Federation or former Soviet republics.

Russian realism has to operate in a globalized world, not to be wished away. Economic autarky was very much a Soviet model, which can hardly be reproduced on any major scale in post-Soviet Russia. The Soviet economy was absolutely alien to the market. This posture is not of much use for today's capitalist Russia, even if its capitalism is largely state-directed. Russia is not an economic powerhouse; yet it is part and parcel of the global economy. It largely lives off its energy and other raw materials exports, plus trade in agricultural products and arms transfers. Unlike the USSR, it produces relatively few manufactured goods, and it depends heavily on imports. Even the widely publicized campaign for import substitution in the wake of US-led sanctions has been narrowly defined—with a focus on national security issues—and has had a limited impact on the economy as a whole.

Despite the Russian economy's phenomenal resilience, its relative economic weakness of course makes the country vulnerable to external economic and financial constraints, such as Western sanctions. Conscious of this, Moscow is not initiating a reduction in contacts, either economic or political. On the contrary, it is on the receiving end, from terminating its membership in the former Group of Eight to restrictions on technology transfers and on US dollar transactions. In Putin's memorable phrase, "It is not us who are fleeing the dollar, it is the dollar that is running away from us" ("Plenary Session" 2019). So "go it alone" politically does not entail Russia withdrawing from economic or indeed other arrangements with the West, such as the Council of Europe.[5] Moscow is being punished by attempts to isolate it politically and economically, but it does not lock itself in.

Thus, while seeking to circumscribe what the Russian authorities regard as malicious interference from abroad such as the promotion of democracy and support for opposition-minded nongovernmental organizations, Moscow simultaneously wants to preserve and expand the contacts that it deems positive, such as trade and investment, scientific and technological exchanges, educational and cultural interaction, and sports and tourism. To promote the last sector, the Kremlin organized large-scale projects such as the 2014 Sochi Winter Olympics and the 2018 Soccer World Cup. Even as the government celebrates agreements on visa-free travel with other countries (all of them non-Western), it proceeds to relax the visa process for tourists traveling to Russia.[6] As for Russians themselves, they are still free to travel abroad, except for certain categories of civil servants, military, security, and law enforcement personnel, whose freedom to travel abroad was curtailed after 2014.

Although the national Russian mass media, particularly television, are dominated by the state, the Internet—and thus access to opposition and foreign sources—is still largely free. Restrictions have been introduced, but they are anything but critical. There are concerns that legislation—which, it is said, is designed to prevent the Russian segment of the Internet from being switched off from the outside—is actually aimed at isolating Russia from the global system from the inside. The government reassures Russian citizens that this is not the case, but Moscow's recent actions certainly enhance the trend toward the regionalization of the Internet.

On balance, however, instead of being progressively more isolated from the world, Russia is actually becoming more, not less, entangled with it. The important caveat is this now mostly means the non-Western world. Since 2014, political, economic, and security relations with China have grown to a level that can be described as an entente. China, the biggest economy not to have joined the sanctions regime against Russia, is now its main trading partner and technology provider. Russians, of course, are aware of the risks of too close proximity to a superpower like China. Even if Russia has no reason to fear a Chinese military invasion, Beijing's economic, financial, and technological influence on Russia is set to grow. Russians are becoming concerned. They are looking for ways—for example, by strengthening ties to India and Japan—to balance economic and political relationships. By reaching out to Cisco (US), Nokia (Europe), and Huawei (China) to build 5G communications networks, they are seeking to maintain a balance while developing their own capabilities. However, this is admittedly more difficult now that relations with Europe are damaged, and those with the United States are openly confrontational.

The 2015 Russian military intervention in Syria led to an explosion of Russia's contacts with a plethora of parties—local Syrian; regional Middle Eastern; neighbors like Turkey and Iran; Israel; the Gulf States; and Egypt. These diverse and usually difficult relationships require daily care and a lot of flexibility. Moscow is also expanding its footprint elsewhere in the world, from Africa to Latin America. Its international commitments are much more limited than in the Soviet era, but Russia is definitely "going global" again, after a thirty-year break. Russia professes that it is not averse to cooperating with all others, and it only insists on its interests and views being taken into account. Of course, for those in North America, Europe, and Australia who see Russia's policies as aggressive and directed against the liberal world order, the room for compromise with Moscow is limited to nonexistent. The Kremlin, for its part, is adamant that it will not surrender to Western demands.

This state of confrontation with or alienation from the West will likely persist for many years. Reviving political dialogue and enhancing economic exchanges with individual European countries may be easier, and faster, if Moscow is able to display a degree of resourcefulness and flexibility, but NATO discipline and EU solidarity will limit what is possible there. As for the US-Russian rivalry, which is a "hybrid war," it will probably continue to be fought with increasing intensity in the economic, financial, technological, information, ideological, and military domains, including cyber warfare.

Unlike the Cold War, this hybrid confrontation will largely eschew regular high-level dialogue, periodic détente, and the occasional compromise. In the current environment, nuclear arms control has lost its significance as a stabilizer of strategic relations. With the Anti-Ballistic Missile Treaty dead since 2002, the Intermediate Nuclear Forces Treaty being formally canceled in 2019, and the New Strategic Arms Reduction Treaty in danger of being left to expire in 2021, traditional arms control is practically over. For the foreseeable future, the most important item on the US-Russian agenda will be preventing an inadvertent military collision, which might result from an escalation of conflicts, incidents in the air or at sea, or a misunderstanding. Reliable around-the-clock communications between the top US and Russian military commanders and their staffs, and the two countries' leading national security authorities, will be the main instruments for keeping the peace between the old/new adversaries. Dialogue will be essentially limited to the working level.

In today's world of increasingly assertive states, Russia will see the United States and China as fellow major power actors. It will try to play its own game vis-à-vis the two twenty-first-century superpowers, and not become China's vassal. For the time being, Moscow would have to lean on Beijing, but it would be careful not to depend on its strategic partner too much. With the United States, Russia would seek a relationship squarely based on interests, which might become possible in the longer term future as the US redesigns its new place and posthegemonial role in the world and modifies its foreign policy accordingly.

Russia's approach, with a clear emphasis on the national interest, works well in relations with a number of countries that also see themselves as would-be global powers, such as India, or regional players, such as Turkey, Iran, Pakistan, Saudi Arabia, Egypt, and Israel. It is widely applicable throughout the world, except for the one region where the Russians would be most interested in applying it—Europe. The European Union, a halfway house between a trading bloc and a federation, presents a challenge for Russia's foreign policy. Moscow would be prepared to form a partnership with Berlin or Paris or the other capitals of Europe, but it must accept that there is no such thing today as Germany or France—outside the EU. With this important exception, Russia is comfortable with the world of strengthened states as it has emerged in the twenty-first century. In 2000, it appeared that Russia was bucking the world trend by choosing the other door to leave the twentieth century—back into the nineteenth rather than into the twenty-first. Now it appears Moscow has blazed the trail.

COLLABORATIVE PROBLEM SOLVING

Today, the scenario of a liberal world order appears to be backward-looking. In fact, it largely represents, in an idealized form, the state of the world system since the end of the Cold War and the collapse of communism as an economic, political, and ideological alternative to liberal and democratic capitalism. It was marked by the Washington consensus between the US Treasury, the International Monetary Fund, and the World Bank on economic policy; by rapid democratization and active democracy promotion in the political realm; by the dominance of Western-based and mostly liberally minded global media; and by the rise of the "international community," which essentially stood for a group of advanced North American and European democracies led by the United States. Almost three decades ago, this scenario went off to a seemingly auspicious start.

In 1992, the UN Security Council met for the first time at the level of heads of state. More than that, for a number of years all permanent members of the UN Security Council worked in unison. They shared the basic principles and norms of international behavior and sought to reconcile their differences by means of friendly dialogue and consultations. This was a high point of international unity. Russia fully joined the trend, acceding to various international institutions, such as the International Monetary Fund and the World Bank; informally bidding even for NATO membership; and hoping that solutions to the world's problem would be found in friendly interaction among all like-minded players.

In the early 1990s, Russia actively engaged in UN peacekeeping, sending blue helmets to Croatia. After the Dayton agreement ended the Bosnian war in 1995, Russia even placed its peacekeepers under US/NATO command—an unprecedented gesture of Moscow's desire for integration with the West. In 1999, a Russian contingent helped keep the peace in Kosovo after the NATO air campaign against Serbia. This, however, was the point where Russian confidence in the West finally snapped: Moscow loudly protested against the use of force by the United States and its allies. In 2003, Russia withdrew its peacekeepers from the Balkans. Since that time, it has not sent troops to serve under the UN flag again.

"One world" did in fact replace the bipolar system, but this new world was also unipolar, with one power, the United States, in a uniquely dominant position. This was a period of Pax Americana—the time of peaceful cooperation among all the major powers. US allies were happy to be "in," and former adversaries and their satellites were invited to join—after going through an elaborate process of admission.

The situation of the 1990s is unlikely to be repeated. Of course, the severe setback suffered by global liberal democracy does not constitute its demise. The principal lesson to be learned, however, is that the world is not going to be uniformly liberal, or democratic, or culturally Western. Liberal democracy will not be roundly defeated or expunged from this world, but it will not again dominate it. Western countries will go through domestic transformations, and their political systems may become reconfigured as a result, but essentially, they are unlikely to revert to their illiberal past. Liberalism may be tempered, and democracy may have to be reinvented. There is a good chance, however, that in the twenty-first century North America, most of Europe, and Australia will stay essentially liberal and democratic. By contrast, the so called rules-based order they advocate is unlikely to triumph worldwide. The reason for this is that in the future, rulemaking will no longer be the prerogative of the like-minded Western nations. Others, which are growing stronger and more assertive, are unlikely to accept the role of rule takers.

The idea that, to be successful, non-Western nations inevitably must embrace liberal democracy, or become responsible stakeholders of a still Western-led global liberal order while undergoing domestic democratization, has crucially failed in China. Russia, after a botched experience with Western-style democracy, reverted to an autocratic rule supported by a popular legitimation mechanism. Also, political institutions and society values in a number of nominally democratic non-Western countries, from Brazil to India to Indonesia to Nigeria to South Africa, continue to differ widely from the Western model. Even Turkey is evolving away from the European pattern that it long used to follow. Thus, the Euro-Atlantic world will have to coexist with many neighbors.

No less important, China, Russia, Iran overtly, and other leading non-Western countries, such as currently US-friendly India, do not or will not accept US leadership/hegemony in the global system. This is crucial, because it was precisely this leadership that was the key ordering factor both in the post–World War II "Free World" liberal system and in its post–Cold War global equivalent. This makes the idea of a global resurgence of liberalism that would lead to the emergence of a system dominated by a few liberal states—some Western, some non-Western—moot, not to say defunct, overtaken by events.

A scenario of several genuinely liberal and democratic Western countries imposing a liberal order on the rest of the world looks equally unrealistic. The European Union, which has economic and demographic power roughly equal to that of the United States, has proven incapable of turning itself into a federal state and a full-fledged strategic player. The idea of "two Wests"—North America plus Europe—which has looked appealing to some Russian observers since the early 1990s, is now being discarded, in the first place by the Europeans themselves. No matter how irritated the Germans or the French may be with elements of US foreign policy, particularly under President Donald Trump, they will remain fully dependent on Washington for their external military security and general foreign policy guidance. NATO is there to stay, in its present form of an alliance between the protector/leader nation and the protected followers. The EU's strategic autonomy is essentially an aspiration. The EU is attractive and influential in a number of respects, but in grand strategic terms it remains effectively an add-on to NATO, which is the central platform for Western collective decision-making and is single-handedly led by the United States. Other countries in the global Western camp—Japan, South Korea, Canada, and Australia—are even less prone to strive for strategic independence from the United States.

Thus, the emerging configuration of the global system will include the expanded post–Cold War West and a broad range of non-Western countries. At present, their principal meeting place is the United Nations system, including the international financial institutions such as the International Monetary Fund and the World Bank, and the newer creations such as the Group of Twenty. From their inceptions, most of the global institutions are Western in their basic concept and design. However, the balance within them is gradually shifting toward non-Western players, above all China. Beijing is also starting its own international institutions, such as the Asian Infrastructure Investment Bank, and is coming up with unorthodox projects like the Belt and Road Initiative.

For a decade or so, Russia enjoyed a unique position in this hybrid system as a country that had a notional presence in both camps: Western, through its participation in the Group of Eight, a partnership with NATO, and strategic nuclear relations with the United States; and non-Western, through its close links with China, India, and other nations. Plus, it continued to enjoy de facto special relationships with a number of former Soviet republics, from Armenia to Belarus to Tajikistan. For Moscow, this was a happy merger between multipolarity and multilateralism.

In 2014, this situation came to an end. As by now clearly a non-Western country, Russia should be interested in strengthening non-Western multilateral institutions and enhancing those institutions' contribution to, and impact on, global governance. Yet this is not a key priority for Moscow. There are several reasons for this. As a great power, Russia is essentially a loner. So are several of its partners: China, India, and Brazil. Forming an institution in which several key players collaborate on an equal basis is challenging. The institutions that bring together such players, such as the BRICS (Brazil, Russia, India, China, and South Africa) and the Shanghai Cooperation Organization, are still more symbolic than really productive. India and Pakistan, which joined the Shanghai Cooperation Organization in 2018, continue to view each other as adversaries, and even launched air strikes against each other in 2019. Not only does the non-West lack a single leader, like the United States in the Western system; it is not a community of values or interests. A desire to have more rights and privileges within the existing global system is not enough. Thus, not only is the scenario of close international collaboration within the global liberal order unrealistic; close collaboration within the non-West is likewise hardly a viable option.

PRAGMATIC COOPERATION

The pragmatic cooperation scenario occupies the middle ground between the realist and liberal internationalist scenarios. It brings together elements of both. In a practical sense, it assumes that nation-states that have already reasserted themselves as key actors in the twenty-first-century global system will find it imperative to collaborate within various institutionalized frameworks. This scenario has a chance later in the twenty-first century, but not before the current round of Sino-US rivalry and the US-Russian confrontation will have run their courses, creating a new global equilibrium.

Some form of a concert of nations will be required for the pragmatic scenario to become reality. However, it will not be a latter-day expanded replica of the early-nineteenth-century Concert of Europe, with its periodic congresses of the great powers; nor would it be an implementation of Franklin D. Roosevelt's 1940s idea of a handful of global policemen-cum-judges at the pinnacle of the United Nations system acting in unison. There are likely to be multiple flexible arrangements, or ad hoc "concerts" of somewhat different composition.

The United States and China, as the two leading—and actively competing—powers of the twenty-first century, will form a unique if informal relationship. This relationship will be of a different kind than the US-Soviet one in the second half of the twentieth century, as there is unlikely to be a new bipolarity. The United States will continue to lead a large, but somewhat loose, group of "Western" nations that will rely on Washington for security protection. The hard core of the system will include the English-speaking nations: the United Kingdom, Canada, Australia, New Zealand, and the United States itself. As "Five Eyes," these countries already have intimate intelligence cooperation. China, by contrast, will hardly be a pole for many countries. More likely it will stand alone, maintaining close relationships with a few neighboring countries, including with Russia.

More formal groups would continue to deal primarily with global economic issues, like the current Group of Twenty. Within the Group of Twenty, there is a Western group of Group of Seven nations, and a non-Western faction of BRICS. There is a palpable need for informal coordination among the world's principal economic and financial centers—the United States, the European Union, and China. At some point in the future, India might join them. On global security issues, there will continue to be the UN Security Council, with its permanent five members the P-5, although their present composition could change. On issues of global strategic stability there is a need for close contact and a measure of cooperation between the world's premier military powers, the "M-3": the United States, China, and Russia. On Internet governance, the democracies will be generally pitted against autocracies, with Russia generally in the latter group, but the two camps will have to collaborate. On climate, the European Union might have a chance to play the leading role, with the largest economies—America, China, and India—mainly protecting their national interests.

At the regional level, from the European Union to Association of Southeast Asian Nations to the North American Free Trade Association, the world is already a collection of economic blocs and a wide number of "unaffiliated" countries. Some important economic relationships, however, will be rather informal, like China's Belt and Road Initiative. Russia will continue trying to reap benefits from "harmonizing" the BRI with its own integrationist project, the Eurasian Economic Union.[7] There are regional groupings in Africa, Latin America, and Asia. Several projects will be bringing together one integrated unit, on one hand, and a whole region, on the other hand: China plus Africa; the EU and Africa; the EU's Eastern Partnership; or China+16 countries of Eastern and Central Europe. There are multiple regional arrangements that play modest but generally useful roles in managing joint neighborhoods, from the Arctic to the Mediterranean, and the Baltic to the Black Sea.

These mechanisms will be increasingly in demand, because unlike in the period of the Cold War, all major powers will tend to focus much more on their domestic needs. The United States, the world's most entangled power, has been on a strategic retrenchment since the Barack Obama presidency.

This is not isolationism, but a major realignment of resources and a redesign of relationships, primarily with America's many allies. China is unlikely to take up the responsibilities that the United States is vacating. Maintaining spheres of influence will become prohibitively costly, including for Russia. In place of former empires, formal or informal, security vacuums will emerge, inviting contests between regional or local rivals.

The major powers, their ambitions transformed, will compete mostly on the strengths of their individual capabilities. As they proceed with their contests, however, they will have to work together to deal with various conflicts that may threaten several or all of them or impinge on their interests. In the field of nuclear proliferation, the United States, Russia, and China, the leading nuclear powers, have already been collaborating on the nuclear issues of Iran and North Korea. In the area of countering terrorism, many more nations will have a reason to share information and occasionally join forces with one another. High degrees of collaboration may result from a commonality of interest in such issues as managing climate change and dealing with pandemics. In general terms, the less politicized an issue, the better the chance of international cooperation. Political issues will continue to be divisive and contentious.

IMPACT OF THE SCENARIOS ON PEACE AND CONFLICT DIPLOMACY

The three scenarios described above lead to very different types of world order. They also create different conditions for managing international disputes.

The space for peace and conflict diplomacy, which shrank with the resumption of major power competition, may again expand—as a result of the individual major powers' inability to establish the sort of order they would prefer solely through their own mainly hard power efforts. From North Korea's nuclear issues to the simmering conflict in Donbas, and from Syria to Libya to Afghanistan to Yemen, joint diplomatic efforts of several powers are necessary to reduce and end violence and bring the situation to a political solution. Cooperation will not be overly friendly or run smoothly; but as something born out of necessity, it may have a chance to yield practical results, despite the continuing rivalries and competition. These results may be limited, yet real. For example, in the case of Donbas, implementing the 2015 Minsk Agreement is not likely, for the agreement is widely interpreted in Ukraine as giving Russia an advantage. What can be achieved, however, is making sure that there is no shelling or shooting across the line of contact between the opposing sides, and that the prisoners captured by the belligerent parties return home. As for Crimea, its status is unlikely to be internationally recognized for many decades. Yet, Crimea may continue to live in peace, despite the legal constraints.

New confrontation with the West has had a double-edged impact on the Russian state. On one hand, Western sanctions have produced a rallying-around-the-flag effect and a surge in Russian patriotism. On the other hand, the same sanctions have been testing the solidity of the corruption-ridden Russian state, the resilience of the country's sluggish economy, and the national cohesion under conditions of crass inequality. The longer-term effects of the sanctions are going to be more consequential than their immediate impact, but they also stimulate the political regime to be more inventive, creative, and attentive in order not to perish. The situation is further complicated by the looming political transition to a post-Putin regime. Predictions about Russia's future are foolhardy, but it is likely that the Russian nation, economy, and state are more likely to get stronger under pressure than to crack.

As just demonstrated, this pragmatic cooperation will not necessarily mean the establishment of an order based on mutually agreed-upon rules, but a degree of institutionalization of conflict resolution and postconflict rehabilitation will be required. Some commonly designed and commonly policed norms and principles may be indeed practiced, but only as a result of an agreement among the major powers. This version of a rules-based order will be markedly different from what this phrase means today. Such compromise can only be based on an equilibrium reached as a result of ongoing power rivalry and confrontation. Its exact parameters cannot be foreseen at this point.

However, peace and conflict diplomacy is already working, despite the resurgent major power rivalries. The Joint Comprehensive Plan of Action with Iran was concluded in 2015, more than one year into the US-Russian confrontation. From 2017, China and Russia have been voting at the UN Security Council to impose sanctions on North Korea for its nuclear and missile testing. They also supported the top-level dialogue between the United States and North Korea, even as Washington officially branded both Beijing and Moscow its rivals, and the Pentagon has viewed them as adversaries. Having achieved a military success in Syria, Russia has been reaching out, albeit with no success so far, to the European Union with a plea to engage in reconstruction of the war-ravaged country. In 2019, all major powers reacted with uniform pleas of caution and restraint to a fresh flare-up of military tensions between nuclear-armed India and Pakistan. In a rare act of cooperation in that same year, the United States, Russia, and the European Union acted together to evict an oligarchical ruler of post-Soviet Moldova and support a coalition composed of pro-European and pro-Russian parties.

In the future, peace and conflict diplomacy will continue to be practiced, less as a result of a common desire to achieve a better global order but more as something that is deemed necessary to avoid scenarios that bring no good to anyone. That nation building is off the agenda is a positive development. Outsiders, such as the United States in Iraq and Afghanistan, or the NATO alliance in Libya, have proven themselves utterly incapable of planting their systems and values on alien soil. However, helping other nations with strengthening internal security and improving governance—as well as engaging in conflict prevention, management, and resolution—is both necessary and feasible, as a number of cases in Africa suggest.

Experience shows that peace and conflict diplomacy needs to work closely with the parties to the conflict to patiently find ways toward solutions, not to try to impose ready-made programs from above onto the heads of the locals. It has to be inclusive; all relevant players should be involved, with a rare exception of universally defined terrorist groups, such as al-Qaeda and the Islamic State. It must reach out to neighbors and other foreign countries intimately involved, to make sure that any solution is supported in the neighborhood and the wider region. And it must rest on a minimum of a consensus among the world's major powers to be solid.

NOTES

1. In 1854, Napoleon III paid back Nicholas I, Alexander's brother and successor, by aligning with Great Britain, the Ottoman Empire. and others, to fight against Russia in the Crimean War. But another general European war had to wait a hundred years.
2. "Hyperpuissance" is the word of Hubert Vedrine, French foreign minister (1997–2002). "Ueberpower" is the word of Josef Joffe, publisher of Germany's *Die Zeit* weekly. This was the title of his 2006 book, *Ueberpower: The Imperial Temptation of America* (W. W. Norton).
3. This was first suggested by the economist C. Fred Bergsten, and was advocated by, among others, Robert Zoellick and former US national security adviser Zbigniew Brzezinski.
4. This was attributed to Russian emperor Alexander III (who reigned 1881–94).
5. In 2019, Russia managed a successful campaign to keep its membership in the Council of Europe without making political concessions.
6. In a departure from past practices that demanded strict reciprocity, in 2019 Russia allowed foreigners longer visa-free visits to Saint Petersburg and the region.
7. The Eurasian Economic Union includes Armenia, Belarus, Kazakhstan, Kyrgyzstan, and Russia.

CHAPTER 7

Peace and Conflict Diplomacy in Latin America

Marcos Tourinho

International order in Latin America has gone through dramatic change over the past three decades. As the Cold War faded out in the region, the continent was able to gradually address political instability and conflict in various areas along its borders as it went through widespread, if uneven, processes of democratization and regionalization.[1] These trends created conditions favorable to the resolution of actual and potential armed conflict in the region, such as the solution of territorial disputes between Chile and Argentina in 1984, the Central American Peace Accords in 1987, and the peace agreement between Peru and Ecuador in 1995–98, after the brief Cenepa War. As a result, the region has seen no direct military conflict since 1995, with the exception of the long-standing civil war in Colombia.

The transition toward a more peaceful order in the region was enabled and reinforced by a deepening of regional institutions in Central America, the Andes region, and the Southern Cone. Although these initiatives were differently motivated and took place at their own time and pace, they all contributed to the establishment of a complex network of overlapping agreements and institutional arrangements that were repeatedly used to address peace and conflict challenges in the region. In the past decade, however, this network of institutions has started to deteriorate. This has been most clearly manifested in the inability of any regional institution to effectively address the Venezuelan crisis since the death of President Hugo Chávez, in spite of the country's membership to Mercosur, UNASUR, and the Organization of American States (OAS).

The issue is further aggravated by the long-standing resistance of Latin American states to have the UN Security Council address peace and security challenges in the region. Although various UN bodies have a strong presence in Latin America (UNICEF and the UN Development Program in general, but also, in particular, the UN Office of Drugs and Crime in Colombia and the International Commission against Impunity in Guatemala), states have acted diplomatically to avoid having regional issues considered on the UN Security Council's agenda. For those policymakers, the Security Council is an unpredictable governing body dominated primarily by great power politics, from which they are largely excluded. Including a regional issue on the agenda of the Security Council means, therefore, playing a smaller role in deliberation and ultimately losing control of potential outcomes on issues that may be of substantial regional security importance. It is typically only if a crisis is of immense importance for a permanent member that it will be considered by the Security Council (e.g., Haiti in 1993–94, and again since 2004).[2]

In this context, what are the prospects for peace and security diplomacy in Latin America, in particular given the complex global scenario of paralysis and disfunction in the UN Security Council, an increasingly explicit rivalry between the United States and China, and the reemergence of authoritarian tendencies in national governments worldwide?

This chapter argues that though regional and domestic orders prevailing in Latin America since the end of the Cold War have brought about a period of peace (although with high levels of domestic violence), trends in the current political scenario globally and in the region raise concerns about the stability of the current arrangement. The argument unfolds in two steps. The first section describes the evolution of peace and security institutions in the region, notably in the context of widespread democratization, and explains how these institutions supported conflict diplomacy during crises. The second section discusses global and local trends that might destabilize the peace on the continent: (1) the possibility of a new "global cold war"; (2) spillover effects of domestic instability, especially in Venezuela; and (3) the strengthening of authoritarian tendencies in the region, on both the left and right sides of the political spectrum.

THE EVOLUTION OF PEACE AND SECURITY INSTITUTIONS IN LATIN AMERICA

Latin America is home to a complex network of overlapping regional agreements, institutions, and arrangements directly or indirectly related to peace and conflict diplomacy. Throughout the twentieth century, in particular after the Cold War, states in the region did not hesitate in establishing competing

or complementing regional agreements seeking to promote peace and political cooperation, and to engage with or protect themselves from an increasingly integrated global economy. Although these institutions were primarily
dealing with economic and societal cooperation, they typically held a promise of political integration and were central to the management of conflicts
in the region.

Integration took place in a fragmented way, centered in three main regions:
Central America, the Andes, and the Southern Cone. In Central America,
the process that led to the resolution of the civil wars in the 1980s served as
an impulse for further cooperation and a renewal of the area's long-standing
promise of deep integration.[3] By removing the main obstacles to cooperation,
the Esquipulas Peace Process laid the foundations for the Central American
Integration System created in 1991, which led to a series of cooperation treaties in the years that followed. These agreements took place in parallel with
Central American efforts to further integrate in the global economy, a process
that by the late 1990s had dominated that subregionalization and culminated
in the establishment of a free trade agreement with the Dominican Republic
and the United States in 2004 (Bull 1999).

The Andean Community, conversely, developed gradually after the establishment of the Andean Pact of 1969. It was rather motivated by a need to
prepare less developed countries to join the then-promising Latin American
Free Trade Association and became until the late 1980s the most far-reaching
integration scheme in Latin America. As regionalism evolved in the region,
the group became more political through the creation of the Andean Presidential Council in 1990. Though a free trade area has been in place since 1993
and a common external tariff has been formally operative since 1995, actual
economic integration has been inconsistent (Malamud and Schmitter 2011).[4]

In South America, the renewal of regional integration was triggered primarily by the bilateral rapprochement between Brazil and Argentina taking
place throughout the 1980s. Rivalry between the two countries was such
that between 1935 and 1980, no sitting Brazilian president visited neighboring Buenos Aires. A thawing in relations started in 1980 and, in particular
following democratization in the two countries, led to numerous bilateral
agreements of integration and cooperation, including in the sensitive nuclear
field, to culminate in the creation—with Uruguay and Paraguay—of Mercosur ten years later.

These developments and the long period of peace observed in the region
led, by the late 1990s, to a debate about whether South America or one of
its subregions could be characterized as a security community. For Deutsch
(1957, 5), a security community is constituted when "a region where there

is real assurance that the members of that community will not fight each other physically, but will settle their disputes in some other way." Though there is no irrefutable answer for that question, it is clear that at least around Mercosur, political developments have led to the construction of an area in which war is unthinkable, in particular considering the history of conflict and rivalry in its recent past (Kacowicz 1998; Hurrell 1998a).

The United States has long played a central role in the peace and conflict diplomacy of Latin America, although far more intensively in Central America than further south. Although its presence and potential action remained a factor in Latin American governments' policy planning, the country oscillated in its approach to peace and conflict in the region (Hurrell 1998b). Although, in the 1970s and 1980s, US intervention was robust, starting in the 1990s, the United States remained relatively disengaged from international peace and conflict diplomacy after the end of the Cold War, particularly in South America. Prominent exceptions are instances in which international issues are clearly linked to US domestic politics (as with Cuba and Haiti) or associated with drug trafficking (as with Colombia).[5] The relative lack of engagement of the United States with regional peace and conflict diplomacy is not unrelated to the fact that since the 2000s the OAS, the main institutional connection between the United States and Canada and the rest of the continent, was sidelined by states as the principal forum for peace and conflict diplomacy in the region.

During the 1980s and 1990s, the OAS played an important role in peace and conflict diplomacy in the region. Although it was never the single center for regional policymaking on the continent (it competed with the organizations described above), the OAS was a major player in resolving the Central American civil wars and was central to the condemnation of the coup in 1991 coup d'état in Haiti. In the process, it also took advantage of the "liberal moment" in the hemisphere to hold several international conferences that helped to constitute the most robust institutional and normative framework to address conflict among all international institutions in the region. Institutionally, the organization has a fixed secretariat in Washington that is able to push policy forward on the bureaucratic level (Barnett and Finnemore 1999). In normative terms, the OAS gradually built up in the 1990s a series of robust instruments intended to solidify the Americas as a zone of peace and democracy. These included the 1991 Santiago Declaration on the Collective Defense of Democracy (Resolution 1080), which empowered OAS bodies to respond to breaches of democracy, including through the imposition of sanctions, and efforts to increase state-level military activities. Though the mechanism was invoked in the 1990s—for instance, in the cases of Haiti in

1991 and Peru in 1992—its effectiveness was uneven, and the track record is better explained by domestic politics than institutional developments in the Inter-American system (Levitt 2006). Still, these efforts evolved and culminated in 2001 in the adoption of the Inter-American Democratic Charter, which further institutionalized procedures for cases of formal disruption of democracy, or for when democracy is at risk. The procedures were first applied in Venezuela in 2002, when then–president Hugo Chávez suffered an attempted coup d'état (Herz 2008).

As South American states started to pursue alternative spaces of political interaction from the early 2000s, political support for the OAS as the center of regional politics gradually shifted to other organizations in the region. This effort was aligned with a desire to reduce the influence of the United States in South America and the ambition to create something resembling a security community in that subregion. Celso Amorim (2010), Brazil's foreign minister between 2003 and 2011 (and later defense minister), explicitly stated that "it can be easily affirmed that South America has progressively become what I call a security community. . . . [War] is certainly inconceivable in Mercosur, and it is becoming increasingly less conceivable to the whole of South America."

This statement reflects a period of great enthusiasm for regional peace and conflict diplomacy. In South America, the creation the Union of South American Nations (UNASUR), a process initiated in 2004, was the most ambitious attempt to create an intergovernmental organization to promote political, economic, and societal issues in the region—initially modeled after the European Union. Although its most ambitious plans of integration were never likely to succeed, the regional group did serve as a foundation for peace and conflict diplomacy in the region, in particular through its South American Defense Council.

The South American Defense Council was created to facilitate military cooperation in the region and, importantly, to serve as a platform for peace and conflict diplomacy. Although presidential diplomacy remained the central mechanism for resolving conflicts between states, the council sought to take advantage of UNASUR's institutionalization to advance and systematize the use of that mechanism. In practice, the effectiveness of UNASUR and its Defense Council in increasing security cooperation and resolving conflicts depended on the political will of leading heads of state, on an ad hoc basis. Consider, for instance, the Bolivian Crisis of 2008. In that year, movements in the Media Luna region challenged a set of constitutional reforms proposed by the Evo Morales government. This confrontation soon became a movement for autonomy and separatism coming from the wealthier areas of the country. The conflict escalated in violence, culminating in several massacres and the declaration of a state of emergency. In that context, UNASUR played an important role in defusing the crisis. At a time when there were doubts about whether countries in the region (or the United States, for instance) might support the separatist movement, escalating the crisis, an emergency summit was called in Santiago, where UNASUR heads of state threw their unconditional support to the central government in La Paz and created an international commission to investigate the events (Malamud 2008, 9). The Santiago Declaration was a major turning point in the crisis, as the wave of international support was sufficient to strengthen the government and avoid a separatist conflict.

The regional body was also critical in defusing the sharp increase in tension between Colombia and Venezuela in 2010, when Colombia publicly denounced the Venezuelan government for allowing guerrilla groups to operate in its territory as a safe haven. The two countries broke off diplomatic relations, and the possibility of war was publicly speculated on by the parties, and also by heads of state in the region. The process mediated by former Argentine president, and then–UNASUR secretary-general, Néstor Kirchner after the election of Juan Manuel Santos as president of Colombia was crucial to address the crisis and reconcile the two countries on the basis of a mutual commitment to dialogue.

The intended stabilizing role of UNASUR and its Defense Council went beyond crisis management. The institution sought to increase transparency in military spending as well as to advance industrial military cooperation among countries in the region.[6] In addition, UNASUR was present with observers in difficult electoral processes in Venezuela and Paraguay in 2013, and it facilitated giving increased recognition and legitimacy to the elected governments (Vigevani and Júnior 2014). These activities, however, did not have a long-lasting impact in strengthening peace and democracy in the region and might have helped to legitimate dubious democratic processes.

The track record of UNASUR in managing conflict is ambiguous, and shows its institutional limits. On one hand, as described above, the organization was able to diffuse successive political crises, actually avoiding the further escalation of conflict. On the other hand, UNASUR was never able to move beyond ad hoc crisis management to establish itself as a center for mediation and long-term conflict resolution in the region, particularly in relation to Colombia. This is the case for at least three reasons. First, the organization was perceived to be guided primarily by an alliance of left and center-left governments, which on several occasions complicated relations between the organization and the Colombian government. Second, the organization lacked the institutional weight and know-how to conduct long-term, complex peace processes. The expertise provided by Norway, and the neutral sponsorship and mediating role offered by the Vatican and Cuba, respectively, were critical to the success of the years-long peace negotiations. Finally, it is clear that the Colombian government lacked the confidence to share sensitive information about the peace negotiations with neighboring states, some of which allegedly had connections with the Revolutionary Armed Forces of Colombia–People's Army (Fuerzas Armadas Revoluciona-rias de Colombia, FARC), for fears of spoiling the peace process.

Nonetheless, on several occasions the institutions described above were seen as having contributed to conflict resolution in the region. They did take steps to encourage "more intensive and extensive interactions between states through their trust-building properties," and by "establishing, articu-lating, and transmitting norms that define what constitutes acceptable and legitimate state behavior," an accepted benchmark for the establishment of a security community (Adler and Barnett 1998, 418). In practice, institutional legitimacy was leveraged strategically by political leaders to transcend more equivocal forms of presidential diplomacy in order to manage crises in the region more systematically.

It is for this reason that despite its limits, the recent weakening of insti-tutions in Latin America is a cause of concern from the perspective of peace and conflict diplomacy. Currently, no international institution in the region commands sufficient authority to manage major conflicts or political crises. Throughout the 2000s, the emergence of UNASUR (and a South American strategic space, more broadly) as well as the creation of the Community of Latin American and Caribbean States (Comunidad de Estados Latinoamer-icanos y Caribeños) was associated with the decline of other institutions as principal spaces for conflict management in the region. The OAS, for instance, suffered much from the antagonism between the United States and Venezuela and, with the establishment of political alternatives, lost some of its protagonist role as a diplomatic center for peace and conflict diplomacy in the region, despite its robust legal foundations (Cooper 2017).

The decline of regional institutions in Latin America was further compli-cated by the collapse of UNASUR starting in early 2017. A dispute over the successor of former Colombian president Ernesto Samper as secretary-general has left the institution without leadership for two years. The dispute, which is implicitly about how to address the Venezuela crisis, has provoked the vol-untary withdrawal of Argentina, Brazil, Chile, Colombia, Ecuador, Paraguay, and Peru from the organization, which is now almost empty. The absence of a regional institution able to throw its weight behind consensual solutions for critical regional issues has been most missed in the ever-escalating Venezuela crisis, a threat to the peace of the entire region.

CHALLENGES TO PEACE AND CONFLICT DIPLOMACY IN LATIN AMERICA

In a context of profound institutional fragility, the combination of global and regional trends of discord and instability could pose substantial threats to the regional peace and security environment. This section explores three of these critical trends: rivalry between great powers, the reemergence of authoritarian tendencies globally as well as in the region, and the potential spillover from domestic stability, especially in Venezuela. It also considers how these trends might affect Latin American politics and society. As noted above, this is a vulnerable moment for peace and conflict diplomacy in the region because established institutions have been unable to mediate major conflicts across the region.

In recent years, the increasingly public polarization between the United States and China has raised concerns about the possibility of direct or indirect conflict between the great powers. Their escalating economic and military rivalry opposes a still dominant status quo power with an emerging economy with different sociopolitical and economic models. This dispute is also a battleground for global influence. As in the Cold War (Westad 2005), much of the dispute is likely to take place not in a direct clash between the great powers but in the peripheries of the international system.

Similarly, hostility between the United States and Russia has already affected international peace and security deeply, far beyond their borders. At least since their strong disagreements over the UN-authorized military intervention in Libya in 2011, the UN Security Council has become increasingly divided and remains unable to effectively address some of the most critical international crises of this century, including the civil wars in Syria and Yemen (Brockmeier, Stuenkel, and Tourinho 2016). There is evidence that this continued polarization will also affect any attempt by the UN Security Council to engage with any seriously contentious Latin American political crisis.[7] The boycott by Russia, China, and others of a meeting to informally include Venezuela on the Security Council's 2017 agenda, as well as their position at a formal debate on the situation in Nicaragua in 2018, indicate that the Security Council remains an unlikely center for conflict resolution in the region.

The extent to which the hostility expressed in these relationships is structural is unclear. In particular, with regard to China, it is possible that the belligerent attitude adopted by the United States helped to escalate the crisis to a point at which existing incentives toward accommodation are overshadowed. Though claims that we are currently living in a second Cold War (Kaplan 2019) remain overstated for now, if a confrontation between great powers were to escalate to become a new zero-sum game associated with containment policies by great powers, the results for Latin America are likely to be disastrous. This is for two reasons.

First, if such a confrontation took place, states would likely feel the need or inclination to take sides. This would narrow their space for commercial or political maneuvers, and force a broader shift in the region toward a zero-sum mentality that harms the potential for cooperation beyond the principal players in the dispute. This is especially problematic because the United States and China are the top two trade economies for Latin America, with China being the largest export market for Brazil (20.3 percent), Chile (25.8 percent), Peru (24.4 percent), and Uruguay (19.4 percent); and the second-largest for Argentina, Costa Rica, and Cuba (Gonzalez 2018). Though it is likely that there will always be some space for each country to make suboptimal choices in their own political economy, global polarity raises the costs for small and medium-sized states to act fully autonomously.

Second, global polarization and great power support could radicalize existing policy-based disagreements domestically and between neighboring governments throughout the region. Latin America is composed of fragile democracies that struggle to mediate social conflict, including between the right and left. The reignition of a broad world narrative of ideological confrontation and incompatibility, together with an expectable inflow of funds and propaganda on both sides, is likely to increase tensions domestically and internationally. As of today, there are growing anti-China sentiments across the region to compete with already-existing anti-US perspectives within the region, reflecting both countries' high levels of economic engagement and political influence in Latin America.

The potential social harm and physical violence provoked by global political polarization may be further exacerbated by the resurgence of authoritarian political tendencies in the region. In the past decade, on both the left and right, Latin America has seen the emergence of new forms of autocratic inclinations, following the emerging global trend of gradual degradation of democratic institutions to reconstitute them as illiberal or only nominal democracies or full-on authoritarian governments.

On the left, Venezuela has, since the death of Hugo Chávez, completed a gradual degradation of democratic institutions and moved decisively toward authoritarianism. The Maduro administration's systematic arrest of political opposition and, ultimately, its decision to take over the powers of the elected National Assembly in 2017, is an unquestionable mark of democratic collapse in Venezuela and the reemergence of authoritarianism in the region. In Central America, Nicaragua is also an important case to consider in this context. The government led by Daniel Ortega also sought control of all branches of government, barred opposition members to participate freely in elections, and pursued continuous reelections (Stuenkel and Feldman 2017). In 2018, a wave of popular protest was met with great violence by the Ortega government, provoking the death of hundreds of people, and with thousands more seeking to leave the country. In Bolivia, the Evo Morales government did not hesitate to seek unlimited reelections (a classic move in the authoritarian playbook), and disputes about fairness in the conduct of the 2019 elections, and its ultimate invalidation, have pushed the country to a path of further instability and institutional risk.

On the right, a renewed flirtation with authoritarianism is more recent, and though there is still uncertainty about the extent to which antidemocratic discourse will translate into constitutional disruption, democratic institutions have deteriorated. It is indisputable that growing frustration with the region's astronomical levels of armed violence and corruption has led some of the population toward a nostalgic desire for heavy-handed rule. This has reignited political sentiments based on overt nationalism, antiminority attitudes, and overbearing law enforcement, often praising a return to an authoritarian past. Human Rights Watch (2019) has interpreted this movement as part of a threat to democracy and civil society.

The change in equilibrium provoked by a rise in authoritarianism on the left or the right is likely to increase domestic instability and, as a consequence, potentially raise international tension across the region. Indeed, domestic instability can be a significant trigger for international conflict. In his study of security communities in the Great Lakes region, Laurie Nathan (2006, 280) highlights the potential spillover effects between intra- and interstate conflicts: "Large-scale internal violence can lead to cross-border violence in the form of hostilities between states, rebel attacks from neighboring countries, military action by governments against rebel forces, or collective enforcement action aimed at restoring domestic order. Even if local violence has not had any of these effects in a given case, the risk that they might arise in the future cannot be excluded. Dependable expectations of peaceful change are therefore unattainable."

In the case of Latin America, one could add risks of increased tension and militarization of borders to address smuggling, drug-related crime and violence, and illegal arms trade. As Hurrell (1998b, 530) noted, "One of the results of regionalization and of economic integration is to make neighbors more vulnerable to instability across their borders and to increased levels of political interdependence." The most serious security problems and threats to regional order are domestic and transnational, including primarily arms and drug trafficking and criminality.

Therefore, while Latin America offers a very different security scenario from the Great Lakes region, the possibility of such spillover effects should not be overlooked. Not only is internal instability not at all uncommon (the previously mentioned case of Bolivia being a relevant one), experience shows that the region has been relatively close to such triggers for war.

This was the case, for instance, in two significant crises taking place in South America over the past decade. In 2008, as a part of its decades-long struggle against narcoguerillas and paramilitary organizations in its territory, Colombia decided to raid a well-established camp of the Colombian group FARC in Ecuadorean territory. The governments of Venezuela and Ecuador responded with outrage to the operation, breaking diplomatic relations with Colombia and sending military troops to their Colombian border. That same year, Hugo Chávez suggested that the Colombian guerrilla groups FARC and the National Liberation Army of Colombia (Ejército de Liberación Nacional) be granted the more legitimate "belligerent status" (as opposed to terrorist designation) in Venezuela. At the time, Colombian president Álvaro Uribe privately declared that "the best counter to Chávez remains action—including the use of the military" ("CJCS Admiral Mullen" 2008).[8] Thus even with significant economic interdependence—Colombian exports to Ecuador reached their historic peace that same year (Weisbrot and Johnston)—and stable multilateral institutional frameworks, internal security instability evolved to become a source of regional instability.[9] Only two years later, another crisis between Colombia and Venezuela took the region to the brink of war as a result of one country's domestic instability. In 2010, in the crisis described above, Colombia accused Venezuela of providing safe haven to guerrilla groups operating in its border.

These cases show how, particularly in a region with great internal social instability and political violence, an interstate approach to security is not sufficient. Internal and transnational problems such as drugs, crime, and political repression, when sufficiently escalated, may be a trigger for regional conflict. As Nathan (2006, 280) argues, "At the very least, domestic violence generates uncertainty, tension and suspicion between states, preventing them from achieving the mutual trust and sense of collective identity required to create and maintain a security community."

Although the Colombian Civil War—by far the most serious peace and conflict challenge in the region—is close to complete peacemaking today, other substantial challenges remain. Venezuela, in particular, is a major source of regional concern and has an immense potential to destabilize Latin America, both Central and South. Since the death of President Hugo Chávez in 2013, the political crisis in Venezuela has both broadened and deepened. Nicolás Maduro, his successor, accelerated the degradation of democratic and economic institutions in place and threw the country into profound political and economic crises.

The collapse of democracy and the radicalization of the political crisis in Venezuela has thus far had three major effects on regional diplomacy. First, it significantly exacerbated the weakening of institutional order in the region. Venezuela under Chávez was a major proponent of weakening the OAS as a pillar of regional stability, a move which was supported by Kirchner's Argentina and Lula's Brazil. Its influence over Caribbean states has to this date made it impossible for the organization to address this and other crises on the continent. Mercosur was divided over the entry of Venezuela, a process that was only completed with the questionable maneuver of suspending Paraguay temporarily, which encouraged that country to join the Pacific Alliance, another regional group. The case of UNASUR, introduced above, is furthermore complicated. Because it was deliberately built with low levels of bureaucratic independence and institutionalization, a dispute over the appropriate leadership for the group in relation to the country has brought UNASUR to a dead end; and a new organization, still incipient, was established under the leadership of Chile (Oliveira and Gonçalves 2019).

Second, the crisis in Venezuela provoked a major refugee crisis in the region. Both political repression and drastic economic mismanagement have led to extreme shortages of food and medicine. About 5 million Venezuelans have already fled, mostly to neighboring states, and an additional million are expected to depart in 2020 (Stott and Long 2020), although the COVID-19 pandemic might slow down the outflow. Though the region has a strong history of support for asylum seekers, migrants, and refugees (Esquirol 2012), this most recent wave is causing political tension and uncertainty across the region's borders.

Finally, the crisis in Venezuela has become a problem on its own with regard to its potential transformation in a civil war. The creation of government-sponsored militias across the country and the profound engagement of armed forces officials in civilian affairs in government and business are risk factors that make a peaceful political transition less likely. The crisis has further escalated with National Assembly leader Juan Guaidó's claim to power and the subsequent political recognition of multiple states across the region, including the United States, Canada, Brazil, Argentina, and Colombia. The choice for robust economic sanctions imposed by the United States on oil revenue indicate that the country is seeking the collapse of the Venezuela regime, but that has not resulted in substantive political change.

CONCLUSION: A REGION VULNERABLE TO A NEW CYCLE OF INSTABILITY

Latin America is a region with powerful disincentives for conflict. Having had most of its territorial borders settled for over a century, and a remarkable history of few wars in its past, countries on the continent do not engage in major political rivalries. Yet this does not mean that peace can be taken for granted: war often takes place without any of its main actors wishing for it.

Latin America had, since the end of the Cold War, a virtuous cycle of international (but not domestic) peace and security. There were two principal pillars for this development. First, the general (if imperfect and incomplete) process of democratization across the region renewed the political environment in various states, reestablished a balance in civil-military relations, and, more broadly, removed obstacles for peace where conflict and rivalry was dominant. The impact of this factor is particularly notable in the resolution of the civil wars in Central America, as well as in the rapprochement between Brazil and Argentina in the 1980s. Second, the continent developed a complex network of overlapping regional institutions that were able to manage political conflict in the region, either formally or on an ad hoc basis.

This chapter has argued that two recent trends (in the region as well as globally) have actively undermined these two pillars of international peace and cooperation in the region. First, the last few years saw a drastic decline on regional institutions' capacity to mediate conflict. With the relative decline of the OAS as the center of regional policymaking in the 2000s, regional organizations became the focal point of peace and conflict diplomacy. Because they were poorly institutionalized (e.g., a relatively weak secretariat and treaty-commitments) these institutions have been unable to withstand the divisiveness provoked by Venezuela's authoritarian escalation and political differences between states and more generally. This weakness is reflected in Colombia's choice for having the UN Security Council as the guarantor of its historic peace agreement with FARC, a highly unusual move in the region.

Second, authoritarian tendencies have been on the rise in the region, both on the left and right. As explained above, radicalization in domestic politics can be a source of instability internally and abroad. The risk and promise of "external solutions for internal problems"—a central pillar of populist nationalism, particularly in periods of domestic instability—is consequential for the possibility of peace in Latin America. The ability of populism to generate and benefit from volatility and instability in relation to others goes directly against the need for the peace to have consistency and predictability in the international conduct of states. These factors leave the region vulnerable to spillover effects from the multiple fronts on which internal stability could take place.

With the significant potential for global discord and instability observed, the interplay between global and regional dynamics exacerbates the risks associated with armed conflict in Latin America. It is possible that a new political equilibrium in the region will provoke renewed regional integration, just on different terms. At the time of writing, however, there is no clear path for peace and conflict diplomacy in the region (or outside) capable of addressing the major crises currently facing Latin America.

NOTES

1. The argument offered here does imply more generally that democracy and regionalism necessarily lead to peace. For a discussion on the applicability of liberal democratic peace theory in the region, see Hurrell (1998b).
2. The Colombian peace process is a relevant exception here. To protect the agreement with the FARC from both potential regional spoilers (e.g., Venezuela) and internal opposition, in 2016 Colombia formally requested, with the FARC, that the UN Security Council endorse the agreement and establish an international monitoring mission, thereby increasing costs for spoilers and strengthening normative commitments to implement the agreement.
3. The history of regional integration in Central America is profound, starting with the common Federal Republic of Central America after independence from Spain in 1824 and, after its dissolution, repeated attempts to reconstitute it entirely or partially, through common courts, markets, and other institutions.
4. More recently, in 2011, the creation of the Pacific Alliance trade bloc involving Colombia, Peru, Chile, and Mexico has renewed efforts toward political integration and economic prosperity in the region.
5. Throughout this period of peace in Latin America, the crises in Haiti (in 1994, and again in 2004) were the only instances when the UN Security Council took direct action in the region. More recently, the Security Council played an active role in supporting the Colombian peace process.
6. The advancement of industrial military cooperation was also motivated by commercial interests of regional powers as well as by a desire by ruling governments to create opportunities for corruption. For the logic of corruption in such cases, see Mello and Spektor (2018).
7. The UN Security Council's engagement with the Colombian Civil War was made at the request and with the consent of the Colombian government as a strategy to establish the peace agreement in international law and to protect it from potential spoilers domestically, and did not face any significant international opposition.

8. As reported by Ambassador Brownfield of a meeting between President Uribe and Admiral Mike Mullen, who was then chief of the Joint Chiefs of Staff.

9. In spite of the fact that drug trafficking is, in broader terms, a transnational issue and that there are suspicions of Venezuelan support for the guerrillas, the Colombian war against the FARC was not fully internationalized.

CHAPTER 8

African Peace and Conflict Diplomacy in Uncertain Times

Solomon Ayele Dersso

Writing on the ten crises to watch in 2019, Robert Malley (2018) of the International Crisis Group noted that the "international order as we know it is unraveling, with no clear sense of what will come in its wake." The institutions upholding the post–World War II international order are in a state of decay. With the retreat of Western liberalism, as Edward Luce (2017) put it, and the rise of China and resurgence of Russia, the power relationship underpinning it has witnessed major shifts. The rules governing international relationships are fraying. These major dynamics entail very poignant consequences for international peace and for conflict diplomacy in particular. As the disasters in Syria and Yemen and in other places attest, in this interim period (of what appears to be a transition from the old order into another one that has yet to be made) international peace and security diplomacy are delivering badly, if not totally failing.

Africa's past experiences show that major shifts in the international context tend to directly affect peace and security on the continent. Africa, for example, became a theater for the Cold War with very dire consequences for peace and security (Mbeki 2012). Similarly, the war on terrorism has also had major adverse effects on the dynamics of and approaches to peace and conflict diplomacy in Africa, including the militarily heavy approach to conflict management and resolution. Unlike the 2008 global financial crisis, Africa is not likely to escape the adverse effects of the unraveling of the international order.

This chapter seeks to comment on how three different scenarios that may emerge from the current period of the realignment of the international order may affect peace and security diplomacy in Africa. My proposition in this chapter is that the impact of the three scenarios depends on two major factors. The first factor relates to developments within Africa, including the trends and dynamics of peace and security threats in Africa, and the role of African states and institutions for peace and security diplomacy. The second factor is the interface between Africa's peace and security situations and institutions and the international environment.

To contextualize the analysis of the impact of the three scenarios, it is important to start with presentation of the current state of peace and security diplomacy in Africa. The second section of the chapter thus provides a review of Africa's peace and conflict diplomacy.

THE AFRICAN PEACE AND SECURITY ARCHITECTURE, AND PEACE AND CONFLICT DIPLOMACY IN AFRICA

Since the turn of the century, the peace and conflict diplomacy of Africa has been anchored in the new normative and institutional organization of the African Union (AU). The norms and the institutional structure making the peace and security system of the AU constitute what is popularly known as the African Peace and Security Architecture (APSA). It is therefore important to start this analysis with a discussion of the APSA as the hub of Africa's peace and security diplomacy.

The APSA and the International Order

In the post–Cold War period, Africa is one of the regions that witnessed major transformation in peace and security arrangements. This is particularly reflected in the context of the transition of the Organization of African Unity (OAU) to the AU (Maluwa 2012). In this regard, two developments have reconfigured the peace and security landscape of Africa. The first is the establishment, and efforts at the operationalization, of a reasonably sophisticated and comprehensive peace and security architecture, known by the collective name of the African Peace and Security Architecture (Engel and Porto 2010; Dersso 2013a; Vines 2013; Bah et al. 2014). Second, and alongside the building of the APSA, the AU and subregional organizations have come to take increasing responsibilities in responding to the various peace and security challenges that have emerged on the continent.

It is to be recalled that the emergence of the APSA is a product of both internal and external factors (Dersso 2012). Internally, there were at least three major factors apart from the conclusion of the OAU's objective for the liberation of the continent in 1994 with the demise of the apartheid regime in South Africa (Tieku 2009, 2014; Dersso 2017).[1] The external factors include most notably the failures of United Nations operations in Somalia and Rwanda and the ensuing withdrawal of international support, "leaving new crises in Africa largely in the hands of under-resourced regional countries" ("Working Together for Peace" 2011).[2] As Steven Holmes put it in March 1993 in the *New York Times*, under the intriguing headline "Africa: From Cold War to Cold Shoulders," "having been carved up and colonized by European powers and turned into pawns, knights and rooks on a cold war chessboard by the superpowers, Africa now faces a devastating new problem: indifference."

Although, as a result, Africa was left to pick up the pieces from the disastrous external interventions and the crisis of leadership and statehood, the ensuing enormous void served as a major impetus for the countries of the region to rise to the challenge and assume responsibility for Africa's peace and security, culminating in the transition of the OAU to the AU and establishment of the APSA. The APSA has two components. The first one consists of the normative and policy thinking that underpins the APSA. The second one is the institutional dimension.

As Alex Vines (2013) has rightly pointed out, the normative and policy dimensions of the APSA significantly draw on the liberal peace model (Curtis 2012). This is given expression through the values and principles enunciated in the legal and policy instruments of the AU that govern peace and security diplomacy in Africa, notably the Constitutive Act (also known as the AU Act) is the foundation of these instruments (Magliveras and Naldi 2002, 415) and the subsidiary instruments, which primarily include the Protocol on the Establishment of the Peace and Security Council of the African Union (PSC Protocol) and the Common African Defense and Security Policy (CADSP).[3] Of the eighteen principles listed in the AU Constitutive Act, eight form the central planks of the AU security regime (Williams 2007).[4]

Although some of these principles reflect continuity from the OAU, the new ones introduce a paradigmatic change. Respect for democratic principles, human rights, the rule of law, and good governance is the first of these new principles. The Common African Defense and Security Policy also identifies human security as an important basis and measure of the continental collective security system. The policy also identifies intrastate conflicts or tensions as common security threats, hence envisaging an interventionist approach to the prevention, management, and resolution of conflicts (De Oliveira and Verhoeven 2018). The sharp edge of the interventionist streak of the new principles enshrined in the AU Constitutive Act is embodied in the paradigm-changing norm establishing the right of the AU to intervene. Article 4(h) of the Constitutive Act thus stipulates the AU's right to "intervene in a member state pursuant to a decision of the Assembly in respect of grave circumstances, namely war crimes, genocide and crimes against humanity" (Kioko 2003, 807; Aneme 2011; Kuwali and Viljoen 2015; Dersso 2013b). This marks a sweeping break from the OAU's noninterventionist, normative orientation and diplomatic tradition of indifference. As the key normative illustration of the fundamental change in the field of peace and security, this principle manifests the desire of the framers of the act for the AU and its member states to assume responsibility for peace and security on the continent. Expressed in those terms, this principle not only creates the legal basis for intervention but also imposes an obligation on the AU to intervene to prevent or stop the perpetration of heinous crimes anywhere on the continent (Yusuf 2003).[5]

There are aspects of the norms of the APSA, which, though linked to the democratic norms of the liberal international order, have been given unique application. A case in point is the AU norm on unconstitutional changes of government, the only aspect of the AU norm on constitutional rule and democratic governance that is given clearly established mechanisms of enforcement both in the Constitutive Act of the AU and in the PSC Protocol. This is a norm without parallel in the international system, and it has been given much more consistent application even when lacking adequate support from the international system, as the recent decision of the AU slapping Sudan with sanctions after the seizure of power by the army illustrates ("Emergency Session" 2019). Of course, in recent years the application of this norm on unconstitutional changes of government have faced major challenges due to contested extension of constitutional term limits by governments (Dersso 2017).

Giving credence to the view of Vines noted above, the foregoing review highlights both the influence and the incorporation into the APSA of some of the tenets of the liberal peace framework that have shaped the post–Cold War peace and security diplomacy globally. The aspects of the norms and policies of the APSA manifesting this liberal peace agenda clearly show the close association with and the reliance of the APSA on the international peace and security order (Opongo 2013).

Going beyond the normative realm that reflects significant borrowing and regional adaptation of the liberal peace framework underpinning the international order, there is also substantial institutional affinity and interdependence between the APSA and the institutions serving the global security order. Indeed, one of the features of the APSA is that it is premised on both the recognition of the indivisibility of security and on its complementarity with the multilateral global collective security system anchored in the United Nations Charter.

Accordingly, the PSC Protocol underscores "the need to forge closer cooperation and partnership between the United Nations . . . and the African Union, in the promotion and maintenance of peace, security and stability in Africa." The PSC Protocol also defines as one of the powers of the PSC: the promotion and development of "a strong partnership for peace and security" between the Union and the United Nations." Article 17 of the PSC Protocol outlines the mechanisms for how the PSC pursues its role in promoting "partnership for peace and security" between the AU and the United Nations.[6]

Beyond the normative and institutional inseparability of the APSA from the international peace and security system, the APSA has also become functionally tied to the international order. The operationalization of the various components of the APSA and its implementation during the past decade and a half have drawn on and involved the building of partnerships that mobilized the necessary strategic, financial, technical, and logistical support for its functioning (Darkwa 2016). Although these partnerships notably with the UN and the European Union reveal an acknowledgment that the international order cannot on its own and without support from regional mechanisms effectively address peace and security challenges, they are also predicated on the recognition of the APSA as a regional arrangement anchored in and complementary to the international collective security order ("Uniting Our Strengths" 2015).

It is important to recall that the intimate bond between the APSA as Africa's regional security arrangement and the international order has a solid historical pedigree (Williams 2007), although the appropriation of the liberal peace agenda is a more recent development. This close affinity with the international system is normatively asserted in the OAU Charter (via the reference to the UN Charter). It also enjoyed support in the work of leading pan-African figures of the independent period, notably Kwame Nkrumah of Ghana. In one of his celebrated works, *Africa Must Unite*, Nkrumah (1963), arguing that "it is impossible to separate the affairs of Africa from the affairs of the world as a whole," asserted that "although confidence in the United Nations has suffered several shocks since its foundation, and particularly of late in connection with the Congo crisis, it remains the only world organization in which the many problems of the world have a chance of finding reasonable solution. It must, therefore, be supported by all interested in the preservation of peace and the progress of human civilization."

Trends in the Nature of Conflicts, and in the AU's Peace and Conflict Diplomacy

Over the years, the peace and security landscape of the African continent has witnessed shifts in the nature and dynamics of conflicts. In the early 1990s, Africa witnessed a shift from interstate to intrastate conflicts with a surge of civil wars. Although the incidence of such violent conflicts steadily declined from late 1990s to the mid-2000s, coinciding with the establishment of the AU and its interventionist peace and security regime, this trend has since experienced major reversals.

Intrastate conflicts remain major sources of conflict to this date, although a lot has changed in recent years in terms of the character and form of conflicts. Unlike in the 1990s, traditional rebel groups involving large-scale organization and mobilization for control of state power are increasingly becoming rare. More and more, the actors active in many of the conflict situations are irregular and loosely organized groups, such as clan militias, guerrilla forces, criminal networks, religious or ethnic militias, and terrorist groups operating in peripheral areas taking advantage of the absence or weak presence of the state. Yet, despite their decline, civil wars involving armed rebel groups continue to persist. As the experiences of the Central African Republic, Mali, and South Sudan show, contemporary civil wars in Africa are strongly driven by the recurrence in new forms of intrastate conflicts rather than by the emergence of entirely new violence.

One notable feature of contemporary intrastate conflicts is that they are not entirely internal. Invariably, all such conflicts continue to exhibit significant external dimension. It has been reported that 79 percent of civil wars in Africa are characterized by cross-border violence, and 29 percent of conflict actors operate across borders (Deltenre and Liégeois 2016). This "very high level of clandestine cross-border military operations and various forms of support to proxies by neighboring countries (some covert, some openly acknowledged)" has led one study to redefine what it called "the paradigmatic armed conflicts" in Africa "from 'internal' to 'internal conflicts with important internationalized political and military components'" (Bah et al. 2014). It can thus be argued that the dearth of interstate conflicts is not the total absence of interstate tensions but is in part attributable to the use of proxy wars by states (Twagiramungu et al. 2019).

Over the past decade, the expansion of transnational threats involving terrorism and violent extremism, armed banditry, and organized crime has come to constitute a major threat to peace and security in Africa (Anning and Abdala 2016). Although in 2008, when the AU first issued a report on terrorism, only a few pockets of territories in East Africa and North Africa were affected by terrorist violence, during the past several years the threat of terrorism expanded to cover almost all parts of the continent, affecting regions that have hitherto been immune, including Southern Africa. Large swaths of territories in the Lake Chad Basin region, the Sahel, North Africa, Central Africa, and East Africa have become affected by terrorist groups and criminal networks. These threats are not bound to national territories. As the case of Boko Haram shows, they operate across a number of national boundaries and traverse at least two geopolitical regions.

The other source of threat for peace and security increasingly results from major breaches of the governance and human rights norms reflecting the "downward trend in democratic governance in Africa" (Crocker 2019a). One of the manifestations of this is the rise in conflict events involving contested transitions and protest activities. These are associated with electoral violence, crisis over extension of presidential term limits, coups d'état, and other forms of unconstitutional changes of government. As events in Burundi, the Democratic Republic of Congo, Ethiopia, Algeria, and Sudan, among others, illustrated, protests and riots have become the dominant forms of conflict events in Africa. According to the Tana Forum (2018), accounting for a total of 5,660 events in 2017, protests and riots have become the leading conflict events on the continent.

The AU has since the early 2000s been engaged in deploying responses to deal with the various peace and security threats facing the continent, establishing itself in a matter of less than a decade as a major peace and security actor deploying diplomatic and security tools in response to the various threats highlighted above. Since coming into operation in 2002, it has deployed or authorized the deployment of more than a dozen peace support operations to Burundi, the Central African Republic, Comoros, Darfur, Mali, Somalia, Central Africa, the Lake Chad Basin, and the Sahel region. In 2013, for example, a total of about 40,000 uniformed and civilian personnel were mandated to serve in AU peace operations, which increases to approximately 71,000 if the joint African Union–United Nations hybrid mission in Darfur is also taken into account (Lotze 2013). An important development related to this increasing role of the AU in peace support operations has been the emergence of an evolving division of labor, whereby African countries contribute the critical element of peacekeeping personnel while partners including the UN and the EU as well as individual countries provide support for filling the financial, logistical, and mission support capabilities gaps of the AU (Darkwa 2016).

The number of AU peace support operations has since plummeted. Corresponding to this decline in the number of AU peace operations, we have witnessed increase in UN peacekeeping operations. The UN launched the new operations in the Central African Republic and Mali in 2014 and 2015. Yet these operations, rather than being brand new, have been transferred from the AU to the UN. It is also worth noting that in both the Central African Republic and Mali, the AU has transformed its presence into special political offices, continuing to play major roles in the peace processes in those countries. In the Central African Republic, through its political mission, the AU has initiated the Africa Initiative for Peace and Reconciliation in the Central African Republic, which facilitated the peace deal signed between the government and fourteen armed rebel groups in February 2019. In Mali, the AU Mission to Mali and Sahel has continued to play a role in the peace process in Mali.

The transnational threats, particularly those relating to terrorism and violent extremism, have additionally involved military operations including by military personnel of notably the United States and France. In a streak of innovation, these expanding transnational threats have also led to the emergence—in the Central African, Lake Chad Basin, and Sahel regions— of ad hoc regional joint forces mobilizing the security forces of affected countries.[7] These are not necessarily positive, particularly where such military heavy responses lack clear political strategy in pursuit of which they are deployed. Indeed, they can have very adverse consequences for protection of civilians.

Both in the operations in Somalia and Mali and in these ad hoc regional joint forces, the AU and regional actors have demonstrated willingness to undertake peace enforcement, counterinsurgency, and counterterrorism tasks that the UN is unable to engage in. As the expansion in the threat of terrorism and radical extremism noted above shows, this profile of the AU and subregional frameworks is sure to remain increasingly important. Indeed, it has been well recognized through its deployments—notably in Somalia, Mali, and the Central African Republic—that one of the major comparative advantages of the AU is its ability to get in more quickly and with more force than the UN does. However, this comes at a heavy cost, because such operations often result in a huge loss of lives and limbs of the personnel of those operations.

Many of the other forms of conflicts also attracted responses involving a combination of sanctions and mediation in the case of situations of unconstitutional changes of governments and the use of peacemaking and mediation processes including in cases of crises involving protest and riot events. The peacemaking or mediation responses have taken different forms, such as ad hoc panels (the high-level ad hoc panels for Côte d'Ivoire and

Libya), high-level panels (the AU high-level panels for Sudan and Egypt), chief mediators of the AU or special representatives or envoys of the chairperson of the AU Commission (in the Central African Republic, Comoros, Côte d'Ivoire, Darfur, Madagascar, Mali, Somalia, and South Sudan) (De Carvalho 2017). Additional forms of interventions have also been initiated in more recent years. These notably include the deployment of human rights observers and military monitors in Burundi and human rights investigation missions or commission of inquiry sent to South Sudan in 2014 and Burundi in 2015.

PEACE AND SECURITY DIPLOMACY IN AFRICA IN A SCENARIO OF DISCORD

In a scenario of discord, at least three trends will have serious ramifications for peace and conflict diplomacy, particularly in Africa. The first is the return of the assertion of state sovereignty. The second involves the legitimacy it lends to authoritarian governments. The third is the deepening polarization among states, particularly major powers, in a development that mirrors the Cold War and the risk of this leading to the internationalization of regional conflicts.

This period has now become a time characterized by "the rise of populist sovereignism" (De Spiegeleire, Skinner, and Sweijs 2017). From Brexit to Trump, populist sovereignism has put an immense strain on the liberal world order and multilateralism in general (Luce 2017). It was in the name of "taking back control," or sovereignty, that the "leave" camp won in the UK referendum on its membership in the European Union. The electoral victory of President Donald Trump in 2016, with his trademark slogan of "Make America Great Again," also unleashed an approach that eschewed multilateral frameworks and relies heavily on the flexing of muscles in pursuing international relations. This was accompanied in Europe by the major gains that right wing populist parties made in national politics.

The rise of populist sovereignism has had at least two major consequences in other parts of the world, such as Africa, Asia, and Latin America. The first is what may be called the contagion effect. As a result of a rise in populist authoritarianism, a nationalist or authoritarian populist revival is visible in various countries, including India, Turkey, and Brazil. In Africa, this phenomenon has been visible, among others, in Egypt, in Zimbabwe under Mugabe, in Uganda, and increasingly in Tanzania. The second and related consequence is the enthusiastic reception by strong leaders in various parts of Africa of President Trump's counsel from his inaugural speech that "it is the right of all nations to put their own interest first." Robert Mugabe of Zimbabwe welcomed Trump's sovereignism when he told the state television that "America for America, America for Americans—on that we agree" and, he added, "Zimbabwe for Zimbabweans" (MacKinnon and York 2017). "Authoritarian leaders of Burundi and Uganda were among the first to congratulate Mr. Trump on his election." President Museveni of Uganda expressed his "love for Trump." Egypt's president, Abdel Fattah Al-Sisi, praised Trump "on his unique personality"(Gray 2017).

There are now signs that support for the liberal peace framework that shaped peace and conflict diplomacy in the post–Cold War period is dwindling, putting it mildly. In a departure from previous US administrations that embraced and championed the promotion of democracy and human rights, President Trump vowed in his first speech never to "impose our way of life" on any country. And in his first speech to Congress, he also declared that all countries have a right to "chart their own path." In a step with direct implications for peace and conflict diplomacy, his administration proposed reducing US contributions to the UN by 40 percent, and forced the UN General Assembly to cut $600 million from its peacekeeping budget.

These developments affect peace and conflict diplomacy in Africa in various ways. The first and most obvious impact of the scenario of discord is its tendency to tip the balance in favor of sovereignty and national interest, to the detriment of the collective security order. Within the framework of the PSC, member states have in the past few years have come to take over control of agenda setting, reversing the practice of the past, when the AU Commission dominated the crafting of the PSC's agenda. Respect for sovereignty and assertion of the AU's intergovernmental character has become a common refrain in the statements and interventions of member states.[8] As highlighted in the example of the decision on deployment of an intervention force to Burundi, the assertion of the sovereignty-based intergovernmental character of the AU has come to stifle effective AU action. It is to be recalled that when—on December 17, 2015—the PSC, meeting at the level of ambassadors, decided to deploy the African Protection and Prevention Mission in Burundi with or without the consent of Burundi, the AU Commission was at the forefront of the decision-making process, with representatives of member states largely following the lead of the AU Commission (Dersso 2016). On January 29, 2016, when the PSC met at the heads of state and government level, representatives of member states were in the driving seat when the ultimate decision on moving ahead with the proposed deployment of the mission was taken (International Crisis Group 2016). Although the changes in sentiments around risks of Burundi sliding back to a genocidal civil war played a role, considerations of sovereignty and consent of Burundi were major factors in the decision of the heads of state of the PSC overturning the December 17 ambassadorial-level PSC decision (Dersso 2016; Williams 2016).[9]

As Chester Crocker (2019a, 2019b) observed, the long-term, global pushback by the leading authoritarian powers against liberal governance norms has consequences in Africa and other regions. It in particular lends legitimacy to authoritarian tendencies, undermining the regional peace and security order. One such manifestation has been the attempt by Egypt to lend an AU support on the military seizure of power in Sudan (Elders 2019). To this end, President Al Sisi of Egypt convened, in his capacity as chair of AU, a consultative summit in Cairo on April 24, 2019. The recommendation from the summit for the PSC to extend the two-week period set for transfer of power by the junta to a civilian-led authority to a three-month period led to the extension of the timeline to two months. Despite continuing efforts by Egypt to forestall PSC action on the junta, the PSC sanctioned the junta with suspension from participation in AU activities (Dersso 2019). Rather than inducing it, the scenario of discord mostly has the effect of reinforcing existing tendencies on the part of member states to resort to the old diplomatic tradition of indifference and of support for regime security.

There is also an emerging trend of governments of member states refusing to engage with regional and international peace and security processes. Burundi has been particularly adept at frustrating regional and international engagements. The government in Bujumbura refused to sign a memorandum of understanding on the deployment of AU human rights monitors and military observers, insisting on having an oversight role on its reports. In 2015, Bujumbura also rejected a UN-appointed mediator after a critical report of the UN office on the elections conducted in the country. It also successfully defied the proposed deployment of UN police to the country. During 2018, Burundi's president refused to engage the AU commissioner for peace and security when the commissioner undertook a visit to Bujumbura. The Democratic Republic of Congo declined to receive the planned visit of UN secretary-general Antonio Guterres and AU Commission chairperson Moussa Faki Mahamat (Nichols 2018). Sudan also declined the proposal from Guterres to appoint Nicholas Haysom as his personal envoy to Sudan.

Additionally, in this context, multilateral frameworks or approaches are viewed in transactional terms. They are to be used only to the extent that they serve the national interest or foreign policy preferences of individual countries. This has already become visible in some of the major conflict situations in Africa. Indeed, it is this prominence of a sovereignty and transactional foreign policy approach on the part of key countries in the Intergovern-mental Authority on Development region that has led to the failure of this regional authority to mediate a successful peace in South Sudan and to have the peace implemented once it has been signed (Vertin 2018).

Another manifestation of this trend that is already under way is the increas-ing reluctance within the AU to have country situations on the agenda of the PSC (International Crisis Group 2019). Instead of mirroring the prevailing peace and security dynamics on the continent, the trend in the content of the agenda of the PSC has increasingly shown the tendency of monthly chairs of the PSC to include national preferences in the focus of the monthly program of work of the PSC. As a result, the PSC has failed to put on its agenda and consider ongoing crisis situations such as the conflict in Cameroon.

The other development in this scenario shaping peace and conflict diplo-macy, as noted in the introduction, is the end of the unipolar world order of the post–Cold War period and the apparent rise of poorly regulated multipolar competition. Dubbed by some as the new Cold War, big power rivalry and ten-sion has increasingly become a major feature of the international system, with major consequences for conflict prevention, management, and resolution.

In early 2018, while unveiling the US National Defense Strategy, then–defense secretary James Mattis announced that great power competition—not terrorism—is now the primary focus of US national strategy. As reported by Taylor (2018), the National Defense Strategy states that "long-term stra-tegic competitions with China and Russia" are the "principal priorities" for the Defense Department.

This inaugurates a new era marking the end of a period when the differ-ent centers of power sought some form of, albeit ad hoc, accommodation. It heralds the beginning of a period when they are poised to pursue antagonis-tic rivalry for hegemonic dominance and supremacy. "The empirical reality makes it abundantly clear that relations between the major powers have become more tense and potentially more dangerous than they have been since the end of the Cold War," as Tekeda Alemu (2019) put it.

That Africa has become one of the main theaters for such competition became evident when the United States' "new Africa strategy" was launched in December 2018. While unveiling the strategy, John Bolton, President Donald Trump's national security adviser, pointed out, following the logic of the US Defense Strategy, that the greatest threat for US interests came not from poverty or Islamist extremism but from China and Russia (Landler and Wong 2018).

Highlighting the centrality of big power competition in the United States' Africa strategy, the *New York Times* (Landler and Wong 2018) published an article headlined "Bolton Outlines a Strategy for Africa That Is Really About Countering China," and the Editorial Board of the *Financial Times* (2018) dubbed the strategy "America's scrambled approach to Africa."

At a time of rising and unregulated big power antagonism and rivalry, the willingness of and minimum consensus among major powers to defend and operate within the framework of multilateralism is also fading. In this context, troubling signs of regional tensions descending into major conflicts—in which major powers are sapped leading to the breakdown of world order—have been witnessed as reflected in the cases of Syria and Yemen.

In this context, a major risk for peace and conflict diplomacy in Africa would therefore be the risk of an internationalization of conflicts, with rival major powers standing on opposing sides of the conflict. At best, this would lead to a situation where the required minimum consensus for collective action within the framework of the APSA could not be found. At worst, it could lead to the descent of regional conflicts into major international conflicts, wherein rival major powers would insert themselves. As the situation in Libya in 2011–12 illustrated and continues to show currently, in this situation there is a likelihood of the role of the AU and the interest of the affected region being totally ignored, leading to very disastrous outcomes.

This deepening polarization among the permanent five members of the UN Security Council (P-5) ("Working Together for Peace 2011, 2), likely to expand in a scenario of discord, also carries adverse consequences on peace and conflict diplomacy within the UN affecting the UN Security Council's role with respect to second-order conflicts, in which major powers have no significant interest. In this regard, Richard Gowan (2019) observed, in an incisive opinion piece, that "the big powers that give the UN its clout are increasingly unable to find enough common ground to make credible collective action possible." He goes on to explain that the "rift between China, Russia and the Western members of the Security Council that opened up over Libya and Syria in 2011 and 2012 have now spread to diplomacy over crises from Venezuela and the Central African Republic to Iran."

The polarization in the P-5 is also set to affect the role of the three African nonpermanent members of the UN Security Council (the A-3) in representing and pursuing a cohesive position on African issues in the UN Security Council. A recent report of the International Crisis Group (2019) in this respect observed that the attempt of major powers to split the A-3 up "will grow especially intense as the P-5 increasingly vie for influence and pressure A-3 members to either help them get the nine votes needed under UN rules to adopt their favored resolutions or join blocking coalitions to deny their rivals the nine votes that they require."

The withdrawal of funding by the US for peace and security work of the UN has also affected peace and security diplomacy in Africa. While unveiling the Africa Strategy of Trump's administration, John Bolton stated that Washington's goal was "for the nations of the region to take ownership over peace and security in their own neighborhood" (Calamur 2018). The first victim of this budget cut was peacekeeping operations, which are among the most important instruments for peace and conflict diplomacy in Africa. Indeed, the United States has already forced the UN General Assembly to cut $600 million from the UN peacekeeping budget. This will affect major missions in Africa, including those in the Central African Republic, the Democratic Republic of Congo, and Sudan (Carver 2018).

The posture of the Trump Administration in terms of cutting funding for peace and security had a direct impact on Africa, particularly within the context of the negotiation between the AU and the UN for a framework on the financing of UN-authorized, AU-led peace support operations in Africa. During 2018, the African nonpermanent members of the UN Security Council prepared a joint draft resolution on the financing basis of UN-authorized AU peace support operations. Despite the overwhelming support for the draft resolution within the UN Security Council and the unprecedented co-sponsorship of the draft by nearly ninety UN member states, voting on the draft did not proceed as planned, on account of the US threat to veto the resolution ("Vote on Draft Resolution" 2018). The US refused to support the draft resolution, despite the fact that the A-3 believed that "they have done all they can to bring the US on board and that the draft to be voted on tomorrow has been revised to accommodate almost all of the US concerns" ("Vote on Draft Resolution" 2018). The previous US administration was supportive of the adoption of a framework resolution carrying no specific financing obligation on the UN but only a commitment to finance on a case-by-case basis and subject to various stringent requirements.

The shift in the focus of the EU from providing support for peace and security to addressing the so-called migration crisis, together with the US push to cut funding for multilateral peace and security work, is set to give rise to funding gaps for the APSA. Apart from reinforcing the ongoing effort to mobilize funding from within the continent, this situation has the potential of increasing a shift to seek support and enhance a partnership with China. China's role has already been deepening. As pointed out during the first China-Africa peace and security forum, apart from the donation of equipment, and funding support of about $1.2 million annually to the African Union Mission in Somalia since 2011 and the provision of equipment that forms part of the strategic stock for the African Standby Force, to the tune of

$100 million, China has pledged additional support of $80 million (Chergui 2019). Although this increasing partnership is sure to determine the nature of the AU's peace and security responses, with emphasis on stability and a bias for regime security, it is unlikely that this would completely erode the APSA's liberal values. This has come out recently from the divergent position that the AU and China took on the situation in Sudan. Though the AU's PSC slapped the military junta in Sudan with sanctions of suspension from membership in the AU, upholding the norm banning unconstitutional changes of government, China opted to throw its support behind the junta.

Although the foregoing establishes that the scenario of discord will have major adverse effects on peace and security diplomacy in Africa, it should be underlined that this impact is not a function only of the weight of the conditions prevailing in that scenario. The extent of the adverse impact of these conditions also depends on how African actors are able to sustain the tenets of peace and conflict diplomacy under the AU and limit the effect of these adverse conditions. That the AU imposed sanctions on Sudan for unconstitutional changes of government following the seizure of power by the military is a clear example that even in a context where there is no supportive international environment, the AU can meaningfully pursue peace and conflict diplomacy on the continent.

PEACE AND SECURITY DIPLOMACY IN A SCENARIO OF COLLABORATION

This scenario envisages the continuation of the post–Cold War liberal international order and the strengthening of global institutions. This is based on the emergence of a coalition of international actors that mobilize as a countervailing force in support of the liberal international order. These actors, nation-states, and civil society actors share in liberal values and seek to promote these values through existing or strengthened institutions of collective security and cooperation.

Within the framework of a scenario of collaboration, the AU has been able to establish and achieve some degree of operationalization of the various peace and security mechanisms making up the APSA. The AU, in collaboration with subregional organizations and the UN, has managed to deploy a number of peacemaking and peace support operations across the continent and has initiated peacemaking efforts in many of the conflict situations, including most recently in South Sudan through the Intergovernmental Authority on

Development, in Burundi through the East African Community, and in the Central African Republic.

In operationalizing the APAS while the AU mobilized diplomatic resources and the requisite personnel for peace support operations, its external partners have contributed—through the provision of finance, logistics, and training—to African operations. Paul Williams (2017a, 2017b) had a point when he argued that many of the peace support operations deployed within the framework of the AU "would not have been possible without a range of international partnerships, including unprecedented levels of cooperation, particularly between the UN and AU." Indeed, the AU and the UN have over the years succeeded in deepening their partnership on peace and security (Williams and Dersso 2015). Beyond and above the high level of coordination processes between the UN Secretariat and the AU Commission and the annual consultative meetings between the AU's PSC and the UN Security Council, the various resolutions that the council adopted on the AU-UN partnership is further evidence of progress in pursuing policy and operational coordination in addressing peace and security challenges on the continent.

In a scenario of collaboration, this partnership will continue to receive support from the EU and its member states. It is also expected that China and India will also lend their support for further enhancing coordination with and support for the APSA and the AU's work on peace and security. In this context, negotiations for a UN Security Council resolution establishing the framework and parameters for UN support, using its assessed contributions to AU-led peace support operations authorized by the UN Security Council, will continue with a strong prospect of success.

Even in this scenario, it is unlikely that there will be a reversal of the reluctance on the part of the UN Security Council for mandating new missions. In this context, new peace operations in Africa are likely to be those mandated or authorized by the AU, with the UN engaging in new operations in Africa only by taking over from such AU missions, as has been done in Burundi and Darfur in the past and in Mali and the Central African Republic recently. This and the trend in the nature of conflicts highlighted in the previous section illustrate the continuing importance of the peace and conflict diplomacy of the AU and subregional organizations.

Despite recent recessions manifested in measurements of good governance and democratization, as well as the APSA's sustained commitment, it is expected that the support for and acceptance of APSA norms on the continent will also expand. Apart from the promotional work of the AU and its various bodies, this will likely come about due to the expanding engagement and work of nonstate actors—including policy research bodies, civil society organizations, academic institutions, and the media. Also important in this context are the rise in public support and demand for more responsive and accountable governments.

At the continental level, this scenario will also likely make it possible for the AU and the regional economic communities / regional mechanisms (RECs/RMs) that play a major role in peace and security to negotiate and achieve a framework for a division of labor, burden sharing, and coordination that is key for effective collective action. Currently, the interface between the AU and the RECs/RMs is fraught with major issues in various conflict situations, including in Mali, the Central African Republic, South Sudan, and Burundi. The lack of a clear and workable modus operandi for coordinating policy action and mobilizing responses has meant that it was not possible to pursue effective peace and conflict diplomacy by the AU and RECs/RMs in these situations. Given the recognition within the AU and on the part of the RECs/RMs of the need for achieving an effective framework for policy coordination, a scenario of collaboration (with the UN, the EU, and others supporting coordinated action among African actors) avails some of the conditions that make it possible for the AU and RECs/RMs to negotiate and achieve such a framework.

It is, however, important to note that the emergence of this scenario does not on its own address the challenges facing peace and conflict diplomacy in Africa arising from the leadership deficit on the part of AU member states.

PEACE AND SECURITY DIPLOMACY IN A SCENARIO OF PRAGMATIC COOPERATION

In this scenario of pragmatic and selective cooperation, major powers would not interfere to any great degree in other countries' domestic situations but would uphold common principles of dispute resolution and intermittently cooperate in order to solve common pool resource problems, such as climate change and humanitarian crises.

À la carte and opportunistic approaches to peace and security collaboration appear to be a major feature of this scenario. This ad hoc nature of cooperation would make the possibility of peace and conflict diplomacy unpredictable. Although this scenario does not share the rejection of or opposition to multilateral approaches to peace and security of the scenario of discord, there is no enthusiastic support under this scenario for the full package of the existing international order.

For purposes of African peacemaking actors, the result of this scenario is that it would make partnership with and reliance on the international system difficult. This, together with the reluctance in this scenario of major powers to interfere in the situation of others, would necessitate the assumption of increasing responsibility by the AU and RECs/RMs for peace and conflict diplomacy on the continent. This would thus deepen increasing regionalization of collective action on peace and security, but in a context where the scope for dissonance with the internationally established norms and practice of peace and conflict diplomacy is increasing.

It is possible under this scenario that there may not be an appetite for peace and conflict diplomacy to be concerned with the ambitious objectives of promoting democracy and human rights, or even nation building. Instead, the ambition of peace and conflict diplomacy would be limited to measures for stopping violence and achieving a modicum of stability (negative peace), for facilitating humanitarian relief, and for limiting the adverse effects of new security threats. The result is that the elements of the APSA that have been appropriated from the liberal peace framework may not be pursued actively in the AU's and RECs/RMs' pursuit of peace and conflict diplomacy on the continent. In other words, this is a scenario that strengthens the hand of those African actors who remain skeptics about the APSA's human security ambitions. However, as noted above, this is not a situation with a linear trend. Instead, the influence of the increasing public support for democratic norms on the continent can operate as a countervailing force able to sustain a peace and conflict diplomacy supportive of democratic and human rights norms.

CONCLUSION

Despite the fundamental importance of the multilateral system, how this system can promote and maintain peace and security in Africa is a function of the work of African nation-states and the relationship of the African continental organizations with the multilateral system, particularly within the UN framework. In recent years, peace and conflict diplomacy in Africa has not performed as well as it could. Apart from the challenge that the changing dynamics of conflicts has presented to peace and security diplomacy—such as the diversity of conflict parties and the level of regionalization/internationalization of conflicts—peace and conflict diplomacy has faced major difficulties due to the rise in the assertion of sovereignty, a weakening consensus for collective action, and the dearth of political leadership on the continent.

The emergence of a scenario of discord in the international system is likely to exacerbate some of these difficulties, thereby severely limiting the pursuit of peace and conflict diplomacy on the continent. As witnessed during the Cold War, a major risk for peace and conflict diplomacy in Africa would be the internationalization of conflicts, with rival major powers standing on opposing sides of the conflict, thereby making it highly difficult, if not totally impossible, to resolve conflicts. As the failures from the Libya crisis illustrate, the APSA could stand the chance of limiting the impact of the scenario of discord in reducing the space for peace and conflict diplomacy in Africa only if the leadership of member states succeeds in ensuring that situations on the continent are shielded from becoming theaters for major power rivalry based on a solid common position. Thus, though this scenario could carry adverse effects for the effective functioning of the AU's peace and security order, it is possible to maintain the space for peace and conflict diplomacy, with the AU and regional actors assuming even greater responsibility, although not necessarily delivering effectively. Rather than being totally at the mercy of exogenous factors, peace and conflict diplomacy in Africa hugely depends on endogenous factors. It is the convergence of these two factors that seems to be most decisive.

The scenario of collaboration is the most optimal condition for pursuing a successful peace and conflict diplomacy in Africa. This can be gathered from the historical experience of the continent, and indeed from the level of interdependence between the AU's peace and security framework—APSA—and the international system. However, even in this scenario, the inadequacies and failures of AU member states and institutions, as witnessed in the various conflict situations such as Burundi and South Sudan, play a major part for the performance of peace and conflict diplomacy in Africa. Accordingly, despite the permissive conditions that this scenario avails, peace and security diplomacy could fail to deliver on account of the internal political conditions of African peace and security actors. Yet Alemu was spot on when he observed that "Africa benefits when there is amity among nations, most particularly between the major powers, for it is those countries that have the means to mess things up for others. Their cooperation is beneficial, for opening up possibilities for the creation of better opportunities for international cooperation for development financing, among other things. This is in the interest of all African countries" (Alemu 2019, 14).

Overall, the prevailing uncertainties in the direction of the international system do not bode well for peace and conflict diplomacy in Africa. To the extent that the AU peace and security framework is premised on the international peace and security system, it could not completely escape the adverse effects of the emergence of the scenario of discord. The best that can be hoped for in this scenario is that the APSA can create the possibility for limiting the adverse effects and keeping some space, albeit limited, for pursuing peace and conflict diplomacy with some degree of success.

NOTES

1. First is the impact of democratization of the 1990s on the OAU's state-centric principles of sovereignty and noninterference leading, for example, to the banning of unconstitutional changes of government, the rise to positions of influence and the convergence of political thinking and interests of leaders of key African states, and the shift in the nature of conflict involving the emergence to dominance of intrastate conflicts of major regional ramifications necessitating regional response.
2. As the late former secretary-general of the UN, Kofi Annan, put it in his 1998 Report on the Causes of Conflict, "Africa was left to fend for itself."
3. The listing of the instruments is not exhaustive and an additional list of instruments is available in the preamble to the PSC Protocol. The 2005 AU Non-Aggression and Common Defense Pact also forms part of the peace and security normative instruments of the AU.
4. The identification of these eight principles as the constituent elements of the normative component of AU peace and security system is based on what Paul Williams called the seven norms that make up the central tenets of the AU security culture.
5. This principle represents more than an agenda for interventionism. Seen from the perspective of the emerging norm of the responsibility to protect, as espoused by the AU under the Ezulwini Consensus of 2005, it also expresses the aspect of the sovereignty of states, which involves the underlying principle that the first and primary responsibility of protection lies with the state.
6. Apart from the establishment of close working relationship between the PSC and the UN Security Council, as per subarticle 1 of Article 17, one of the mechanisms envisaged under subarticle 3 is the maintenance of "close and continued interaction with . . . its [the Security Council's] African members, . . . including holding periodic meetings and regular consultations on questions of peace, security and stability in Africa."
7. In the Central African region, Uganda, South Sudan, the Central African Republic, and the Democratic Republic of Congo initiated the Regional Task Force which came together to form the African Union Regional Task Force (AU-RTF) of the Regional Cooperation Initiative for the Elimination of the Lord's Resistance Army (RCI-LRA); in the Lake Chad basin Nigeria, Chad, and Cameroon came together to form the Multinational Joint Task Force (MNJTF) to deal with the threat posed by Boko Haram; and in the Sahel Burkina Faso, Chad, Mali, Mauritania, and Niger initiated the G5 Sahel Joint Force.
8. Although the sovereignty and territorial integrity of Burundi was not at issue, the PSC in its communiqué of its 808th session felt compelled to "reaffirm . . . the respect of the sovereignty and territorial integrity of the Republic of Burundi."

9. Williams observes that the majority of PSC heads of state "did not deem it appropriate to send troops to Burundi without the government's consent. . . . Gambia's president, Yahya Jammeh, and Tanzania's foreign minister, Augustine Mahiga, made particularly strong statements against the need for MAPROBU, but they reflected a majority view in the room."

CHAPTER 9

Resilient Statism in a Changing Middle East

Shadi Hamid

Contrary to how it might have briefly seemed in the 1990s and 2000s, the state is still central—especially in the Middle East. There are of course the well-known examples of state failure in Libya, Yemen, and Syria. However, even here, the Syrian state—after the intervention of two stronger states, Iran and Russia—appears more resilient than anyone would have likely dreamed in the early days of the 2011 Arab uprisings.

Somewhat paradoxically, it was the Arab Spring that gave new life to seemingly moribund Arab states, although that would only become obvious several years later. They had grown bloated, unresponsive, and in love with their own existence, but at the same time ambivalent about preserving it. Fortunately, for their own citizens, countries like Egypt had grown more repressive—the fraud-ridden November 2010 elections were a nadir—but were unwilling to take that repression to its logical conclusion of firing onto protesters en masse. But it was the threat of upheaval and overthrow that pushed several key states to embrace and emphasize both their "state-ness" and their "nation-ness," including countries that had previously defined themselves in explicitly Islamic terms. The most obvious case is Saudi Arabia, which in addition to developing a new "Saudi nationalism" (Smith Diwan 2018) adopted a more muscular foreign policy vis-à-vis Bahrain (by intervening in March 2011 to neutralize mass protests), Egypt (through its support for counterrevolution in the spring and summer of 2013), Yemen (by spearheading military action against the Houthi-led government), and its old rival, Iran.

This should not be too surprising. In a given region, domestic instability within individual countries tends to fuel state-driven regional conflict. The collapse of parliamentary democracy in Japan in the 1920s, resulting in the rise of military dictatorship, sparked an extended conflict across Asia that did not conclude until well after 1945. In 1959, the Cuban Revolution set off a string of insurgencies and coups, with militaries viewing themselves as guardians of the state countering popular mobilization and demands for economic and social representation (Felbab-Brown, Trinkunas, and Hamid 2017). In short, though disorder within states of course weakens those states, it can also strengthen other states, even as this strength seeks to cover and compensate for longer-term weaknesses deriving from a lack of popular representation and democratic legitimacy.

In different ways and to different degrees, Arab regimes have aggressively used the authority—and machinery—of the state to reify nationalism and the nation-state. These are all cases of nationalism strengthening the state and vice versa. This puts international observers in something of a bind: stronger, more effective states are better for implementing economic reforms, combating terrorist networks, and claiming a monopoly over the use of force. Yet improving states' effectiveness, at least in the context of the Middle East, tends to also strengthen and entrench the repressive capabilities of those same states. Hard power is certainly an important element of the projection of influence both at home and abroad, but less attention has been paid to what Peter Mandaville and I (2018) refer to as "religious soft power" in the Middle East.

The United Arab Emirates, Jordan, Morocco, and Egypt have all draped themselves in the flag of "moderate Islam," each giving their own nationalist spin to the concept. In doing so, they seek to counter domestic and regional ideological challenges emanating both from mainstream Islamist groups like the Muslim Brotherhood and extremist organizations like the Islamic State, or ISIS.

Pointing to the instability that the Arab uprisings wrought, authoritarian regimes argue either implicitly or explicitly, or both, that this is not the time for democracy, political reform, or anything that might challenge *haybat al-dawla*, or the "the prestige of the state" (Marks 2017, 239). As part of the projection of religious soft power—by and through the state alone—they prioritize religious reform, including through coexistence forums and training programs for imams. In other words, this is not the time for anything rash, as officials from these countries caution international audiences time and time again. The United Arab Emirates, for its part, has emerged as a primary sponsor of interfaith summits on religious pluralism and coexistence overlaid with a strong Sufi tenor. In Morocco, too, Sufi traditions— which were once associated with rebellion in the colonial era but today tend toward deference to political authority—figure prominently in the

Moroccan monarchy's brand of domesticated Islam. As Sarah Alaoui writes, "This quietism is necessary in a country where the king rules over both the secular and spiritual spheres, and heavily relies on Islam—and a purported lineage to the Prophet Muhammad—to legitimate his rule. This control of the religious sphere has only increased post–September 11" (Alaoui 2019).

AMERICAN "DISENGAGEMENT" FROM BUSH TO OBAMA

Although the United States has encouraged these seemingly innocuous and unobjectionable efforts, the broader context in which Arab allies have felt the need to aggressively assert themselves is more telling. The surge in state-driven regional competition is the product of a drastically different geopolitical and security context than what analysts took for granted after the Cold War. As the editors of this volume note in chapter 1: "Toward the end of the Cold War and for some months thereafter, lessened contention between the United States and the USSR led to cooperative engagement in winding down regional conflicts" (Crocker, Hampson, and Aall 2020). If, per the editors, peace and conflict diplomacy constitutes things like mediation, humanitarian intervention, peacekeeping, capacity building, and strengthening social cohesion, then we have witnessed a significant decline of such efforts in the Middle East, if not necessarily elsewhere. Reversing this decline requires a combination of political will and leadership and significant financial and diplomatic resources. To state the obvious, peace and conflict diplomacy is difficult, even in the best of circumstances. In the Middle East, it is *more* difficult.

The George W. Bush administration's invasion of Iraq in 2003 was, in many ways, the original sin that prompted a long, almost uninterrupted decline in the ability of global institutions to collaborate in response to regional conflict. The editors define the second of three plausible scenarios—*strengthened global institutions*—as "a system comprising a collection of states, reinforced by transnational civil society, that share liberal values and promote those values through, for example, existing or strengthened instruments of collective security and cooperation at the global and/or regional levels" (Crocker, Hampson, and Aall 2020). This goes hand in hand with popular notions of liberal internationalism preserving what is commonly referred to as the "liberal international order" (Wright 2018). President Barack Obama and his senior advisers no doubt saw themselves as internationalists in the service of this vision—at least in theory. As Obama succinctly told *The Atlantic*'s Jeffrey

Goldberg (2016a) in the most expansive exposition of his foreign policy doctrine: "Multilateralism regulates hubris."

Statements like this on the importance of action and leadership in concert with allies complement, but also occasionally belie, a deeper strain in Obama's foreign policy vision, which was best described by Nina Hachigian and David Shorr (2013) as the "responsibility doctrine"—the idea that stepping back allows others to step in and take responsibility for their own region. In the Middle East, the success of such an approach depended on having allies that share American interests or American values, when, in reality, most shared little of either.

Due to the formative experience of the Iraq War, along with domestic political considerations, Obama hoped to reduce America's footprint in the Middle East. If this was the overarching desire in theory, this could only mean a general bias toward disengagement in practice, irrespective of whether greater US involvement could produce better outcomes in particular crises. The one potential exception to Obama's preference for less, rather than more, involvement was his dogged—and ultimately successful—promotion of the Iran nuclear deal, formalized in the Joint Comprehensive Plan of Action. Yet even here there was a catch.

HOW DISENGAGEMENT FUELED ARAB ADVENTURISM

The Iran deal—and how to interpret it—remains especially contentious. It is portrayed by both former Obama administration officials and their staunchest critics as central to President Obama's foreign policy legacy. Yet even such an active foray into diplomacy, negotiation, and multilateral cooperation was a means to the end of removing the possibility of an American or Israeli war with a nuclear (and therefore presumably more aggressive) Iran. It was, in other words, a way to preempt any potentially deeper involvement in the Middle East rather than to serve a broader vision of American leadership in the region.

The overall geopolitical context produced by the Iran deal, then, was one of greater insecurity—at least from the standpoint of America's allies in the Middle East. This perceived insecurity, in turn, emboldened numerous states, namely Saudi Arabia and the United Arab Emirates, to play an increasingly aggressive and ultimately more destabilizing regional role. This became most evident in the case of the Saudi-led intervention in Yemen, which, despite its popular association with the Trump administration, began under the Obama administration, which despite its moral qualms provided critical military and logistical support for the Saudi effort. Hal Brands (2017, 63) points to the "panicked behavior by an exposed Saudi Arabia, whose effort to push back unilaterally against Tehran in early 2015 led it into a war in Yemen that further destabilized the region."

Uninterested or halfhearted American engagement is likely to persist to some degree under future administrations, whether Republican or Democratic, and even more so in a world where pandemics, economic crises, and domestic polarization dominate policymakers' attention. There is little public appetite for a strategy that diverges significantly from either the Obama or Trump administration's approaches, which, though generally very different, nonetheless shared a general distaste for overinvolvement in the domestic affairs of Arab authoritarian states, stabilization efforts, and state building (or, more pejoratively, "nation building"). The Middle East, in part because of policy failures from 2003 onward, has come to be viewed by policy elites on both sides of the aisle and the American public alike as an unsalvageable mess, a near-constant invitation to "damned if you do, damned if you don't" critiques, or a faraway place consumed by "ancient hatreds" that drags down the legacies of American presidents.[1] As Mara Karlin and Tamara Wittes (2019) note: "The United States thus exists in a kind of Middle Eastern purgatory—too distracted by regional crises to pivot to other global priorities but not invested enough to move the region in a better direction. This worst-of-both-worlds approach exacts a heavy price. It sows uncertainty among Washington's Middle Eastern partners, which encourages them to act in risky and aggressive ways." Karlin and Wittes come to a different conclusion from the one offered here on how to address this in-between situation; but at the very least, anyone interested in peace and conflict diplomacy must contend with the inefficacy of doing either too little or too much.

If current trends continue—and, if anything, they are likely to intensify, considering the changes wrought by the COVID-19 pandemic—America's Middle East policy will persist in a primarily defensive mode, attempting to minimize the damage and danger emanating from the region's ongoing conflicts. The domestic, regional, and international contexts will not be conducive to a bold, distinctive Middle East strategy that proactively tries to address the causes of regional conflict—namely, authoritarianism, adventurism abroad from authoritarian regimes, and failures of governance and legitimacy. To address these deeper structural problems would require an ambitious and at least somewhat "interventionist" Middle East policy, something that is simply not possible without strong financial and political will from American presidents.

As mentioned above, the complex relationship between the domestic and foreign policies of Middle Eastern states is a critical starting point for any analysis of regional dynamics. To think that the internal conduct of authoritarian nations can simply be dismissed or put to the side is to misunderstand how domestic disorder can spill over beyond and across borders, as it did most dramatically during the Syrian civil war and the resulting refugee crisis. Population outflows in the hundreds of thousands had profound effects on individual European nations and the European Union more generally, fueling, for example, the rise of right-wing populist parties (Postelnicescu 2016).

However, this relationship between the internal and the external is also critical for how we understand America's current and future role in the Middle East. Under the Trump presidency, the United States—at both the public and elite levels—has found itself consumed by seemingly existential questions of national identity and the very foundations of democracy (and whether democracy might "die" under the authoritarian and norm-breaking leadership style of someone like Donald Trump) (Britton-Purdy 2018). This diverts attention and resources from developing an alternative Middle East strategy. And even if such a strategy were developed by policymakers or candidates, high levels of polarization would make implementing it extremely challenging. This polarization has increasingly affected the conduct of foreign policy, which had long been seen (at least in theory) as a more bipartisan endeavor, with frequent exhortations that partisan politics "stops at the water's edge."

President Trump, and by extension the Republican Party, have sought to unravel Obama's foreign policy legacy with unusual dedication and intensity. Traditionally, there would be at least some respect for foreign policy continuity both during and after presidential transitions. Trump's aggressive politicization of foreign policy has led to what might be called "partisan balancing," where whatever the president does, the other party will define itself as representing the opposite. We see this dynamic playing out with Trump's close and personalized embrace of Saudi Arabian crown prince Mohamed bin Salman, on one hand, and Democrats becoming increasingly critical of Saudi policies, on the other hand. Partisan balancing also affects one of the Middle East's most enduring conflicts—the Israeli-Palestinian conflict, where the Trump administration, reacting to Obama's perceived toughness on Israel, has unquestioningly endorsed right-wing Israeli narratives and, again, personally embraced a polarizing leader in Prime Minister Benjamin Netanyahu. A Democratic administration is likely to reverse course at least to some degree.

In practice, this means that any foreign policy strategy will be difficult to sustain after any alternation of power at the presidential level. In effect, then, attempts to develop and pursue a US grand strategy will not "endure past an election cycle" (Drezner 2019). This is not entirely due to polarization, however. There has also been a slow but significant shift in how the United States conducts foreign policy. In recent decades, presidents who might otherwise be constrained on domestic policy due to partisan polarization have found themselves with greater room for maneuver on foreign policy, and they themselves have worked to entrench and reinforce their own prerogatives. As Daniel Drezner (2019) writes: "Foreign policy analysts largely celebrated this concentration of power in the executive branch, and prior to Trump, their logic seemed solid. They pointed to the public's ignorance of and Congress's lack of interest in international relations. As political gridlock and polarization took hold, elected Democrats and Republicans viewed foreign policy as merely a plaything for the next election. And so most foreign policy elites viewed the president as the last adult in the room."

European democracies, though less polarized on foreign policy due to multiparty systems and coalition governments, are similarly consumed by domestic challenges and constrained by the rise of right-wing populists who are more likely to defer to Arab authoritarian allies. But even if this were not the case, European countries would find themselves doing less with less. European partners, after all, have generally taken their lead from US policy priorities. This means that they have little tolerance for being overexposed in the Middle East, unless they can be confident of either American support or leadership—something that they are unlikely to be confident of anytime soon.

COLLABORATION AND THE LIBERAL INTERNATIONAL ORDER

It is possible to imagine some shift in the direction of greater international collaboration (with the United States and European powers reasserting themselves), if not necessarily in the near future then perhaps in the medium term. The rise of right-wing populist parties, which see the "liberal" in the liberal international order as a bug rather than a feature, has raised the urgency, for center-left and center-right elites, of reviving or at least preserving the liberal order.

In the Middle Eastern context, however, the effects of any shift back in this direction will be limited for some of the reasons already mentioned. In this sense, the Middle East presents an extreme version of the difficulties of international engagement in regions like Asia, Latin America, and Sub-Saharan Africa. The usual slate of obstacles is more pronounced, due to the threat of terrorism, the alliance with Israel, the role of Islam (and fear of Islamist ascendance), long-standing interests vis-à-vis oil, and the durability of authoritarian rule. As we saw under the Obama administration, a president who saw himself as a liberal internationalist and a multilateralist did not necessarily apply the principles of liberal internationalism to a region that he saw as inherently resistant to American leadership. Still, it is helpful to view the overall geopolitical context in the Middle East—and the United States' role in shaping this context—as a spectrum rather than a binary between opposed scenarios. Along this spectrum, a Democratic or traditional (i.e., non-Trumpian) Republican president may promote a more proactive approach in the Middle East than Obama did—as Hillary Clinton or, say, Senator Marco Rubio would likely have done.

This potentially more collaborative environment—with the United States reasserting its lead role in the Middle East, in contrast to the Obama administration's relative "minimalism"—could have significant effects in a number of ways. First, the United States, and by extension the European Union and stakeholders like the World Bank and the International Monetary Fund, would reduce their reliance on authoritarian Arab allies for the management of regional conflicts. Instead of outsourcing Yemen policy to Gulf allies, the US officials would exert sustained pressure on Saudi Arabia to make significant concessions as part of a negotiated solution with the Houthis.

Stabilization in Syria and Libya would also be a key priority, particularly as the economic fallout from the COVID-19 pandemic is likely to amplify the human cost of years of civil conflict. The United States' role could be decisive in breaking the current Libyan stalemate, which is being sustained in part by American allies like Saudi Arabia, the United Arab Emirates, Egypt, and even France supporting the forces of General Khalifa Heftar against the internationally recognized government in Tripoli. The United States itself, under both Obama and Trump, has remained relatively detached from events in Libya, yet because it can influence European and Gulf partners, it is among only a few actors that can play the role of credible arbiter between competing parties. As in Yemen, if hostilities can be reduced, reconstruction efforts and returning Libya's political and economic transition to a sound footing would need to be the focus of international involvement.

A recent Brookings Institution report, for example, makes the case for a city-based approach to rebuilding Libya, led by more active American engagement coupled with close coordination with the UN and other international organizations (Allen et al. 2019). With a weak central government and significant economic and political discrepancies among various Libyan municipalities, the focus of Western donors, nongovernmental organizations, and international organizations would shift to municipal governments, civil society groups, and local militias. As the authors of the report outline (Allen et al. 2019, 3): "Significant economic, political, and security activity would then center on the country's dozen to 15 major cities. Criteria would be established for how local entities could qualify for their fair-share allotment of oil revenues and international aid. An oversight board . . . would assess eligibility based on the actual behavior of the local actors. They would have the power to dock militias and other local actors a percentage of their monthly allocation of funds in the event of serious misbehavior." This could proceed in parallel with the deployment of a UN-sanctioned peacekeeping force, if requested by the Libyan government.

What can realistically be done about Syria, now that the regime of Bashar al-Assad has effectively won the war, is more complicated, because any reconstruction plan would require engaging and even financially supporting either the regime itself or entities and organizations associated with it. With this in mind, reconstruction aid to the central government should be conditioned on facilitating humanitarian access, releasing political prisoners, and allowing Syrian civil society and opposition groups to have a say in the formation of a transitional Syrian government.

A QUESTION OF VALUES

The examples of Yemen, Libya, and Syria bring into focus the question of whether a revival of the international community's role in resolving regional conflicts will be driven by liberal and democratic values—or whether liberal or ostensibly prodemocracy states will, in the name of pragmatism, seek to work closely with authoritarian powers. The latter would mean liberal states deemphasizing ideological differences with authoritarian states and avoiding involvement (or, more pejoratively, "interference") in the domestic affairs of states, including on human rights and political reform. Fen Osler Hampson has referred to this as the "diplomacy of stability" in contrast to a "diplomacy of transformation."[2] Such an approach could bring dividends on less controversial, but still quite critical, priorities like environmental threats, pandemic response, climate change, and perhaps even addressing humanitarian crises (albeit without confronting the regimes responsible, directly or indirectly, for those very same humanitarian crises). But this will be akin to crisis management without addressing the deeper causes of polarization, conflict, and extremism, which inevitably relate to the inherent weaknesses of authoritarian regimes that are overreliant on repression and suffer, by definition, from legitimacy deficits.

Whether a sort of values-neutral "concert of nations" is even actually possible is another question. In light of the intensifying tensions with the world's two leading nondemocratic powers, China and Russia, something resembling a reset seems unlikely for the foreseeable future. But there may be deeper ideological and structural reasons that make "pragmatic cooperation" with less powerful autocracies difficult too—simply that the latter view the world and their preferred international order fundamentally differently (e.g., see Kagan 2019). Regarding potential avenues for collaboration, the editors of this volume highlight dispute resolution and environmental challenges like climate change, for example. In theory, these are issues that do not involve specific questions of the internal, democratic conduct of states. The Obama administration, at least initially, attempted to emphasize diplomacy and strengthen relationships with Russia and China, while deemphasizing human rights and political reform. This approach, however, did *not* lead to improved cooperation, because the ideological differences between liberal and authoritarian states are reflected not just in their stated policy preferences but also in regime type.

CONCLUSION

What is likely to persist in each of the three scenarios under consideration in this volume is a standard and ultimately unimaginative toolkit of counterterrorism programming, deference to the stability of ostensibly "stable" authoritarian regimes, and relatively small-scale support for civil society. Promoting religious tolerance is one area that, being already somewhat popular, is likely to grow more so. This is the low-hanging fruit that the international community can agree on in the absence of other agreements, offering at least the illusion of progress.

There is a deeper political philosophical question here: Can authoritarian regimes, which are, by definition, suspicious of dissent and free inquiry—the very bedrocks of religious freedom—truly be champions of religious liberty and pluralism?

Such efforts, however, face other limitations. First, they can easily distract from the real drivers of conflict. As Annelle Sheline (2019) writes, the Muslim leaders who convene religious tolerance gatherings and promote moderate Islam as a counter to extremist groups "may contribute to the view that Islam is collectively at fault." She explains: "This is due, in part, to the willingness of Muslim political leaders to blame a 'misinterpretation' of Islam for violence. If a corrupted form of Islam is seen as culpable, leaders in the Middle East can avoid acknowledging the ways in which political and economic inequalities in their own states reinforce authoritarianism, domestic coercive apparatuses, and state-sponsored brutality, all of which can generate hostile responses from individuals targeted with repression."

Even if these efforts vis-à-vis religious freedom were something more than cynical gambits to control religious production at home or to curry favor with Western constituencies and donors abroad, they seem to assume that rhetoric, ideas, and good faith, on their own, can reduce conflict. Even if they could, this would not leave global powers or international institutions with much to do besides wait. There is, after all, little that non-Muslim nations or international or supranational organizations can do to influence Islam's evolution (it is challenging enough for Muslim countries). What they can do is focus on the things they actually have experience with and the ability to influence. And this is where refocusing on the "conflict" part of "conflict resolution" offers much-needed perspective. This leads us inevitably to questions of territorial control and governance—or the lack thereof.

Religion and religious ideology matter, but they are rarely enough on their own to motivate volunteers to join militant groups. To put it a little bit differently, its governing ideology aside, the Islamic State would not have been able to govern large swaths of Syria and Iraq if there had been a legitimate, responsive state there already governing. To focus narrowly on counterterrorism or countering violent extremism as a stopgap measure when few international powers are willing to focus on failures of governance and repression is to mistake symptoms for causes. As Kenneth Pollack (2016) writes, emphasizing counterterrorism "as a *goal* of foreign policy" is an error in its own right. Terrorism, like most other global problems, is a product of other things, and those other things—whatever we think they may be—must be addressed. To put it differently, you cannot fight terrorism just by fighting terrorism. And you cannot stop humanitarian crises by stopping humanitarian crises. And you cannot believe in or rely on states that, themselves, have a vested interest in *not* solving the very problems they claim to be fighting.

NOTES

1. In his final State of the Union Address, President Obama was criticized for seeming to endorse a version of the "ancient hatreds" thesis, saying that "the Middle East is going through a transformation that will play out for a generation, rooted in conflicts that date back millennia."
2. Fen Osler Hampson's direct communication with the author, May 16, 2019.

CHAPTER 10

Southern Asia's Realist Future

Kanti Bajpai

South Asia is one of the most war-prone and crisis-prone regions in the world. India and Pakistan fought in 1947–48, 1965, 1971, and 1999, and they had war scares in 1950, 1986–87, 1991, 2001–2, 2008, and 2019. There are several drivers of conflict, but protracted territorial quarrels are key. In addition, since 1998, both countries have been overtly armed with nuclear weapons. Terrorist strikes in India traceable to entities operating out of Pakistan have periodically led to military crises between the two neighbors, most lately in February 2019. In short, South Asia could blow up if creative global and regional diplomacy fails to manage and eventually resolve conflict.

Global diplomacy has played a role in India-Pakistan relations. The Centre for International Governance Innovation project suggests that in uncertain times, global diplomacy features three trends or choices: discord between realist-minded big powers; collaboration between powerful liberal internationalist states; and global public goods cooperation by a concert of powers.[1] How would these diplomatic systems affect South Asia? Drawing on the past experiences and present conditions of South Asia, this chapter presents a thought experiment on how the three forms of diplomacy might address the issues of peace and stability between India and Pakistan. It argues that given the deep differences in South Asia, periodic extremist attacks on India by groups based in Pakistan, and the presence of nuclear weapons, great power efforts to manage deterrence and crises and to get Pakistan to curb violent Islamists are the most viable diplomatic interventions. In addition, the increasing power of China in South Asia and the Indian Ocean region is setting in motion a triangular relationship between India, China, and the United States in a more extended southern Asia that needs careful management. All this suggests a realist future for the region.

THREE DIPLOMATIC SCENARIOS:
THE IMPLICATIONS FOR REGIONAL
PEACE AND STABILITY

The project's three possible global diplomacy futures are presented as alternatives. In fact, they may coexist to varying degrees over time and space.[2] What are their implications for regional security?

Scenario 1 features great powers turning more competitive minded or retrenching from international responsibilities. In such a world, one possibility is that the great powers will aim for spheres of influence, particularly in nearby regions. Another possibility is that as competing great powers seek allies, they divide regions. Last, if the great powers choose to retrench, they may well retreat from regional involvement, leaving regional states to look after themselves. A spheres-of-influence outcome would assure regional peace and stability through hegemony. Dividing a region between great powers could produce local peace and stability by means of a balance of power and deterrence. If great powers retrench, regional peace and stability would be left to regional states. The predominant state in the region may pacify the region through its power, by coercion or largesse. Alternatively, regional states may choose regionalism as a way of regulating their relations.

Scenario 2 of the project features strengthened global institutions led by powerful liberal-minded states. A liberal minded hegemon and a league of democratic states could promote liberal internationalist values and practices worldwide, which would foster regional peace and stability. Liberal internationalist values and practices would include formal equality between states; openness to the flow of goods and capital; dispute settlement through negotiation; international rule of law; and enforcement of standards by international institutions. The role of the great liberal powers would be to propagate these values and practices, to support them by a combination of suasion and coercion, and to oppose contrary values and practices. Concretely, a liberal internationalist approach would reject spheres of influence and instead would promote free trade and investment, encourage regional conflict resolution, and support dispute settlement through international law (e.g., arbitration and judicial rulings) and international institutions (particularly the United Nations).

Scenario 3 envisages a concert of great powers that produces global public goods. Although the great powers are rivals, they have an interest in collaborating to provide global public goods. This functional cooperation could have implications for regional peace and stability. In a world where the most powerful states provide public goods, regional states could be drawn into webs of cooperation with the powerful as well as with neighbors. In this situation, regional tensions and conflicts may be limited by the need to access various global public goods: regional discord and violence would be seen to disrupt access to these vital facilities, and reconciliation and nonviolent methods of change may result. In addition, some global public goods in the sphere of international security—for example, humanitarian intervention and counterterrorism—may target regional rogue states that mistreat their own people or that promote or tolerate terrorism. A great power concert that can threaten intervention on behalf of human rights and political stability and that can punish states that promote or tolerate terrorism could help achieve regional peace and stability.

REALIST DIPLOMACY AND SOUTH ASIA

A realist world where states are more unilateralist and international institutions are weakened is the first possibility at a time when the United States and China as well as the United States and Russia are locked in an increasingly competitive relationship. In such a world, regions face three possible futures. The first is to be part of a sphere of influence of one great power or another. A version of this is living under a regional satrap allied to a great power. A second future is regional deterrence, with the contending great powers ensuring that their regional friends achieve deterrence against neighbors and against rival great powers, either by extended deterrence commitments or by building the military capacities of regional friends. A third future is great power retrenchment, which leaves regional states to their own devices. What are the prospects in South Asia?

Sphere of Influence

Could the competition between the United States on one side and China and Russia on the other side push them toward seeking an exclusive sphere of influence in South Asia? This seems unlikely, for two reasons, and therefore coerced cooperation between India and Pakistan is only a remote possibility.

First of all, South Asia is not a central region for the United States, China, or Russia. Regions have many uses for great powers. They may have key natural resources such as petroleum products and strategic minerals. A region may be a vital market for the great power's goods or investments. Regions may be geopolitical zones that need to be controlled—for instance, for military bases. They may also need to be denied physically to rival great powers. A region may pull in a great power for cultural reasons, too—regions may be cultural kin, and if physically contiguous may exert irredentist pulls on the great power.

South Asia fails on all these counts. The region has no natural resources of any consequence. Nor was the region economically terribly attractive until India's economic reforms of the early 1990s. In 2018, India was the world's seventh-largest economy in nominal gross domestic product (World Bank 2019). It is also poised to have the largest population, surpassing China by midcentury ("India to Dethrone China" 2017). Nevertheless, the idea of controlling a market for one's goods and capital ended in the 1940s. The great powers are not above using economic levers to get their way, as dramatized most recently by US policies under Donald Trump; but an exclusive sphere of economic influence is no one's game. Nor do any of the great powers have cultural links of any depth with South Asia, and there are no irredentist pulls on them.

Second, though South Asia is not strategically central to the great powers, they may yet want to deny control of it to each other. However, geography and India's power prevent the region from succumbing easily to external domination. Geographically, South Asia is not in the United States' or Russia's backyard, and imagining it to be a sphere of influence is a stretch for both Washington and Moscow. South Asia is in China's backyard, and in the 1950s and 1960s, as Beijing struggled to control Tibet, it worried about the influence of the United States. However, India's deepening nonalignment and Pakistan's growing alignment with China gradually reduced Beijing's anxieties. In any case, even if a South Asian power had turned hostile and provided the United States or (later) the Soviet Union with bases and other facilities, the separation of China from the subcontinent by the massive Tibetan plateau, the Himalayas, and the Karakoram mountains militated against any serious strategic threats from the region, particularly after China defeated India in the 1962 war.

At the same time, China's ability to assimilate South Asia to its sphere of influence is limited. Physical involvement in South Asia, including military intervention on any scale, is virtually impossible to sustain. Chinese forces would have the "exterior lines" and face huge logistics challenges. Also, political geography limits China's influence. The small states all touch India and have no borders with each other. Indian goodwill and forbearance are therefore vital to their security and well-being. China's power notwithstanding, none of India's neighbors, except Pakistan, can count on Beijing to offset Delhi. Finally, perhaps uniquely among regional powers, India is powerful enough to resist any attempt by the United States, China, or Russia to dominate the region and to obtain its allegiance as a regional satrap. Despite the growing power gap between China and India, it seems unlikely that Beijing will be able to dominate South Asia.[3] China's sphere of influence efforts are in any case directed toward East Asia, which has been strategically, economically, and culturally far more important for it historically (Kang 2009; Zhang 2015).

Regional Deterrence

If South Asia is unlikely to be pacified by sphere-of-influence dominance, the United States, China, and Russia could help stabilize the region either by extended deterrence or through arms transfers. After 1998, when the two South Asian powers went nuclear, extended deterrence became irrelevant. Since the 1950s, India and Pakistan have sought to build their conventional military capabilities through arms transfers from the United States, the United Kingdom, the Soviet Union / Russia, and China. This has certainly achieved a rough-and-ready level of conventional deterrence. Looking ahead, the key challenge for the three external powers is not so much extended or conventional deterrence as ensuring deterrence stability in a crisis-prone region.

India and Pakistan face at least three deterrence situations: nuclear deterrence; conventional deterrence; and subconventional deterrence (preventing cross-national terrorist or insurgent strikes). The three levels of deterrence are interrelated. Deterrence at the nuclear level has made the region safe for conflict, up to a point, at the conventional and subconventional levels (Ganguly and Kapur 2012). With both countries in possession of nuclear weapons, cross-border terror strikes into India have proliferated. Whether the Pakistani establishment actively instigates terror strikes, militants are encouraged by fact that India's decision to retaliate against terror groups in Pakistan has to weigh the risk of conflict escalation, potentially up to the nuclear level. The experience of the *mujahideen* in Afghanistan is instructive. Anti-Soviet *mujahideen* were able to operate from Pakistan protected by the US and Chinese nuclear shield.

In response to this threat from Pakistan, India's military has prepared for conventional cross-border retaliatory strikes on the calculation that it has escalation dominance and it is Pakistan that faces the risk of escalation. India's so-called Cold Start doctrine and its air strikes on the Balakot camp in Pakistan in February 2019 show that India is willing to use retaliatory violence despite the presence of nuclear weapons on both sides (Ladwig 2008; Abi-Habib and Ramzy 2019). In short, nuclear weapons have made the region relatively safe for militants from Pakistan to launch strikes against India; and the fear of escalation to nuclear war has created room for India to retaliate at the conventional level.

Given that the region has avoided nuclear war, large scale-conventional war (at least since the Kargil war in 1999), or subconventional strikes above a certain level of lethality, it has achieved what Ashley Tellis (1997) calls "ugly stability." However, this is a brittle situation. During the February 2019 crisis, in addition to its initial aircraft-led strikes on the Balakot militant camp, New Delhi apparently threatened to unleash a missile attack if the Indian pilot captured during a subsequent dogfight was not returned expeditiously. Pakistan was reportedly prepared to counter with retaliatory missile strikes (Miglani and Jorgic 2019). At this point, the United States and Saudi Arabia were involved in urging Pakistan to quickly return the Indian air force pilot unharmed (Sood 2019).

This is not the first time that outside powers have become involved in South Asia to prevent conflict escalation. In virtually every India-Pakistan crisis under the shadow of nuclear weapons, outside powers have intervened diplomatically. This will likely continue. First of all, the permanent five members of the UN Security Council (P-5) will be keen to preserve the taboo on nuclear use. Lowering the nuclear threshold and having a nuclear-armed state use nuclear weapons could put at risk the generalized deterrence between P-5 rivals. Second, in case of nuclear war, radioactive fallout could drift beyond South Asia (Reisner et al. 2018). Third, a regional crisis could draw the great powers into confrontation with each other. In a situation where the military tide was turning against one side or other, its great power friends might be tempted to intervene militarily. Specifically, China might intervene on behalf of a weaker Pakistan. If so, the pressure on the US and Russia to become involved could increase, leading to a much wider conflict spiral.

It bears saying that with respect to South Asian deterrence, China complicates calculations. Although it has an interest in ensuring that deterrence is stable in South Asia, its own quarrels with India and its massive military infrastructure in Tibet and overall military modernization mean that the India-Pakistan deterrent relationship is not the only deterrence game in the region. India must ensure that it can dissuade China from attacking it along the contested border. The military standoffs with China in 2013, 2014, 2017 (the Doklam standoff), and 2020 (in Ladakh) suggest that stability along the Line of Actual Control (LAC) is by no means assured, and a small incident could morph into a much bigger confrontation.

India therefore faces a two-front problem. To be sure, scenarios of a Chinese invasion are exaggerated. China's supply lines will be dauntingly long. If the People's Liberation Army (PLA) does manage to break through India's front lines, it will find itself along twisting Indian mountain roads and would be vulnerable to artillery and air power. Should it manage to reach the Indian plains, it would lengthen its exterior lines even further and face devastating counterattacks. In any case, the PLA must fear escalation up to the nuclear level. Having said that the possibility of a large-scale Chinese invasion is exaggerated, clashes and escalation along the LAC cannot be ruled out. Among other things, Beijing needs to make clear it will not take advantage of an India-Pakistan war to launch an attack on India. In a two-front war, Delhi might be tempted to make some very dangerous choices. China can help South Asian deterrence by stabilizing behavior along its border with India.

Great Power Retrenchment

In a world of realist diplomacy, the great powers might choose to retrench from regional involvements to look after their own narrower interests. The United States, China, and Russia do not have formal alliance commitments to India or Pakistan, but any one or more of these powers could choose to retreat from South Asia even further. Will they?

The three powers have enduring interests in the region. These interests are not central to their security—South Asia is not a strategically vital region for any of them, as argued above—but they do keep the United States, China, and Russia connected to regional affairs. Although the three powers may not turn active peacemakers, they will remain engaged. China above all has little choice but to be involved in South Asia, given that it is territorially contiguous to India and Pakistan and fears the destabilization of Tibet and Xinjiang from Indian and Pakistani soil, respectively. If great power retrenchment does occur, therefore, it will likely be asymmetric, with China unlikely to retrench very far.

The United States, China, and Russia have an interest in ensuring (1) that nuclear confrontation and war do not occur in South Asia and (2) that Islamic extremism is kept in check in Pakistan and Afghanistan. Beyond this, their interests diverge. The United States sees India as a key player in balancing a rising China (Tellis 2015). For China, Pakistan plays a similar role in balancing India, saddling Delhi with a two-front military problem. This allows Beijing to focus its attention on East Asia (Small 2015, 52–65). Russia wants to ensure that neither India nor Pakistan falls into the United States' or China's sphere of influence (Oliker 2017). In addition, all three external powers have varying economic interests in the region, particularly the United States and China. The United States has sizable private investments in India and a growing arms sales relationship. China has invested over $60 billion in the China Pakistan Economic Corridor (CPEC), and it is Pakistan's largest arms supplier (Zhou 2018; Sahu 2019). Russia is the largest exporter of arms to India and is eyeing arms sales to Pakistan (Rajagopalan 2018). In the case of the United States, there is an additional interest: Indian immigrants are increasingly a force in US politics, including through the India Caucus in Congress (Betigeri 2019).

These interests mean that the United States, China, and Russia cannot afford to retrench altogether. The United States had a formal alliance relationship with Pakistan in CENTO and SEATO. This operated to provide Pakistan with weapons, military training, and extended deterrence. From 1979 to 1989, Pakistan was an informal ally in the fight against the Soviet occupation of Afghanistan. It was also a partner after the September 11, 2001 terrorist attacks on the United States in the global war on terrorism and continues to be a conduit for US supplies into Afghanistan. In the 2000s, the United States developed a strategic relationship with India to counter China's power, with increasing military sales, high-level defense dialogues, and intelligence sharing. China has been an informal ally of Pakistan since the early 1960s (though it has never come to Pakistan's aid directly in India-Pakistan wars). It has steadfastly supported Islamabad diplomatically in its quarrels with India and with the former Soviet Union. It has armed Pakistan since the 1960s and, as noted above, continues to be its main arms supplier. The Soviet Union / Russia had a twenty-five-year Treaty of Friendship and Cooperation with India signed in 1972 that established a quasi-alliance.[4] Currently, Moscow tilts toward India but maintains good relations with Pakistan out of concern for extremism in the region and as a reminder to India that Russia could change its tilt if Delhi gets too close to Washington. For instance, Russia has shown an interest in resuming arms sales to Pakistan and has cooperated with Islamabad in brokering peace talks with the Taliban (Kapoor 2019).

The levels and type of engagement of the United States, China, and Russia currently vary. Diplomatically, they have a common interest in keeping regional conflict from escalating to the nuclear level and in engaging Pakistan to keep extremism at bay. The two issues, as noted above, are related. Beyond this common interest, the three powers are at cross-purposes, with the United States closer to India, China closer to Pakistan, and Russia tilting to India but flirting intermittently with Pakistan. The result is a delicate balancing game between the three powers that leaves India as the dominant power but not so dominant that it can control its rival, Pakistan (Paul 2006).

The roles of China and the United States are crucial if this delicate balance is to be maintained. Of the big three, China is the least likely to retrench; indeed, its regional presence is likely to expand. This is partly for structural reasons: with great power comes growing involvement everywhere. But it is also partly related to South Asia's particular features. India is a rising power with nuclear weapons adjacent to China's western provinces; India and Pakistan harbor Tibetan activists and radical Islamists, respectively; the border quarrel with India is unresolved; and there are economic opportunities in these very populous countries. Although Beijing may not be in a position to assimilate South Asia to its sphere of influence, since 2008 and the coming to power of Xi Jinping it has made strategic inroads into the region.

New Delhi has conceded it can no longer keep China out of South Asia (Xavier 2018). In part this is due to the United States. India-US cooperation has grown steadily, but since 2016 so have differences—over visas for Indian professionals, the trade imbalance in India's favor, US insistence that New Delhi cut connectivity and energy ties with Iran and arms from Russia, and America's peace talks with the Taliban. Difficulties with Moscow have compounded Delhi's challenges. Russia has mended relations with Pakistan, is testy over India's military ties with the United States, and is increasingly close to China. In short, India cannot count on either the United States or Russia to provide balance against China. Though neither power is hostile to India, they have created a space for increasing Chinese influence in South Asia.

China could therefore become the arbitrating/mediating power, as the United States and the Soviet Union were at their peak during the Cold War. New Delhi's China diplomacy since the Doklam crisis of 2017 shows that it has moved away from a confrontational stance built around obstreperousness on the border quarrel and the forging of an anti-China coalition of the United States, Japan, Vietnam, and Australia (Bajpai 2017). By the time of the "informal summit" at Wuhan in 2018, it was clear that India had decided to mend fences over territorial differences and to downplay the emerging Japan- and US-led Free and Open Indo-Pacific (FOIP) in favor of a diplomacy of engagement led by the Association of Southeast Asian Nations (Modi 2018; Trivedi 2019).

India's post-Doklam détente with China occurred even as Chinese influence in the Indian Ocean region has grown. The two main prongs of influence are Beijing's Belt and Route Initiative (BRI) and its naval expansion. Two parts of the BRI affect India: the CPEC, which transits parts of Kashmir on the Pakistani side (which India claims); and the Maritime Silk Road, which connects China all the way to the Gulf and eastern Africa. The BRI is being rolled out in parallel with the unprecedented expansion of the PLA Navy (PLAN). By 2030, China could have over five hundred vessels. India by contrast will have roughly two hundred vessels (Lague and Kim 2019; Press Trust of India 2018b). In addition, PLAN has an overseas base in Djibouti in the Horn of Africa, has access to Gwadar port in Pakistan and Hamban-tota port in Sri Lanka, and has stated it will seek facilities elsewhere in the neighborhood.

India's shying away from a partnership with the Australian, Japanese, and US navies in FOIP and its related forum, the Quad, rests on Delhi's calculation that China is too powerful to confront openly. This marks a return to a more equidistant, "hide-and-bide" posture that has marked Indian policy since 1962. The difference from classical nonalignment is that India is simultaneously deepening its military and especially naval links with the United States. Although it seems to have edged away from coalition defense in the FOIP/Quad grouping, it has signed on to various bilateral agreements with the United States: the Communications Compatibility and Security Agreement, known as COMCASA; the Logistics Exchange Memorandum of Agreement, known as LEMOA; and the General Security of Military Information Agreement, known as GSOMIA. In negotiation are the Basic Exchange and Cooperation Agreement, or BECA, on geospatial intelligence, and the Industrial Security Annex. These are all key requirements for cooperation with the US military. In addition, India and the United States exercise together in the Bay of Bengal and the Indian Ocean as a way of improving interoperability: indeed, the United States exercises more with India than any other navy (Miglani 2017). The challenge for India is to stealthily deepen military relations with the United States, despite President Trump's periodic outbursts and gaffes on India, and to do so without overly angering China.

This analysis suggests that while the ingress from China is sharpening, a naval balance of power could evolve in the Indian Ocean area. As China pushes in, India and the United States will act in a loose coalition to check its power. China's naval strength will grow, but its long exterior lines will limit its ability to project power. It will seek bases in the region to compensate for the logistical deficiency, but these bases will be vulnerable to the Indian and US navies. In short, as long as no power is overly aggressive, a stable naval equilibrium could be achieved.

Coerced Cooperation?

In the longer term, the great powers may choose to go beyond stabilizing deterrence and managing crises in South Asia. From 1947, during the first Kashmir war, to the late 1950s, the great powers tried to resolve subcontinental conflict—through the United Nations and sometime their own direct diplomacy. The last of these efforts was after the 1962 India-China war, when the United States and United Kingdom prevailed upon India to reopen

Kashmir talks with Pakistan; and after the 1965 war, when the Soviet Union, at Tashkent, attempted to broker a long-lasting peace (Riedel 2015; "Tashkent Declaration" 1966). With the failure of these efforts, the great powers retired from peacemaking efforts.

In a future realist world, the great powers might be tempted to coerce cooperation. Although Pakistan would likely welcome external intervention, India's suspicion of third-party intervention would cause it to dig in its heels. In addition, Delhi insists there can be no serious dialogue with Islamabad until Pakistan takes strong steps against extremist groups operating from its soil. India's Balakot airstrikes on February 26, 2019, were followed by pressures from the United States, United Kingdom, Saudi Arabia, United Arab Emirates, and some European governments to address India's concerns. Pakistan has taken some actions, but these fall short of Indian demands (Saifi and Regan 2019). International actions have included a resolution in the UN Security Council designating Masood Azhar a terrorist.[5] Despite its opposition in the past to actions against Azhar, China joined the five other permanent members of the Security Council (P-5) in voting for the 2019 UN resolution (Nichols and Sayeed 2019; Roche 2019a). It is only this form of great power intervention that India will accept.

LIBERAL INTERNATIONALIST DIPLOMACY AND SOUTH ASIA

If the world chooses the diplomacy of a liberal internationalist order, could South Asia come to be marked by normal diplomatic interactions between India and Pakistan and typified by collective and cooperative security, regional economic openness, and dispute settlement through bilateral, regional, and multilateral means? Rather than coercing India and Pakistan into cooperation, could the great powers promote norms and practices that create the conditions in which Delhi and Islamabad would choose cooperation of their own volition?

Promoting Democracy and Cooperative Security

Although the United States has historically promoted an international order where democracy and the rule of law in domestic politics is the condition for long-term peace and stability in international relations, neither China nor Russia emphasizes this. Even Washington has backed illiberal powers when this has suited its strategic or economic interests. In South Asia, throughout most of the Cold War, the United States was closer to Pakistan than to India. Conversely, authoritarian China in the 1950s and authoritarian Russia / the Soviet Union until 1989 were closer to India.

Delhi has always been wary of promoting democracy internationally, partly on the argument that sovereignty must trump democracy promotion and partly because it did not want to be seen as endorsing a US-led endeavor (Raja Mohan 2007). By contrast, in South Asia, India has argued for the importance of democracy as the basis for sustained peace and stability; yet it has worked with authoritarian neighbors and intervened against democratic governments in its neighborhood when necessary (Cartwright 2009; Raja Mohan 2011). Pakistan has gone in and out of democracy about every decade, and the ability of its civilian governments to control foreign and security policy is limited, given the power and assertiveness of the Pakistani military. Understandably, democracy promotion has never featured in its foreign policy.

To sum up, except for the United States, the external powers have no particular interest in a democracy route to peace and stability. Even the United States is not wedded to the idea beyond a point. Regionally, neither Delhi nor Islamabad backs democracy promotion in international affairs. Nor do they make it a condition of bilateral India-Pakistan interactions. There is a view in Indian strategic circles that a democratic Pakistan is in India's long-term interest because in a democratic setup the military would be susceptible to constraints. Conversely, there is also a recognition that peace and stability can only be delivered by the Pakistani military, which has a veto on relations with India (Parthasarathy 2018).

Leaving aside democracy promotion, the big three have all endorsed a policy of India and Pakistan narrowing their differences through normal diplomatic interaction and state-to-state negotiations. All three external powers would be suspicious of regional collective security arrangements unless these were targeted at their rivals. Conversely, as noted above, they would all back cooperative security where this is understood to mean regional understandings to reduce the threat of war and crisis by means of arms control, confidence-building measures (CBMs), and crisis management protocols.

India and Pakistan have a history of cooperative security. In four wars, casualty rates have been very low. This is partly due to hardware limitations and the short duration of their hostilities but also to an unwillingness to attack population centers and military installations close to civilian facilities (Ganguly 1995). In addition, they have instituted hotline communications between high-level military and civilian authorities, including prime ministers. They have also agreed to notify each other before major military exercises and ballistic missile tests and to ban air force flights within a 5-kilometer band of the front lines. In 1999, they decided to negotiate a broader range of restraint measures; but after the Kargil war, the talks derailed. In the nuclear realm, since 1988 they have had an agreement not to attack each other's nuclear facilities. India has a no-first-use pledge in its nuclear doctrine, whereas Pakistan rejects the idea. Pakistan has argued instead for a strategic restraint regime comprising nuclear limits (on the development and deployment of nuclear weapons as well as missile defense), the negotiation of a conventional military balance, and resolution of political disputes. In turn, India has rejected the notion of bilateral strategic restraint given China's superiority in nuclear weapons (on various India-Pakistan CBMs, see Salik 2010).

Although the three big powers would support South Asian cooperative security going further than the current regional regime, their behaviors can make an impact on the region negatively. On the positive side, the agreements on arms control and CBMs, both conventional and nuclear, that the big three have reached since 1945 have inspired India and Pakistan. After the Comprehensive Test Ban Treaty (CTBT) came into force, India and Pakistan tested nuclear weapons in 1998 but made it known that they would not test again. Both countries had already signed on to the various multilateral test bans before the CTBT, such as the bans on atmospheric and seabed testing. Doctrinal commitments to restraint also have influenced India and Pakistan. For instance, India has committed to negative security assurances (Ministry of External Affairs 2003).[6] Its no-use-against-non-nuclear powers and no-first-use commitments have been inspired by the promises of other nuclear powers. From the second-tier nuclear states—the United Kingdom, France, and China—India and Pakistan seem to have learned that a small, robust nuclear force is compatible with deterrence.

Against this positive record, the great powers' reversals or ambivalence on multilateral arms control suggest to India and Pakistan that they too do not need to sign up or to stick to commitments. The United States' inability to ratify the CTBT and its withdrawal from the ABM Treaty as well as the Intermediate Nuclear Forces (INF) Treaty raise questions about the sanctity of international agreements. On the negative side, too, is the US and Russian investment in a new generation of nuclear weapons, with China likely to follow (Zhao 2019). This could encourage India and Pakistan to reconsider their commitment to relatively small arsenals. So, also, inconsistencies in nonproliferation policies make an impact on South Asia. China's transfer of nuclear technologies to Pakistan certainly hardened India's resolve to go nuclear in 1998 (Paul 2003, 6). The United States' nuclear deal with India and its refusal to reach a similar agreement with Pakistan intensified Islamabad's determination to enlarge and ramify its nuclear forces (Dalton and

Krepon 2015, 7–12). China's conventional military modernization and massive infrastructural investments in Tibet are a major worry for India. New Delhi responded by boosting its forces along its northern border but also by continuing to build its nuclear capabilities, especially its long-range missile capabilities in order to deter China (Sahgal 2018; Kapur and Wueger 2018). This in turn gives Pakistan an incentive to enlarge its arsenal.

In sum, India and Pakistan have shown an ability to limit violence between themselves and to institute CBMs. It is in the interest of the great powers to push India-Pakistan arms limitations as part of global nonproliferation and stability, but this runs into Indian opposition because India eyes its military balance with China. South Asian restraint is also undermined by great power inconsistencies and ambivalence toward arms limitations. Worth noting too is that US interest in Indian arms limitations may have reduced over time with the rise of Chinese military power. The larger problem in the region is the relationship between terrorist strikes in India, Indian conventional retaliation, and the threat of escalation. No amount of arms control and CBMs can altogether stop this dynamic once the two parties embark on it. Fundamental conflict resolution in the region is therefore crucial.

Regional Economic Openness

Could South Asia move toward conflict resolution through the freer movement of goods, capital, and services such that both sides have a stake in resolving their seemingly intractable conflicts? South Asia has long been one of the least integrated regions if one judges by the India-Pakistan case. India and its smaller neighbors, by contrast, have been quite integrated with the Indian economy. In the case of India and Pakistan, trade was relatively open from 1947 to 1965, with some hiccups. After the 1965 war, trade went into a slump as a result of conflict and mistrust, and it has never returned to pre-war levels: in 2018–19, bilateral trade was just over $2 billion (Sharma and Kapoor 2019). To put this in perspective, in 2017, India-China trade was $84.44 billion (Press Trust of India 2018a).

Strategic, political, and economic factors hold trade back. Strategically, the worry is the obverse of the liberal promise: trade will create constituencies for peace who will undermine national security for the sake of private economic gain. This is a strong view in Pakistan. It is not vented in public and polite company, but anyone who has interacted with Pakistani policy elites will testify to its existence. Politically, over time, there has been a view that it is morally incorrect and therefore politically infeasible to trade with India when Indian policies on Kashmir and other matters are inimical to Pakistan.

Once again, this view will rarely if ever find expression in Pakistani writings on trade, but it is articulated primarily by Islamists but also by some liberal opinion. What is publicly articulated is the economic argument in support of protectionism for Pakistan's relatively weak industries. Every attempt to give India most-favored-nation (MFN) status has foundered on these kinds of strategic, political, and economic views.

Not everything is Pakistan's fault. Although India has given Pakistan MFN status (back in 1996), there are sectors in India that resist free trade. As for cross-border investment, this is almost nonexistent. Though Pakistan has always permitted Indian foreign direct investment (FDI), India only permitted outward and inward bound FDI in the case of Pakistan after 2012. Since then, Delhi has allowed Pakistani firms to invest in India but only in the public sector (though not in defense, space, and atomic energy). Yet investment levels are negligible: Indian companies worry about Pakistani political instability; and Pakistani companies fear Indian procedural hurdles (Bimal 2014; Shahzad and Shams 2012).

India-Pakistan trade and investment were further depressed after the Pulwama terrorist strike on Indian security forces in February 2019. Delhi withdrew MFN status and slapped a 200 percent tariff on all Pakistani goods in retaliation. Trade had reached $1.2 billion in 2018–19, which represented a 5 percent increase over the previous year (Press Trust of India 2019a). After India's military retaliation, trade across the Line of Control in Kashmir was resumed in March 2019. In August 2019, after Delhi changed the constitutional status of its part of Kashmir, Islamabad stopped all bilateral trade. Trade will probably resume at some point, but the problem is that the volume is so low that for the foreseeable future the exchange of goods will not foster cooperation. Estimates are that it could reach $30 billion, which would be a significant amount, but it is nowhere near that figure ("India, Pakistan Can Take" 2018).

Negotiated Dispute Settlement

Liberal internationalists argue that states can negotiate their differences through bilateral negotiations, regional mechanisms, and international law and mediation. The general view is that South Asia has a poor record here. But in fact, this is not the case, though with time these possibilities have receded, above all because India has concluded that it did badly in bilateral and international efforts at dispute settlement (Bajpai 2013).

Between 1947 and 1967, India and Pakistan negotiated solutions to every bilateral dispute arising out of partition except Kashmir. They also almost agreed to a UN-organized plebiscite in Kashmir in the 1950s. In 1964, even as

Indian prime minister Jawaharlal Nehru lay dying, Sheikh Abdullah, the veteran Kashmiri leader, was in Pakistan to resurrect bilateral talks (Gupta 1966; Khan 2018). After the 1965 and 1971 wars, the two sides inked agreements on future relations. In the 1972 Simla pact, this included a commitment to pursue bilateral negotiations on Kashmir. In the 1990s (and again in the 2000s), they came close to settlements on river water and territorial differences (Saran 2017, 77–105). In 1992, they began the process of a composite "six plus two" dialogue, the "two" being Kashmir and security (Dasgupta 2015). In 1999, at the Lahore summit, they signed yet another major declaration. It dealt with nuclear security, Kashmir, and terrorism, among other issues. The agreement was undermined by the subsequent Kargil war, the terrorist attack on India's parliament in December 2001, and the Indian military mobilization that followed. Despite these setbacks and the November 2008 terrorist attack on Mumbai, the two countries continued with the composite dialogue and a back-channel dialogue on Kashmir that brought them close to a settlement (Coll 2009). Along the way, they used the arbitration mechanism in the Indus Waters Treaty to settle several water conflicts (Bajpai 2013, 119–22). In sum, India and Pakistan have repeatedly used bilateral and international mechanisms to settle disputes (High Commission of India 2019).

Nevertheless, Delhi has grown increasingly suspicious of international efforts at dispute settlements, even though it originally took the dispute to the United Nations and committed itself unasked to a plebiscite in the state. After the Mumbai terrorist attacks, it has also grown allergic to sustained bilateral discussions with Pakistan. Looking ahead, India remains ambivalent about the role of the international community and the great powers in particular. Although it traditionally rejects a third-party mediating role, Delhi has increasingly urged external powers to use their influence with Pakistan. In the Kargil war, during the 2001–2 mobilization crisis, in the aftermath of the Mumbai attacks, and after Balakot, it has mobilized international opinion against Pakistan. A similar ambivalence marks its approach to bilateral talks. It insists that bilateral talks will be impossible until Islamabad reins in extremist groups (Press Trust of India 2019c). Yet since 2014, India has periodically relented, with Prime Minister Narendra Modi, Foreign Minister Susham Swaraj, and National Security Adviser Ajit Doval meeting counterparts (Bajpai 2017, 73–75; "Secret Meeting" 2018).

With Balakot behind the two countries, Modi's massive general election victory of May 2019, and Imran Khan's election victory in Pakistan in August 2018, India and Pakistan could return to bilateral negotiations. For example, in 2018, India and Pakistan suddenly agreed to a visa-less corridor for Sikh pilgrims visiting Kartarpur in Pakistan. Away from the glare of public scrutiny, they could well return to quiet, more private discussions: the two national security advisers apparently continue to meet and communicate. The back channel between trusted advisers nearly delivered a settlement of Kashmir back in 2007. Talks apparently foundered on worry over domestic opinion, followed by the terrorist attacks in Mumbai in November 2008, and Pakistani president Pervez Musharraf's fall from power (Coll 2009). With Modi's election victory, and his desire to leave a legacy, India might be in a mood to pursue a Kashmir settlement. Under pressure from the great powers and regional friends such as Saudi Arabia, and against the background of its economic difficulties, the Pakistani military might also be instigated to find a long-lasting solution. President Trump's offer to mediate between India and Pakistan in July 2019, though gauche, could in time push India to restart bilateral negotiations, even if Kashmir is not immediately on the table (Roche 2019b). A combination of political change, personal ambition, and great power encouragement could see a return to bilateral talks.

Cooperative Security and Great Power Nudging

In summary, big power diplomacy backing regional efforts at cooperative security—arms control and CBMs—has a track record. Regional economic openness as a means of conflict management and resolution has little future, given the very low level of trade and investment flows and Pakistani political and strategic worries above all. Bilateral negotiation, despite interruptions, has proved to be the most enduring form of conflict management since the 1960s. International mediation has a history of success and near-success and, if conducted privately and with care, could play a part in restarting bilateral talks. Given Indian resistance, it can probably do little more than nudging. Any attempt to shape the substance of an actual settlement would likely be counterproductive.

GREAT POWER CONCERT AND FUNCTIONAL COOPERATION IN SOUTH ASIA

A third possibility globally is great power concert diplomacy, which involves intermittent and issue-based cooperation for global public goods. This functional cooperation could have implications for regional security. India and Pakistan could be drawn into cooperating with powerful outsiders as well as with neighbors, with positive spillovers into bilateral conflicts. Historically, as developing countries, the two have usually been on the same side in climate change negotiations, other multilateral agreements related to development and economic issues, and international deliberations in UN agencies. They have also both been big contributors to UN peacekeeping forces and have worked together for nearly sixty years across continents (Mitra 2018). In theory, a great power concert that delivers global public goods could attract both India and Pakistan.

Collective Inaction

One possibility is that India and Pakistan limit their conflicts in the face of climate change. In order to access global facilities dealing with carbon mitigation and climate adaptation, they could cooperate in a South Asian "Marshall Plan" backed by external powers. Another area of cooperation could be global public health. Global health crises and responses may require India and Pakistan to mitigate their differences in order to cope with, say, a pandemic. In the interest of global health governance, the great powers would cajole and coerce the South Asian powers to set aside their quarrels and collaborate. A third possibility is that the Indian and Pakistani militaries, as key members of UN peacekeeping efforts around the world, could be nudged into developing inter-military ties that dampen conflict along their common borders. Finally, global public goods in the sphere of international security—counterterrorism, particularly—could be aimed at extremists, specifically in Pakistan, and might entail Indian and Pakistani intelligence cooperation.

A key problem with the concert-led, global public goods route to functional cooperation in South Asia is the ability of the United States, China, and Russia to cooperate and to bring regional states together. At best, there are periods of remission and concertation among them. Under President Trump, remission more than concertation has been the norm. Since 2016, the US has pulled out of the 2015 Paris accord on climate change; the Iran nuclear deal; the INF agreement with Russia; the Trans-Pacific Partnership; the North American Free Trade Agreement; the United Nations Educational, Scientific, and Cultural Organization, UNESCO; the United Nations Relief and Works Agency for Palestine Refugees; and the United Nations Human Rights Council. Although the other big powers have not followed the United States' remission from international accords, concertation seems unlikely with Trump in the White House.

The second problem with the functional argument is that even though India and Pakistan have often been on the same side in global negotiations, their parallel interests and actual collaboration have not spilled over into greater diplomatic and strategic convergence. Overall Indian and Pakistani involvement in global public goods arenas—for instance, in dealing with some of the consequences of climate change such as humanitarian disasters, a transnational health epidemic affecting both countries, and UN peacekeeping—is likely to be temporary, with little prospect of reducing conflict over long-standing quarrels. Encapsulation of cooperation is more likely than positive spillovers.

Counterterrorism, Peacekeeping, and South Asian Cooperation?

Against this gloomy prognosis are two possible areas of light. The first is if the great powers join together against Islamic extremism and see South Asia as a key battleground against militancy. The second is to build on the Indian and Pakistani involvement in peacekeeping and try to foster greater inter-military ties.

Could the United States, China, and Russia transcend their global public goods differences and cooperate on counterterrorism? In the aftermath of 9/11, US-Russia cooperation continued until the Obama-Medvedev period but broke down over Russia's intervention in the Ukraine and Syria. Currently, while President Trump has supported counterterrorism cooperation with Russia, US sanctions for Moscow's role in the Ukraine, Syria, and putative interference in the US presidential elections of 2016 have stalled collaboration (Saradzhyan 2017). The US and China also cooperated after 9/11, largely in diplomatic terms. From time to time, they have worked together on China's Uighur concerns. Africa is an area where they might collaborate further given their stakes there. Conversely, China has concerns about the US military presence in Afghanistan and Iraq. Recently, the US has criticized China's domestic counterterrorism in Xinjiang. Competition for global influence has also hampered cooperation (Park 2017).

The United States, China, and Russia all worry about extremism in Pakistan but are reluctant to push beyond a point, fearing that they might destabilize the country further with blowback to their own interests. In an extreme state of internal turbulence, the safety and control of Pakistani nuclear weapons would be a worry. For the United States, extricating itself from Afghanistan would become more complicated if Pakistan were wracked by internal troubles. China and Russia could see greater regional instability in Central Asia and Xinjiang if Pakistan went on the boil. Yet, after Indian actions in Balakot in February 2019, the three big powers did urge Islamabad to act against militant groups. China, reversing its earlier stand, eventually joined the other P-5 members in passing a resolution against Masood Azhar, the extremist based in Pakistan. Whether this action and Pakistani crackdowns against extremists significantly reduces militant activities remains to be seen, but the record, going back to 2001, is not encouraging. Pakistan may not be the only target of great power demarches. The big three might conclude that India's Kashmir troubles and differences with Pakistan have fueled extremism. If so, the fight against Islamists in Pakistan is linked to Indian actions on Kashmir and other bilateral disputes. This raises the possibility that global counterterrorism necessitates South Asian conflict resolution. Once again, as in the discussions above on the realist and liberal diplomatic paradigms, the issue of fundamental conflict resolution surfaces.

The other area in which a great power concert could bring South Asians together is peacekeeping. Cooperation between the two militaries in peacekeeping operations could have brought the two militaries together institutionally and bolstered confidence building, perhaps even conflict resolution, given the Pakistani military's central role in national security. Unfortunately, there is no evidence that, despite a degree of camaraderie during peacekeeping, operational bonhomie has translated into congenial military-to-military relations.[7] Indeed, even as their troops work together in third places, the two militaries periodically accuse each other of atrocities along their common border (Jacob 2019).

Would China's growing peacekeeping involvement bring change to Indian and Pakistani peacekeeping? Among the P-5, China already contributes the largest number of peacekeepers and is second only to the United States in terms of financial contributions ("Is China Contributing" 2016). Chinese deployments might reduce the need for South Asian troops, which could annoy both India and Pakistan, thus actually bringing them together—but it would take some fairly inept diplomacy to unite India and Pakistan against China. PLA units rubbing up against Indian troops in actual operational environments could lead to frictions. However, judging by the positive India-Pakistan experience in peacekeeping, it is likely that Indian and Chinese military encounters will be cordial. China might use its growing weight to favor Pakistani over Indian UN deployments, leading to further India-China and India-Pakistan tensions; but again, it is hard to conceive of why Beijing would seek to alienate India. At a time when peacekeepers are in high demand, it would be an act of pettiness that would be counterproductive when China is projecting internationalist leadership. Conversely, there is no reason to think that Beijing will use its peacekeeping leadership to encourage greater South Asian military-to-military cooperation. Overall, Chinese leadership of peacekeeping diplomacy is unlikely to affect India-Pakistan participation.

COVID-19 and the Limits of Concert and Functional Cooperation

COVID-19 illustrates the limitations of the concert and functional route to cooperation in South Asia. The quarrel between the United States and China over the origins and handling of the pandemic underlines how deep the remission in cooperation at the global level has become. Even if the pandemic had led to US-China cooperation, India and Pakistan might be at odds. Indeed, they quickly were. When India invited the South Asian heads of government to a virtual summit, Pakistan responded by deputing its health minister. At the meeting it was agreed that all states would contribute to a regional emergency fund. Pakistan insisted that its contribution would only go to the South Asian Association for Regional Cooperation (SAARC) and not the India-led initiative (Bhattacharya 2020). Worse, since the COVID outbreak, India and Pakistan have accused each other of intensifying cease-fire violations at the LOC (Basu 2020). When terrorists struck in Indian Kashmir, Delhi insisted Islamabad was behind the attacks. Pakistan claimed the attacks were Indian "false flag operations" (Gupta 2020). COVID-19 has also led to India-China frictions. Delhi accused China of making it difficult to evacuate its citizens from Wuhan. Since then, it has criticized the quality and price of masks and other equipment it bought from China. China has rejected these criticisms. Delhi subsequently joined other countries in insisting on an independent inquiry into the origins and handling of the pandemic. It also subjected all FDI from "neighboring countries" to government approval to prevent Chinese takeovers of Indian companies in financial distress during the COVID-19 crisis—to which Beijing has objected. Meanwhile, in a parallel to the India-Pakistan case, a spate of border incidents occurred in different sectors along the India-China LAC (Madan 2020; Smith 2020).

In sum, global concertation between the big powers is increasingly under stress. COVID-19 seems to have accentuated differences. India and Pakistan do not have a history of positive spillovers from their participation and cooperation in global public goods initiatives. The early indications are that COVID-19 has not brought them together and that it has been assimilated to existing fault lines. The global concert and functional route to peace and stability in South Asia seems unlikely.

CONCLUSION: SOUTH ASIA AND WORLD ORDER

The India-Pakistan relationship remains a dangerous one. The crisis of February 2019 suggests that terrorist attacks against Indian targets could well lead Delhi to retaliate with conventional strikes against extremists in Pakistan, which in turn will lead to Islamabad ordering some form of counter-retaliation. This could escalate to a full-blown war in the shadow of nuclear weapons. Of the three global diplomatic modes, both the liberal and the functional great-power concert hold out little for peace and stability in South Asia. Liberalism's advocacy of democracy promotion and regional economic openness is of limited utility; its espousal of cooperative security is more apposite. Encouragement of bilateral or international-led negotiations has had more success historically but no longer seems capable of delivering peace and stability in the face of extremism and terrorism as well as Indian suspicion. Nor will global public goods diplomacy draw India and Pakistan into networks of cooperation that spill over positively into bilateral relations. The COVID-19 crisis is only the most recent instance of lack of global concertation and the inability of India and Pakistan to collaborate even in the face of a common, non-traditional security threat.

With extremists continuing to operate in Pakistan, with Kashmir continuing to serve as a rallying cry for Islamist extremists, and with nuclear weapons on both sides, South Asia is strategically brittle. The growing diplomatic, strategic, and economic presence of China in South Asia and in the Indian Ocean region is causing India worry. Delhi is trying to manage this new regional challenge by a nonprovocative stance toward China and a stealthily growing military relationship with the United States. Differences between India and the US on one side and China on the other could spill back into India-Pakistan relations. Beijing could choose to deepen strategic relations with Islamabad to counter a Delhi-Washington entente, thereby exacerbating differences between the subcontinental neighbors.

As against this, South Asia would be better served if the great powers avoid taking sides overly, manage crises that will periodically erupt, and encourage CBMs and normal diplomatic interactions with the hope that escalation attendant on a terrorist attack will be controlled. South Asia is not a case for spheres-of-influence dictation; nor is great power retrenchment and leaving the region to its own devices likely or desirable. Trying to stabilize deterrence and strengthen crisis management is vital. Beyond this, China above all, given its strong links to Pakistan and the Pakistani military in particular, is best placed to exert pressure against extremism—which is also in its interest given the troubles of Xinjiang. Actions by the United States and its allies to curb or stop the flow of funds to extremist organizations in Pakistan is also vital.

What are the implications of a realist South Asia for the great powers and world order? All this suggests a future that is more realist than either liberal or intermittently functional. A South Asia where the great powers continue to back their own preferred regional partners, sometimes cooperating and other times going it alone to ensure military stability, would be positive for global order. In the Indian Ocean, a balance of power between India, China, and the United States would also be positive for global order. Southern Asia seems likely to be a theater of contention between regional states and great powers, but balances of power, deterrence, and restraint and conflict management could maintain at least a cold peace. This more likely realist future for South(ern) Asia could well coexist with different types of diplomatic possibilities in other regions and in different issue areas. International order is unlikely to be a flat, homogeneous space but rather an undulating one, varying by the mix of realism, liberalism, and functionalism across space, time, and issue area.

NOTES

1. For more on this, see www.cigionline.org/.
2. See, e.g., Bull (1977) for the coexistence of Hobbesian, Grotian, and Kantian elements of international society.
3. In 2018, China's gross domestic product in nominal terms was $13.6 trillion, while India's was $2.72 trillion (World Bank 2019). China has 290 nuclear weapons and India has 140 (Arms Control Association 2019).
4. The treaty expired in 1997 and was not renewed.
5. Azhar is head of the group that carried out the terror strike in Kashmir that led to the Indian air strike.
6. Pakistan has not published a nuclear doctrine; but see Tasleem (2016) on its doctrine-in-practice.
7. Pakistani Army chief Qamar Bajwa, who had served with the UN peacekeeping mission in the Congo under an Indian general, reportedly reached out to Indian Army chief Bipin Rawat in 2018; but this was later denied by India. See Abi-Habib (2018); and for the denial, see Baweja (2019).

CHAPTER 11

Can ASEAN's Institutions Do Preventive Diplomacy?

See Seng Tan

The contemporary Asia-Pacific is a region not easily reduced or reducible to any of the three scenarios of discord, collaboration, and pragmatic cooperation that serve as the conceptual categories in this volume. No region truly is, but the Asia-Pacific (encompassing East Asia and Australia) is especially so, due to its vastness, diversity, and granular complexity. Their analytical language and terms of reference may differ, but the combined received wisdom on Asia-Pacific in international politics strongly suggests that elements of discord, collaboration, and pragmatic cooperation coexist within the region, mostly in a stable but at times uneasy fashion, as on/off regional flashpoints such as the Korean Peninsula, the Taiwan Strait, and the South China Sea would suggest (Taylor 2018). The aim of this chapter is to inquire about the ability of two Asia-Pacific-wide arrangements—the Association of Southeast Asian Nations' ASEAN Regional Forum (ARF) and the ASEAN Defense Ministers Meeting–Plus (ADMM-Plus)—to conduct preventive diplomacy (PD), which refers to conduct undertaken by actors aimed at preventing the rise, escalation, and/or spreading of conflicts or humanitarian catastrophes. Home to a number of flashpoints, domestic crises, and natural disasters, the Asia-Pacific is a prime candidate for PD, as identified in a 1995 concept paper issued on behalf of the ARF, the region's first multilateral security forum formed in 1994, whose present membership comprises twenty-six countries and the European Union. However, thus far the ARF has shown itself incapable of mounting and implementing PD measures, despite having formally adopted a PD work plan back in 2011 (Emmers and Tan 2011; Yuzawa 2006). Yet, as a number of studies have indicated, the ARF's inefficacies should not be taken to mean that

Asian-Pacific countries are thereby loath to the idea and practice of PD, which has in fact flourished in a number of instances within the region (Huan and Emmers 2016; Banim and Pejsova 2017). This is arguably true as well where the potential for PD through the ADMM-Plus, an eighteen-country arrangement formed in 2010, is concerned, even if its trustees have never publicly identified PD as an objective for their institution.

This chapter takes a comparative look at the prospects of the ARF and the ADMM-Plus respectively as PD actors.[1] It concludes that the ADMM-Plus is far likelier to succeed in implementing and conducting PD—a goal to which the ARF has aspired but failed so far to achieve—given the ADMM-Plus's investments in its capabilities as a security actor.[2] Whether ADMM-Plus members possess the requisite collective will to fulfill the arrangement's potential, as conceived here, remains uncertain because a number of roadblocks could derail this outcome from being realized. Conversely, the possibility that the ARF can still participate in PD cannot be ruled out. Arguably, the efforts of both these institutions—indeed, for any form of security multilateralism built around ASEAN—is best understood as pragmatic cooperation, albeit not quite in the terms laid out in this volume, not least when great power rivalry and tension have threatened on occasion to destabilize the region toward regional discord (Allison 2017; Friedberg 2012). And though great power collaboration is a part of the equation, it has mostly been limited to the pursuit of a kind of "grand bargain" that, among other things, involves recognition of the so-called centrality of ASEAN in Asian-Pacific multilateralism (Goh 2011; Tan 2017a). Hence, given the minimalist brand of institutionalized collaboration that has hitherto characterized Asian-Pacific multilateralism, the approach of ASEAN and that of its wider regional offshoots to PD is best conceived of as a quest for practical and functionally oriented cooperation sans the lofty aims and ambitious designs associated with liberal-institutionalist conceptions of multilateralism. Yet this also means that in contrast to its rhetoric, the aims of multilateral security cooperation in the Asia-Pacific—as evidenced by the outcomes—are not especially ambitious. ASEAN-led multilateralism has long been characterized by a perdurable gap between declared aspirations, on one hand, and actual achievements, on the other hand, leading one analyst to label it a "frustrated" enterprise (Nair 2009). This modest state of affairs would not surprise longtime watchers of the region; Michael Leifer, the late doyen of Asian-Pacific security studies, often warned against undue optimism over what ASEAN-led multilateralism can actually achieve, especially when a liberal idea is left in realist hands (Leifer 1999). The following analysis is therefore rendered against these important caveats.

IS PD RELEVANT TO THE ASIA-PACIFIC?

Before examining the two regional institutions in question, a look at the relevance of PD to the Asia-Pacific more broadly is in order. There is no question that the contemporary Asia-Pacific region suffers from security dilemmas stemming from disputes over territory and rising trends in military spending (Emmers 2009a; "Chapter Ten" 2018). Conversely, the region's susceptibility to a host of nonmilitary risks and threats—financial shocks, pandemics, climate upheavals, natural disasters, piracy, terrorism, and the like—have also drawn considerable policy and scholarly attention to the many nontraditional challenges that equally define the region's well-being (Caballero-Anthony and Cook 2013; Pardo and Reeves 2015). The relevance of PD to preventing, managing, and/or resolving military conflicts worldwide is clear enough, even if its success has at best been mixed (George 2000; Lund 1995). But as the following discussion suggests, where the ASEAN-led security arrangements of interest here are concerned, the incessant preoccupation of their member states over sovereignty and noninterference considerations has rendered extremely difficult the building of an institutional consensus on the application of PD to hard security problems confronting the Asia-Pacific region. Rather, the outcome has been a limiting of PD to nonconventional or nonmilitary challenges, even if parts of the region have shown a greater openness to PD more generally.

According to the literature, PD is diplomatic, political, military, economic, and humanitarian action undertaken by governments, international organizations, and/or nongovernmental actors with the aim to prevent the rise of disputes and conflicts between and within states; the escalation of such disputes and conflicts into armed confrontation; the spilling over or spreading of violence from such disputes and conflicts to other countries or areas; and the rise of acute humanitarian crises and, failing that, their management (Acharya 1994). As the former secretary-general of the United Nations, Boutros Boutros-Ghali (1992, 5), put it in *An Agenda for Peace*, PD is "action to prevent disputes from arising between parties, to prevent existing disputes from escalating into conflicts and to limit the spread of the latter when they occur. It typically involves proactive rather than reactive responses to international crises and/or precrisis situations" (Cahill 1996; Lund 1996). During peacetime or a precrisis time, PD involves measures like confidence building, institution building, early warning, and preventive humanitarian action. Along these lines, Dag Hammarskjöld, another former UN secretary-general, envisaged a number of instruments—such as hotlines, risk-reduction centers, and transparency measures—for the purpose of mitigating mutual misperception and suspicion between states. In times of crisis, PD typically takes the form of fact-finding, good offices and goodwill missions, crisis management (including reconciliation, mediation, and arbitration), and other tension-defusing measures, as well as preventive deployment—that is, the dispatch of units to trouble spots to prevent the widening/escalation of a conflict with or without the mutual consent of the rivals—which differentiates it from peacekeeping.[3]

As noted above, the inability of the ARF hitherto to implement PD, despite having adopted a PD work plan in 2011, should not be taken to mean that the Asia-Pacific countries are thereby against the idea and practice of PD. This much is clear where the relative success of the European Union in applying PD practices to a number of conflict situations in Southeast Asia are concerned (Huan and Emmers 2016; Banim and Pejsova 2017). For example, the EU deployed its Aceh Monitoring Mission to Aceh, Indonesia, in 2005 to assist in the demobilization of Gerakan Aceh Merdeka fighters and the decommissioning of their arms (Shulze 2007). The EU also contributed to the peace process in Mindanao between the Philippine government and the Moro Islamic Liberation Front through its provision of aid programs, the application of its instrument contributing to stability and peace (the EU's mechanism in support of security initiatives and peacebuilding activities in partner countries) and its broader efforts in monitoring, mediation, and confidence building (Houvenaeghel 2015). Finally, the EU has also played a major role in the peace process in Myanmar through its deployment of PD measures in support of the long transition from military rule to the rule of law and accountable government (Banim 2014). Some have also detailed ASEAN-based efforts at PD within Southeast Asia while highlighting their ad hoc nature and dependence on the activism of a single ASEAN member country (Della-Giacoma 2011). For their part, some ASEAN states have demonstrated an individual propensity for PD in their foreign policies. Indonesia has shown time and again a readiness to engage in PD, including, for example, its former foreign minister Marty Natalegawa's diplomatic effort to salvage ASEAN's standing in the wake of the failure of the group's member states to reach a consensus in 2012 over the South China Sea disputes (Emmerson 2012). It has also been argued that Malaysia played a crucial mediating role, through its leadership of the International Monitoring Team of peacekeepers, in supporting the October 2012 Framework Agreement on the Bangsamoro between the Philippines and the Moro Islamic Liberation Front (Franco 2013). These illustrations reflect the relevance of PD to the Asia-Pacific region insofar as state and international actors possess the requisite capacity and resolve to conduct PD in ways appropriate to the particular contexts and challenges in question.

However, the question of PD's relevance to the Asia-Pacific region is complicated by the "stickiness" of the noninterference/nonintervention norm in regional diplomacy and security (Jones 2010). A key component of the so-called ASEAN Way—the diplomatic convention that governs interactions between and among member countries in ASEAN and its spin-off arrangements such as the ARF and the ADMM-Plus (Acharya 1997; Leifer 1996)—noninterference has often been invoked by Southeast Asian and other countries to block attempts by external parties—or, for that matter, regional neighbors—to introduce into their midst new diplomatic norms and/or security practices deemed inimical to their national interests and/or threatening to their sovereignty. As the ARF's failure to implement PD (recounted below) has shown, conservative ARF members readily wielded the noninterference norm to temper the enthusiasm of their counterparts that wanted their forum to push ahead with more ambitious types of security cooperation. To the extent that the Asia-Pacific region has succeeded in hosting PD, it has done so less through contravening noninterference—although that has happened, on occasion—than by accommodating the norm, namely, by responding to the requests by (or invitations from) affected countries in need of outside assistance (Tan 2019, 6).[4]

THE ARF: DOWN BUT NOT OUT AS A PD ACTOR?

The story of the ARF's stalled attempts to implement PD is well known. Established in 1994 as the Asia-Pacific region's first region-wide multilateral security arrangement, the ARF comprises a membership that has since grown to twenty-six countries and the EU.[5] With ASEAN at the heart of an institution that includes the world's leading great powers, it is not surprising that the ARF has not progressed as a security actor, not only because of ASEAN's relative weakness as an organization but also because of divergences and polarities among its members that significantly constrain interstate cooperation. The ARF set for itself an ambitious three-stage road map that envisaged its participation in security cooperation in three progressive stages—namely, confidence building, then PD, and finally conflict resolution. Its failure to realize this goal—for all intents and purposes, the ARF remains stuck in a loose confidence-building mode and has not ventured into PD, other than adopting a conservative PD work plan in 2011—has become a cautionary tale of unfulfilled expectations. The innovations in PD proposed by its advocates—such as Australia, Canada, and the EU—clearly rubbed against enduring concerns among more conservative ARF members—such as China and a number of Southeast Asian countries—over potential interventionism legitimated and justified by a PD regime (Yuzawa 2006).

It has further been suggested that the institutional design and decision-making protocols of the ARF, combined with power-balancing gamesmanship among its members, effectively consign the forum's efforts to lowest-common-denominator outcomes at best and outright failure at worst (Emmers and Tan 2011). Moreover, even from the early days of the forum's existence, it was apparent that ASEAN, as the hub of the ARF, was not above engaging in the politics of privilege against the non-ASEAN counterparts, some of which complained publicly about their perceived treatment as "second-class citizens" in the forum (Leifer 1996). The ARF is not without its champions. Nonetheless, the purported irrelevance of the ARF to regional security is so keenly felt around the region that a number of its middle-power members—Australia, Japan, and South Korea—proposed alternatives in the late 2000s to complement the ARF, if not replace it altogether. Fortuitously for the ARF, when the membership of the East Asia Summit grew to include Russia and the United States in 2011, then–Australian leader Kevin Rudd and his supporters quickly rationalized that that enlarged summit was what they had been advocating all along (Tan 2015, 51).

ADMM-PLUS: GOING WHERE THE ARF HAS FEARED TO TREAD?

Comprising eighteen members, the ADMM-Plus is fast gaining the reputation of having gone where the ARF has feared or failed to tread.[6] Like the ARF, the ADMM-Plus is designed both as a mechanism for multilateral security dialogue and consultation as well as a framework for nontraditional security cooperation. To date, seven concerns—namely, maritime security, humanitarian assistance and disaster relief (HADR), counterterrorism, peacekeeping operations, military medicine, humanitarian mine action (or demining), and cyber security, each with a designated experts' working group (EWG)—have been mandated by the ADMM-Plus as areas for practical collaboration by its member countries. The progress made underscores an unexpected occurrence few imagined possible in the Asia-Pacific context: in contrast to the ARF, what has been interesting about the ADMM-Plus is its development of a capacity to engage in PD, even though the group has never formally declared its intentions to be a PD actor. Since its inauguration in 2010, joint activities undertaken by all eighteen members have grown in frequency and complexity. Since 2011, the ADMM-Plus has convened an impressive array of EWG planning sessions, table-top exercises, and "full troop" exercises. The scale and scope of some of these activities are by no means trivial; for example, in a combined maritime security and counter-terrorism exercise held in Brunei Darussalam and Singapore (as well as in the waters between them) in 2016, a total of 3,500 personnel, eighteen naval vessels, twenty-five aircraft, and forty special forces teams participated. The following discussion examines a series of ADMM-Plus accomplishments— and, importantly, the challenges and constraints that stand in the way of further and deeper cooperation—in maritime security, HADR, and counter-terrorism cooperation that conceivably serve as the building blocks for PD.

ADMM-Plus's efforts in maritime security collaboration, as the 2016 combined exercise mentioned above suggests, have not been insignificant. In 2018, ADMM-Plus members reaffirmed their commitment to enhancing operational safety, which includes subscribing to the Code for Unplanned Encounters at Sea (CUES) and accepting the 1972 Convention on the International Regulations for Preventing Collisions at Sea.[7] Hitherto the application of CUES by the ADMM-Plus has assumed the form of a CUES-based maritime exercise involving the navies of the ten ASEAN states and China offshore from the Chinese city of Zhanjiang, while a corresponding exercise with the US Navy took place in 2019. A litmus test for ADMM-Plus is whether there is a consensus to conduct a CUES exercise in the South China Sea, a major confluence where commercial and military shipping dissect and converge. Indeed, the militarization of the South China Sea by the navies and coastguards of countries involved therein could lead to unwanted incidents (Panda 2018). The key challenge, therefore, is how the collective commitment of all relevant parties to CUES can not only be proactive but also sustained (Tan 2017b).

The adoption of CUES by ADMM-Plus has been highlighted as an act in confidence building ("Joint Statement" 2018). Arguably, it represents a formal confidence-building measure (CBM)—and thereby a peacetime or precrisis PD measure—that goes some ways beyond the largely informal confidence-building activities for which the ARF has been known (Emmers and Tan 2011; Yuzawa 2006). The ADMM-Plus's adoption of CUES builds upon similar agreements, such as that between ASEAN and China, which reportedly is supported by an emergency hotline (ASEAN 2017). Indeed, in the light of the difficult, even torturous, effort by ASEAN and China to establish the long-awaited Code of Conduct (COC) for the South China Sea— both sides have agreed to a "single draft" code that will serve as the basis for the COC if and when it eventuates—the region's CUES arrangements have taken on added significance. In their survey of efforts to apply PD in Southeast Asia, Huan and Emmers (2016) observe that the success or failure of PD implementation in the region depends as much on the level of great power interest in particular disputes as the nature of the agreement being sought. Great power interference tends to complicate the strategic calculations of concerned Southeast Asian countries and is therefore likely to make it harder for PD attempts to succeed. Notwithstanding China's apparent cooperativeness in the COC negotiations, it is likely not in Beijing's interest to have a strong and binding COC (Valencia 2017). This insight recalls Dag Hammarskjöld's understanding of PD as a way to keep local conflicts from becoming entangled in superpower rivalry (Boutros-Ghali 1993). In the South China Sea, the pervasive presence of an assertive great power, China, in the mix is a major challenge. So, too, is a rebalancing America (at least during the Obama years), which alternatively reassured US allies and partners but also raised tensions with China—a situation arguably worsened during the Trump presidency (Choong 2017).

Second, the ADMM-Plus has also enjoyed some progress in HADR cooperation. A turning point in ASEAN-based HADR cooperation was the postcrisis relief effort in the wake of the devastation wrought by Cyclone Nargis on Myanmar in 2008, which underscored ASEAN's ability to persuade and assist Myanmar's military regime to work with the international community to rebuild their country (Tan 2013, 256). According to the late Surin Pitsuwan, who served as ASEAN secretary-general during the Nargis crisis, it was ASEAN's successful mediation—ASEAN's application of PD, in short—that arguably paved the way for Myanmar's subsequent quasi-liberalization (Mitton 2012). In 2015, the ASEAN member states adopted a concept paper on the ASEAN Militaries Ready Group (AMRG) on HADR and endorsed standard operating procedures for the utilization of military assets for HADR under the framework of the ASEAN Agreement on Disaster Management and Emergency Response. Designed as an ASEAN-level military team—coordinated by the ASEAN Coordinating Centre for Humanitarian Assistance on Disaster Management—for quick deployment to areas of crisis, the AMRG has been described, in PD terms, as equally "a preventative mechanism before a crisis occurs" (AHA Centre 2017, 69). The new standard operating procedures are meant to augment the existing Standard Operating Procedures for Regional Standby Arrangements and Coordination of Joint Disaster Relief and Emergency Response Operations, a template defining the roles and terms of reference for both provider countries and recipient countries that would enhance interoperability among

ADMM-Plus defense establishments in collective disaster management. In 2016, the terms of reference for the AMRG were adopted.

In the ASEAN countries themselves, supporting infrastructures and assets include the Regional HADR Coordination Centre based in Singapore and the UN Humanitarian Response Depot based in Kuala Lumpur. As envisaged in the ASEAN Political-Security Community blueprint adopted by ASEAN leaders in 2009, these arrangements can and indeed should be understood properly as PD instruments. Unlike the ARF, which hitherto has produced a work plan on PD but little else, the ADMM-Plus would appear better primed to realize a role in PD. Granted, the fact that the ASEAN Community, originally intended to be completed by 2015, has now been postponed until 2025—with a revised ASEAN Political-Security Community blueprint to boot (ASEAN 2016)—should give one pause against undue speculation about the future prospects of the ADMM-Plus. Its potential to be a bona fide PD actor is there, but so too are manifold constraints. There are reputational costs at stake, as the cautionary tale of the ARF suggests. Regrettably, the lack of action on ASEAN's part in addressing the ongoing Rohingya refugee crisis is not just another black mark for ASEAN-based HADR cooperation (Lego 2017), but also a painful reminder that even institutional actors with experience and success in PD—such as the EU—do not always live up to expectations (Greene and Kelemen 2016).

Finally, in terms of counterterrorism collaboration within the ADMM-Plus, the common threat of ISIS-inspired terrorism—as evidenced by the attacks in Jakarta in January 2016 and the conflict in Marawi (in the Philippines' southern province of Mindanao) from March to October 2017—has intensified and deepened cooperation among the defense establishments of the ASEAN countries (Tan 2018). ASEAN defense leaders have also launched the Our Eyes Initiative (OEI), a cooperative arrangement aimed at countering terrorism. Modeled after the Five Eyes postwar arrangement comprising Australia, Canada, New Zealand, the United Kingdom, and the United States, the OEI involves the sharing of strategic—and, subsequently, operational and tactical—intelligence on terrorism among all ASEAN member countries (Parameswaran 2018). Spurred in part by a shared desire among the ASEAN countries to prevent "another Marawi" from occurring and preclude the region from "becoming like the Middle East" (Allard 2018), the OEI envisages the establishment of centers in each ASEAN member country whose purpose would be to facilitate intraregional communication, intelligence sharing, and counterterrorism cooperation among and across national defense and homeland security establishments—a regional mechanism for surveillance and early warning. Importantly, the OEI closely

follows ASEAN's emphasis on open security regionalism through cooperation with selected ASEAN dialogue partner countries, as exemplified by the
ARF and the ADMM-Plus (Acharya 1997). Reportedly, four "Plus" members of the ADMM-Plus—Australia, Japan, New Zealand, and the United
States—have been identified as the first group of partners with which the
ASEAN states would collaborate as part of the OEI. However, for the OEI
to work effectively, participating countries would first need to manage and
overcome the deep-seated mistrust that persists among them (Chang and
Chong 2016; Loh 2016).[8]

A second and related innovation lies in the development of a cooperative
framework—labeled "3R" for resilience, response, and recovery—to tie the
region's counterterrorism initiatives together ("Joint Statement" 2018; Tan
2018). Reportedly, the 3R framework not only provides a coherent and comprehensive regional approach against terrorism; it also supposedly enhances
ASEAN's centrality, as well as coordination and partnership among the various counterterrorism initiatives of the ADMM-Plus countries. Crucially,
the framework acknowledges the historical differences and varying force
capabilities among the ASEAN states and seeks as such to enhance counterterrorism cooperation among their respective militaries by leveraging their
niche capabilities to better complement the efforts of home front or internal security agencies, which hitherto have led counterterrorism efforts in
most ASEAN countries (Emmers 2009b; Tan and Nasu 2016). The 3R also
calls for regional states to shore up their capabilities to respond to chemical,
biological, radiological, and nuclear threats stemming from terrorist groups
and rogue actors (Santoro 2012). Furthermore, ASEAN has announced the
establishment of the ASEAN Armies Information Sharing Workshop as a
way to enhance cooperation among the region's armed forces in response to
chemical, biological, radiological, and nuclear threats. All said, not unlike the
OEI, the 3R remains a work in progress.

CONCLUSION: PD BY DEFAULT,
IF NOT BY DESIGN?

The ADMM-Plus's achievements underscore an unexpected occurrence few
imagined was possible in the context of ASEAN-led security regionalism,
owing to the drawbacks of the ARF. In contrast to the ARF, the ADMM-
Plus is intentionally developing a capacity to engage in PD, even if the group
has never formally declared its intentions to be a PD actor. Why has the
ADMM-Plus progressed where the ARF presumably failed? Significantly,

both arrangements share the same institutional design, make decisions on the basis of a consensus, and are ASEAN-centered. However, where the ARF has shown itself unwieldy in terms of the size of its membership and the scale of its putative ambitions, the ADMM-Plus arguably consists of a more manageable number of relatively likeminded states with sufficiently common interests and aversions that have eschewed grandiose aspirations in favor of functional, practical, and actionable cooperative activities (Tan 2012). But as we have seen, the ADMM-Plus is not immune to rivalries among its member countries, a number of which have engaged in institutional balancing and will likely continue doing so. Arguably, in order to enjoy sustained success as a security mechanism, the ADMM-Plus would likely require a preexisting stable balance of power among its stakeholders because its present structure—not unlike that of the ARF, with ASEAN playing a central diplomatic role—is incapable of creating such a balance for the reason that ASEAN centrality potentially "confuses power and responsibility and generates frustration" among the non-ASEAN participants in ASEAN-led multilateralism (Rüland 2012). Without the mutual support of the big and regional powers, an ADMM-Plus with ASEAN at the helm can only go so far as a security mechanism. As noted in this chapter's introductory remarks, we saddle unwarranted expectations on Asia-Pacific multilateralism at our peril because ASEAN-led institutions—and the ADMM-Plus is no exception—are assuredly not "peace processes" and therefore should not be treated as such (Leifer 1999). Their aims are relatively modest, and their achievements—where success is best defined and measured in terms of mundane functional accomplishments, such as those described in the foregoing analysis—are even less so (Baldino and Carr 2016). That said, absent ASEAN, it is questionable that any Asia-Pacific arrangement comanaged by the great powers would automatically fare better than an ASEAN-led one, especially in this present era of great power rivalry and discord.

Yet it is also from these trying experiences that regional countries are learning to circumvent difficulties caused by excessive balancing among themselves. For instance, institutional balancing among ARF member states has led to gridlock in the ARF, such that the requisite consensus for the ARF to progress toward PD could not be achieved. As noted above, the ARF suffered setbacks in 2010 and 2014 as a consequence of diplomatic sparring between its Chinese and US participants over the South China Sea. Conversely, the fact that the ADMM-Plus has been able to progress to the extent it has could perhaps be attributed in part to the determination of ADMM-Plus members that are also ARF members to eschew transferring their problems and negative experiences from the ARF to the ADMM-Plus (Tan

2020). As Shoji (2013) has argued, the very types of activities undertaken by the ADMM-Plus imply ASEAN's willingness to differentiate the ADMM-Plus from the ARF, because of the latter's perceived ineffectiveness in promoting conflict prevention. What the ADMM-Plus has shown is its ability, when needed, to bypass—or, at the very least, shelve—security dilemmas that have incessantly prohibited cooperation in the ARF. The fact that the ADMM-Plus has been successfully implementing its goals has presumably encouraged its member states to take seriously their commitment to and investment in this arrangement. Put differently, such dedication perhaps reflects a shared aspiration to rethink sovereignty not just as a right but also as a responsibility (Tan 2017b). Yet therein also lies perhaps the paradox of contemporary Asia-Pacific multilateralism: to the extent that regional countries are gradually getting regional security right through the ADMM-Plus, they could end up doing so at the expense of the ARF. But as noted in the discussion on the ARF, such a risk could be mitigated through a determined quest for greater complementarity and better coordination between these two arrangements—a task that ASEAN, which serves as the secretariat for both, has hitherto not done particularly well.

This chapter has sought to compare the efforts made by the region's two multilateral security institutions, the ARF and ADMM-Plus, to establish and implement PD measures. Although the ADMM-Plus is well ahead of the ARF on this count, this does not mean that the ARF cannot play a role, despite the manifold limitations it faces. Rejuvenation of the ARF does not necessarily entail a major overhaul of its institutional design to make it more like the EU. Management gurus tell us there is a difference between efficiency and effectiveness (Drucker 1963). Efficiency refers to doing things the right way, whereas effectiveness refers to doing the right thing. There is no better time for the ARF, through the focused determination and collective will of its ASEAN and non-ASEAN stakeholders, to do the right thing together by fostering a more effective ARF. Granted, neither the ARF nor ADMM-Plus was built as a PD mechanism, even though the ADMM-Plus seems more suited in this respect in the light of its enhancements. But with the pressing security demands of the Asia-Pacific region, both institutions could end up as PD actors by default more than design.

NOTES

1. My interest here is less the specific types of PD measures that are deployed or deployable by the ARF and ADMM-Plus than the broader concern of whether PD in whichever form is achievable in those institutions.

2. Given the focus in this chapter is on the *potential* of regional institutions as a PD actor, the discussion that follows thereby assesses their ability to implement and conduct PD rather than whether or not their PD efforts have actually proved effective.

3. According to the United Nations, PD is distinct from actions such as peacemaking (i.e., action to bring hostile parties to agreement), peacekeeping (i.e., deployment of "neutral" military, police and/or civilian personnel into a conflict zone with the consent of all parties concerned), and peacebuilding (i.e., action to strengthen and solidify peace in a postconflict situation in order to avoid a relapse into conflict). Nonetheless, there are aspects of such actions that overlap with PD (Acharya 1994).

4. Put differently, the Asia-Pacific region engages in what Amitav Acharya has referred to as "localization"—in this instance, the localization or contextualization of PD practices to the specific local and national contexts at hand (Acharya 2004).

5. The membership of the ARF includes the ten ASEAN member states (Brunei, Cambodia, Indonesia, Laos, Malaysia, Burma, Philippines, Singapore, Thailand, and Vietnam); the ten ASEAN dialogue partners (Australia, Canada, China, the European Union, India, Japan, New Zealand, South Korea, Russia, and the United States); one ASEAN observer (Papua New Guinea); and North Korea, Mongolia, Pakistan, Timor-Leste, Bangladesh, and Sri Lanka.

6. These include the ten ASEAN states and eight of its dialogue partners, namely, Australia, China, India, Japan, New Zealand, Russia, South Korea, and the United States.

7. Most if not all of the ADMM-Plus countries are already signatories to the CUES treaty under the Western Pacific Naval Symposium (WPNS) signed in 2014 at Qingdao, China.

8. In this respect, it is noteworthy that when introducing the initiative back in October 2017, Indonesian defense minister Ryamizard Ryacudu felt the need to defend OEI as having "nothing to do with politics" but would "purely [be] an initiative to fight the existence of terrorist groups and maintain peace in our region."

CHAPTER 12

Sino-US Interactions, Past and Future

Chas W. Freeman Jr.

December 15, 2018 (December 16 in Beijing) marked the fortieth anniversary of Jimmy Carter's and Deng Xiaoping's politically courageous agreement to "normalize" the relationship between Washington and Beijing ("Diplomatic Relations" 1978).[1] This resulted in the replacement of China's demand for revolutionary overthrow of the world order with pragmatic accommodation of it.[2] Two days later, at the Third Plenum of the Eleventh Central Committee of the Chinese Communist Party (CCP),[3] Deng launched China on a path of eclectic borrowing of foreign ideas, policies, and practices called "reform and opening" (改革开放). This liberated the Chinese people—who were then almost a fourth of humanity—from the most suffocating aspects of Soviet Marxist-Leninist dogma and released their formidable entrepreneurial imaginations and energies.

The consequences of Deng's twin decisions for both China and the world have been immense. He saw US-China normalization and "reform and opening" as parts of a single bold gamble with his country's future. His vision enabled China to risk a search for inspiration in America and other capitalist democracies, to which the Chinese elite promptly entrusted its sons and daughters for education.

"Dengism" reinvigorated China's political economy by progressively abandoning major elements of its Soviet-derived model of central planning, state monopolization of commerce and industry, and collectivized agriculture. The results were explosive economic growth amid rocketing living standards, the rebirth of Chinese science and technology, the emergence of a Sino-centric regional order in East Asia, and the debut of China as a major actor on the global stage. American policy had aimed only at altering China's external relationships and behavior. The tremendous changes inside China were a welcome but entirely unexpected bonus.

Contemporary China is the improbable child of neo-Confucian Leninism and the Pax Americana. The defining characteristics of the liberal global order crafted by the United States were a universal commitment to multilateral rulemaking, quasi-judicial dispute resolution, the progressive removal of tariffs and quotas as barriers to trade, open investment flows, some level of selfless development assistance, humanitarian relief, and the principle of Pacta sunt servandan (Agreements must be kept). China has prospered in this international environment and remains comfortable in it.

Despite oft-repeated accusations that Beijing wants to do away with the rule-bound international order, China now seems far more committed to preserving it than its American progenitor.[4] Under the Trump administration, the United States had come to stand explicitly for mercantilist bilateralism and protectionism, economic coercion, an end to support for foreign economic development or refugees, the unilateral abrogation of international agreements, and opposition to multilateralism. By contrast, Chinese dissatisfaction with the international status quo has not been about its rules. China, like many other emerging market economies, has complained about the inability of the International Monetary Fund, World Bank, World Trade Organization (WTO), and regional banks like the Asian Development Bank to expand their reach, funding, and inclusiveness.

When legacy institutions have not risen to the challenges before them, China has worked with others to create parallel structures.[5] American disquiet at seeing countries other than the United States like China emerge as rulemakers and institution builders obscures but does not obviate the fact that the new Chinese-sponsored multilateral institutions have without exception both cooperated with existing bodies and conformed to the norms and practices they espouse. To the extent that the United States' China policy aimed at curbing China's revolutionary zeal and incorporating it into the international system created by the Pax Americana, it has been and remains a success rivaled only by the integration of postrevolutionary France into the conservative order managed by the Concert of Europe.

However, to the disappointment of naive American ideologues, as China modernized, it refused to participate in "the end of history" by embracing either democracy or laissez-faire economics as principles of governance. Instead, Beijing remained stubbornly obsessed with the avoidance of anarchy through authoritarianism. China shows no sign of abandoning the policy and investment-directed market economy that kindled and then sustained the ferocious competition between its enterprises (whether state-owned or privately owned) under "market Leninism." Entrepreneurship guided by preferential access to capital (rather the tax exemptions commonly used in the United States) continues to propel China toward technological innovation and ever greater wealth and power.

Those Americans who criticized US policies of engagement with Beijing as slighting efforts to democratize China and Westernize its human rights and economic practices now cite the failure of engagement to meet their expectations as proof of policy failure. But the success of policies can only be measured in terms of their objectives. However much Americans may have hoped or expected that China would Americanize itself, US policy was almost entirely aimed at changing China's external behavior rather than its constitutional order. The sole exception was the first fifteen months of the Clinton administration (1993–94), when Washington attempted to coerce change in China by linking it to the terms of Chinese foreign trade. When it became apparent that this approach was a dead end, Washington abandoned it, never to resume it (Broder and Mann 1994).

Irreconcilable ideological contradictions between America and China still bedevil the relationship. Chinese accept that foreigners govern themselves differently and should be left alone to do so. Americans see any political system other than constitutional democracy as inherently illegitimate. They will not accept moral equivalence with any authoritarian regime. The United States has concluded that it must, in practice, deal with the CCP, but does so as a politically awkward expedient, not with approval of the CCP's legitimacy.

As an added complication, "democratic peace theory" (a recent addition to American ideology) asserts that democracies do not fight each other, whereas wars are—by implication—to be expected with nations of other political dispensations. This hypothesis translates the absence of democracy in China into a potential menace to US national security.[6] This, in turn, provides a threat that is a welcome alternative to tiresome, low-intensity conflicts in West Asia and North Africa. It makes China a potential "peer competitor" that poses the sort of high-tech challenges to US primacy that the US military-industrial-congressional complex can profitably forfend. Postulating a vague but dreadful menace from China is the latter-day equivalent of paranoia about the supposed "yellow peril." It transforms China's modernization into a reliable driver of increased US spending on complex new weapons systems. Recent events in Xinjiang and Hong Kong have only served to deepen Sino-American alienation. They illustrate how badly each side now mistrusts and misreads the other.

In Xinjiang, Uighur envy of the independence of the Turkic-speaking republics to their west that followed the Soviet collapse, religious fervor born of contact with the so-called Islamic State and other extremists in the broader Islamic world, and resentment of continuing Han migration to the region have fused identity politics with Islamism. Beijing's response to Uighur terrorism has been a draconian evolution of the surveillance state. One could hardly conceive of a course of action more offensive to Western liberalism than the forced religious reeducation and cultural assimilation China has begun to impose on its Muslim minorities.

Hong Kong—as a "special administrative region of China," under the "one-country, two-systems" framework that Beijing applied to it after 1997— enjoyed elements of democracy that London had never thought to give it in its 155 years of rule there. But since its handover to Beijing, Hong Kong has been governed by a local oligarchy that ostentatiously defers to Beijing. In 2019, youth frustrated with this government's lack of attention to their housing, educational, and employment needs joined advocates of secession from China in protests featuring American flags that soon turned violent. Lacking confidence in local governance and blaming Beijing for its failings, the protesters (who had multiple, conflicting spokespersons) concentrated their fury on China ("one country") and demands for apologies from the Hong Kong government for alleged police brutality, making only vague proposals to improve Hong Kong's half of the "two systems" framework.

Americans saw the protests as a thrilling challenge to Chinese authoritarianism. Beijing saw them as foreign-instigated and US-supported riots. Hong Kong having long failed to meet its obligation to enact a national security law, Beijing finally did so for it. The new law banned seditious activities, including speech viewed as insulting to the Chinese nation, raising doubts about the city's prospects as society under the rule of law. Ideological issues are back as a source of conflict in Sino-American relations. However, in contrast to the Cold War, most of the world no longer sees the American system as self-evidently superior to those of its competitors. And, unlike the USSR, which sought to export its model, China does not. Instead, the CCP is on the ideological defensive, as its overwrought reactions to perceived challenges to its authority repeatedly demonstrate. It espouses no ideology other than self-absorption and studied indifference to how other countries govern themselves. In short, Sino-American rivalry does not fit the Cold War pattern. It cannot be managed in the same manner as rivalry with the USSR.

"Containment," the American Cold War grand strategy proposed by George Kennan in 1947, assumed that, if the Soviet system were walled up by sanctions and defensive alliances, it would eventually collapse of its own defects. That turned out to be correct, though it took forty-three years to prove it. Such "containment" is irrelevant to any contest with China.[7] The

Soviet model exalted autarky.[8] China has come to epitomize globalization and broad-based economic interdependence with other nations. It cannot be isolated from a world order where it is so thoroughly integrated and where other countries increasingly look to it for leadership as well as shared prosperity.

Nor is China's economic system irrational, inflexible, enervated, or burdened by unsustainable levels of military spending, as the Soviet Union's was. China has no reason to reenact Moscow's humiliating decision to default on its rivalry with Washington or to accept supervision by Wall Street bankers, carpetbagging Harvard professors, or democracy promoters. Both the Cold War and post–Cold War eras were so different from those of today that they provide no useful counsel for dealing with China's very real challenges to American pride and primacy.

Finally, in many parts of the world, this is an age of pessimism and contraction in the human spirit. But in China, optimism is still in command. Confidential polling reveals little of the destabilizing distrust in government in China that has seized so many parts of the West.[9] The Chinese people's approval of their government and the directions in which it is taking their country is exceptionally high. Chinese may not love the CCP, but very few think their country would be better off without it in charge (Tang 2018). They cannot help contrasting the relatively effective performance of their government with what they, like others, see as devastating political incoherence and dysfunction in the contemporary United States.

So, an obnoxious symmetry has come to pervert Sino-American relations. Neither side shows much empathy in its approach to the other. As it looks at its rival, each sees itself, attributing its own motivations and reasoning processes to the other. Self-righteous American contempt for the legitimacy of the Chinese political system is more than matched by hubristic Chinese disdain for the incompetence of governance in the contemporary United States. American politicians have become aggressively accusatory about China. Chinese struggle to restrain comparably impolitic and counterproductive rhetoric about the United States. These differences are a problem that is likely to persist until the United States gets back its groove, China suffers a sobering setback, or both. Neither development seems imminent.

It is said that Chinese plan in years, decades, and centuries, while Americans calculate what must be done in terms of weeks and months. The Sino-American relationship, till now, has advanced by a series of US finesses of Chinese grievances that left them to fester unresolved. Taiwan is at the center of this pattern.

Taiwan's political relationship with the rest of China now under the governance of the People's Republic remains in doubt. In managing this issue, the United States has expediently evaded long-term strategic choices in exchange for short-term gains, while the CCP has made tactical compromises but held firm to its strategic goal of bringing Taiwan under its dominion. To Chinese nationalists, their inability to resolve the Taiwan question symbolizes their country's ongoing humiliation by foreign interventions intended to divide and weaken it. To the CCP, American protection of Taiwan represents insulting unwillingness by the world's greatest power to respect the People's Republic's political legitimacy.

The balance of power in the Taiwan Strait and adjacent areas continues to shift against the island and the United States, making the use of force by China and war between China and the United States both more plausible and more perilous. The mainland's political system is becoming less open. This has further reduced the appeal of peaceful reunification to the already-skeptical citizens of Taiwan's democracy. The United States might still use its power to move the Taiwan issue toward resolution before Taiwan's bargaining position is fatally weakened and China's capabilities decisively outweigh those of the United States. But, in practice, Washington has consistently chosen complacency over strategy. Against ever-worsening military and economic odds, Americans continue to prefer impasse to evolution in cross-Strait relations.

This strategy-free US approach inadvertently encourages Taipei to ignore its declining negotiating leverage and rapidly diminishing ability to resist coercion from Beijing without invoking Washington's intervention. It makes Taiwan a disaster waiting to happen. In effect, the United States has opted to ignore ever more adverse circumstances, deferring an explosion until actions by Taipei or decisions in Beijing eventually trigger one. Recent moves by the Trump administration to bolster Taipei's defiance of Beijing made such an explosion more, rather than less, likely.

The Taiwan issue is part of a larger unacknowledged problem in US strategic interaction with China. The People's Republic is the only nuclear-armed great power whose frontiers are challenged by the United States. There are no established mechanisms for escalation control between Beijing and Washington. Each has a record of misreading the other in times of crisis. The rioting in Hong Kong has threatened the credibility of a "one China, two systems" as a means of peacefully ending the Chinese civil war, leaving the resumption of the use of force as the only obvious alternative. And if Taiwan is the most plausible casus belli in a war neither side wants or can survive without grave damage, it is no longer the only possible trigger of Sino-American conflict.

Both Taipei and Beijing regard the Senkaku (or Diaoyu / 钓鱼) Islands—uninhabited and barren rocks in the East China Sea—as rightly part of Taiwan, though they are administered by Japan. The modus vivendi that kept arguments over sovereignty from becoming a flash point between China and Japan collapsed in 2010. The dispute now risks dragging Americans into a bloody rendezvous between Chinese and Japanese nationalism.

In any conflict with China, the United States is committed to back Japan. As in the case of Taiwan, exclusive reliance on military means—deterrence—to deal with the Senkaku dispute ensures that it will be perpetuated rather than resolved. There is no American diplomatic strategy for mitigating the risks of war over the issue, and no apparent thought of developing one. Few Americans are aware of the issue. Still fewer have considered the consequences that would flow from an accidental clash or a failure of deterrence.

The year 2010 also marked the outbreak of escalating naval contention between China and the United States in the South China Sea. China (including Taiwan) has long claimed islets, rocks, and reefs there. Beijing did nothing to enforce its claims until rival claimants—Malaysia, the Philippines, and Vietnam—began to do so. It then grabbed whatever they had not, winding up with the least desirable land features in the Spratly Islands. After some time, China enlarged these into artificial, fortified islands from which it cannot be dislodged. Meanwhile, Beijing's inability to muster an internal consensus on the basis and extent of its claims left both ambiguous. This ensured that Americans and others would presume the worst, inadvertently embracing and acting to counter the most extreme positions advocated by Chinese chauvinists.

The United States is not itself a counterclaimant to any territory claimed by China. It has objected to several of China's interpretations of the United Nations Convention on the Law of the Sea.[10] If accepted, these Chinese assertions could restrict US naval operations in the South China Sea.

The initial confrontations between the two sides were over whether China could require prior notification or approval of military reconnaissance activities in its 200-mile exclusive economic zone (EEZ). This argument faded away once China realized that it had an interest of its own in conducting such operations in other countries' EEZs, including in US waters.

The concrete (as opposed to conjectural) point of difference between the Chinese and US navies now concerns China's use of straight baselines to define the territorial seas around the archipelagoes and islands it controls.[11] The US Navy has mounted frequent "freedom of navigation" operations to challenge this Chinese practice. But Washington has failed to articulate clear objectives for these operations, allowing the media to portray them as challenges to Chinese sovereignty rather than to how China exercises it.

Naval interactions in the South China Sea have become a test of wills, punctuated with emotional accusations by each side against the other. Americans charge China with scofflaw behavior. Chinese denounce what they see as an apparent US effort to bully them. There are no diplomatic processes in place to resolve either the territorial disputes among the various claimants or US differences with China over the law of the sea. Both sides are leaving it to might to make right.

China's presence in the South China Sea began as a response to the encroachment of other claimants on previously unenforced Chinese claims. It has become a matter of strategic defense of the Chinese homeland that pits US views of international law against Chinese security interests. Two-thirds of the shipping in the South China Sea is on its way to or from China, giving China a huge stake in defending shipping against interdiction by foreign warships—for example, the US and Japanese navies in Taiwan or Senkaku contingencies. The island bastions China has built in the Spratly Islands facilitate early warning, air, and undersea surveillance operations, and the emplacement of land-based missiles to counter wartime foreign intrusions.

Given the nationalist passion and self-righteousness now at play on both sides, it is hardly surprising that the specific issues at stake in China's near seas have been subsumed in wider Sino-American rivalry. The US desire to continue to call the shots in the Western Pacific, as it has since World War II, now contends with the reality that the People's Liberation Army Navy (PLAN) has already deployed many more warships off China's shores than the United States has worldwide.[12] This quantitative gap is widening even as the quality and range of the PLAN's weaponry approaches and, in some cases, exceeds that of the US Navy. Trends in the South China Sea now drive antagonisms that are broadening and going global.

For many years, there was a striking disconnect between the increasingly contentious Sino-American military relationship and the growing interdependence of the two countries' economies. Although it has a military dimension, China's challenge to US global primacy is mainly economic, not military or political. (China's international appeal, such as it is, does not derive from admiration for Leninism with Chinese characteristics.) The perceived eclipse of American economic primacy by China played a role—though it was not the only factor—in the election of Donald J. Trump as president of the United States in 2016.

President Trump is a mercantilist, with a view of economics that harks back to the era before David Ricardo (whose proof of "comparative advantage" was published in 1817). Trump's economic nationalism led him to an obsession with bilateral rather than global trade balances, a preference for "managed" rather than free trade, an effort to protect the US industrial base through reviews of both inbound and outbound investments based on their presumed implications for US technological leadership, unilateral withdrawal from both plurilateral and multilateral institutions of international economic governance, and reduced immigration. To realize this vision, he launched a war on trade and investment with China (and also all other significant US trading partners).

Links between American and Chinese businesses have long provided the ballast keeping Sino-American relations on an even keel. Trump's trade wars aimed to alter the terms of trade and investment so that economic cooperation through supply chains was succeeded by antagonism. Some of his advisers see this as fostering national economic self-sufficiency in the United States. (Of course, it will also promote self-reliance and sufficiency in China and could transform what had been "ballast" for the relationship into deadweight that drowns jobs and businesses in both countries.) There is no clear path to a negotiated retreat from economic conflict on either side.

The American position was an incoherent blend of unrelated and mutually incompatible demands—the foreign policy equivalent of a haggis.[13] Some on the Trump team wanted to crush China's economic model. Others wanted to punish it for alleged transgressions against the intellectual property of American companies. Still others wanted the two governments to manage trade to ensure that US imports do not exceed US exports to China. There were those who seek the full opening of China's financial sector. Many saw a halt in Chinese investment in the United States and to American investment in high-technology enterprises in China as essential to preserve American leadership in science and technology, especially as it relates to weaponry.

China has been unable to make sense of this fantastic American blend of baneful demands. But Chinese negotiators are concerned that, if they were to accommodate one or more of them, the proponents of competing theses would sabotage any deal because it had not addressed their particular agendas. Chinese officials were left to hope that, as President Trump did in the past, he would seize on minor concessions to declare a preposterous victory. But if he had done so with China, the president would have risked embarrassing revolts by disgruntled members of his notoriously fractious entourage, some of whom have long favored all-out confrontation with Beijing.

There are those on the Chinese side who, similarly, see political advantage in confrontation with the United States. It is a handy excuse to drag their feet on economic reform, undercut American ideological influence in China, favor Chinese over foreign companies, indigenize science and technology, and diversify China's international relationships to reduce reliance on the United States in favor of cooperation with Russia and other less politically erratic and demanding foreign partners. The prospects for a fruitful end to American economic warfare against China do not look good. It is more likely to prove counterproductive in terms of its objectives than to succeed—stimulating Chinese innovation, self-sufficiency, defense spending, and global economic influence while accelerating the decline of science and technology in the United States, impoverishing it, and reducing its role in global governance.

Economic truculence has now joined military antagonism as an engine of Sino-American hostility. As China takes advantage of America's alienation of its foreign allies, partners, and friends, we can expect political antipathy to intensify. It is hard to think of any country anywhere that will not wish to avoid entanglement in long-term Sino-American confrontation. Even regional rivals of China, like India and Japan, see a need to work with Beijing to advance common interests. They do not want the United States to impose its own problems with China on theirs (or China to impose an anti-American agenda on them). No nation is now willing to be forced, Cold War–style, into allegiance to one hyperpower against another.

The twenty-first century is increasingly characterized by entente rather than alliance, ad hoc coalition rather than broad partnership, and transactional rather than relational commitments to cooperation. By failing to adapt to these post–Cold War realities, Washington places its century-old economic primacy in jeopardy. There is no discernible support abroad for the US repudiation of multilateralism in favor of aggressive unilateralism, whether political, economic, or military. There is widening resentment of perceived American abuses of inherited privilege through acts of both omission and commission.

The United States' increasing resort to unilateral sanctions based on dollar sovereignty incentivizes others, including major US allies, to find ways to avoid transactions in dollars.[14] A dollar-free monetary system would protect their companies from extraterritorial punishment by the US Treasury. It would also weaken American dominance of global governance. Building such an alternative system is a project that will draw active support from China, India, and Russia as well as the European Union—which, on September 12, 2018, committed itself to this objective.[15] It has a good chance of eventually knocking the props out from under the "exorbitant privilege" the United States has enjoyed through its unilateral control of the global medium of exchange.

The world to come promises to be one where the United States no longer enjoys many of the advantages to which it has been accustomed: lessened prestige and ability to inspire foreign nations to follow it, declining centrality to global finance and commerce; a greatly diminished role in global governance; and fewer alliances and partnerships to magnify and extend its political and military projection of power. The United States will have few, if any, allies willing to join it in the event of a war with China over Taiwan or the South China Sea. It will also be alone in its intervention in support of Japan in the event of an accidental outbreak of conflict in the Senkaku Islands.

For its part, Beijing has no allies. It has always seen them as unnecessary liabilities rather than assets. Despite a growing partnership with Russia, China seeks to acquire enough power to balance America both economically and militarily on its own. In a universe of transactionalism and à la carte relationships, the relevant questions are whether each country will be able to find partners on specific issues and which states these will be. Meanwhile, the US withdrawal from both plurilateral and multilateral arrangements has left the United States and China with no obvious ways to cooperate in setting the global agenda or its rules, managing worldwide challenges like climate change, or settling disputes through processes that limit bilateral confrontation. Competing American and Chinese technospheres appear to be replacing the post–Cold War globalization of science and technology.

Ideology, including religion, inhibits realpolitik but does not prevent it. We have entered an age of unrealism. Diplomacy shows every sign of devolving toward cynical patterns of pre-Enlightenment statecraft, whereby values count only to the extent they can be exploited to charge interests with energy. This is a world where self-discipline and mental rather than military agility will be the major determinants of events. China has fewer vested interests to overcome as it adjusts to change than does the United States.

The new world disorder is an ecosystem in which no established alignments can be taken for granted. China's Belt and Road Initiative has the potential to reengineer not just the Eurasian but the global economy and China's role in both. Middle-ranked powers like Brazil, Egypt, India, Iran, Mexico, Nigeria, Russia, Saudi Arabia, South Africa, and Turkey occupy strategic positions that enable them to reorient themselves internationally. They are gaining bargaining power vis-à-vis both China and the United States. So are Japan and NATO members. Strategically stranded countries like Bangladesh, Indonesia, Malaysia, Pakistan, the Philippines, and Ukraine can and will offer temporary fealty to foreign powers willing to back their regional agendas. Nothing will be true, and everything will be possible.[16]

Over the forty years that followed the Carter and Deng decisions of December 1978, China and the United States developed a relationship of cooperation within which competition could take place without significant adverse consequences. This relationship is being succeeded by one of malicious coexistence, in which the two sides have yet to find ways to transcend antagonism that permit ad hoc cooperation and limit conflict. In a sense, despite the huge growth in interdependence of markets, bureaucracies, companies, and individuals that has taken place, Beijing and Washington are conceptually back where they were before the Nixon opening of 1972: separated by ideological preconceptions and popular stereotypes uncorrected by any strategic rationale for collaboration in support of common interests, oblivious to the existence of such interests, and politically enjoined from exploring alternatives to military antagonism. On peace and war between them, they are again hostage to the decisions and actions of third parties like Taipei and Tokyo, Pyongyang and Seoul, Delhi and Islamabad. But the international context is radically different, with Chinese power rising as that of the United States declines, and with China now in possession of an assured means of devastating nuclear retaliation against any American threat to it.

In this difficult context, the two must grapple with some of the same dilemmas they did forty years ago: How can they create a dynamic favorable to the peaceful settlement of the Taiwan question? What role should opposition to or partnership with Russia play in their respective national security policies? How can they revise the global and regional balances of power to limit the risks of conflict? What relationships should each seek to develop and sustain relationships with present and potential regional powers like India, Indonesia, Japan, and South Korea and North Korea? Should they isolate or engage each other?

There are new questions as well: How should China and the United States respond to nuclear and missile proliferation in South, West, and Northeast Asia? How can they accommodate differing interpretations of international law, including the UN Charter and the law of the sea? What balance should each strike between exchanges of goods and services to boost prosperity and the relevance of technology to national security? What reforms of institutions and practices would best address emerging challenges to global governance? How are these to be funded or governed, and by whom?

This is a potent list of issues that the two countries can handle cooperatively or competitively. What choices will each make? What, if anything, might increase the prospects for mutually beneficial choices by both sides?

Finally, the shifting balances of power and prestige impose a need for adjustments in US policy. In circumstances where Chinese capabilities and clout are both rising relative to its own, is a confrontational approach by Washington more likely to induce cooperation or to entrench antagonism in Beijing? Is leaving problems to future resolution, when China is more likely to be able to prevail on the battlefield, a wiser approach than trying to resolve them now, however difficult it might be to do so? Should the United States seek to counter or benefit from the reality that all roads in Eurasia and adjacent areas will increasingly lead to Beijing? What sorts of policies would opposition to or support for China's promotion of infrastructure connectivity entail, and where would the resources to implement such policies come from? How can the United States reduce the danger that those nations to which it has made defense commitments will do things that risk recklessly embroiling Americans in unwanted wars? What nuclear deterrent posture and arms control policies are most likely to reduce the possibility of catastrophic damage to the American homeland from China and also Russia?

Sadly, Sino-American relations continued to deteriorate through 2019. At year end, a cease-fire—misportrayed for domestic American political purposes as a "phase-one deal"—briefly suspended the trade war launched by the United States almost two years before.[17] But other aspects of American economic warfare against China continued to escalate. These included US campaigns to shut down investment by China in the United States and by American pension funds in China (Hanemann et al. 2020; "Beijing Hits Back" 2020), to stigmatize Chinese students and cultural centers at American universities as engaged in espionage and subversion ("Statement in Response" 2019; Redden 2019), to halt science and technology exchanges (Psaledakis 2019), to engineer a global ban on Chinese exports of telecommunications technology (Rosenberg 2020), and to dissuade other countries from participating in China's Belt and Road Initiative or accepting its investment and development assistance (Leon 2019). Meanwhile, Washington stepped up naval patrols to challenge China's attempts to exercise sovereignty in its near seas ("US Pursuit" 2019) and chipped away at the bilateral understandings that have kept the peace in the Taiwan Strait for half a century (Albert 2020).

China initially responded with restraint to these attacks on its interests and amour-propre. But as time went on, American actions, accusations, and insinuations evoked a tsunami of nationalist rage that lifted hard-liners to the commanding heights of the CCP propaganda apparatus. Chinese diplomats began to reciprocate perceived American hostility and slights with infantile name-calling, invective, and increasingly preposterous accusations. Other countries that echoed American criticism of China found themselves subjected not just to Chinese verbal abuse but also to the imposition of selective, unannounced barriers to their exports to the Chinese consumer market (now the world's largest) (Chandler 2020). China's actions were so obviously injurious to its relations with other nations that they aroused serious doubt about the ability of its increasingly paranoid domestic autocracy to sustain peaceful coexistence with more open societies.

Days before 2020 began, the previously unknown coronavirus, COVID-19, began to infect some of the inhabitants of the central Chinese city Wuhan. It took local authorities a few weeks to identify it, recognize its highly contagious nature, and overcome political resistance to risking public panic ("COVID-19 and China" 2020; "新型冠状病毒感染的肺炎疫情知识问答" 2020). This fumbled Chinese handling of what became the COVID-19 pandemic was followed by a tragically incompetent American response that soon made the United States the pandemic's global epicenter (Dallas 2020), strained relations with US allies, and severely undercut worldwide perceptions of American capabilities, including in China.

Each side charged the other with cover-ups, politically motivated disinformation campaigns, and obstruction of an effective response to the virus. The United States alleged that China had undue influence in the World Health Organization (WHO). Washington suspended US participation and funding for the WHO, thus turning its complaint into a self-fulfilling prophecy as China upped its own contributions and other countries accused the United States of crippling international efforts to combat the pandemic. Determined to accept "no responsibility" (Oprysko 2020) for the mounting domestic death toll, the Trump administration and Republican Party made China their coronavirus scapegoat of choice in the 2020 elections. US Democrats piled on with charges that the Trump administration had been too "soft on China."

As the summer of 2020 approached, Sino-American relations reached a level of mutual hostility not seen since the Korean War, exacerbating already serious global and regional concerns about the implications for other countries of escalating superpower enmity and setting off a wave of domestic US discrimination against Asian Americans (ASEAN 2020). Evidence-free allegations and political accusations reminiscent of McCarthyism returned to American politics. In China, ever more voices began urging that Beijing take advantage of perceived US weakness, confusion, and international isolation by using force to recover sovereignty over Taiwan. The PLA stepped up its pressure on Taiwan as well as on Japan, Vietnam, and other claimants to land features and fisheries in its near seas. It fielded a nuclear-capable submarine-launched intercontinental ballistic missile and tested a stealth bomber capable of striking targets on the US mainland.

Neither China nor the United States have wanted a war over Taiwan or the other issues dividing them, but each was loudly readying itself to fight one. By May 2020, a world distracted by a pandemic and looming economic depression was arguably closer to an outbreak of armed conflict between nuclear powers than it had been since the Cuban missile crisis of 1962.

Though professional contact between the US and Chinese militaries continued, there were still no effective crisis management or escalation control systems in place between them. In this connection, it was not encouraging for Americans or their foreign security partners that in every recent simulation of such a war, the PLA had prevailed (Gilsinian 2019; Ignatius 2020).

The absence of informed discussion of these issues in and between China and the United States is a clear and present danger to both and also to others. As the fortieth anniversary of their rapprochement nears, the two countries are badly in need of an innovative strategic vision and statesmanship comparable to those they displayed in December 1978. How China and the United States respond to this challenge will determine not only their own futures but also the shape of the world to come.

NOTES

1. This chapter is based in part on a paper prepared for the January 17–19, 2019, conference on Sino-American relations at the Carter Center in Atlanta.
2. The Maoist slogan "People of the world, unite and defeat the US aggressors and all their running dogs!" immediately disappeared. The assertion that "countries want independence, nations want liberation, the people want revolution" was heard no more. And "we will certainly liberate Taiwan" was replaced with initiatives aimed at peaceful reunification with the island.
3. December 18–22, 1978, in Beijing.
4. This is usually accompanied by repetitions of allegations about Chinese strategic objectives and behavior that have been repeated often enough to pose as axiomatic but are backed by no concrete evidence or authenticated Chinese sources.
5. Often, it must be said, because of US foot dragging.
6. The parallels between "democratic peace theory" and past hopes that Christians would not fight Christians, Muslims would not fight Muslims, and socialists would not fight socialists—none of which proved true—cry out for examination. Count me skeptical, to say the least.
7. However, the Chinese word used for "containment" is fundamentally misleading. "遏制" does not accurately convey the sense of a policy of isolation intended to allow an enemy to do itself in through its own ideological rigidity and bureaucratic misdirection of resources. But this very concept of allowing the Soviet warfare state to exhaust itself and die was the core of Kennan's grand strategy of "containment." Applied to contemporary Sino-American relations, "containment," as misunderstood, evokes Chinese fears that US policy is directed at the strangulation of Chinese modernization rather than at balancing China's growing power and deterring its possible abuse in bullying of others in the region. To date, US policy has sought both to engage China and to constrain its external behavior, not to isolate it, suppress it, or overthrow single-party rule in it.
8. Autarky is a system or policy of economic self-sufficiency aimed at removing the need for imports.

9. Unlike the 1930s, when autocracies advocated foreign adoption of their political systems or sought to impose them by force, no autocracy today seeks to export its ideology or form of governance. Contemporary autocracies, including China, leave such messianic approaches to foreign relations to the United States and a few other aggressive promoters of democratic ideology. In the twenty-first century, autocracy is not on the offensive. Democracy is on the retreat as it fails to deliver reliable prosperity, domestic tranquility, effective solutions to problems, and confidence in continued progress to its citizenry.

10. Ironically, China has ratified the Convention, while the United States has not. Since the end of World War II, the US Navy has been accustomed to acting as the regulator of the global and regional maritime commons. It has seen China's emergence as a major, independent naval power as an unwelcome challenge to its primacy in the Western Pacific.

11. A baseline is a contour from which to measure the seaward limits of a state's territorial sea. Normally, a baseline follows the undulations of the low-water mark, but, when a coast is too deeply indented for a smooth contour to follow it, "straight baselines" can be drawn between its outermost points. The United Nations Convention on the Law of the Sea authorizes "archipelagic states" (countries that consist of one or more archipelagoes) to use straight in lieu of normal baselines. China is not an archipelago. It nonetheless uses straight baselines to enclose the archipelagoes it claims. This enlarges the territorial seas it claims. That is of concern to the US Navy and others defending the existing order in the maritime commons.

12. As of 2018, the US Navy deployed 280 vessels worldwide, 60–70 of which were assigned to the Seventh Fleet, whose mission is the projection of US power to the Indo-Pacific region. The PLAN has about 280 deployable battle force ships plus another 200 or more missile and gunboats and 230 support vessels available to defend the approaches to the Chinese coast in support of what Americans term its "antiaccess, area-denial" strategy. By 2020, the US Office of Naval Intelligence forecasts that the PLAN will have 313–42 warships.

13. Those who have not encountered this signature creation of traditional Scottish cuisine may well hope they never do. A haggis is a pudding made of the heart, liver, etc., of a sheep or calf, minced with suet and oatmeal, seasoned, and boiled in the stomach of the animal.

14. The most egregious case in point is the US repudiation of its commitments under the Iran nuclear deal and its effort to strangle Iran's foreign economic relations. See the August 2018 remarks of German foreign minister Heiko Maas reporting on urgent efforts to end US payments dominance, as reported by the Deutsche Welle (www.dw.com/en /germany-urges-swift-end-to-us-payments-dominance/a-45242528).

15. See President of the European Commission Jean-Claude Juncker's September 12, 2018, statement of resolve to turn the euro into a reserve currency to rival the dollar (http:// europa.eu/rapid/press-release_IP-18-5724_en.htm).

16. Apologies to Peter Pomerantsev, whose excellent book of this title is about Russia but might as well be about the world of today as a whole.

17. The Trump administration retained the bulk of its tariffs on Chinese imports in this "deal," only lowering the tariff rates on some imports and reserving the right to restore or increase these at will.

PART III

Discord and Collaboration on Major Security Threats

In this part, each author is asked to comment on the three scenarios and to assess the general implications for future diplomacy and conflict management of challenges flowing from one of the security issues.

CHAPTER 13

The Future of UN Peacekeeping and the Rise of China

Lise Morjé Howard

United Nations peacekeeping serves as something of a litmus test for gauging international cooperation because it does not occur without great power agreement in the UN Security Council. Today, there are more UN peacekeepers than any other type of foreign actor deployed in conflict zones, totaling about 110,000, across thirteen different missions (United Nations Peacekeeping 2020). This fact reflects an underlying common interest among the veto-wielding permanent five (P-5) members of the UN Security Council—China, France, Russia, the United Kingdom, and the United States—that, despite disagreements, they view peacekeeping as a useful tool for mitigating common problems and threats. This consensus has enabled peacekeeping to become surprisingly effective at reducing violence, as demonstrated in a wide variety of recent quantitative studies.

In terms of how peacekeeping fits into the general peace and diplomacy toolbox, three major studies have demonstrated that during complex negotiation processes, the promise that UN peacekeepers will verify peace implementation has a significant effect on the likelihood of arriving at a peace deal (Walter 1997, 2002; Lundgren 2016). In other words, peacekeeping increases the chances that diplomats will be able to negotiate a peace deal, and that it will be implemented. More than two dozen other studies demonstrate that peacekeepers save lives where they are deployed. It is one of the most robust findings in all of international relations. What comes after the establishment of peace, however, remains in question. UN peacekeeping currently holds democratic elections and human rights verification as central goals in peace transitions. These goals, or norms, are currently in flux.

The rise of authoritarian China poses a significant challenge to the *future* of UN peacekeeping, and to the liberal-oriented United Nations system in general. As Chinese influence rises around the globe, peacekeeping may change significantly, reflecting Chinese dominance and preferences for authoritarian rule. In recent years, China has sought to assert itself in and through the UN, and specifically, through peacekeeping (Lee 2020; Gowan 2018). In short, I predict the strengthening of UN peacekeeping (largely fitting the "pragmatic cooperation" scenario), as long as everyone else is willing to go along with Chinese terms. This is a scenario where the only true global institution—the United Nations—is strengthened, because its member states recognize that global threats such as climate change and pandemics are only mitigated by multilateral cooperation. However, the UN's underlying normative justifications will shift toward the ideals and goals of social and political stability, development, and authoritarianism, and away from the liberal values of human rights, most notably, the democratic rights of political contest, freedom of expression, privacy, and religious freedom. Markets will recover from the devastation of COVID-19, and begin to grow again, but based on Chinese, rather than liberal-Western, terms. If, however, the next American, British, and French administrations resist Chinese advances into UN peacekeeping and onto the world stage more broadly, and China chooses to respond in kind, we may well see the unraveling of UN cooperation in general and UN peacekeeping specifically, as a new Cold War takes shape (reflecting the "discord scenario").[1]

This chapter proceeds in four sections. First, I provide an overview of the origins, shifts, and current state of UN peacekeeping. Media reports and qualitative scholarship tend to reflect the significant failings and dysfunction of some operations, but more than two dozen quantitative studies have examined peacekeeping more systematically, across all cases, employing a wide variety of measures and controls, and find that peacekeepers correlate with some extremely important and positive trends in civil wars: the establishment of peace agreements, fewer deaths, a geographic contraction of conflict, shorter wars, and less recurrence of war. Second, I turn to a brief discussion of China's authoritarian rise. The negative aspects of China's rise manifest most notably in the "social credit" system at home; spreading economic dominance through the Belt and Road Initiative and debt traps; seeking military dominance through artificial intelligence; and practicing "mask diplomacy" in the wake of COVID-19. Taking these trends together, China's rise poses challenges to contemporary notions of peacekeeping as a tool for furthering human rights and democratic norms. Third, China has indicated an interest in dominating UN peacekeeping. China is now the second-largest financial contributor to peacekeeping missions, and it has pledged to become the top troop contributor; it has also made moves to assume the leadership of the Department of Peace Operations (formerly the Department of Peacekeeping Operations), when the current undersecretary-general's term is up in several years. Finally, I discuss how peacekeeping can be employed as an instrument to help explain, and predict the future of, important trends in the international system. Currently, peacekeeping continues to reflect the strength of the United Nations as an organization that promotes international peace and security as conceived by liberal, Western powers and their allies. As the United States retreats from the world stage and China rises, China has indicated a continued commitment to the UN and to peacekeeping, but under authoritarian rather than liberal democratic principles. It is possible that China will succeed in transforming peacekeeping as Western powers, especially the United States, experience economic hardship from COVID-19 and accompanying domestic unrest, leading to a western retreat from the international stage.

AN OVERVIEW OF PEACEKEEPING

Peacekeeping was invented more than seventy years ago in order to manage violent conflict. Its three rules—consent, impartiality, and limited force—remain in place today, although the numbers of peacekeeping troops and the UN Department of Peace Operations' budgets have varied over time. These shifts reflect great power cooperation and discord as much as events on the ground. The effectiveness rates of peacekeeping are largely a matter of methodological debate: qualitative studies focusing on a limited number of cases tend to see dysfunction and failure, whereas quantitative studies find overwhelming evidence of peacekeeping's effectiveness. In this section, I address each of these elements in turn: (1) the origins and defining features of peacekeeping, (2) shifts in troop deployments and budgets, and (3) effectiveness rates in peacekeeping.

First, peacekeeping was invented shortly after World War II, when member states in the United Nations realized that, for conflicts where the parties were unlikely to be able to police themselves, sending impartial, multinational troops might promote conflict management, and possibly resolution. Blue-helmeted UN troops deployed to the Middle East with the consent of the belligerents; they pledged to help oversee and implement peace deals impartially (not neutrally);[2] and they were allowed to use force only in self-defense. These three doctrinal rules of peacekeeping—consent, impartiality, and the limited use of force—remain its defining features. They are what distinguish this form of intervention from others, such as counterinsurgency.[3]

Second, peacekeeping troop numbers and budgets have fluctuated over time. As the Cold War took root, UN peacekeeping mirrored great power tensions, even though it remained useful in some circumstances. Reflecting some basic agreement, from 1948 to 1978 the United Nations initiated thirteen missions, mainly to monitor cease-fire lines between states in the Middle East and Asia. However, with the end of détente and the hardening of Cold War bipolarity, from 1978 to 1988, even as wars raged around the globe, not a single new UN peacekeeping mission deployed. This all changed dramatically with the end of the Cold War. In 1992, the five veto-wielding members of the UN Security Council met at the level of heads of state for the first time in history, and decided to work together to end civil wars around the globe by mediating agreements and deploying UN peacekeepers (Howard and Stark 2018). The number of UN troops and accompanying budgets rose dramatically in the early 1990s, but then fell precipitously, as we see in figure 13.1, after the devastating peacekeeping failures in Somalia in 1993, Rwanda in 1994, and Bosnia in 1995, when thousands of civilians perished while UN peacekeepers merely observed. The Bill Clinton administration was reluctant to field peacekeeping missions, cutting the budget dramatically. In the period of post–Cold War unipolarity, the world had no choice but to follow America's lead. Because the United States is the largest funder of peacekeeping, providing nearly 30 percent of the budget, its preferences generally determine the direction of peacekeeping, but not entirely.

Although the second term of the Clinton administration remained reluctant to fund UN peacekeeping, the underlying demand for peacekeeping had not receded. In 1999, the conflicts in Kosovo, Sierra Leone, Timor Leste, and the Democratic Republic of Congo were winding down, and a variety of actors in the UN system requested that the UN send peacekeepers (Howard and Dayal 2018). The United States relented on its previous budgetary stance, and the number of peacekeeping troops increased dramatically. Subsequently, although President George W. Bush initially campaigned on an anti-UN foreign policy platform, again, the demand for peacekeeping persisted. After the terrorist attacks of September 11, 2001, the Bush administration began to support UN peacekeeping like no previous American administration. By 2009, the UN peacekeeping budget had tripled, to nearly $8 billion per year (UN General Assembly 2009). Under the two terms of the Barrack Obama administration, peacekeeping budgets and troop numbers plateaued. Under Donald J. Trump, they have declined to $6.7 billion (UN General Assembly 2018). The Trump administration's reluctance to fund peacekeeping threatens to undermine a tool of international conflict management that has a surprisingly positive

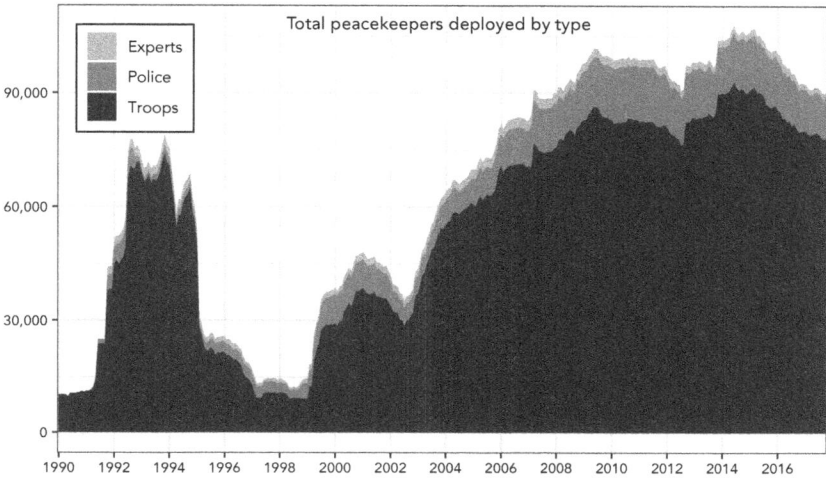

Figure 13.1 The Surge in Uniformed UN Peacekeeping Personnel, 1990–2018

record of accomplishment, across a wide variety of measures, when one looks beyond the headlines.

Third, in terms of peacekeeping effectiveness, most news stories and qualitative scholarship tend to portray an endeavor that is riddled with sexual abuse and exploitation, and other types of pathologies, failures, paradoxes, and dysfunction (Autesserre 2014; Barnett and Finnemore 2004; Campbell 2018; Caplan 2005; Cunliffe 2013; Sengupta 2015; von Billerbeck 2017). The quantitative evidence, however, overwhelmingly demonstrates that peacekeeping works. Using different data sets and statistical models, leveraging slightly different time periods, and measuring peacekeeping in somewhat different ways, more than two dozen studies have found that peacekeeping has a large, positive, and statistically significant effect on reducing violence of all sorts. This includes (1) helping warring parties to reach comprehensive peace settlements, (2) preventing the outbreak and spread of violence to areas at risk of civil war, (3) reducing violence against civilians and combatants in the midst of war, and (4) preventing the recurrence of violence and maintaining peace after war has ended (Beardsley 2011; Beardsley and Gleditsch 2015; Bove and Ruggeri 2016; Carnegie and Mikulaschek 2016; Cunningham 2016; Di Salvatore 2020; Doyle and Sambanis 2006; Eck and Hultman 2017; Fjelde, Hultman, and Nilsson 2018; Fortna 2004, 2008; Gilligan and Sergenti 2008; Hartzell, Hodie, and Rothchild 2001; Howard 2008, 2019; Hultman, Kathman, and Shannon 2013, 2014; Joshi 2013; Kathman and Wood 2016;

Lundgren 2016; Melander 2009; Mironova and Witt 2017; Ruggeri, Dorussen, and Gizelis 2013, 2016, 2017; Walter 1997, 2002). Despite the problems associated with UN peacekeeping—which often dominate the headlines—it is a uniquely and surprisingly effective form of conflict management and even conflict resolution (Walter, Howard, and Fortna 2021).

Although peacekeeping correlates with many positive trends in civil wars, several nagging questions remain, two of which I address briefly here. First, the so-called big five missions—in the Central African Republic, Darfur, the Democratic Republic of Congo, Mali, and South Sudan—are not progressing very well. Though there is evidence that the presence of UN peacekeepers in these countries saves lives, the missions are not able to work steadily toward implementing their mandates and departing. Part of the problem is that these missions are "wandering in the void" between war and peace (Ruggie 1993). In the big five, UN peacekeepers—who are by design not war fighters—have been asked to use robust force against rebels, to protect civilians. Peacekeepers, by and large, remain unable and unwilling to fight. Nevertheless, all current multidimensional missions have been mandated under Chapter VII of the UN Charter to enforce the peace (Howard and Dayal 2018; Howard 2019, chap. 5). As I have argued elsewhere, war fighters are able, and may credibly, fight; peacekeepers, however, have a proven track record of using non-compellent means—persuasion, inducement, and coercion short of offensive force—to accomplish their goals (Howard 2019). Until policymakers recognize the differences between peacekeeping and military action, and hone the two tools separately, the big five missions will continue to wander in the void.

Second, it remains under debate whether peacekeepers enable postconflict democratization. An initial study found that peacekeeping helps to foster at least a minimal level of democracy through the terms of a settlement (Doyle and Sambanis 2006). Others have also found that UN intervention fosters transitions to democracy (Pickering and Peceny 2006; Joshi 2013), and improved observance of the rule of law and governance (Mvukiyehe 2018; Blair 2020). In contrast, some equally rigorous studies have found the opposite: that peacekeeping has negligible or no effects on democratic outcomes (Gurses and Mason 2008; Fortna and Huang 2012). Although the *effects* of peacekeeping on democratization are debatable, since the end of the Cold War, the *goals* of UN peacekeeping in civil wars have unmistakably involved furthering democracy, peace, and open markets. Since September 11, 2001, as I have argued elsewhere, we have seen a systematic shift away from the norms of negotiation and democratization, and toward the goal of stabilization (Howard and Stark 2018). As China rises, I predict that the trend away from negotiation and democratization will strengthen, unless Western governments push back.

THE RISE OF AUTHORITARIAN CHINA

Unlike the other permanent five members of the UN Security Council, China has not sent its military to war in more than four decades. Furthermore, unlike the rise of most other great powers in history, China's rise has not (thus far) been fueled by, nor led to, large-scale bloodshed (Allison 2017). Chinese authoritarianism at home and its spread abroad, however, present deep challenges for the liberal democratic goals of the United Nations in general, and for UN peacekeeping. Both at home and abroad, Chinese authoritarianism seeks to suppress individual rights and freedoms, undermining democracy and an open society. I outline here the main four features of China's rise—social, economic, military, and diplomatic—that strengthen authoritarian governance in China and abroad.

First, in terms of social control, China is systematically undermining basic human rights, such as freedom of religion, political expression, and the right to privacy. The most egregious clampdowns are against various Turkic Muslims, most notably Uighurs, in Xinjiang Province of northwestern China. Under the guise of cracking down on terrorist threats, more than 1 million people have been confined to "reeducation" camps, where they are instructed to disavow Islam and embrace Mao ("Eradicating 'Ideological Viruses'" 2018; Standish 2019). The surveillance techniques used to control Xinjiang have been developed for broader use, such that eventually, all 1.4 billion of China's citizens will be subject to a "social credit scoring system." The system is derived from "finances, social media activities, credit history, health records, online purchases, tax payments, legal matters . . . [and] images gathered from China's 200 million surveillance cameras and facial recognition software" (Marr 2019). The system enables the government to track and rate, and then reward or punish, every citizen under ever-tightening government control.[4] Political dissent, religious expression, and basic privacy are rendered impossible. This capability is attractive to would-be authoritarians throughout the world.

Second, the social credit system extends to economic control, allowing the Chinese Communist Party to exercise greater domination over strategic sectors of the economy, limiting and dominating the private sector, and circumscribing the role of foreign firms, imports, and investment, as well as forcing technology transfers from Western to Chinese firms (Kirişci and Le

Corre 2018; Rolland 2017). Economic control has also extended well beyond China's borders. The Belt and Road Initiative, initially cast as a mechanism for fostering economic advancement globally, is increasingly becoming a tool for China to exercise so-called debt trap diplomacy, as Pakistan, Malaysia, Sri Lanka, and Zambia have discovered (Larmer 2018; Sohn 2012).[5]

Third, in terms of the military, Russian president Vladimir Putin has declared about artificial intelligence, "whoever becomes the leader in this sphere will become the ruler of the world" (Karpukhin 2017).[6] Although China's military will never match the size, funding, or firepower of that of the United States, advancements in artificial intelligence may enable it to neutralize American dominance (Allen 2017; Chen 2018; Horowitz 2018; Lee 2018). China is developing small, cheap swarming drones, new missiles, and submarines, and it is building islands to place strategic "defensive" weapons systems, fueling global military competition (Gajanan 2017; Mehta 2018; Scharre 2018).[7] China's primary goal appears not to dominate the world militarily, but rather to shore up the Chinese Communist Party's control over China itself; regain and maintain economic growth; insulate against perceived foreign military, economic, and political threats; and assert control around its borders, most notably in the South China Sea, Taiwan, and Hong Kong (Fung 2019; Lanteigne 2005; Wuthnow and Saunders 2017).

Although China may not be seeking military domination (other than in artificial intelligence), it is using diplomatic pressure to try to bend global partner support. Some analysts have dubbed this phenomenon "sharp power" (Walker 2018). The current incarnation is in the form of "mask diplomacy," where, especially in Europe, China is pushing a narrative that unlike the United States, China is a reliable and responsible partner for combating COVID-19. China is providing a diplomatic, soft power alternative to liberalism.

In sum, under the Xi government, China is undermining liberalism at home and abroad using social, economic, military, and diplomatic strategies. How might this phenomenon affect UN peacekeeping?

CHINA IN PEACEKEEPING

Historically, China has not sought to play a major role in the UN system in general or in peacekeeping specifically, but this position has gradually shifted such that, as of 2019, China has become a major player in UN peacekeeping, and stands to become the most engaged world power in this domain. China has both material and ideational reasons for supporting peacekeeping.[8] The question remains, however, whether it will uphold the liberal, democratic foundations of peacekeeping; the answer, most likely, is no. In this section, I address each of these elements: (1) China's historic involvement in peacekeeping, (2) China's new leadership in peacekeeping, and (3) *why* China has sought to lead UN peacekeeping.

China has a complex history vis-à-vis the United Nations. In 1951, six years after the UN's creation, China found itself the target of the first US-led, UN-sanctioned enforcement action during the Korean War, predisposing mainland China against external interventions or working with the United Nations. In 1955, the Chinese government issued its "five principles of peaceful coexistence," the most important of which were respect for state sovereignty and nonintervention (Hirono and Lanteigne 2011, 248). After the Chinese Socialist Republic joined the UN Security Council in 1971, it refrained from participating in peacekeeping votes for decades (Morphet 2000). With the end of the Cold War, as the number of UN peacekeeping missions mushroomed, China resisted moves toward increasing robustness in peacekeeping, favoring mandates issued under UN Charter Chapter VI, "Peaceful Settlement of Disputes," over Chapter VII, "Enforcement," which were increasingly favored by the Western P-3 (France, the United Kingdom, and the United States) (Stähle 2008, 643; Howard and Dayal 2018). After China vetoed several mandates, in 1999, its policy toward peacekeeping shifted dramatically: it began to "go along to get along" (Howard and Dayal 2018). Since the early 2010s, Chinese interest in peacekeeping has grown exponentially.

In recent years, China has made moves toward increasing its role in UN peacekeeping in three areas: (1) troop contributions, (2) financing, and (3) institutional leadership. First, for about the last decade, China has sent more troops to participate in peacekeeping missions than the other P-5 members, contravening the long-standing norm that P-5 states do not contribute troops to missions, for fear of undermining the key peacekeeping principle of impartiality.[9] In 2015, China announced that it would create a standby contingent of 8,000 troops for peacekeeping, and it has followed through on this promise ("China Registers 8,000" 2017). If deployed, China would rank as the largest troop contributor of all UN member states (*China's Role in UN Peacekeeping* 2018).[10] Second, in terms of financing, in 2016, China raised its annual financial contribution to UN peacekeeping from 3.9 percent of the annual budget to 10.3 percent (Lanteigne 2018, 2). This increase has rendered China the second-largest financial contributor, after the United States. China has also pledged $1 billion to the UN Peace and Development Trust Fund over ten years for UN-Chinese development initiatives (Lanteigne 2018, 2). Third, China has increasingly sought to have its nationals assume leadership roles in the UN system, and in UN peacekeeping (Lee

2020; "Chinese General" 2011). Although since 1997, France has held the position of undersecretary-general for peacekeeping, during the most recent leadership change in the Department of Peacekeeping Operations in 2016, China made moves toward assuming control of the department (Lynch 2016; Pauley 2018). France's candidate, Jean-Pierre Lacroix, won in 2016, but it remains to be seen what will happen in the next round. The Department of Peace Operations (formerly the Department of Peacekeeping Operations) is the largest unit in the UN system, with a budget that is greater than the rest of the UN's combined. China's leadership of this portion of the UN's bureaucracy would signal a major shift away from Western leadership in the UN. In sum, China has been surging ahead in UN peacekeeping, in troops, funds, and leadership. The question is, why? What motivates China?

There is a significant debate in the scholarly literature between those who see China's advance in peacekeeping as mainly driven by material concerns, and others who locate the origins in ideational factors (Li 2010, 2011). On the material side, although China is increasing naval activity in its neighborhood, its military has not deployed for combat in more than forty years. Participating in peacekeeping is a way for Chinese forces to gain operational experience (Cabestan 2018; Cheng 2010; Gill and Huang 2009). Indeed, China has lost several troops to violence in South Sudan and Mali (*China's Role in UN Peacekeeping* 2018; Zhuang 2016). China also has an important material concern in protecting its national interests in oil installations in Sudan and South Sudan, mining rights in the Central African Republic and in the Democratic Republic of Congo (which holds the key minerals for cell phone production), as well as Belt and Road Initiative passages and trade routes (Becker 2004; Stahle 2008). Thus, the drive may be simply one of national interest defined by material need.

Other scholars, however, see China's quest for advancement in peacekeeping as driven by China's identity as simultaneously a great power and a Global South state (Fung 2016). Participating in peacekeeping is a way to burnish China's international status and reputation (Deng 2008; Howard and Dayal 2018; Larson and Shevchenko 2010). More broadly, China wishes to be seen as a "responsible" world power (Shambaugh 2013; Richardson 2011; "Commentary" 2018; Zhou 2017). Participating in peacekeeping may enable China to advance its ideational interests.

Both sides of the debate have merit. China has material interests that it seeks to protect in developing states, and participating in UN peacekeeping is an advantageous method for keeping track of these while evading charges of neocolonialism. At the same time, during its rise, China has proven receptive to the social influence of its peers and others, especially through its participation in international institutions (Fung 2016; Johnston 2008). This receptiveness is in large part what has driven China to participate in UN peacekeeping: the Obama administration pressured the Chinese government to supply peacekeeping troops and funding. United Nations peacekeeping furthers China's normative interests in peace, stability, and development; however, China is categorically uninterested in furthering human rights and democracy (Communist Party of China 2012; Kent 1999; Lynch 2018a; Sceats and Breslin 2012; Piccone 2018). In 2018, China and Russia, with the assent of the Trump administration, worked to remove human rights and gender provisions from peacekeeping mandates as a way, ostensibly, to reduce costs (Lynch 2018b).

Moreover, China's commitment to Chapter VI notions of peacekeeping may be shifting. China underwrote the research and publication of a major UN report in 2017, spearheaded by Brazilian lieutenant general Carlos Alberto dos Santos Cruz, known as the "Cruz Report" (Cruz, Phillips, and Cusimano 2017). This report advocates a shift away from the "Chapter VI mentality" and toward a more aggressive posture in peacekeeping, where "troops should use overwhelming force and be proactive and preemptive" as a way to safeguard the safety and security of UN troops. Proactive and preemptive force are antithetical to the foundational peacekeeping doctrine of consent, impartiality, and the nonuse of force except in self-defense. It is unclear, as of this writing, the extent to which the Chinese government agrees with Cruz's push to have peacekeepers use force, but it does, generally, fall in line with authoritarian approaches to securing peace.

In sum, China has moved from harboring deep reservations about the UN and peacekeeping to assuming leadership roles in financial contributions, troops, and, possibly, overall administration. Peacekeeping satisfies some of China's material and ideational interests. The question remains, will peacekeeping's normative underpinnings of advancing human rights and democracy survive China's rise?

CONCLUSION: SCENARIOS AND PREDICTIONS

Peacekeeping reflects the will of the majority of the member states in the United Nations, and most importantly, the five permanent, veto-wielding members of the UN Security Council. Without great power agreement, there is no UN peacekeeping. The demand for peacekeeping is not going away any time soon, as wars continue to rage or wind down, mainly in Africa and the Middle East. To what extent will the Western P-3 continue to support China's rise in peacekeeping and its illiberal notions of peace and stability? The Obama administration encouraged China to increase its participation in UN peace-keeping, which meshed well with Chinese president Xi Jinping's UN aspi-rations (Foot 2014; Xi 2017). Since the start of the Trump administration, and its pullback from the UN—mainly in financing—China has sought to fill the void (Gowan 2018; Lynch 2018b). France has resisted a Chinese take-over of the Department of Peacekeeping Operations during the most recent leadership change, but can it hold the line during the next turnover? China's director of peacekeeping in the Ministry of National Defense, Senior Colo-nel Zhou Bo, has argued that China's increased interest in UN peacekeeping is consistent with China's peaceful rise. In his justification, Zhou paraphrases Sun Tzu's axiom that "it is best to subdue one's adversaries without violence" (Zhou 2017). Zhou further contends that greater collaboration between the United States and China on UN peacekeeping could contribute to greater sta-bility in Africa, while simultaneously improving the relationship between the United States and China (Zhou 2017). However, the tools of peace and con-flict diplomacy underpinned by liberal ideas, such as negotiation as a means of fostering democratization after civil wars, will be further eroded in this quest for stability. Thus, it is possible that we could see a strengthened UN, and UN peacekeeping, although not under the premise of liberal internation-alism, suggesting this book's scenario 3, "pragmatic cooperation."

Conversely, if the P-3 decide to resist the spread of China's authoritarian-ism, we may see a world of increasing ideological tension and strengthened states, reverting back to scenario 1, the "discord scenario." The long-standing democratic and human-rights-oriented goals of peacekeeping will come into a direct contest with those of unity, development, and authoritarian control. Although in the past China has often preferred to back down, rather than engage in direct competition on the international stage, it remains difficult to predict the shape and potential outcomes of this contest, especially in the wake of the massive destabilization posed by COVID-19.

NOTES

1. If the United States and China emerge from the COVID-19 pandemic significantly weak-ened and authoritarian-leaning, a coalition of liberal-minded states—including much of Europe, Australia, Japan, and South Korea—may unite. Such a union would most likely not try to work through the United Nations, or on peacekeeping.
2. Note that *impartiality* is distinct from *neutrality*. Like judges in a court of law, peace-keepers are charged with determining when parties violate agreements. Peacekeepers are not supposed to take sides, nor do they remain silent.

3. Although multidimensional peacekeeping and counterinsurgency missions both seek to win over the "hearts and minds" of local populations in order to achieve their goals, counterinsurgency is by definition partial (because counterinsurgents side with the government), deployed without the consent of all parties, and reliant on the use of compellent force. Its basic features thus lie in diametric opposition to the three central elements of peacekeeping.

4. Each citizen starts with 1,000 points. Donating to charity, for example, boots points. Littering, jay walking, fighting, expressing religious sentiment or political dissent, playing video games for too long, or failing to pay a loan on time subtract points. If a person's score falls too far below 1,000, punishments range from, for example, disallowing travel by high-speed rail or plane, inability to access dating websites, limiting school access for children, restricting financial transactions, and incarceration.

5. "Debt trap" diplomacy refers to the process of lending to a developing country in order to build infrastructure, "with the intention of seizing the infrastructure as collateral when the country inevitably defaults on the interest repayment." See Fabricius 2020.

6. I view Russian authoritarianism as a second-order problem. The Russian economy is smaller than that of Italy's, and its military remains weak and poorly organized.

7. See also the 2017 National Security Strategy, and the 2018 National Defense Strategy, which describe China as a "strategic competitor" of the United States.

8. "Ideations" are nonmaterial forces, such as ideas, identity, norms, and culture (Yee 1996).

9. However, France and the United Kingdom did send numerous troops to Bosnia in the early to middle 1990s.

10. China now has peacekeepers deployed in ten of fourteen UN peacekeeping missions. China has deployed at least nineteen separate engineering, helicopter, infantry, transportation, security, and rapid-reaction units (Lanteigne 2018, 4). In 2017, it created its first overseas military base, in Djibouti, which serves as the logistics hub for all of its operations (Neethling 2017).

CHAPTER 14

Nuclear Nonproliferation
at a Crossroads

Toby Dalton

During the coldest days of the Cold War, US and Soviet officials sought means to manage strategic competition, establish international governance of the atom, and avoid a cataclysmic nuclear war. Through bilateral and multilateral diplomacy beginning in the 1950s, the two superpowers led the creation of a nuclear order—an arrangement of states and institutions in the international system based on beliefs about the relationship between nuclear technology and international political power (Dalton, Kassenova, and Williams 2016). This order reached a moment of peak stability in the mid-1990s. Since then, the norms and bargains that underpin the system have come under increasing strain, while stakeholders of the order struggled to address periodic proliferation crises, raising critical questions about the ability of existing institutions to meet future challenges. Future nonproliferation diplomacy will be characterized by tension between states seeking to preserve the existing system, states desiring reform, and states that ignore or neglect the rules.

Reflecting the politics and power dynamics of the Cold War, the nuclear order is fundamentally inequitable. A pillar of this order is the legitimacy granted to 5 states under the Nuclear Non-Proliferation Treaty (NPT) to retain nuclear weapons: the United States, Russia, the United Kingdom, France, and China. (These states are notably also the 5 permanent, veto-wielding members of the UN Security Council, creating a clear linkage between the possession of nuclear weapons and international power and prestige.) The remaining 185 states that are party to the NPT are required to refrain from seeking nuclear weapons. At the fiftieth anniversary of the NPT in 2020, a majority of states show signs of discontent with what is widely perceived to be an unfair order, even as the treaties, agreements, and practices inherent to this order have helped to prevent rampant nuclear weapons proliferation.

Chief among the factors shaping the evolution of nonproliferation diplomacy is the importance of great power cooperation in forming and sustaining the nuclear order. In addition, the way in which institutions and treaties solidified fundamental tensions in the order ensures that so long as nuclear weapons exist, most states will be dissatisfied. Crucially, the interwoven incentive structure established by the nuclear order dampens the potential for systemic collapse—a major breakout, or proliferation "cascade." Yet lagging institutional reform and rising frustration threaten to erode the pillars and devalue the incentives for states not to defect.

How might the evolution of this order shape and channel nonproliferation diplomacy in the three future scenarios this volume explores? The trend lines and analysis given in this chapter suggest a stickiness to the order that could preclude a large wave of proliferation resulting in another half dozen states acquiring nuclear weapons. However, demand for nuclear weapons may still rise, and more states may acquire the technical means to produce nuclear weapons as they hedge national security strategies, forcing states to confront normative decay within the order. For these reasons, a future characterized by strong states and weak international institutions may still see significant interstate cooperation to prevent nuclear proliferation. Conversely, a future in which states vest greater authority in institutions will not be free of tensions that constrain and limit the potential for nonproliferation diplomacy to redress serious grievances and resolve inevitable proliferation crises.

ORIGINS AND ATTRIBUTES
OF THE NUCLEAR ORDER

The institutionalism at the heart of the nuclear order is not especially liberal. The rules and structure were established by and for the big powers and nuclear technology holders, and they have proved relatively immune to reform efforts. Consequently, nonproliferation diplomacy, especially since the mid-1990s, has wrestled with majoritarian efforts to make the system fairer, even as proliferation crises have garnered more attention from the great powers. The resilience of the order, as well as its inability to redress grievances from states that perceive it to be unjust, are artifacts of international conditions at the time of its founding.

The discovery of nuclear fission and resulting scientific efforts to harness its energy for military and civilian purposes coincident with World War II ensured that nuclear competition would become an enduring feature of the US-Soviet competition that emerged from the war's ashes. Though proliferation concerns were clearly present in the first decade of the Cold War, US-Soviet rivalry disrupted efforts to regulate nuclear technology.

Diplomacy to institutionalize a nonproliferation norm began to reach fruition in the late 1950s, even as nuclear technology was spreading rapidly around the globe. The 1962 Cuban missile crisis and other crises spurred US and Soviet leaders to initiate intense negotiations along two axes: bilateral arms limitation to manage strategic competition; and global nonproliferation measures to prevent the spread of nuclear weapons. US-Soviet nuclear diplomacy resulted in a series of foundational bilateral and multilateral treaties and agreements: among others, the Partial and Threshold Nuclear Test Ban Treaties of 1963 and 1974; the creation of the new International Atomic Energy Agency (IAEA) safeguards system to monitor nuclear activity in 1965; the NPT of 1968; the Strategic Arms Limitation Interim Agreement and Anti-Ballistic Missile Treaty of 1972; and the Agreement on Prevention of Nuclear War in 1973. As Steven Miller (2019, 19) observed of this transition period, nuclear disorder gave way to "an increasingly regulated, collaboratively managed nuclear environment in which [US and Soviet] nuclear arsenals were constrained by agreement and the spread of nuclear weapons was inhibited by a negotiated regime rooted in a permanent, legally binding treaty."

When the NPT entered into force in 1970, it established a norm of nonproliferation that tied global security to a shared objective of preventing the further spread of nuclear weapons. Many states view this norm as contingent on what came to be known as the NPT grand bargain. In return for abjuring nuclear weapons, NPT non-nuclear-weapon states (NNWS) secured two promises from the five nuclear-weapon states (NWS). First, the NWS would pursue negotiations on "effective measures relating to the cessation of the nuclear arms race at an early date and to nuclear disarmament" (Treaty on the Non-Proliferation of Nuclear Weapons 1968, Article VI) as well as on a general and complete disarmament treaty. Second, holders of nuclear technology would facilitate "the fullest possible exchange of equipment, materials and scientific and technological information for the peaceful uses of nuclear energy" (Treaty on the Non-Proliferation of Nuclear Weapons 1968, Article IV).

To facilitate peaceful sharing of nuclear technology and nonproliferation, the NPT established two mechanisms that remain among the most important tools in the nonproliferation diplomacy toolbox: IAEA safeguards and nuclear export controls. IAEA safeguards predated the NPT, but the treaty made safeguards a condition of nuclear technology supply, vesting the IAEA with the authority to verify a state's obligations under the treaty to prevent "diversion of nuclear energy from peaceful uses to nuclear weapons or other nuclear explosive devices" (Treaty on the Non-Proliferation of Nuclear Weapons 1968, Article III). In effect, the NPT transfers the responsibility for assessing treaty compliance to the IAEA, on which it can report problems to the UN Security Council under Chapter 7–related peace and security issues (IAEA 1956, Article III.B.4). Additionally, nuclear technology holders established two separate groups—the Zangger Committee and the Nuclear Suppliers Group—to implement the NPT Article III.2 requirement for safeguards on transfers of specific nuclear materials and technologies, and to harmonize export control policies for those technologies (Zangger Committee n.d.; Nuclear Suppliers Group n.d.). By permitting technology holders to set their own rules, however, the NPT created the potential for cartel-like behavior, or at least the perception of it among NNWS.

The NPT's reciprocal commitments binding together nonproliferation, disarmament, and peaceful nuclear uses effectively internalized two tensions within the treaty without resolving either. First, spreading "peaceful" nuclear technology provides states with most of the means to pursue nuclear weapons. Second, states without nuclear weapons agree not to seek them so long as states with nuclear weapons make progress toward giving them up. The treaty provided no criteria for evaluating when a peaceful nuclear program crosses the line into weapons, nor for defining adequate progress by the NWS toward disarmament. Negotiators understood that these gray areas were problematic for enforcing the treaty and ultimately weakened the nonproliferation norm, yet nevertheless were necessary to secure the participation of NWS and NNWS alike.

The US-Soviet condominium alone was not sufficient to convince states to join the NPT and adhere to the nascent nonproliferation norm. For many states, especially in Europe and East Asia, security alliances or other incentives were necessary to garner their commitment not to pursue nuclear weapons. Accordingly, Washington and Moscow gave preferential treatment—security assurances, extended nuclear deterrence, and transfers of sensitive nuclear technology—to their allies and clients, ensuring that the compromises contained in the NPT were complicated further by exceptions and enforcement challenges. Other nuclear technology holders (e.g., Germany, France, and China) shared sensitive equipment and materials with other states, or failed to prevent unscrupulous companies and individuals from profiting through proliferation. By some counts, around thirty states ultimately considered and even experimented with nuclear weapons development before opting not to acquire them (Fuhrmann and Tkach 2015). A few states cheated and were caught, with coercive diplomacy playing an important role in constraining the programs. But neither coercive nor cooperative approaches could prevent determined proliferators. An additional five states eventually acquired nuclear weapons beyond the NPT's five NWS: India, Israel, South Africa, Pakistan, and North Korea.

By the mid-1990s, US-Soviet/Russia efforts (including coercion, cajolery, and bribery) helped form widespread adherence in a regime, with 190 NPT member states today (Coe and Vaynman 2015). As the Cold War ended, several states that had previously eschewed joining opted to sign up. In particular, China's NPT accession in 1992 and promulgation of other antiproliferation measures was a key to consolidating the nonproliferation norm, ensuring that the most powerful states in the international system are aligned in preserving the nuclear order. To the extent that the contemporary order retains its shape and size, therefore, it will be due primarily to the status quo bias resulting from alignment of views and interests among the great powers. Consequently, diplomacy to prevent proliferation, deal with the hard cases, and strengthen existing regimes has and will in the future turn mainly on cooperation among the United States, Russia, and China. At the same time, the defection of just one of these parties from such diplomacy can stymie it—for instance, by wielding a veto in the UN Security Council or withholding support in other institutions that operate on a consensus principle.

The wave of nonproliferation institutionalism that followed the end of the Cold War may ultimately be judged as short-lived. There were some notable successes in the 1990s and 2000s: strengthening of IAEA safeguards; improvement of nuclear export control systems and broadening of membership in / adherence to strategic trade regimes; and high-level summitry and working-level implementation to tighten nuclear security practices and prevent nuclear terrorism. But this same period also witnessed a slow erosion of cooperation among the United States and Russia inside these institutions. Also during this transition period, and driven in particular by the revelations after the 1990–91 Gulf War of Iraq's secret nuclear program, the United States and other Western powers evolved more coercive diplomacy tools, which came to be termed "counterproliferation"—the use of economic sanctions, trade interdiction, and even military force to dissuade states from pursuing nuclear weapons. Counterproliferation actions often elicited sharp criticism from NNWS that championed institutional approaches. As a result, the cleavages among states in the nuclear order have become deeper and wider, posing new and difficult challenges for nonproliferation diplomacy to not only stay abreast of current problems but also prepare for future ones.

TRENDLINES AND DRIVERS

The extent and potential consequences of crisis in the nuclear order is a matter of some debate. Most analysts tend to sound the alarm. The American scholar Nina Tannenwald (2018, 6–7), for instance, argues that "in this emerging nuclear era, key norms that have underpinned the existing nuclear order—most crucially deterrence, non-use and nonproliferation—are under stress. . . . Under pressure from changing military technology and increasing geopolitical tensions, the global nuclear normative order is beginning to unravel." The former Canadian disarmament diplomat Paul Meyer (2017) is more shrill, warning that "today, this [nonproliferation] enterprise is in mortal peril." Even a 2004 report by a high level UN commission—whose publications are not typically known for hyperbole—warns, "We are approaching a point at which the erosion of the non-proliferation regime could become irreversible and result in a cascade of proliferation" (United Nations 2004, 38). Yet such warnings often gloss over state-level factors that suggest a less grim picture. The American nonproliferation expert Lewis Dunn (2010, 193) observes, "expressions of concern about the dangers of runaway nuclear proliferation have again grown in popularity. . . . [But] there are many reasons why one or another country would not seek to acquire nuclear weapons in the next decade plus."

Which of these views proves correct depends on whether key states, on balance, prefer the status quo to the potential chaos that would flow from a collapse of the nonproliferation system. Still, dissatisfaction with perceived inequity in the order has metastasized to nearly every institution and intergovernmental decision-making body in the nuclear order, from NPT Review Conferences to the IAEA Board of Governors. One lagging indicator of this unrest is the negotiation and passage in 2017 of the UN Treaty on the Prohibition of Nuclear Weapons (TPNW, or nuclear ban treaty) despite a boycott by NWS and their allies. Though the order continues to appear rather rigid, the advent of the TPNW indicates at least some potential for disruption and normative change. Five trends bear observation.

First, increasingly fraught strategic relations between China, Russia, and the United States, and divergent diplomatic objectives between the United States and key European and Asian allies, are spilling over into nonproliferation diplomacy. Some of this spillover hampers direct diplomacy on the "hard" cases, namely, Iran and North Korea. Beyond this, Russia's violation of and the United States' withdrawal from the Intermediate-Range Nuclear Forces Treaty—the latter ostensibly over concerns about China's missile buildup in East Asia (Vaddi 2019)—means that the US-Russia New

Strategic Arms Reduction Treaty (New START), which is set to expire in 2021, is the last remaining arms control measure governing strategic competition between the erstwhile Cold War rivals. Power asymmetries and technological advances are making it much harder to conceptualize future arms control regimes that would replace these treaties. The prospective end of US-Russia arms control also removes the one indicator of progress toward and fulfillment of disarmament aspirations embodied in the NPT. This would exacerbate tensions within the NPT grand bargain and amplify the dissatisfaction among many states, especially those in the Non-Aligned Movement, which would rightly question whether the NWS will ever make "good faith" efforts to achieve nuclear disarmament.

Second, memberships, governance rules, and decision-making procedures in multilateral nonproliferation institutions increasingly do not reflect the contemporary global power distribution. The diffusion of power after the Cold War permitted many states to assert greater interest and authority in nonproliferation institutions, the result of which is difficulty in finding sufficient common ground or compromise among expanded memberships. Some institutions, such as the IAEA Board of Governors, began to make more decisions by vote. Others, like the UN Conference on Disarmament (CD) in Geneva and the Nuclear Suppliers Group (NSG), remain bound by a consensus principle. The CD in particular is a cautionary example. The CD serves as the UN's multilateral disarmament negotiating forum, but the last successful nuclear negotiation concluded by the body was the 1996 Comprehensive Nuclear Test Ban Treaty. Most years since, CD members have not been able to agree on a prioritization of issues that could be negotiated, let alone a program of work for the negotiations (Meyer 2009). The diffusion of power is also reflected in the TPNW, an effort by a majority of states to strengthen disarmament norms. The TPNW creates a parallel normative architecture to the NPT that accords no privilege to powerful states. It is therefore doubtful that the NWS will join the prohibition treaty in the near future, though it is possible that the NNWS will opt to leave the NPT in favor of the TPNW, a move cheered by some scholars who argue for a more equitable nuclear order (Pretorius and Sauer 2019).

Third, the desirability of nuclear energy technology among developing states is highly uncertain, while the locus of nuclear technology innovation and associated supply chains is shifting away from traditional Western vendors and toward Russian and Chinese state-owned enterprises. Currently, nuclear energy forecasts suggest a concentration of new reactor construction, mainly in China and India, over the next several decades, and fewer likely new builds among developing countries than had been forecast before the 2011 Fukushima accident (International Atomic Energy Agency 2016). Reduced global demand for nuclear energy could mean less potential for a peaceful nuclear program to provide a cover for nuclear weapons intentions. At the same time, as China and Russia dominate access to new nuclear energy markets, some question whether they will uphold existing nonproliferation standards as conditions of supply, or give preferential treatment to "friends," thus creating more exceptions and double standards in the system (Levite and Dalton 2017). US officials and the nuclear industry often raise these concerns, though their motivations are clearly influenced by competition. To be fair, Russia and China are both members of the NSG and have (with some exceptions in South Asia) tended to uphold its strictures. However, whether they will continue to do so in a future of declining nonproliferation institutionalism or sharper global competition is less clear.

Fourth, sensitive nuclear and missile technologies are nearing ubiquity over time. Partly this is a result of general advances in technology and manufacturing and the spread of these capabilities around the globe. After all, the equipment needed to produce first-generation nuclear weapons is now over seventy years old, hardly at the cutting edge. Today, most countries, if so determined, could acquire and develop the technologies to make nuclear weapons. This ubiquity was demonstrated in the late 1990s and early 2000s by the A. Q. Khan network, which supplied uranium enrichment technology to Iran, Libya, and North Korea, sourced from Pakistan's nuclear program, which was in turn derivative of European technology and suppliers. Khan's cohort procured components from a number of countries (including Malaysia and South Africa) after having transferred the schematics and manufacturing specifications to subsidiaries in those states (Broad, Sanger, and Bonner 2004). Since then, new additive manufacturing technologies have enhanced the potential that some key, hard-to-acquire components could be "printed" from a digital build file, thus bypassing supply chokepoints and controls (Volpe 2019). Arguably, prospective proliferators will have an easier time overcoming technical hurdles than did their predecessors, which started fissile material production programs in the 1960s and 1970s.

And fifth, although transnational civil society activism and middle power diplomacy reached a new threshold with the adoption of the nuclear prohibition treaty in 2017, there are many hurdles to effective nonproliferation activism in the future. Historically, a transient and ephemeral policy space limited the impact of civil society on nuclear policy, and most often consigned it to the margins, given the national security framework within which nonproliferation diplomacy takes place. Periodically, social movements have gained traction to alter the course of policy—such as the nuclear freeze movement in the United States and the European Nuclear Disarmament campaign in Western Europe in the early 1980s, which helped spur renewed US-Soviet arms control negotiations. A new nuclear abolition movement arose after the 2010 NPT Review Conference to pressure nuclear weapon possessors to disarm on the basis of concerns about the potential global humanitarian consequences of nuclear war. The diverse coalition driving the movement featured both middle powers and nonaligned states (led by Norway, Austria, Mexico, Brazil, and Indonesia, among others), backed by the International Coalition Against Nuclear Weapons, which mobilized civil society, youth, and peace groups from around the world. Despite opposition by the NWS, these groups successfully moved the humanitarian consequences of nuclear weapons onto the agenda of the UN General Assembly, which authorized a conference in which UN member states negotiated the TPNW in 2017. The passage of the treaty may be a watershed, permitting civil society to carve out more space to make an impact on nonproliferation diplomacy. Or attention could fade in the face of the practical challenges to implementing and enforcing a ban on nuclear weapons, and the space for civil society may again close.

PROPOSITIONS AND FUTURE SCENARIOS

What do these trends suggest about the conduct of nonproliferation diplomacy in the three alternate future scenarios considered in this volume? As with other functional issues for which states are the primary agents, the limits and possibilities for nonproliferation will depend greatly on both domestic sources of foreign policy and the specific character of interstate relations—especially among the great powers around whose interests the nuclear order was built. For instance, a future characterized by strong states and the adoption of offensive realist strategies by the great powers (scenario 1) could well drive weaker states in the system to seek nuclear weapons for protection, spurring more frequent proliferation crisis. Conversely, a future in which states devolve sovereignty in favor of strengthened international institutions (scenario 2) probably means that fewer states would perceive a need for nuclear weapons, thus limiting the number of future "hard cases" that pose the greatest nonproliferation diplomacy challenge. And a future in which leading powers are able to cooperate in issue-specific concerts, even as bilateral relations remain competitive (scenario 3), may facilitate diplomacy on the proliferation hard cases, and perhaps also allow more space for activism by middle powers and civil society. Following are five propositions about the future that help to clarify where and why nonproliferation diplomacy pathways diverge in these future scenarios.

Security Alliances Are the Most Important
Determinant of Future Proliferation

The small number of cases of states that developed nuclear weapons, standing at just ten, means that generalizing proliferation causality is necessarily problematic. The scholarship on proliferation drivers tends to coalesce around three models for explaining why states pursue nuclear weapons: security; domestic politics; and norms or identity (Sagan 1997). Nonproliferation institutions, however, tend to ignore the variety of motivations for seeking nuclear weapons, and instead work mainly by regulating the supply of nuclear technology and deterring its misuse through international inspections. There are comparatively few tools aimed at minimizing the potential demand for nuclear weapons. At the global level, the norm embodied in the NPT aims to devalue nuclear weapons as a symbol of power. That leaves alliances as the most important means by which states seek to manage potential security-related demand for nuclear weapons. (The second theorized driver, domestic politics, is inherently difficult to mitigate, unlike security and normative rationales.) Indeed, some states expressly use ambiguity about their potential acquisition of nuclear weapons to elicit stronger security commitments or other concessions from security partners (Volpe 2017). Thus, the continuation and health of security alliances in the future will have a big impact on prospective proliferation (Fitzpatrick 2016). This is especially the case for the United States, which extends nuclear deterrence to its NATO allies in Europe, as well as to Japan and South Korea. Apart from Iran, if there is a next proliferator, it would quite likely be a current US ally or partner.

In a future characterized by strong states and autarkic tendencies in the international system (scenario 1), alliances will come under greater strain, and potentially even dissolve. Even if alliances remain in some form, security commitments are likely to be viewed as less credible. As a result, states will probably hedge their security strategies, to include by acquiring a latent nuclear weapons capability through development of the technologies needed to build a nuclear weapon under the guise of peaceful programs. Some may go further, by also creating the political and military infrastructure to induct nuclear weapons if circumstances were to require it, to create a nuclear hedge (Levite 2003). It is notable that the taboo on public debate over potential nuclear weapons acquisition eroded in Germany and South Korea with the rise of doubts about the United States as a security partner under President Donald Trump (Dalton, Byun, and Lee 2016; Kühn, Volpe, and Thomson 2018). It is possible that in either scenario 1 or scenario 3, the United States may opt to "share" nuclear weapons—perhaps an extension of the NATO nuclear-sharing arrangement, or some other model that involves allies in nuclear planning and employment decisions—with additional allies as a means of forestalling their acquisition of an independent nuclear capability. It seems less likely that the United States (or any of the other states with nuclear weapons apart from North Korea) would outright transfer nuclear weapons to a third country. (There are long-standing rumors—though sparse public evidence—of a secret agreement under which Pakistan would transfer nuclear weapons to Saudi Arabia.)

Alliance diplomacy under the more institutionalist future in scenario 2 could look very different. Then, the key question would be less about alliances as a means of mitigating nuclear weapons demand, and more about how to manage divergent intra-alliance views on disarmament commitments and extended nuclear deterrence. Already, the TPNW has prompted such debate in Japan and the Netherlands, which are covered by US extended nuclear deterrence, as well as Switzerland and Sweden, which are not part of NATO but still benefit from its protections by geographic association. In pressuring these governments to sign the TPNW, civil society organizations aim to force US allies to reduce their reliance on nuclear weapons and extended deterrence. However, one possible unintended consequence of a weakening of US extended nuclear deterrence, especially within NATO, may be to drive more European states toward a nuclear hedging strategy.

Great Power Competition Means Less Arms Control and Disarmament, Not Necessarily More Proliferation

Deepening great power competition, to include strategic arms racing unconstrained by bilateral or multilateral restraint regimes, is probable in any conceivable future scenario. Manifest challenges diminish the prospect of the United States, China, and Russia negotiating new types of control arrangements: evolving offensive and defensive technologies, asymmetric power balances, cyber threats and technology entanglements, and shifting from a bilateral to a multilateral configuration. Nuclear arsenals are more poised to grow than shrink in the future.

Assuming this trend holds, even in the most institutionalist future (scenario 2), the prospects for arms control will remain low. To the extent that arms reductions are still viewed by many states as an important proxy for progress toward disarmament, this suggests increasing international discord between the NWS and the NNWS in key nonproliferation forums. In other words, a lack of "good faith" efforts by the great powers on disarmament will hamper efforts to strengthen nonproliferation institutions, reinforcing the existing tendency toward incremental, least-common-denominator change.

Yet, great power competition does not necessarily mean a dearth of great power cooperation on nonproliferation diplomacy. Even as the United States and Soviet Union were engaged indirectly in a war in Vietnam, for instance, their diplomats were negotiating the Nuclear Non-Proliferation Treaty. Apart from the alliance management issues cited above, the incentives for great powers to continue to stymie proliferation efforts will remain. The scenario 3 environment, with episodic cooperation or great power concerts, is already the norm for diplomacy on the hard nuclear cases, such as the Six-Party Talks with North Korea and the EU3+3 negotiations with Iran. Such concerts are likely to continue.

Even in a future system dominated by great power competition (scenario 1), it is imaginable that Washington, Moscow, and Beijing would still seek to prevent other states from acquiring nuclear weapons as a way to maximize national power. The analysis of this scenario turns more on the extent to which they would cooperate to enforce nonproliferation rules, and the tools they might opt to utilize. Unilateral coercive strategies are perhaps more likely than concerts or multilateral approaches in this scenario, which raises questions about the effectiveness of multilateral economic and trade sanctions. If the great powers opt for offensive realism, then it seems plausible that a great power (and of these, most probably the United States, based on historical proclivities) could use military force to prevent proliferation. Further, they may opt for unilateral approaches precisely because sanctions or military force avoid the perceived burdens of a rules-based order.

Nuclear Technology Ubiquity Places Increasing Stress on the Nonproliferation Norm

The number of latent nuclear states is likely to grow in coming years. This projection is based on several linked developments: the spread by the Khan network of the technology and equipment to enrich uranium; the probability that states that procured this technology illicitly would have fewer compunctions about selling it, especially North Korea; the demand for nuclear technology in the Middle East, in particular; and the possible relaxation of some global nonproliferation standards as the commercial market becomes increasingly competitive (Levite and Dalton 2017). More countries are likely to demand access to sensitive nuclear technologies as part of their civil nuclear enterprises in the future, Saudi Arabia being a prominent case in point (El Gamal and Paul 2017). Of course, Saudi officials on numerous occasions have also stated plainly that they would acquire nuclear weapons if Iran does (CBS News 2018). Thus, a rise in nuclear latency, even if the states in question are implementing safeguards and related nonproliferation commitments faithfully, will increase fears that civil nuclear programs are enabling states to "break out" of the NPT and very quickly develop nuclear weapons, thereby eroding confidence in the nonproliferation norm. There could even be a "latency cascade," in which one state's technology status, even if ostensibly peaceful, drives other states to acquire the same capability.

In a future of strengthened global nonproliferation institutions (scenario 2), states may find new means of managing proliferation concerns that stem from an increase in the number of latent nuclear states. In this scenario, IAEA safeguards are more likely to be fully funded and politically supported by key member countries. The agency already devotes more inspection resources to highly latent states, such as Japan, and is evolving its safeguards practices to take account of other potential indicators of nuclear weapons programs beyond its traditional focus on verifying declared nuclear materials. These practices may permit the agency to be more vigilant and provide earlier warning if latent states begin to shift toward nuclear hedging. In addition, whether through formal institutions such as the Nuclear Suppliers Group or through informal means, states may develop additional reassurance mechanisms, such as providing greater transparency on some specific activities of concern (Dalton et al. 2017). As noted above, however, the politics of IAEA safeguards probably preclude further institutional strengthening of the IAEA's mandate to permit it broader inspection rights. Simply put, the NNWS are unlikely to agree to any further increases in safeguards requirements if they perceive it as an effort to limit access to nuclear technology, and probably not without demonstrated progress by the NWS toward disarmament.

In a future dominated by strong states (scenario 1), and especially if it is more autarkic, key nonproliferation institutions will probably lose funding and relevance. Nonproliferation diplomacy, channeled through the remaining institutions, will not prevent an increase in the number of latent nuclear states. Nor is it likely to result in additional tools for managing international concerns about latency, for states would place greater value on protecting their sovereignty than assuaging the fears of others. This is a recipe for faster erosion of the nonproliferation norm.

Nonproliferation Diplomacy Concentrates in Key Regions, Less at the Global Level

Most global nonproliferation diplomacy—whether at the UN General Assembly First Committee, the NPT Review Conference, the CD, or the IAEA Board of Governors—is more performative than substantive. With the recent exception of the TPNW and its preceding conferences on the humanitarian effects of nuclear weapons, regional dynamics are now the most important driver of nonproliferation diplomacy, not global norms and institutions. Whether in South Asia, East Asia, or the Middle East, intraregional security dilemmas feed interest in nuclear deterrence and catalyze the intervention of outside powers. After the Cold War, most nonproliferation diplomacy concentrated on the proliferation "hard cases": India and Pakistan; Iraq; North Korea; and Iran. Today, the nuclearized security spiral in South Asia is deepening to the point of being effectively immune to diplomatic initiatives from outside powers. East Asia features three states with nuclear weapons (Russia, China, and North Korea) and three with high nuclear latency (Japan, South Korea, and Taiwan) whose future status turns mainly on the credibility of US security commitments and extended nuclear deterrence. The Middle East has one state exercising opacity with nuclear weapons (Israel, which all analysts believe possesses them but says it will not be the first to introduce nuclear weapons in the region); one high latency state (Iran); and at least one potential nuclear weapons aspirant (Saudi Arabia). Only Europe, with three nuclear weapon states (France, Russia, and the United Kingdom, as well as US nuclear weapons in NATO), experiences normative disarmament debate amid profound regional security issues.

Different regions are likely to be prominent for nonproliferation diplomacy in each of the future scenarios considered here. In scenario 1 and probably scenario 3, the Middle East could see a proliferation cascade from Iran, to Saudi Arabia, to perhaps others such as Turkey, Egypt, or Syria. (East Asia might also be prominent in scenario 1, depending on whether the United States pulls back from its security alliances as part of a more defensive realist strategy.) Consequently, states will focus nonproliferation diplomacy on managing regional security tensions in the Middle East. Scenario 2, conversely, is a European future. As the center of liberal democratic order, European governments are the presumptive leaders of efforts to mend and strengthen nonproliferation institutions. Yet Europe is also at the center of the global disarmament debate, with parliamentary bodies and civil society groups pressuring their governments to join the TPNW. The tension between these forces indicates that European governments will be both the subject and object of nonproliferation diplomacy in such a future.

Depending on how the diplomacy with North Korea over the future of its nuclear weapons program evolves, this issue could cut different ways in the future scenarios. One plausible outcome is a negotiated constraint on the size and readiness status of North Korea's arsenal, with some measure of international verification activity. It seems less conceivable that North

Korea completely disarms as a result of diplomacy, unless and until there is a more cooperative security system in place on the Korean Peninsula, probably involving confederation of the two Koreas. With Kim Jong Un's consolidation of power in North Korea, that outcome seems increasingly remote. If diplomacy fails, the default condition is a return to deterrence and attempted containment by Washington and Seoul; less likely (though not impossible, especially if accidents or miscalculations are involved) is a United States military operation to denuclearize North Korea (Lewis 2018). In a future of strengthened states (scenario 1), deterrence and containment seem a more likely outcome, with a higher probability that South Korea will also ultimately seek nuclear weapons. A sustainable nuclear restraint agreement with Pyongyang has proved elusive to date, but could be a result in scenario 3, with the great powers using concert diplomacy (both coercive and cooperative) to incentivize North Korean compliance. How this issue plays out in a future of strengthened institutions (scenario 2) is less clear cut, but is likely to be highly frustrating under any circumstances. A negotiated agreement under which North Korea retains nuclear weapons—a de facto recognition of nuclear weapons possession, even if temporally limited—would constitute yet another exception to the norm of nonpossession of nuclear weapons that could bedevil global diplomacy to build institutions. However, an unfettered North Korean nuclear weapons program, and the periodic security crises that would attend this condition, would demonstrate the inadequacies of institutions to address the proliferation hard cases and thus the continuing need for great power coercive diplomacy at the expense of institutions.

Change Agents Must Circumvent Existing Nonproliferation Institutions to Succeed

As a lagging indicator of dissatisfaction with the ability of existing mechanisms to deliver outcomes perceived as just, the TPNW is an important sign of what may come. To establish the nuclear ban, frustrated middle powers and civil society groups built a global campaign and used majoritarian tactics at the United Nations to bypass institutions in which nuclear weapon states wield vetoes, namely, the Conference on Disarmament and the UN Security Council. Future activist coalitions may see in this model a means to work outside the existing nonproliferation system to bring greater disarmament pressure on the NWS and other states that seek the protection of extended nuclear deterrence.

The greatest space available to innovators (or instigators, depending on the perspective) may exist in a future of pragmatic cooperation among states (scenario 3). In such a future, coalitions could form to circumvent efforts by the major powers to protect the status quo. The TPNW is one model for this, but others may be available. It is questionable, however, whether a coalition could deliver significant reform of existing nonproliferation institutions, at least without the acquiescence of the NWS. For this reason, change agents are likely to look for paths outside the existing bodies to create new norms or practices. A major limitation of this approach, however, is that enforcement mechanisms must be tied to the UN Security Council in order to be effective, which again requires the support of the NWS.

A future of increased institutionalism (scenario 2) would still offer space for civil society groups and middle powers to seek change, but they will struggle against the least-common-denominator attribute of diplomacy channeled within existing nonproliferation institutions. Moreover, efforts to build a fairer order will amplify tensions among states over disarmament issues, and especially the failure of the NWS to implement a broad range of disarmament-related steps to which they agreed during the 1995, 2000, and 2010 NPT Review Conferences. If the trend of previous NPT diplomacy continues, it is possible that this impasse would result in nonproliferation institutions functioning less effectively, even in a future of deeper institutionalism.

CONCLUSIONS: RETHINKING THE NONPROLIFERATION DIPLOMACY TOOLKIT

The trends described above suggest substantial challenges ahead for nonproliferation diplomacy, regardless of the future scenario in question. With these challenges in mind, what steps could strengthen the tools and practices that would help mitigate worst outcomes?

First, states should debate whether the consensus principle that beleaguers diplomacy in several institutional contexts should be limited to certain issues or procedural matters, such that states could not block a consensus merely to prevent negotiations. For example, rather than continuing to let the negotiation of a fissile material cutoff treaty remain hostage to the opposition of Pakistan (and perhaps also China) in the Conference on Disarmament, interested states could agree to implement informal measures outside a formal treaty to create a de facto norm. They could also negotiate protocols for sharing information about existing stocks of fissile material, and even interim means of verifying a freeze. This need not be done outside the CD if states could agree on different ways of conducting negotiations under the CD umbrella. A more ambitious option would be to shift a fissile material negotiation to the UN General Assembly and follow the TPNW model, although that could risk the participation of the NWS.

Second, nongovernmental groups and states, including in regional groupings, can increase collaborative work to fill gaps in existing regimes or strengthen key norms. Practically speaking, given the structure of the nuclear order and the advantages it accords the NWS, any global efforts to improve the toolkit must involve at least the tacit support of one or more of the NWS. A useful example in this regard is the International Partnership on Nuclear Disarmament Verification, which brings together technical and policy experts from governments, universities, and research institutions to collaborate on developing technologies and methodologies for verifying key steps in a nuclear disarmament process. Similar efforts could address, for instance, the growing need for reassurance mechanisms to address the insecurity that might flow from an increase in the number of states with high nuclear weapons latency (Dalton et al. 2017). Regional confidence-building measures could be quite useful, including transparency arrangements modeled on the Open Skies Treaty. Small, incremental changes, seeded on a regional basis or via collaboration among states and nongovernmental organizations, could provide much-needed stability.

And third, states must begin to wean themselves from economic sanctions as the default coercive means of deterring nuclear proliferation. Sanctions can be part of a strategy to affect incentives, but they are a wasting asset. Instead, states should explore comprehensive approaches to address the range of plausible proliferation demands. Security alliances can remain an element of such approaches, but they have limitations in regions that are prone to a future proliferation crisis, especially the Middle East.

CHAPTER 15

Great Power Rivalries in 5G Technology Markets

Stacie Hoffmann, Samantha Bradshaw, and Emily Taylor

Peace and conflict diplomacy also play out in the virtual world, where both state and nonstate actors use the Internet to attack others with the aim of causing disruption, undermining democracy and political institutions, but also stealing intellectual property.[1] Because of the Internet's anonymity and the lightning speed of cyberattacks, there are strong incentives for states and other nonstate actors to game the system. Accordingly, it will take a considerable period of time to change state behavior and negotiate new norms and rules that limit or proscribe cyber warfare.

However, there is another dimension to cyber diplomacy and conflict management that warrants close attention, which is reflected in the key business choices that countries are now having to make regarding the adoption of the next generation of technologies to operate mobile networks and the Internet. These technologies are proving to be another major source of friction and contention in international relations. Much of this global contention is centered on 5G networks and the physical equipment, software, technical standards, and business models that will support the fifth generation of wireless communications technologies supporting cellular data networks. The Chinese global information and technologies firm Huawei has developed a commanding lead as a global provider of 5G technologies and networks. This has sounded alarm bells in the United States and other countries about potentially giving China unparalleled access to and control over sensitive data that travels over those networks.

Great power rivalry with respect to 5G presents a fascinating case study of the high politics and diplomatic challenges that now infuse the highly technical and complex world of communications technology. It is a textbook case of the critical, competing strategic choices that many countries are having to make as they struggle with the wider implications of buying and using technologies that may be at odds with their traditional security and intelligence interests and partnerships. The struggle to find a balanced accommodation of mutual economic interests, without compromising fundamental differences on values or genuine security concerns, increasingly presents one of the major challenges of cyber diplomacy and conflict management in today's world. For this reason, a detailed case study of these challenges that is centered on 5G and that explains how great power rivalries have played into the geopolitics of the Internet and communications networks is a valuable complement to the other essays in this volume.

INTRODUCTION

Michael Kovrig, a former Canadian diplomat, has found himself at the center of a geopolitical firestorm. Kovrig was arrested in Beijing in December 2018 by the Chinese authorities for activities that "endanger national security." Interrogated throughout the day, without access to legal advice, held in isolation and barred from taking exercise outdoors, Kovrig's arbitrary detention has caused deep concerns among Canadian officials (Vanderklippe 2019).[2] His arrest came days after Canadian officials detained Meng Wanzhou, the chief financial officer of the Chinese telecom giant Huawei, for extradition to the United States on charges of conspiracy to violate American sanctions on Iran and theft of a competitor's intellectual property: "Tappy" the robot, developed by TalkTalk. Analysts have suggested that Kovrig's detention was a tit-for-tat retaliation for the arrest of Meng, but China has denied this. Huawei and Meng deny the charges, and a senior spokesperson called the indictments "unfair and immoral," urging the United States to stop the "unreasonable suppression" of the telecommunications company (*Guardian* 2019).

Since then, the cadence of strike and counterstrike between China and the United States has not abated. In March 2019, Huawei issued proceedings against the United States, claiming that US import laws are unconstitutional. In May, President Trump declared a national security state of emergency, and added the company to a US Entity List barring the supply of US-origin technology to Huawei. What had been a public dispute intersecting with key moments in complex trade negotiations between the two nations rapidly spread through international supply chains. Intended or not, the US government was imposing its will on the rest of the world by means of alarmist rhetoric and long arm regulatory measures.

The diplomatic fireworks underscore long-standing tensions about trade, intellectual property, international competition, and national security. But they also highlight great power rivalries currently being fought in cyberspace. The fight threatens to undermine the evolving global dialogue on legitimate national security concerns related to the deployment of 5G networks and the critical services they will support. Enveloping 5G in the wider power struggle risks drowning out significant and documented concerns of particular companies' security practices and accountability structures—most notably Huawei and ZTE.

The US strategy in this diplomatic chess match is unclear. The white noise from trade negotiations, intellectual property theft, detainments, and sanctions has prevented the US from articulating a convincing "clear and present danger" regarding 5G technologies. This impairs the country's ability to make the case for an American-led international order as it did in the Cold War (Trubowitz and Harris 2019). The US has also failed to recognize that for other countries, the reality of an outright Huawei ban may not be practical, or even possible, due to existing networks and nations' bilateral trade and diplomatic relationships. As a result, the United States is impairing wider, internationally coordinated engagement on the issue.

The US administration's erratic interventions have impoverished an important public debate, placed stress on long-standing alliances such as the Five Eyes, and risk alienating a cross section of nations sympathetic to Western values and approaches to Internet governance. As a result, the United States is missing an opportunity to highlight benefits of Western-built (and largely non-American) communications networks while advising on risks associated with particular vendors or approaches to 5G. Instead, by drowning out allies' evidence-based inputs, the United States is isolating itself and preventing other like-minded nations from joining in the discussion constructively. A worst-case scenario could ultimately be a fractured Internet based on the 5G technology nations choose to adopt at the application and bespoke network layers.

As states struggle for power in cyberspace, many of the traditional structures and norms that shaped the Internet thus far are under pressure (O'Hara and Hall 2018). Although there has been progress in establishing high-level principles, most states have yet to turn these commitments into national practices, and recent global efforts have highlighted more differences than common approaches (Hitchens and Gallagher 2019).[3] The situation vis-à-vis 5G—its physical equipment, software, technical standards, and the business models that underpin its global rollout—has become a lightning rod for these international power struggles.

The way in which 5G is developed and implemented could have significant implications for the future of the open Internet, the norms and rules that govern it, and the ideological assumptions hidden deep within its technical infrastructure. At the national level, a delay in the adoption of new 5G technologies may also result in reduced economic development at home, harm to local industries' ambitions in international markets, and delayed economic and social benefits. The case of 5G also surfaces long-standing international tensions surrounding US dominance of key Internet systems and conflicting visions for the future of Internet governance: whether that is an open, multistakeholder approach or a closed, top-down approach led by government. Taking a play from the United States' playbook of global tech monopolies, China is attempting to shift this balance in its favor by creating a vertically integrated 5G monopoly.

This chapter looks at three facets of these geopolitical struggles. The first section presents 5G technology and how this could have an impact on Internet governance and existing relationships and roles of stakeholders. The second section considers national security issues related to 5G through two lenses: cybersecurity and local/global markets. The third section contrasts Chinese and Western approaches to technology and 5G development, elucidating the wider geopolitical landscape of the current dispute.

The battle over 5G development is being played out as a zero-sum game, particularly by the United States and China. The resulting technological cold war could hinder local development and the adoption of 5G, create new fracture points for the Internet, and weaken the security of networks and services it enables ("Best of Today" 2019).

INTERNET GOVERNANCE AND THE POLITICS OF 5G

Once the preserve of arcane processes involving multistakeholder groups, Internet governance used to be reassuringly boring. With the arrival of 5G, it has suddenly become a crucible for geopolitics and great power rivalries.

Internet Governance, Standards, and 5G

The Internet is not a single homogeneous network, but instead is an ecosystem comprising technology, software, hardware, content, and institutions—which 5G is set to disrupt. The design and implementation of these infrastructures are not neutral, but instead reflect particular economic interests or social values held by the engineers who design them (Bradshaw and DeNardis 2018; Lessig 2006; Winner 1980; Zittrain 2008).

For most of the Internet's existence, its values were shaped by engineers, educational consortiums, government institutions, and commercial forces located in Western democracies. There have been long-standing concerns over US dominance of the Internet, its legal environment, support for multistakeholder governance, and values such as privacy and freedom of speech (Abbate 1999; Goldsmith and Wu 2006).[4] One example was the perceived influence of the US government over the International Corporation for Assigned Names and Numbers before the Internet Assigned Numbers Authority transition. Frustrated by the decentralized and multistakeholder approach to Internet governance, some governments—including authoritarian regimes—have been advocating for state-led multilateral approaches through the United Nations and its specialized agency, the International Telecommunications Union (ITU).

In essence, it is not uncommon to debate the influence that a technology's "home" environment and legal structure have on an organization and its impact on trust (Marks 2019). With a new, Chinese, leader in 5G, Chinese vendors are now being placed under similar scrutiny from government and industry as American technologies and industry have previously experienced, particularly in a post-Snowden era. Western commentators are skeptical of the accountability and transparency of companies with opaque legal structures, operating within a single-party authoritarian state, shielded from Western free market dynamics. With 5G promising to connect more people, things, and services than ever, it would only make sense that Chinese technologies reflect a Chinese approach, including reinforced government control over the Internet, data, information, and even users. The example of the Chinese Social Credit System enabled by the digital economy illustrates that there is no guarantee that Chinese-origin technologies embody Western values (Liang et al. 2018).

Shorthand for "fifth-generation" mobile networks, "5G" is the baseline standard that will revolutionize mobile networking technologies. Like the previous 4G and 3G technologies, 5G is a technical standard that connects devices to a network. But whereas previous technologies supported handset-to-handset voice and data communication (figure 15.1), 5G is being designed to handle the connection of billions of devices and data transfer at much faster and more reliable rates. In practical terms, this will mean a proliferation of masts, aerials, and connected devices from CCTV, to drones,

Figure 15.1 A 4G City: Traditional Connectivity Infrastructure with Cables and Towers

Figure 15.2 A 5G City: New 5G Mobile Infrastructure with More Masts,
Aerials, and Connected Things

wearables, connected cars, refrigerators, game consoles, and robots (figure 15.2). 5G will become the technical foundation upon which we carry out our daily lives, not just as technology users but also as citizens and participants in society.

5G also represents the evolution of telecommunications architecture from static networks of wires and switches to responsive, high-powered computers

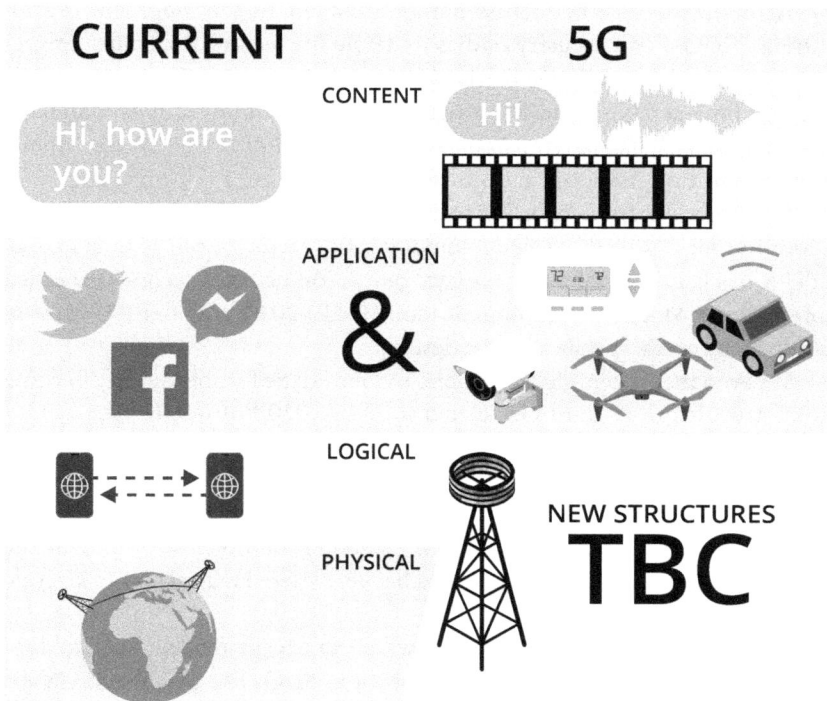

Figure 15.3 Internet Layers

and networks managed by software. Ultimately, 5G is resulting in a consolidation of the Internet's layers, bringing physical, logical, and, in some cases, application layers closer in proximity. The ways in which the Internet's layers are realigned will largely be affected by a particular deployment of 5G. Figure 15.3 shows the consolidation of the logical and physical layers that is likely to occur in most instances.

The development and testing of 5G is carried out by a constellation of actors including operators, equipment and parts providers, governments, and other interested stakeholders.[5] China's Huawei alone invested about 89.7 billion yuan (about $13.4 billion) in research and development in 2017 ("Research & Development" 2017). A leader in 5G technology, Huawei aims to have stand-alone 5G deployment by 2020, five years ahead of the rest of the world (Triolo, Allison, and Brown 2018). Western telecommunication equipment manufacturers—such as Ericsson, Nokia, and Qualcomm—had been leading the way developing patents but were recently eclipsed by Huawei (Pohlmann 2018).

Actors come together across numerous standards development organizations (SDOs) and industry bodies to define the technical specifications of 5G. Some important SDOs in this space include the 3rd Generation Partnership Project (3GPP) and the European Telecommunications Standards Institute, as well as industry bodies such as the Global System for Mobile Communication Association (GSMA).[6]

Governments are negotiating technical specifications and radio spectrum allocation for 5G in the Radiocommunication Sector of the ITU (ITU-R). ITU-R has launched a project on next generation network technology called International Mobile Telecommunication (IMT)-2020, and 3GPP is contributing the technical specifications it develops.

Yet even these seemingly technical and mundane forums quickly become politicized. Work in the ITU related to IMT-2020 but outside the ITU-R sector, such as edge computing and network management, are primarily steered by just China and South Korea. This is giving China the opportunity to legitimize and promote its own flavor of 5G (Lazanski 2019b). In addition, China has created its own IMT-2020 Promotion Group outside the ITU for "research and international exchange," where Huawei plays a key role (Huawei 2018).

The choice of standards bodies in which to engage reflects stakeholders' and states' ideology. Concentrating on work in SDOs like 3GPP and GSMA reflects a preference for industry-led and a multistakeholder approach to standards setting (a Western preference), while working in bodies like the ITU reflects a preference for a government-led and multilateral approach (favored by those wanting greater state control over the Internet) (Lazanski 2019b). A summary of these initiatives and their key 5G work is given in table 15.1.

The Politics of 5G

This subsection highlights five ways in which 5G is susceptible to politics: the impact of standards on security, the adaptive nature of the network, net neutrality, competition policy, and intellectual property.[7] Each element is discussed in turn.

First, we look at the manner in which 5G technologies are elaborated through standards. Acting as the foundation of a technology, standards development embeds a range of public interest issues, including security and others explored in this section. With an untold number of devices and types of data connected by 5G, there are increased risks of data theft, espionage, or compromise with real-world physical effects—particularly if technology is not developed with such issues in mind. Accordingly, the politics of 5G

Table 15.1 Where Are 5G Standards Being Developed?

Body	5G-Related Work
3GPP	Developing technical specifications for 5G (so-called non-stand-alone and stand-alone specifications[a]).
ITU-R	Negotiating technical specifications and international regulations for harmonized radio spectrum use for 5G.
ETSI	Developing standards for technologies that will enable and optimize 5G, such as network function virtualization, multiaccess edge computing, next-generation protocols, and millimeter-wave transmission.[b]
GSMA	Developing frameworks, guidance, and best practices through industry collaboration on key 5G topics, such as migration to virtual networks,[c] security,[d] and spectrum policy.[e]

Note: 3GPP = 3rd Generation Partnership Project; ITU-R = Radiocommunications Sector of the International Telecommunications Union; ETSI = European Telecommunications Standards Institute; GSMA = Global System for Mobile Communication Association.
a. Non-stand-alone 5G specifications are designed to use existing 4G LTE infrastructure for 5G mobile communications, whereas stand-alone specifications support 5G independent of existing 4G technology and were due for release in early 2020.
b. ETSI n.d.
c. GSMA 2018.
d. GSMA n.d.
e. GSMA 2019.

security are not only about confidentiality, integrity, and the availability of information and resiliency of networks but also about the protection of the underlying services that 5G enables. 5G is not only susceptible to the same variety of threats as any system connected to the Internet, but also introduces a broader range of security threats to communications networks. Standards play a vital role in mitigating the risks posed by these threats.

Second, 5G converges computing and communications, pushing network intelligence closer to the "edge" of the core network.[8] Intelligence in the core of the network, supported by massive data centers, will manage and configure the network in real time to optimize efficiency—making it responsive instead of static.[9] As a result, there are greater opportunities for censorship and control over specific segments of the network: rather than cutting access to the entire Internet, specific neighborhoods, government offices, or businesses could be isolated or targeted.

Third, 5G manifests the most recent reincarnation of contentions surrounding net neutrality (Crawford 2018) and fundamentally changes business models (Obiodu and Giles 2017). For example, mobile operators' business models are shifting toward those of connectivity and cloud service providers, increasing operators' control over networks and services. Networks will be run and managed by software (a software-defined network) and hosted by large data processing centers (e.g., Amazon Web Services). Connectivity, platforms, or services will be leased out to or resold by third parties—like a smart city, health care services, or content providers like Netflix. The focus will shift from individual consumers, to new business-to-business service models. This could result in prioritizing certain companies' speeds and services over others, distorting the marketplace.

Fourth, 5G technology embeds issues related to competition policy. The shift from network provider to service provider creates an attractive, vertically integrated business model, where an operator becomes the intermediary between hardware, software, network management, and services. Tech companies with a diversified portfolio, like Huawei, are in good standing to provide a full end-to-end solution for business and consumer alike. This could result in the rise of a vertically integrated, global 5G tech monopoly or further entrench existing dominant market positions.

Fifth, although 5G's initial technical specifications are open and freely available, intellectual property for hardware and software still plays a key role.[10] This potentially impairs traditional Internet values around permissionless innovation, leading to disputes over intellectual property rights and access to information. Firms are rushing to register patents which can generate future revenue streams, help secure a dominant position in 5G markets, and generate ongoing revenue from infrastructure maintenance and support.

Although 5G equipment procurement and standards development might appear to be neutral, 5G represents a fundamental evolution of the underlying architecture of the Internet. Importantly, its rollout is tightly coupled with questions surrounding the ideological dominance and governance structures of an Internet that will support future connectivity and critical services, which many in the West have taken for granted. This evolution also creates new stress points—for example, at the network edge and spectrum use—that could fracture the current global Internet ecosystem. It is not surprising, then, that diplomacy is strained when the stakes are high for both states and domestic industry—including first-mover advantage, economic growth, intellectual property ownership, and resources required to deploy 5G networks.

5G and National Security

In Western media, much of the political positioning around 5G is framed around fears over political and corporate espionage via backdoors and the threat of withholding intelligence from allies (Bryan-Low et al. 2019; Lecher 2019). Though these positions are sometimes motivated by genuine security concerns, they are sometimes co-opted to cloak protectionist measures in response to international economic power struggles (Steinbock 2017). Unfortunately, stress is being placed on existing alliances, disengaging and alienating much of the world from the discussion. As nations become reliant on digital technologies, 5G will be integral to national well-being and security.

The next section explores national security concerns into two buckets: cybersecurity; and economic concerns—primarily local industry and access to foreign markets.[11] The aim is to understand where risk really lies in the 5G ecosystem, not only those fears expressed in the media. Admittedly, China is one of many possible threat actors in such scenarios, but there are particular factors that highlight the potential negative impact on national security of a global Chinese leader in 5G.

CYBERSECURITY AND 5G

The 3GPP and its international membership of industry and national partners (including the United States and China) has adopted a "security-by-design" approach to developing 5G technical specifications.[12] This means that security tools are being built into the technology—something that was not done for earlier mobile technologies. However, security-by-design alone will not resolve the security conundrum. Standards can still contain in-built security flaws or unexpected side effects and will not address all future threats. Additionally, some governments and other actors deliberately interfere with standard-setting processes and networks to advance their interests (Parton 2019).

Governments must consider long-term effects of today's decisions. 5G will support critical infrastructure and services in an increasingly unknown environment due to bespoke deployments and responsive networks. Therefore, procurement choices for 5G infrastructure need to take into account both immediate concerns such as social and economic development and long-term issues like commercial relationships with third parties. A key difference between building communications networks and other physical infrastructure (e.g., roads) is required, constant, and highly specialized maintenance and support. In addition to supply chain concerns—in which China plays a key role—security complexities are augmented by 5G. These include unique and widespread deployments of high-capacity computers, the software-based core network's susceptibility to cyberattacks (e.g., malware), the reduced effectiveness of traditional risk mitigation techniques (e.g., product and systems testing), and an increased attack surface.[13]

Unlike previous networks that relied heavily on hardware, 5G will be primarily software-based, run and managed in a cloud environment. This opens the entire network to new sources of cyberattacks.[14] Recent years have seen a ramping up in the severity of cyberattacks—including the NotPetya, Wannacry, and Mirai attacks—disrupting websites and services. However, an attack on 5G could lead to physical harms, and disrupt a wider range of critical services, such as the network management servers, a factory network, or a city's transportation system.

Due to the nature of 5G, the attack surface is significantly greater than previous networked technologies.[15] It is projected that there will be twenty times more radio antennae to relay information, each representing a potential source of vulnerability (Crawford 2018). This will increase the threat from devices connected to and data on the network, putting the services and systems the network enables at risk. For example, a compromised smart water supply system could result in contaminated water and public health issues.

Securing 5G systems will require specialized tech firms to have ongoing access to networks, software, and data processing centers—bringing with it opportunities for bad actors to exploit those networks for strategic gain (Hemmings 2018). Governments are questioning the degree to which a single provider should be entrenched in critical national infrastructure. A lack of component diversity will increase the risk of a single point of failure. Network equipment can be a backdoor in itself, potentially giving vendors access to data, information, services, and systems (Cerulus 2017). Additionally, 5G could allow for more targeted manipulation of that network. Though it will be difficult to build a 5G network without Huawei, the principle of purchasing parts from rival suppliers supports resiliency and protects against a single point of failure ("Huawei is at the Centre" 2019).

Every system will have bugs and vulnerabilities that can be exploited by adversaries ("Huawei is at the Centre" 2019). Edward Snowden revealed that the United States hacked Chinese telecommunications firms and the network backbone of Tsinghua University (Lam and Chen 2013). China is alleged to have siphoned off data from the African Union's networks to China for years—networks built, paid for, and managed by Chinese companies including Huawei (Fidler 2018). Regardless of intention, the fact it took so long to identify this security flaw calls into question the quality of Huawei's security practices.

Mitigating risks will be more difficult with 5G. Testing and monitoring is a common risk mitigation technique for systems and equipment and adds a degree of protection from supply chain exploitation (Schneier 2018). The UK's Huawei Cyber Security Evaluation Centre (HCSEC) was built for this purpose. Although there are different views on the HCSEC's effectiveness, it provides an evidence-based, technical assessment of networks and components ("FCC Proposes to Protect" 2018; Intelligence and Security Committee 2013).

However, existing testing and monitoring programs will not be as effective for 5G (Donaldson 2018). First, there is the challenge of inspecting an enormous volume of code for vulnerabilities or defects—which in itself could take years to analyze. Furthermore, "developer's advantage" makes it more difficult for customers (i.e., governments and operators) to analyze the code. Testing reviews a system at a particular point in time, but 5G will be constantly adapting, and seemingly mundane maintenance such as software updates can cause unforeseen issues or be used for malicious purposes (Lin 2019). Security evaluations also fail to address deployment diversity—a key aspect of 5G—which can affect the behavior of a device or system (Donaldson 2018; Rogers and Ruppersberger 2012).

In any industry there is a difference in quality and company culture between vendors, both of which have a direct impact on product resilience and incident response. Although Chinese officials try to downplay the issue, there is plenty of evidence related to Huawei's substandard security and support practices (Lin 2019). The United Kingdom's HCSEC and Australian government have voiced concern over the company's products and processes following technical reviews (Huawei Cyber Security Oversight Board 2019; Fifield and Morrison 2018). NCSC's technical director, Ian Levy, called Huawei equipment "shoddy" and its engineering outdated, both of which impacts the resiliency of the network (Hancock 2019). Instead of highlighting security concerns substantiated by testing and experience, the media has focused on economic power struggles, claims of sanctions violations, and corporate espionage. In contrast, the United States' approach of scare-mongering and threatening allies without highlighting hard evidence has been unhelpful. Ultimately, the global dialogue on 5G cybersecurity has been undermined by making the debate irrelevant to the vast majority of countries around the world—and is partially due to a lack of coherent strategy and evidence by the loudest voice, the US government.

MARKETS, STANDARDS, AND 5G

China is poised to assume first-mover advantage in 5G technology. This is buoyed by the fact that Chinese companies have the resources—including a favorable regulatory structure and financial capital—to run large 5G test beds, tightly control supply chains, develop vertical markets, and access a wide variety of global markets. In technology markets, first-mover advantage generally leads to a winner-takes-all scenario, due to economies of scale, network effects, and switching costs—factors that help to explain why the race to 5G has become a zero-sum game (Barwise 2018). 5G will bring decades of vendor lock-in for critical infrastructure providers. It could also result in walled gardens of devices and services; capture of markets; further reduction in market competition; and the emergence of a vertical, Chinese 5G tech monopoly.

The emerging 5G ecosystem is already hardening preferred business models. Huawei, with its ability to bundle 5G-enabled services and network solutions, is an attractive prospect and moves the world toward a more concentrated 5G marketplace. Paired with vendor lock-in, a generation would be enough time for tech companies like Huawei to effectively quash foreign competition—particularly if markets are not carefully protected from distortion, and local research and development is not sufficiently supported.

Some experts wonder if Western companies should adopt a riskier strategy, such as leapfrogging to 6G innovation. 6G, the name given to the next-but-one technology, will further develop 5G software and services while using 5G infrastructure. However, this risky strategy could result in Western companies losing existing market shares in Internet infrastructure. In addition, the West would still need to engage in and devote resources to technology development and standardization to protect national interests, such as spectrum allocation and future market share.

Critical 5G spectrum allocation negotiations at the ITU's World Radio Congress in November 2019 were to highlight points of contention in 5G standards development. In 5G, different spectrum ranges can be given priority for core communications or supplemental use cases. The choices will make an impact on the technical requirements for network equipment and devices connecting to the network, which could be another fragmentation point (Obiodu and Giles 2017). Unsurprisingly, the United States, China, and other countries are at loggerheads on the exact ranges to allocate.[16]

Although a fracture point in spectrum allocation increases the threat of a splinternet, more likely is a geopolitical division in markets for the hardware and software of Internet infrastructure. This would result in reduced access to some markets for Western equipment providers, especially in the developing world. It would also relegate China's market access to developing countries and states that prefer Internet governance to be done along the lines of the ITU's "UN bloc politics," as opposed to the open, industry-led, multistakeholder approach supported by Western countries and the 5G models they promote (Nye 2014, 7).

Competing visions of the Internet are echoed in the standards development process and reflected by the SDOs or technical groups specifically chosen by different parties. There are long-standing concerns related to SDOs being used as a political tool to build in vulnerabilities, sabotage standards, or make design decisions to benefit specific stakeholders (Forrell and Solaner 1986; Wessel 2019). More recently, it has emerged that China is increasing participation in and acquisition of key roles in intergovernmental and standards bodies—such as the United Nations, ITU, Internet Engineering Task Force (IETF), and 3GPP—in order to fast-track their own "flavor" of Internet technology, legitimize the corresponding standards, and sell it to the world (Lazanski 2019a; Okano-Heijmans, van der Putten, and van Schaik 2018).

Such an alternative Internet governance model would give certain governments and industry players greater control over citizens' data, impair access to information, and have a chilling effect on expression. Chinese approaches to Internet technology include centralized and indiscriminate data aggregation, increased control over aspects such as user profiles or information flows, and social engineering tools such as China's highly criticized Social Credit System and surveillance technology used to monitor minorities (Byler 2019; Lazanski 2019a). These attributes are particularly attractive to authoritarian governments (e.g., in the Gulf) that have long been fighting for greater control over the Internet and access to user data and profiles—effectively reinforcing digital divides between Internet users based on access to information or services and human rights protections.

Western governments have an interest in protecting market access and local industry to avoid a 5G marketplace dominated by Chinese-origin technology. China has proved successful at building globally competitive indigenous companies. Part of this is thanks to a decline in Western equipment and network technology providers—which many attribute at least in part to Huawei's growth in global market share.[17] As a resulting effect of smaller market shares and revenues, Western companies are unable to allocate sufficient resources on research and development to maintain their competitiveness with Chinese actors. Chinese companies also have an uncanny ability to undercut the competition by offering network equipment at half the price of its competitors, such as Ericsson and Nokia. Critics claim that this amounts to predation, enabled by China's "illegal government subsidies" and stolen intellectual property (Tong 2019).

Predatory market practices do not fully account for Huawei's competitive edge. China's foreign development Belt and Road Initiative enables access to markets and bundling networks with other Belt and Road Initiative projects. China, through a patient, long-term strategy, is creating an asymmetric market environment by using its power to bind nations to its financial and technological solutions (Manuel 2017). The Belt and Road Initiative has built networks across Africa, South America, and Asia. Sometimes this is paired with anticompetitive lending practices backed by Chinese state-owned banks. For example, in Mexico a 1 percent interest loan with the Bank of China was offered if 80 percent of the funding was spent with Huawei when building a 4G network (Johnson 2019). In Brazil, Huawei bid on a radio network project and provided the broadband network, service, and support at no extra charge—effectively locking in a generation of Brazil's Internet technology (Johnson 2019).

Although contracts with Chinese companies may not require substantial investment at the outset, the potential long-term effect paints a different picture. China has been called out for its predatory loan practices that undermine sustainable financing and often result in China's acquisition of valuable national resources (Hurley, Morris, and Portelance 2018). For instance, China has assumed shares of a Sri Lankan port in return for $584 million in debt forgiveness (Sirilal 2018). This could foreshadow further absorption of key national resources by Chinese entities, which may then be used to float its own complex economy if and when other at-risk countries fall short on debt repayment.[18]

The evidence suggests that China is pursuing a multipronged strategy whose medium-term objective is to lock out foreign 5G competition internationally. Key levers include generous information and communication technology infrastructure projects, and the bait-and-switch lending practices described above. The strategy is supported by the dwindling number of network equipment providers.[19] Resulting effects include the widespread uptake of technologies that reflect Chinese approaches to Internet governance and disregard for international human rights frameworks. This could result in the fracturing of Internet technologies at the spectrum and services layers, while a global monopoly tolls the bell for non-Chinese competitors.

NATIONAL STRATEGIES AND 5G

Economic stability and national security are increasingly linked by governments, with technology billed as a key supporting factor (*Lawfare* 2018a, 2018b). In the case of China, a long-view foreign policy is intertwined with national policy, using foreign markets and assets to build local economic stability and increase global power. This is in contrast to the United States, where national policy informs foreign policy but is largely reflective of—and changes with—the party politics of the president. As the world becomes ubiquitously connected, the ability to disentangle the technical from the political is increasingly difficult. With international economic rivalries manifesting in 5G, governments are tasked with making decisions—and alliances—that will make an impact on local industry, critical infrastructure, and citizens for years to come.

Chinese Approaches

Historically, China is known as a major manufacturer and exporter of goods, but also for corporate espionage, protectionist policies, government influence in private industry, and its Great Firewall.[20] Over the past twenty years, China has adopted a strategic focus on diversifying its economy to include digital technology innovation and exporting.[21] Development targets include plans to be 70 percent self-sufficient and hold a dominant position in global trade—highlighting the entanglement between national and foreign strategies (McBride and Chatzky 2019).

Supporting China's ambitions is a complex weave of public-private relationships, national policies, and foreign development enacted through various forms of soft and hard power. These policies have a direct impact on the development of 5G and related markets through intellectual property, technical standards, and competition policy. Although Western countries also take measures to support local industries, they are more transparent and within the bounds of internationally agreed-on norms (e.g., rules from the World Trade Organization, or WTO). A closer look at China's strategy uncovers a more complex and multilayered approach in an attempt to skirt those same norms while maintaining the facade of complying with international rules-based systems (McBride and Chatzky 2019). It is not difficult to imagine the successful implementation of China's strategies resulting in a vertically integrated global tech monopoly—echoing the emergence of American tech monopolies and their role in shaping today's Internet. China does not intend to relinquish its current level of control over the Internet with the adoption of 5G, and Chinese-origin technologies should be considered within this light.

Opaque Public-Private Relationships

Deliberate actions taken by the Chinese government to support innovation, manage local markets, and skew foreign markets have been described as "political engineering" (Rosen and Kennedy 2019). Strong government influence is also reflected in China's authoritarian approach to Internet governance, characterized by pervasive surveillance and promotion of "government micromanagement of the Internet" (O'Hara and Hall 2018, 8). Close coordination between industry and government, including civil-military integration, remains opaque (Cheung 2018, 321). Huawei is a key market actor in this arena, focusing on Chinese approaches to data, infrastructure, and cloud security. It is one of ten firms that account for 40 percent of the national cybersecurity market (Cheung 2018). Chinese companies that do not follow the appropriate line in international forums risk difficulties back home. In 2016, Lenovo initially voted for a US-origin (Qualcomm) technology being developed for 5G by the 3GPP; but this vote was switched in the final round after public, and likely government, pressure to support Huawei's standard (Hersey 2018). The public-private relationship is worsening the business climate in China for foreign firms, and the country's relationship with other nations (McBride and Chatzky 2019; Zarroli 2019).

Additional insight into the blurring boundaries between public and private in China can be gained from examining the flow of financial capital through government subsidies, as well as diversified funding streams, including venture capital, private equity investors, and stock markets (Kennedy 2017, 18).[22] These financial links can be exploited to exercise soft power on private industry (Intelligence and Security Committee 2013; Rogers and Ruppersberger 2012). Huawei usually counters claims of government ties with carefully worded statements about employee ownership and the absence of government on its board (Huawei 2019). However, during an investigation of Huawei by the US government in 2012, internal company documentation was deemed "state secret," and Huawei reported a Chinese Communist Party Committee within the company—a common occurrence in China (Johnson et al. 2019; Rogers and Ruppersberger 2012). More recently, in June 2019 China requested a stop to a WTO review of its market economy status—a battle China was losing—brought forward by the United States and the European Union (Miles 2019c). Overall, the secrecy around Huawei's business practices have made it difficult to determine the relationship between state and firm. This heightens Western distrust of claimed separation between public and private entities, particularly in light of recent changes to national security policies.

National Policies, Strategies, and the Technology Industry

Over the past two decades, a raft of national policies and strategies have been put in place to proactively foster, promote, and protect the technology sector. These well-documented protectionist policies effectively promote local providers and disadvantage foreign investors, and they have implications for privacy and access to data (Hoffman and Kania 2018; Sacks 2018). Policies support key emerging technologies—including 5G, artificial intelligence, the Internet of Things, and facial recognition. On the international stage, this national strategy has resulted in increased involvement of Chinese tech players in international SDOs, and the holding of strategic positions within those organizations. Strategies include:

- Intellectual property ownership through research and development, mergers and acquisitions, joint partnerships, or technical standardization;
- Support for strategic industries including funding, market restructuring, and manipulation;
- Use of competition policy and national security rhetoric to promote local companies and constrain foreign competition (Kennedy 2017);[23] and
- Building Internet infrastructure (e.g., as part of the Belt and Road Initiative) globally.

China's recently enacted Cybersecurity Law (2017), requires data localization, restricts cross-border data flows, and requires technology reviews for foreign firms (Cheung 2018, 322). To comply, foreign companies need to form partnerships with local data storage providers or build their own local resources. Both require the handing over of proprietary information (e.g., data, hardware, and software) for review, risking the potential loss of privacy and intellectual property. An additional impact is the loss of business for entities located outside China, such as those providing data analysis or cloud services, thus constricting the global marketplace.

The drive to develop indigenous intellectual property is a common thread in China's recent policies.[24] Paired with the technical standards, this would enable the mass exporting of a Chinese approach to Internet technologies. Combined, Chinese entities currently own 10 percent of new 5G intellectual property (IP), compared with only 7 percent in total for the predecessor 4G technology (Scott 2018).[25] The Chinese share of 5G IP is likely to grow. This could result in even cheaper Chinese products, reduced royalty payments and reliance on imported IP, increased inward flow of capital by foreign adoption of Chinese IP, and less reliance on global supply chains susceptible to geopolitics (Cheung 2018, 311). These market advantages will be mirrored by increased costs to foreign competitors of integrating a de facto standard based on Chinese IP, and governments like that of the United States having one fewer bargaining chip with China.

Western countries have reacted to the Chinese strategies by blocking certain acquisitions. The United States blocked the acquisition of Qualcomm by a Singaporean firm for fear it would move a key tech industry away from the United States, and closer to Beijing (Rushe 2018). Germany also blocked the Chinese acquisition of a machine tool manufacturer, noting concern over strategic foreign takeovers pursuant to the Made in China 2025 program (Delfs 2018).

The Case of Huawei

Companies like Huawei are a perfect example of the successful execution of China's various national and foreign strategies. Taking into account the variety and potential severity of security concerns related to 5G, the United States and Australia have tightened existing policies regarding the presence of Chinese companies in networks. Huawei has not hidden its frustration at its curtailed access to foreign markets, and it claims a lack of publicized "intentional security vulnerabilities" (Ghosh 2019; Huawei 2019). It is also calling upon strategic friends to support its position. The ITU secretary general, Houlin Zhao (originally an information and communications technology engineer from China), departed from the ITU's position of technological neutrality to make targeted statements against the "unfair" blacklisting of Huawei—showing a disregard for the interests and experiences of the ITU's other industry, academic, and governmental members (Miles 2019a).

However, a variety of long-standing concerns regarding Huawei's business and its equipment have been made public. In 2012 Australia requested that Huawei not bid on its national broadband network, effectively banning the company (Chirgwin 2012). In 2013, after a government review, the United States banned Huawei and ZTE from participating in national 4G rollout (Muncaster 2013). Both cited national security concerns—not an uncommon move for governments.[26]

The United Kingdom's 2019 HCSEC report, which reviews current equipment in UK networks, is among the most critical public statements regarding the technical quality and security of Huawei's network equipment (Huawei Cyber Security Oversight Board 2019, paragraph 3.16).[27] The analysis highlights Huawei's lack of good security practices and capabilities, calling out "serious and systematic defects in Huawei's software engineering and cybersecurity competence." Australia's technical security simulation on the company's 5G equipment resulted in a ban on Huawei products in its networks (Bryan-Low et al. n.d.).

The 2018 and 2019 HCSEC report and Australian simulation were not the first inklings of the company's technical shortcomings. There are a number of reported basic security flaws in devices and poor security management by Huawei—all seemingly lost in the media storm, despite being the hardest evidence of cybersecurity risks inherent to Huawei. In 5G the risk is heightened from a flaw in a home router to a more serious flaw in the network itself (Corfield 2019). Huawei's carefully worded indictment of the United States focuses on "intention," not the existence of vulnerabilities. Intention is difficult to prove, and is made even more difficult by millions of lines of code and moving parts (Science and Technology Committee 2019). The United States might have evidence of collusion between China and Huawei, but that evidence is classified. The upcoming court case may result in the US government revealing more information on vulnerabilities or other risks associated with Huawei, which would likely benefit the ongoing international dialogue on the topic and bring a much-needed evidence base to other countries poised to invest in 5G infrastructure. Until then, a variety of concerns, if exploited, could result in serious harm.

WESTERN APPROACHES

The presence of Chinese components in Western Internet and telecommunications infrastructure is not new—a point the United States seems to be overlooking. Unfortunately, the complexity of the issue is lost in Twitter diplomacy and ongoing trade negotiations between the United States and China.[28] Key events in the US-China trade negotiations and the developing Huawei story intertwine as 2019 progresses. This reinforces the view that the United States is using Huawei as a pawn in the diplomatic chess game, but revelations during the period from other countries also show real security concerns relating to the Chinese company.

Amid the sound and fury of US rhetoric, hard evidence and technical reports like those by the United Kingdom and Australia have been overshadowed in the media. The United States has also failed both to recognize the different environments in which other countries must operate and to create an inclusive dialogue on the issues.

There is vocal concern from some governments vis-à-vis risks of further embedding Chinese firms in critical national infrastructures. Governments must weigh the costs and benefits of their positions. Geopolitics, trade relationships, and diplomatic ties play a role in positions, as does the potential damage to public services and the economy of a significantly delayed national 5G rollout. Governments must also consider the risks of being drawn into China's Internet policies promoting government control, human rights infringement, anticompetitive behavior, and the threat of helping to create a vertically integrated Chinese 5G monopoly.

Emerging positions reflect assessment of the extent to which Chinese providers such as Huawei might be incorporated in the 5G rollout in order to benefit from early adoption. This includes drawing lines between edge equipment and the core network's hardware and software. Nations may not need or want to take the United States' strong-armed approach, emphasizing the need for a clear story on 5G security matters. Conflating too many tangential issues specific to the US-China context—such as corporate espionage and sanctions violations—without clear positioning within the wider landscape risks diluting essential dialogue around national security and other issues, such as net neutrality and human rights, that are relevant the world over.

In response to China's strategic moves, Western countries are displaying a wariness toward Chinese firms. Table 15.2 provides an overview of the reported positions and actions taken by some Western countries with regard to Chinese technology companies.[29] A common approach by governments is to undertake a technology review, with simulations and an evaluation of supply chain risks. Some countries are considering or have implemented protectionist policies, reminiscent of those already established in China, albeit with a lighter touch (e.g., equipment testing and contracting requirements), sometimes under the pretext of national security.

The national responses reveal a range of soft and hard power strategies. Cautious steps call for official multilateral positions (e.g., Poland's call for an EU-NATO position (Reuters 2019) or internal security reviews (e.g., Canada). At the time of writing, Germany and Belgium are the only countries not to proactively restrict Chinese companies' access to national 5G deployment, after a security review.

The hard-line responses to date are blanket bans at national (Australia) and/or targeted corporate (US) levels—an unsurprising outcome from countries that since the early 2010s have publicly voiced concerns about Chinese telecoms companies' involvement in national networks (Lu-YueYang 2012; Rogers and Ruppersberger 2012). The United States' tough policies are paired with bilateral diplomacy approaches, aimed at engendering a global shift in national 5G strategies to exclude Chinese firms (Johnson 2019).

However, the failure of the United States' closest allies to rally to their cause threatens to destabilize long-standing alliances such as the Five Eyes. First, the US threatened to reduce intelligence sharing with allies that allowed Huawei into local networks. Then, Huawei was added to a US Entity List, barring companies around the world from trading with or supplying American-origin goods or services to Huawei. This blunt tool had huge ripple effects

Table 15.2 National Inquiries into Network Security and Huawei

Country or Bloc	Ongoing Reviews	Completed Review	Announced/ Official Position	Policy/ Procurement Changes	Warning on Chinese Firm(s)	Ban on Chinese Firm(s)	No Action
United States		X	X			X	
Canada	X						
Australia		X	X			X	
New Zealand	X					Blocked Huawei contract[a]	
France	X			Likely	X		
United Kingdom	X			Likely	X		
Italy	X			X			
Germany		X	X				X
Norway		X		X			
Netherlands		X		Likely	X		
Czech Republic	X						
Poland	X						
Belgium		X					X
European Union			X			National decision	
NATO	X						

Note: The countries and blocs are in order of the Five Eyes, EU members and the EU, and the NATO bloc.

a. The European Union has not issued a ban on Chinese firms, but instead has left the decision to governments. Reports highlight that some security officials feel the broad range of risks "posed by Chinese technology in general" are not addressed by the banning of a single supplier (Bryan-Low et al. 2019). At time of writing, New Zealand had not announced a ban on Huawei, but had blocked Huawei from a contract with a domestic mobile operator, Spark New Zealand, on national security grounds (*Guardian* 2018).

outside the 5G arena and American borders. Google quickly revoked Huawei's access to licensed material, including software updates; the United Kingdom's ARM and Japan's Panasonic halted trade or initiated reviews of their relationship with the Chinese company; and the Institute of Electrical and Electronic Standards, an SDO, placed a temporary hold on Huawei's participation in standards reviews to assess compliance with the United States' Entity List. Although the Entity List is an American policy, like Chinese policies, it has extraterritorial impact. Unfortunately, and also in parallel with China, this is likely to damage the United States' relationship with foreign governments and industry.

Evidence-based, moderate policy approaches aimed at procurement and contracting processes are emerging—namely, in Norway, the United Kingdom, and Italy.[30] These approaches are relatable and attainable for most governments and could develop a best practice approach for others to follow. This could also lead to a realignment of like-minded nations working together to address a collective resource issue—cyberthreats in an increasingly connected world.

MARKETS AND TRADE RELATIONS

It is not surprising that each country has taken a slightly different approach to the threat of a China-dominated 5G market. Ongoing diplomatic and trade relations between countries play a key role. For instance, in addition to the tensions caused by detentions of Canadian citizens and Meng Wanzhou, a 2012 Canada-China agreement allows Huawei to bring claims against the Canadian government in response to restrictive regulatory action (McGregor 2019).[31] In the meantime, as Canada executes its security review, China has blocked key Canadian exports such as canola oil and pork (Blatchford 2019; Patton and Nickel 2019). In other parts of the world, disruption to travel and ongoing trade negotiations between New Zealand and China have been linked to the banning of Huawei from a local operator's 5G rollout (Withers 2019). Italy was the first of the Group of Seven to sign a Belt and Road deal with China, yet telecoms was reportedly purposefully left out of the deal (Fonte and Piscioneri 2019).

Procurement, contracting and policy approaches such as those being put forward by the United Kingdom, Italy, and Norway offer important flexibility for governments in treading around politicized and complex issues by setting minimum, universally applicable requirements. First, they may reduce some vendors' access to contract competitions through legitimate and transparent means. Second, security becomes a primary purchasing point—something that was not done for previous networks (Intelligence and Security Committee 2013). And third, such approaches can provide a way forward for governments that wish to have a degree of control over which technology is used in 5G networks, but that may not be able to enact a ban for political or practical reasons. Such an approach could fairly and efficiently deliver the quiet exclusion of Chinese firms like Huawei, at least from critical parts of a network.

The United Kingdom's National Cyber Security Centre (NCSC) has published advice on adopting good cybersecurity practices. For example, NCSC has called for the use of vendors with a track record of minimizing vulnerabilities, impact, and harm (Levy 2019). One way for the industry to operationalize this advice is to work with vendors that follow best practices in security-by-design, have good transparency practices, and vulnerability reporting initiatives, such as Microsoft's Government Security Program (Microsoft 2003). To further address concerns, the United Kingdom is also stressing the need to manage risk and increase vendor diversity in the ecosystem in order to prevent a single point of failure (Donaldson 2018; Levy 2019). Governments and operators adopting such an approach will take into consideration the extent to which Chinese equipment providers are already integrated into local infrastructure (Morris 2018).

Reducing Huawei's 5G network presence will be more difficult for small community network operators or countries with less capital to invest. Western companies (e.g., Qualcomm, Nokia, and Ericsson) should consider how to make their 5G technology accessible and affordable in developing markets, for example, through joint ventures to deliver a more competitively priced product. In addition, governments could help subsidize rollouts, offer tax relief, or loosen policies on network deployment in order to increase purchasing power and make a wider range of 5G technology providers accessible to a greater number of market actors. Combined, these actions could help to rebalance an asymmetric and complex global 5G marketplace.

CONCLUSION

5G will transform current business models and financial flows around Internet infrastructure and network provision. This transformation engenders concerns over security and surveillance, IP rights, net neutrality, and Internet censorship. There is a shifting landscape of threats and risks related to mobile communications, such as the growing complexity and size of a network's attack surface and the potential for a single incident to result in physical damage—all of which have an impact on 5G's ability to support critical infrastructure. The interconnected and global nature of the Internet means that it could become the next tragedy of the commons if not governed appropriately. A likely fracture point is at the system and services layer, which will reconcentrate power in the hands of infrastructure providers. As such, there should be a wider discussion of the threats and benefits of 5G that go outside bilateral trade negotiations and economic power struggles.

In the first half of 2019, there was a flurry of governmental statements, actions, and finger-pointing as China and the United States brought the 5G race up to the brink of an all-out techno cold war. East and West seem to be adopting earlier moves from each other's playbooks—not many would have foreseen China leveling five complaints in a year at the United States and threatening Australia via the WTO a few years ago (Miles 2019b; WTO n.d.–a).[32] China is hoping that first-mover advantage will result in an indigenous global monopoly that shapes the next generation of Internet technologies, business models, and our daily lives—much the way American tech companies have shaped the current Internet. The US is using opaque claims of national security, reminiscent of a Chinese approach, to advance its protectionist position. Other Western nations are implementing protectionist policies that impede China's access to local markets, yet these approaches better reflect cybersecurity best practices and buoy an admittedly small, but strategically important, marketplace. Ironically, the fallout from the Trump executive order on securing the information and communications technology and services supply chain (White House 2019) is likely to motivate Chinese tech companies to create an entirely indigenous supply chain, further impacting global supply chains. Differences in the US and Chinese approaches come down to perceptions of openness, transparency, quality, and the degree of separation between public and private entities, including legal and national security frameworks.

How we resolve geopolitical tensions regarding 5G will impact the future of cyber security and national economies. Companies play a "fundamental role in shaping" technology as well as the norms and rules of the Internet (Hurel and Lobato 2018, 66). As a result, the state-firm diplomacy that has evolved over the past three decades is now taking center stage in geopolitics as the US government and Huawei go head to head (Strange 1992). An example of effective state-firm diplomacy is the United Kingdom's Huawei Cyber Security Evaluation Centre, paid for by Huawei and overseen by the NCSC. Although not without its critics, the mutual benefit of such a solution (e.g., market access and oversight of critical infrastructure) speaks to the ability of actors to find common ground on specific aspects of contested issues (Katwala 2019). Good practices such the HCSEC can be replicated elsewhere and evolve with technology. The benefit of centers like HCSEC goes beyond finding vulnerabilities to building assurance and understanding of a system (Science and Technology Committee 2019). However, the limitations of such a testing and review center should be acknowledged.

At the national level, hard-line responses such as naming and shaming, the addition of tariffs, or other trade-related actions that potentially breach international norms such as WTO trade rules, risk stifling innovation and the opportunities offered by 5G. A likely outcome of the national and regional inquiries currently being undertaken (table 15.2) is stricter requirements on procurements and contracting that adhere to the WTO's most-favored-nation principle and national security exemptions, and that support recommended norms (Global Commission on Internet Governance 2016; WTO n.d.–b). Policy updates could include requirements for compliance with principles such as security-by-design (Day et al. 2018); the ability to provide evidence on risk mitigation techniques; vulnerability disclosure and transparency reports (Global Forum on Cyber Expertise 2018; IoT Security Foundation 2017); or the use of conformance, testing, or certification requirements for market entry (Johnson et al. 2019).

Governments can also form new strategic partnerships to promote a more moderate, evidence-based policy dialogue on 5G, to promote best practices in cybersecurity, and to increase overall awareness of national security and other concerns (e.g., human rights) encapsulated in 5G. Japan, Israel, Taiwan, the United Kingdom, Canada, Norway, the Czech Republic, New Zealand, and other countries have voiced similar concerns, but these voices have been lost in the media noise. These countries could work together to deliver a broadly accessible line of reasoning that is reflective of the varied risks associated with companies like Huawei. It may also result in new international alliances for the 5G era. The May 2019 summit in the Czech Republic is a good first step in this direction, but measured and practical actions like this lack the Twitter-friendly media frenzy of US-China relations.

In essence, the public conversation needs to change—moving away from bilateral trade wars toward arguments that are relatable to governments and people the world over. This includes the increased ability for targeted communications interception or network shutdowns, the collective commons issue of cybersecurity, the need to adopt best practices, and improving network resilience through principles such as supplier diversity, discouraging the adoption of substandard practices, and raising awareness about the policy context in which Chinese companies operate. A more constructive approach should also address the "elephant in the room" of market protectionism by the West and market manipulation by Chinese firms. However, possibly the hardest-hitting approach would be the declassification of information regarding additional security threats that have until now been discussed behind closed doors.

Norms development in this space will necessarily be an iterative process due to the ongoing evolution of technology and risk management, but not least the sensitivity of the topic to national security. Finding solutions to these issues does not necessarily need to be state-led. Stakeholders should also redouble efforts across relevant standards bodies and expert groups, particularly those that are multistakeholder, open, and transparent—such as the IETF, the European Telecommunications Standards Institute, and industry forums such as GSMA and the Global Networking Initiative.

The UN is making a concerted effort to find its place in Internet governance, and 5G is no exception. In Internet governance, this would place the open, multistakeholder approach at risk and does not engage the large body of actors that are key to the Internet. The recent UN High-Level Panel on Digital Cooperation (HLPDC) focused heavily on a UN flavor of coordinated cooperation (United Nations 2019). With the upcoming UN Group of Government Experts and Open-Ended Working Group, there will be even more governments involved in processes at the UN level. However, these groups, and most likely initiatives to arise from the HLPDC, remain government-led and closed in terms of participation and agreed outputs. The arenas in which China is pushing its 5G standards, such as the ITU, lack the remit and expertise to work on human rights issues such as privacy. Yet recent high-level conferences show the drive by some nations to dangerously expand the ITU's remit to work on legally and culturally sensitive issues, embedding particular approaches to these topics into technology, away from public oversight (Article 19, 2017). Centralizing efforts in a closed, intergovernmental environment under increasing influence by those that do not share Western approaches to Internet governance does not bode well for Western values or vision of the Internet. It minimizes the role of, and to an extent excludes, industry experts and technologists that innovate, build, and run technologies and services that underpin daily lives. Academia and civil society provide important sources of research, information sharing and watchdog roles that are curtailed in closed, intergovernmental forums. Their participation is reliant on the benevolence, and perspective, of those governments shaping the discussion.

Both governments and users should be wary of a Chinese 5G internet. Countries like China that champion government control of the Internet, information, data, and users will not relinquish that control with future technologies. The realist in this situation would expect Chinese-origin technology to instead design and develop new technologies to better fit China's needs and end goals. A technology's home environment, including legal and policy landscape, also enables particular behaviors. Heretofore, public disagreements between tech giants and governments have often focused on access to user accounts and devices, as seen between the US government and Apple in 2016 (Khamooshi 2016). However, with 5G the use of national law like China's National Intelligence Law could grant the government access to an entire cloud service running a network—and all the data on that network, not just a user's device.

The United States is one of—if not the—strongest powers when it comes to utilizing tools enabled by the Internet. However, the United States perceives the possibility of China taking first-mover advantage in 5G as a means to further shift power to the East, solidify its leadership in emerging technologies, and abuse that power. China is a complex business, trading, and diplomatic partner with opaque public-private relationships, a history of exploiting the Internet's architecture for political and economic gain, a concerning track record of market manipulation and a fundamentally different approach to Internet governance and human rights. To some extent, the race comes down to a question of whom governments prefer to be rooted in their critical infrastructure. Separating parties into camps will include an element of subjectivity. Each country will need to navigate different waters—including diplomatic relationships, market interest, existing equipment in and resiliency of their networks, and short- and long-term benefits of 5G rollout.

NOTES

1. The authors thank Patrick Taylor for the images in this chapter.
2. Kovrig was a prominent political commentator with a focus on Chinese military strategy.
3. There have been several attempts at establishing norms for responsible state behavior in cyberspace, principally through the UN Group of Governmental Experts and the Organization for Security and Cooperation in Europe. Although the Group of Governmental Experts established joint commitments in 2010, 2013, and 2015, the 2017 negotiations fell apart, reflecting growing divisions among states surrounding how global cybersecurity should be governed.
4. From the Internet's early origins as a US Cold War military experiment (Naughton 2016), to the International Corporation for Assigned Names and Numbers—the California-based nonprofit organization responsible for coordinating global policy for the Domain Name System—to global commercial forces such as Google, Apple, and Facebook, the Internet has been strongly influenced by American perspectives.
5. Government-led efforts have been complemented by big operators and other players in the East—such as Samsung, KT, SK Telecom (South Korea), Huawei, ZTE, China Mobile, China Unicom, and China Telcom (China). In the West, network operators like

AT&T, Verizon, Vodafone, Telefonica, Telenor, and Deutsche Telekom have been testing 5G technologies for deployment.

6. The Internet Engineering Task Force, a key multistakeholder Internet standards body, is currently developing the next generation of Internet protocols that deserve their own review through the lens of geopolitical issues. Although these protocols will be used in 5G, the task force is not working on 5G-specific standards.

7. There are additional concerns such as Internet consolidation ("Future Thinking" 2019) and human rights (Freedom House 2018) that are not fully explored here but are equally important and deserving of a detailed analysis.

8. This is where the term "edge computing" comes into play in 5G networks.

9. The network "core" is responsible for operations and critical security functions such as network management and device authentication.

10. Intellectual property rights are protected under international trade law—for example, by the World Trade Organization's Agreement on Trade-Related Aspects of Intellectual Property Rights, known as TRIPS.

11. For the purpose of this chapter, we take a general approach to cybersecurity and the reduction of risk of cyber attacks. Considerations include the protection of networks and systems (including hardware and software), services, and data from threats. Threats manifest through a variety of means, including but not limited to unauthorized access (e.g., hacking), malware (e.g., the WannaCry virus), or distributed denial-of-service attacks (e.g., the Dyn Attack).

12. *Security by design* is a process whereby security concerns are taken into account from the outset of conception and design, resulting in security tools and risk mitigation being built into the end product instead of added on after development.

13. An *attack surface* is the sum of the vulnerabilities, or points susceptible to attack—in, for example, devices, software, hardware, or systems.

14. These include malware, hacking, man-in-the-middle, and distributed denial-of-service attacks.

15. This is due to an increased amount and variety of physical network equipment like cell towers and connected "things," as well as vulnerabilities related to computer software, cloud computing, and data.

16. The United States prefers high frequency for core communications, while China, in particular, prefers low frequency. Within regions, there is also a lack of alignment over the exact bands to be released (e.g., Europe), and sometimes even national players differ in opinion (e.g., Japan) (Mavrakis 2018; Triolo, Allison, and Brown 2018). Africa's position is unique, because it has yet to complete digital migration of television, which would release critical bands for 5G (Reed 2018).

17. Companies such as Alcatel, Lucient, and Marconi closed down or were absorbed by remaining competitors like Nokia.

18. Eight of the most vulnerable countries include Djibouti, Maldives, Laos, Mongolia, Tajikistan, Kyrgyzstan, and Pakistan (Hurley, Morris, and Portelance 2018).

19. Simplistically, this includes a small mix of American, European, Japanese, South Korean, and Chinese vendors.

20. The Great Firewall creates a national intranet only connected to the global network through a limited number of highly monitored gateways, creating a connected environment (including data, information, and users), which is easier to monitor, manage, and track.

21. From 1997 to 2017, China's high-technology exports increased from approximately $20.5 billion to $504.4 billion (World Bank n.d.).
22. In 2016 a $46 million "cybersecurity investment fund" was established by the China Internet Development Foundation, which has links to the Cyberspace Administration of China (Cheung 2018, 322). In the context of Chinese companies' foreign investments, a Chinese state-owned investment company, CITIC, was effectively handed a financial stake in the Czech Republic after assuming the assets of a Chinese conglomerate, CEFC (Muller 2018).
23. These include the National Intelligence Law, Counter Espionage Law, and State Security Law. It is also worth noting that the Xi Jinping government takes a broad interpretation of "national security," including eleven areas: political, territorial, military, economic, cultural, social, economic, science and technology, information, nuclear, and natural resources (Wong 2017).
24. Some motivation behind the drive to build China's high-technology industry and for self-sufficiency was highlighted by President Trump's now-repealed ban on semiconductor sales to ZTE, which would have resulted in the company's demise (*Lawfare* 2018a).
25. Industry leader Qualcomm reportedly owned 15 percent, followed by Nokia with 11 percent, at the end of 2017.
26. E.g., Lenovo has had restrictions placed on it in Australia, the United Kingdom, Canada, New Zealand, and the United States (Robertson 2013). Products from Russia's Kaspersky Labs have also experienced restrictions (Schneier 2018).
27. The 2019 report, building on security concerns first expressed in 2018, flagged difficulties related to risk mitigation and "defects in Huawei's software engineering and cybersecurity processes" (Huawei Cyber Security Oversight Board 2019, 4).
28. For a chronology of the US-China trade talks and Huawei events in 2018–19, see https://oxil.uk/publications/geopolitics-of-5g/.
29. This information is as of June 2019. Some non-Western countries are taking action to restrict Chinese companies' access to 5G markets. E.g., Japan has blocked Chinese equipment, Taiwan renewed an existing ban on Huawei and ZTE equipment (Morris 2018), and Israel has legal restrictions on Chinese equipment (Triolo, Allison, and Brown 2018).
30. Norway implemented changes to its laws and regulations, including the Security Act and sectoral laws, to give heavier weight to security assessments (Wijnen 2019). Similarly, the United Kingdom initiated a Telecoms Supply Chain Review (which was due in the spring of 2019) looking at market incentives and security risks (UK Department for Digital, Culture, Media & Sport 2018), while Italy's government passed a law listing 5G network technology among the nation's "strategic assets for national security," requiring notification of intent to use foreign telecoms equipment and includes veto power (Giarda, Lattanzio, and Liotta 2019).
31. This is from the Agreement for the Promotion and Reciprocal Protection of Investments.
32. This is up from an average of about one per year from 2002 to 2016.

CHAPTER 16

Terrorism and the Decay
of the Liberal Order

Daniel Benjamin

Terrorism, it is often said, is the transnational issue par excellence. Terrorists train in one country, plot in another, use complex global communications and transportation linkages, and strike anywhere in the world. Certainly that has been the case for the two types of terrorism that have been dominant since the end of the Cold War—jihadist and state-sponsored terror. It should follow that the quality of international relationships and the strength of multilateral institutions ought, by rights, be an essential determinant of counterterrorism cooperation and global security.

To a great extent, that is the case, and a high level of international cooperation has been an essential element of Western nations' success in limiting the impact of both forms of terrorism in the period since September 11, 2001. Despite continued breathlessness in some journalistic reporting and fear mongering by politicians, achievements in the realm of counterterrorism have been real. State sponsorship of terrorism has declined dramatically, especially in the last two decades; however, as we shall see, the practice may be reviving. Jihadist attacks still occur with some frequency in Europe, and there also continue to be occasional strikes in the United States.[1] The incidence of thwarted attacks remains noteworthy, and though public opinion on both sides of the Atlantic is somewhat calmer than just a few years ago, there remains a strong emotional latency, and a resurgence of great anxiety would likely follow a series of renewed attacks.

Nonetheless, within the counterterrorism community, there is a sense that several major goals have been achieved:

1. The threat of the high-end, catastrophic attack has been much reduced. Fear of a terrorist strike involving weapons of mass destruction has

receded, even if the possibility of such an event cannot be fully eliminated (Rasmussen 2015).

2. The ISIS caliphate no longer exists; its territorial hold was extinguished by a coalition of US, Western, and local forces.

3. Border security, especially in the United States, is highly effective at keeping out jihadist terrorists—so much so that terrorist operations with foreign command and control are virtually unknown. Homegrown operations carried out by American citizens or permanent residents have become the rule.

The Western experience is nothing like what countries in the developing world continue to endure. Global terrorism casualties grew significantly between 2012 and 2014, driven primarily by events in Iraq, Afghanistan, Syria, Pakistan, and Nigeria. Since 2015, the numbers have drifted downward and/or plateaued, albeit at a historically high level ("Number of Fatalities" n.d.). These countries have been afflicted overwhelmingly by internal dynamics that have made terrorism a tool of choice for antigovernment groups. The numbers may decline further in these countries. But it will not be surprising if they spike elsewhere, in places such as Egypt or Algeria, where public dissatisfaction with regime policies is rife. The resilient fact is that misgovernance, repression, and economic stagnation—key drivers for jihadist violence—remain endemic across most of the broader Middle East, with no sign of change on the horizon. State weakness—in Africa especially, but also elsewhere—combined with growing intercommunal tensions and resource scarcity, make terrorism a chronic problem.

Given this bifurcated picture, what are the prospects for maintaining the security gains in the West and reducing the violence that continues to plague significant swaths of the globe? A critical variable will undoubtedly be the nature of the international system, and it is worth considering how the international community would perform under two possible scenarios—specifically those of "strengthened states," which involves renewed nationalism and more competitive interstate relations, and that of "pragmatic cooperation," in which there is ad hoc, intermittent cooperation to solve common problems.

BEHIND THE SCENES, SOME THINGS WORK

Under either scenario, a high degree of cooperation on tactical counterterrorism—those activities that aim at preventing individual attacks—will likely persist. That is, international counterterrorism collaboration is unlikely to be greatly affected by any change in the nature of the international system, and there should be little erosion of the cooperation involved in intelligence sharing, surveillance, law enforcement, and even border security. Decay of the liberal international order due to resurgent nationalism, xenophobia, and antiglobalization sentiment might at first glance appear to threaten to current practices. But counterterrorism cooperation is insulated in a way that few other forms of multilateral cooperation are—a reflection of the unusual nature of the international counterterrorism architecture.

That architecture has evolved considerably since 2001 as the UN, NATO, and many regional multilateral organizations have focused more energy on terrorism, and new institutions have been established, such as the Global Counterterrorism Forum (GCTF), which was created in 2011 to propagate best practices and enhance capacity building, and GCERF, a donors' forum, that grew out of the GCTF. But the institutions at the core of counterterrorism cooperation are intelligence services, and the network that has evolved is not attached to any multilateral agencies. Rather, it is a shadow network linked together by a web of principally bilateral liaison relationships. This network is resilient and surprisingly extensive. Former US director of central intelligence Michael Hayden reflected on this state of affairs in a recent memoir (Hayden 2016, 313), in which he spoke of his foreign intelligence counterparts: "We trade off each other for mutual benefit, even when there isn't much agreement at the policy level between governments.... In fact, these partnerships are remarkably durable, operating below the surface, even when political relations are stormy." Everyone has an interest in preventing terrorist attacks within their borders and neighborhoods. Even when political relations are roiled, countries will exchange sensitive intelligence to thwart terrorist conspiracies and want to ensure they are receiving information from others. Although jihadist violence played a catalytic role in creating the global network of intelligence partners, cooperation is not limited to countering this form of terrorism. White supremacist terrorism—a growing menace in North America, Europe, and Australia / New Zealand—is also a matter for increasing collaboration, and if the more dire predictions about ecoterrorism, antiglobalization activism, and/or other forms of terrorist activity come true, these too would become shared concerns.

The number of countries completely excluded from the global intelligence network is small: Iran and Syria, both designated as state sponsors of terrorism, are outside the walls, as is North Korea, another recently redesignated state sponsor. As of this writing, the fourth member of the undesirables club, Sudan, appears to be on the verge of being delisted—Sudan had remained on the list for collateral reasons having to do with human rights violations in Darfur and South Sudan, but years of certified counterterrorism cooperation with the United States and the overthrow of longtime strongman Omar al-Bashir have accelerated the momentum for delisting.

Cooperation with the many other members of the international community comes in many varieties. Key desiderata include the volume and quality of information shared by the partner country and how carefully the partner country handles information. A partner that uses intelligence to enable repressive measures against its own population may see the sharing restricted, and the same is true for one that leaks sensitive information. In a few cases, the relationship is limited because of the competitive, often hostile nature of the bilateral ties. Russia, for example, has sought to use counterterrorism cooperation as a way to improve its understanding of US intelligence capabilities, so exchanges have been limited. Cooperation with China is limited for similar reasons and because of Beijing's repressive policies, especially against its Uighur minority. Overall, however, urgent threat information has traditionally been passed on without hesitation and has been invaluable in disrupting plots around the world.

That kind of routine cooperation would likely survive a decaying of the global order due to the resurgence of nationalism. In theory, heightened competition between nations could lead to curtailed intelligence sharing. Jihadist violence, however, remains anathema to virtually every government on earth, and it is a widely believed that a string of successful attacks could have destabilizing consequences for individual nations, regions, and the global community as a whole. The jihadist movement today enjoys no significant state sponsorship, even if some Gulf countries have yet to fully regulate financial transactions that may benefit these groups, and the Pakistani government, in particular, still has ties to radical Islamist groups that carry out attacks against India.

An advantage of intelligence cooperation is that it is conducted out of the public eye and therefore is insulated from political pressure. But many counterterrorism activities are conducted in the open and could be affected by the kind of political pressure that is rooted in heightened nationalism. Extradition arrangements and law enforcement exchanges, the purview of justice and interior ministries, occur thanks to mutual legal assistance treaties that have been negotiated in sizable numbers in recent decades, and could be affected by bilateral tensions. Exchanges of information on international travelers, which have been institutionalized through agreements between interior ministries and the US Department of Homeland Security, could similarly be jeopardized. Still, so long as the prospect of jihadist attack inspires the kind of alarm that it currently does, governments will be disinclined to diminish cooperation.

Intelligence agencies are at the heart of the counterterrorism enterprise, but no discussion of the issue would be complete without mention of military engagement. Setting aside the 2003 invasion of Iraq—falsely advertised as a counterterrorism effort—two major military actions and a large scattering of others have been undertaken to deal with a terrorist threat. Of the large-scale ones, the first is Afghanistan, where hostilities have continued for almost nineteen years, and the second was the campaign to destroy the Islamic State of Iraq and the Levant (ISIS) caliphate. Both involved extensive coalition efforts—at least sixty nations took part in Afghanistan beginning in 2001, while some eighty partners joined forces to fight ISIS in the wake of its dramatic rise in 2014. These campaigns have had a powerful impact on the terrorist threat: In Afghanistan, US and allied forces drove al-Qaeda from its safe haven, killing large numbers of the group's operatives and removing from power the Taliban, the group that allowed al-Qaeda to use Afghanistan as a base. These successes greatly reduced the ability of the group to plot complex, long-range operations like the attacks of 9/11, even if those successes soon gave way to mission creep and a long, grinding conflict with the Taliban. In the Middle East, the US-led coalition halted ISIS's march across Iraq and then reduced and ultimately destroyed the caliphate, which had demonstrated a remarkable ability to inspire young Muslims to travel to the region and take up arms to support the fledgling extremist polity.

The defeat of ISIS was a catalytic, positive experience for Iraq, and a triumph for the international coalition that was assembled for the task. In theory, the experience ought to provide a model for similar future challenges—and the persistence of a low-level insurgency in western Iraq as well as terrorist successes in West Africa suggest that there could be a need for such an outside force within a few years (Seligman 2019; Hassan 2018). The changing nature of the international system will undoubtedly condition the chances for assembling such large coalitions again.

Much will depend on timing and circumstances. But when it comes to military coalition building, the United States has historically played the role of the necessary convener; given the current unpredictable leadership in Washington, which has signaled its determination to draw down in Afghanistan and reorient its forces to deal with great power rivalry, it is not certain that the United States would lead such an effort, particularly if the situation was viewed as anything less than exigent. Washington's willingness to assemble a coalition in a post-Trump world will depend on a variety of factors, including who occupies the White House and the balance of power in Congress. In a more fractious international system, with more countries looking inward, assembling a coalition against ISIS 2.0 could be much more challenging.

NET ASSESSMENT

The picture that emerges of the terrorist threat in the coming years is, therefore, mixed. North America and Europe will likely see continued danger from jihadist violence, but they are unlikely to see a return of the threat of catastrophic violence or of campaigns involving multiple destabilizing attacks. Elsewhere, the reality may be more violent. In the Middle East, South and Central Asia, and Africa, high levels of violence will probably continue so long as key drivers of extremism—including civil conflict, gross economic inequity, and misgovernance—persist. How effectively Western nations can wall themselves off from developments in these more volatile parts of the world remains to be seen: Intelligence, law enforcement, and border security proficiency ensure a high degree of security, but there is a question of what happens if the fires burn ever hotter abroad. There is always the possibility that some terrorist group will again decide that it has an interest in targeting the "far enemy" in the West to advance its cause, and a perfect defense is, of course, not possible.

RETURN OF THE SUPPRESSED?

Although the jihadist threat is what most people think of when they think about terrorism, it is not the only form of the threat. Indeed, the brand of terrorism that preoccupied policymakers before 2001—state-sponsored terrorism—could well revive if the global system continues to slide toward a more conflictual, "strengthened states" mode.

State sponsorship has receded from the spotlight in recent years because of improvements in the intelligence and forensic work that help fix attribution for such attacks. Quick attribution gives nations that have been struck by terrorists a window for military response. Even if it takes some time to determine authorship of an attack—as, for example, in the aftermath of the Iranian backed attack on Khobar Tower (1996) or the Libyan bombing of Pan Am Flight 103 (1988)—the increasing effectiveness of international economic sanctions regimes has made such strikes less attractive as instruments of policy. Both Iranian and Libyan efforts to target the US interests declined after those countries were identified as being responsible for those attacks. Today, state sponsorship of terrorism persists primarily only in two theaters where such violence has been committed for decades: against Israel, principally by the Iranian-backed Hezbollah; and against India, by Pakistani-based groups.

A revival of state-sponsored violence against the United States thus is unlikely. But that does not mean the day of state-sponsored terror is past. On the contrary: the erosion that has occurred to date in the international system suggests we may be headed toward an increase in the frequency with which a few states plot acts of violence against individuals and groups that reside in other, less powerful countries.

The most dramatic violation of the liberal, rules-based order in decades is Russia's seizure of Crimea and incursion into eastern Ukraine, the first case of borders being changed by force in Europe since the end of World War II. These actions were not achieved by massed armies but through infiltration and special operations—"hybrid warfare," in the terminology of Russian military leaders. The Crimea campaign involved deployment of "little green men," individuals who, like terrorists, do not wear military uniforms or other types of identification. And, in fact, scholars often include terrorism in the array of tactics used in hybrid warfare. In the words of Ahmed Hashim (2017), hybrid warfare "occurs when an actor practicing it against an opponent brings into play a 'cocktail' of conventional military capabilities, political warfare, terrorism, subversion, guerrilla warfare, organized crime, and, in contemporary times, cyber warfare. It may also include violations of international laws of war by the practitioner of hybrid warfare."

Given its success in Crimea, there is little reason to believe that Russia would forgo comparable acts in future efforts. Russian leaders might, for prudential reasons, be unlikely to launch terrorist attacks against NATO members. But in light of the current government's willingness to take risks, Moscow might well launch unconventional attacks against neighboring, non-NATO countries that were resisting Russia's efforts to exert control over their affairs.

In fact, it was precisely because Russia wanted to prevent a country from joining NATO that it undertook a covert operation in Montenegro that also might be located on the spectrum between military operations and terrorism. In October 2016, Russian intelligence agents conspired to arrange an occupation by proxies of the Montenegrin parliament and assassination of Prime Minister Milo Djukanovic. The goal was to prevent Djukanovic from fulfilling his pledge to bring the small Balkan nation into the Alliance. The plot was ultimately thwarted, and the key conspirators were convicted of a variety of crimes. Among those sentenced were two Russian GRU (military intelligence) officers, who were tried in absentia.

Against this backdrop, it is worth recalling that before 9/11, the last truly heightened period of terrorist activity in the West came during the Cold War—before the liberal, rules-based order was a genuinely global phenomenon. From the 1960s through the 1980s, the Soviet Union supported terrorist groups that plagued Western Europe and the Middle East, many of which were often seen as sui generis expressions of the Arab-Israeli conflict and the political upheaval of the late 1960s and 1970s. As Christopher Andrew and Vasili Mitrokhin (1999) and other historians of the KGB have shown, Moscow used its intelligence network, together with the services of Warsaw Pact partners such as Czechoslovakia and the GDR, to support groups including the Palestinian Front for the Liberation of Palestine, the German Red Army Faction (aka the Baader-Meinhof Gang), the Italian Red Brigades, and the Provisional Irish Republican Army. This support included safe haven, training, cash, and weaponry. Terrorism in Western Europe claimed between 150 and more than 400 lives annually from 1972 to 1988. Although this may seem like a small number compared with events such as 9/11, the toll in Western Europe has exceeded 150 only four times since 1998 and has never exceeded 200. The consequences of terrorism in this earlier wave were profound. West Germany, then a young democracy, experienced the Deutsche Herbst, the violence-filled fall of 1977, as a series of earthquakes, prompting Chancellor Helmut Schmidt to make a televised speech to the nation to provide reassurance that its democracy was not in danger.

More than forty years later, the landscape is much changed. But as Daniel Byman (2005, 37) has written, "One of the most common reasons to support a terrorist group is to destabilize a neighbor. Weakening a neighbor is often part and parcel of a brutal competition among states, useful for gaining concessions regarding disputed territory, as punishment for joining a hostile alliance, or as a way of augmenting a conventional military campaign in a war." Byman counts nineteen cases when a state backed a terrorist, at least in part because of a desire to destabilize a neighboring country. One can easily imagine nations that practice sphere-of-influence politics resorting to terrorist tactics to bring wayward neighbors in line. Given how far Russia has gone to disrupt politics in more distant countries, it is hard to draw a line past which Moscow would not tread.

RUSSIA, BUT NOT ONLY RUSSIA

Russia is not unique in violating existing norms. The taboo on one country killing inhabitants of another appears to be weakening. It is a reasonable hypothesis that this trend points toward a possible increase in the incidence of state-sponsored terrorism.

Evidence for this development is somewhat limited—prediction is difficult because the number of events that can be studied is small. Still, the data for this hypothesis are intriguing and disturbing. Historically speaking, assassinations, typically by intelligence services, in foreign countries have occurred for decades, though in small numbers. Some of these cases involved killing dissidents who had fled their native countries: the Chilean activist Orlando Letelier was murdered in a car bombing in 1976 in Washington by agents of the Pinochet regime. Two years later, Georgi Markov, a Bulgarian exile, was killed in London with a poison-tipped umbrella, allegedly by the Bulgarian intelligence service. After the Islamic Revolution, Iran assassinated dozens and possibly hundreds of dissident expatriates, many of them in Western Europe.

Another category involves killing operatives of terrorist groups. Some of the Iranians targeted were members of the Mujahedin e-Khalq, a group that had participated in the revolution, then had a falling out with the clerical leadership and carried out numerous attacks against the new Iranian power elite. Israel also carried out targeted killings of terrorists abroad, including eight of the original eleven Black September members who carried out the massacre at the Munich Olympics (Calahan 1995). Other Israeli operations have met with uneven results. The attempted killing of Hamas leader Hamad Meshal in Jordan in 1997 caused a crisis in Israeli-Jordanian relations and an ultimatum that resulted in the provision of an antidote to the poison that Mossad agents had injected in him. The bungled killing of Mahmoud al-Mabhouh, another Hamas leader, in Dubai in 2010, led to international censure for Israel.

In recent years, Russia has been the leader in the growing effort to kill regime critics. These include the case of former KGB spy Alexander Litvinenko, who died in London from radiation sickness after his food was poisoned with polonium as well as a number of cases in which Moscow's hand has been suspected though not proven: Alexander Perepilichnyy, a Russian businessman who had been helping Swiss prosecutors, is believed to have been poisoned in London in 2012, while the following year oligarch Boris Berezovsky was found hanging in his London mansion under mysterious circumstances. German Gorbuntsov, an expatriate banker, was shot in London in 2012 but survived. More recently, the 2018 attempted killing of former Russian spy Sergei Skripal and his daughter in Salisbury with an advanced chemical weapon—which sickened two others and killed a third—underscored Russia's growing lack of caution.[2] In Ukraine, Russian lethal activities away from the battlefields have been substantially more widespread (Schwirtz 2019).

Russia is not alone. Saudi Arabia's killing of Jamal Khashoggi in 2018 became—and continues to be—an international cause célèbre. Remarkably, despite all the opprobrium aimed at Riyadh and Crown Prince Mohammed bin Salman, it appears that he has not been deterred from further conspiracies aimed at critics. Recent reporting indicates three regime critics based in Norway, Canada, and the United States have also been targeted for assassination.[3] North Korean agents arranged the assassination of Kim Jong-nam, the half-brother of Kim Jong Un, in 2017 in a complicated plot that involved the nerve agent VX. North Korea had carried out other killings in the past. The use of VX, in the view of the Trump administration, was reason enough to relist North Korea as a state sponsor of terrorism. Interestingly, Iran, which had largely ceased targeting regime opponents after the election of reformer Mohammad Khatami as president in 1997, has also resumed its practice of lethal operations abroad.

Under US policy, assassination is not an act of terrorism *unless* it is carried out by an already-listed state sponsor. The policy has allowed Israel, in particular, to avoid being listed as a state sponsor despite the many targeted killings of terrorists outside its borders. Assassination nonetheless provides a good indicator of the respect that a country has for the traditional rules of the road in international intelligence operations. One can imagine that, with energetic US and Western efforts, the taboo on such behavior could be revived and strengthened. But the surge in killings suggests an increased willingness to violate norms regarding the use of violence below the level of warfare and is a worrisome harbinger for the future. In any global order in which the standards that obtained until 2016, are weakened, it is easy to imagine a continuing increase in such state-backed violence.

THE FUTURE OF "STRATEGIC COUNTERTERRORISM"

Although there is a good basis, as discussed above, for optimism about the future of tactical counterterrorism cooperation, in the case of continued deterioration of the liberal, rules-based order, one likely casualty is strategic-level improvement in counterterrorism in the principally Muslim-majority nations where the jihadist movement is strongest. By strategic-level improvement, we mean anything that would address the major drivers of contemporary terrorism: poor governance, repression, a lack of political voice, underdevelopment, economic inequity, and stagnation. Leaders in the West—especially the European Union and the United States—have dedicated significant funding to development projects in some of these countries, and there have been efforts to press some of the worst offenders to reduce the violations of human rights that have driven extremism. More ambitious efforts to condition bilateral assistance and support from international financial institutions on broader-based reforms have not occurred because governments have not offered aid packages that would provide sufficient leverage to press for far-reaching change. In the era of COVID-19, with exceptionally strained budgets, the outlook for enhanced resources for such efforts is grimmer than ever.

Indeed, resurgent populism will likely imperil support for existing economic assistance. In the United States, the Trump administration has sought to cut funding for development dramatically, only to be thwarted by Congress. It is a safe bet that this part of the federal budget will remain under attack if Trump or like-minded nationalists succeed him. The fate of antiterrorism assistance programs, which have played an important role in capacity building, may eventually also be in jeopardy, and this applies on the military side of the budget as well as the civilian.[4] Troop drawdowns in conflict-ridden parts of the world appear imminent in Afghanistan, where a hasty departure could provide the opportunity for terrorist groups to reestablish themselves in the country and in West Africa. An American retreat from these programs and some of these parts of the world could disincentivize others from maintaining robust policies. In some cases, such as French engagement in the Sahel, a perception that vital interests are at stake would likely lead Paris to extend its military presence. In Afghanistan, it is harder to see who would step up.

With little chance of broad-based reform efforts that might ameliorate the conditions that breed extremism, there are also signs that some grievances may become more acute. The growth of nationalism has been accompanied by a decline in international norms regarding human rights—no surprise, given the nationalist emphasis on sovereignty—and that threatens to stoke the extremist threat. So much is evident in the Trump administration's dealings with the Egyptian government of Abdel Fattah al-Sisi. The administration's resumption of hitherto suspended military assistance—despite manifest human rights abuses—provided a signal of acceptance of the regime's extrajudicial killing and unlawful incarceration. Among scholars and practitioners, there is broad agreement that repression has been a catalyst of jihadist sentiment. The Trump administration's approach, which leaves the decision over domestic security issues entirely to that country's ruler, is a natural concomitant of the competitive nationalist approach to international relations, and it will only increase the size of the radical Islamist movement, which has grown in size many times over in the last twenty years.[5] The global jihad was born in Egypt's notorious Tora Prison, where Sayyid Qutb wrote his most influential works, and others, such as Ayman al-Zawahiri, were hardened in their hatred of the regimes of Nasser and Sadat. The current crackdown, which exceeds anything from those eras, will not contribute to global security.

Increasing nationalism could exacerbate radicalization in other indirect ways. A decline in the international community's capacity for conflict resolution, peacekeeping, and reconstruction means that conflicts in Yemen, Syria, and the Sahel will continue to burn. It is a law of international affairs that war is the father of extremism, and so the production of radicalized fighters will continue apace. It is increasingly clear that climate change also drives conflict in marginal areas. So as long efforts to limit global warming are stalled because of a skepticism about science that seems embedded in populist nationalism—witness Trump's America and Bolsonaro's Brazil—extremism will likely grow. As has been seen in Africa, for example, when conflict does break out, there is a good chance that one side or another will ally itself with a terrorist group such as ISIS or al-Qaeda to enhance its credibility.

In sum, we can imagine a near-term future in which Western countries can manage, though not eliminate, their terrorism problems. But for much of the rest of the world, growing extremism is a highly probable, if unintended, consequence of increased nationalism and a retreat from multilateralism and the rules-based order. Contemporary terrorism, which relies on the fruits of globalization and technological advance, demands a high degree of international integration to combat effectively. Any future in which the ties between nations are weakened by nationalism and competition will see some degradation in security at the global level. The real question becomes how extensive this degradation will be, and how well its consequences can be handled.

NOTES

1. Overall threat levels remain somewhat higher in Europe than in North America due to issues related to integration, border security, and lower investment in security. Nonetheless, terrorist violence in Europe remains a small fraction of what exists in parts of the developing world and much closer in nature and frequency to what is found in the United States.
2. Reporting on Russian assassinations is given by Pasha-Robinson (2018) and Price and Ghosh (2018). There are a number of other killings in Britain and elsewhere in the West in which Russia's hand is suspected (Eckel and Schreck 2019). One involves a former senior Kremlin official, Mikhail Lesin, who appears to have been murdered in the United States (Schwirtz 2019).
3. Journalists' accounts of Saudi Arabia's efforts to silence critics are discussed by Meyer (2019) and Akkad (2019).
4. For a discussion of US efforts to draw down counterterrorism efforts, see Schmitt (2019).
5. The White House's decision to pursue the designation of the Muslim Brotherhood as a foreign terrorist organization is another—and possibly pivotal—error. More than a year after its announcement of its determination to designate the Ikhwan, no formal action has been registered.

PART IV

Conclusion

CHAPTER 17

Diplomacy and World Order

Chester A. Crocker, Fen Osler Hampson,
and Pamela Aall

A VARIEGATED DIPLOMATIC ENVIRONMENT

Must we conclude that the time has passed for diplomacy in the service of peace? We should recall Zartman's (2015, 5–6) reminder that the world order, however troubled, is far from collapsing into "total anarchy, wasting all time and energy in unregulated conflict and unprevented violence." We believe it is simplistic to argue that the architecture of the liberal international order has collapsed in the face of resurgent forces of populism, authoritarianism, and nationalism and the actions of major emerging powers such as China and India, which are flexing newfound sources of power. There remain strong vestiges of the post–World War II order as well as powerful incentives for international cooperation and diplomacy to manage and resolve the world's conflicts. We should also recall our initial definition of peace and conflict diplomacy as involving both the art of high-level engagement between governments to shape, manage, and resolve disputes and also a process characterized by the involvement of intergovernmental, nonstate, and civil society actors in such activities.

In the peace and conflict diplomacy space, we see three basic types: *competitive and instrumentalist diplomacy, stabilization diplomacy*, and *governance diplomacy*. The first is diplomacy aimed at advancing and defending the interests—both material and ideological—of the major powers, using such tools as sanctions, deterrence-based threats, claims of spheres of influence, and support of proxy forces. Such behavior often occurs in conflict environments, though its main goal may have little to do with ending the conflict. Rather, its purpose may be to exploit or manipulate the situation in one's own interests or to pursue damage limitation goals. This *competitive and instrumentalist* type of diplomacy invariably heightens the potential for proxy warfare rather than peaceful settlement. It is quite clearly different from the two other forms of peace and conflict diplomacy, which are focused on creating stabilization and governance mechanisms to reduce the potential for armed conflict and violence.

Stabilization diplomacy involves activity that is directed at stabilizing and deescalating conflict through, for example, agreeing to recognize the territorial status quo; introducing peacekeeping troops to maintain a negotiated cease-fire; sending envoys to initiate a dialogue between warring parties to allow for the delivery of humanitarian aid; "freezing" an arms race through negotiated commitments not to deploy certain kinds of weaponry; or agreeing to specific "rules of the road" regarding the deployment of current and emerging military technologies. Above all, a central precept of stabilization diplomacy is the importance of state sovereignty and the belief that its preservation is the key to regional security and international order.

Governance diplomacy refers to the wide range of activities undertaken by state and/or nonstate actors to promote the expansion of human rights, civic rights, and greater pluralism or to create new political institutions that are democratically accountable and inclusive.[1] At the interstate level, *governance diplomacy* involves the creation of new international institutions (at the regional or global level) where member states formally commit themselves to abide by certain norms and rules as well as proscribe certain kinds of activity and behavior. The concept of governance diplomacy is also based on the notion that state sovereignty is not an absolute principle or right of states, though its actual boundaries will typically vary from one context to another.

We do not imagine that our types of diplomacy are rigidly aligned with individual scenarios, or that they are always mutually exclusive. For example, a practitioner of a *competitive and instrumental* proxy war might argue that its purpose is, in reality, aimed at achieving future stability or a negotiated peace deal. We also recognize that regions differ in terms of their diplomatic cultures: that is, their views on the relative emphasis to place on international law, on external intervention in the internal affairs of states, and on the role of the United Nations in legitimizing of the use of force (Crocker, Hampson, and Aall 2011b).

To complete this picture, regional variations occur in several dimensions; regions may vary by the local prevalence of a dominant scenario, but may also vary as a result of the diplomatic preferences of leading powers. The interaction between the regional and global scenario preferences of powerful states is already visible today and may become more so. Variation is also visible in the way that functional challenges—terrorism, technological competition, weapons proliferation, and fragile state peacekeeping—affect state behavior in different regions. The discussion of scenarios in this volume is not intended to force future thinking into mutually exclusive directions but, rather, to explore a range of possibilities. Such an approach must also take into account the likelihood that major unforeseen events—for example, a war in South Asia, a global pandemic killing hundreds of thousands, a massive migrant crisis triggered by conflict or climate stress—could push states and societies in one direction or another.

SCENARIO 1: REALISM IN A DANGEROUS WORLD

In scenario 1, we would expect to see states pursue both *competitive/instrumentalist* as well as *stabilization diplomacy*. Priority would be given to balancing competing states or groups of states and maintaining support for state sovereignty principles. As during the last half of the twentieth century, there could be both heightened international tensions and an overriding quest for stability. The tempering influence of international institutions in conflict management would continue at a much reduced level as major powers take a narrowly instrumentalist view of the United Nations. In these circumstances, the tension between competitive and stabilizing diplomatic approaches would be evident. Geopolitical confrontation and heightened conflict potential could play out alongside cautious, self-protective decision-making and a limited form of stabilization diplomacy in areas of common interest to the major powers, such as those described in chapter 16 by Daniel Benjamin on counterterrorism and chapter 14 by Toby Dalton on nonproliferation.

However, these forms of *competitive/instrumentalist* and *stabilization diplomacy* would appear to raise as many questions as they answer. Will powerful states simply back whichever local strongmen emerge in proxy states that lie within their sphere of influence? In an environment of geopolitical rivalry, will major powers favor stability or instability when a competitor's proxies get in trouble (Crocker 2019b)? The return of geopolitical polarization can spread across the international system, making an impact on a wide range of decision-makers, none of whom are immune from its effects, producing a chilling effect on the chances for peacemaking or conflict prevention.

The pursuit of rival manipulative agendas in, for example, Libya or Syria may cut directly against the chance to open channels of communication between the conflicting parties. As great powers flex their political muscles and extend their influence by "stealth," including noncoercive means, this will have an impact on decisions about the shape and even the future of UN peace operations, as chapter 13 by Lise Morjé Howard and chapter 3 by Jean-Marie Guéhenno point out. Containing or suppressing conflict in places such as Kashmir and Cyprus may also be a feature of such diplomatic efforts of aspiring regional powers seeking to assert their influence in their own neighborhoods. This scenario could aggravate current conflicts and lay the seeds of future violence, even while making the conduct of peace and conflict diplomacy more difficult to organize and implement, as Hans Binnendijk observes in chapter 4.

SCENARIO 2: A RETURN TO INTERNATIONAL COOPERATION

Scenario 2 features a reinvigorated pursuit of liberal international order priorities, including conflict prevention, respect for institutions, and support for better governance. Such *governance diplomacy* would address both interstate and intrastate challenges to peace and security. It would seek out negotiated political solutions to thorny conflicts and also ongoing intractable violence. The sorts of innovative, multistakeholder practices seen in Colombia, the Philippines-Mindanao strife, and the Iran nuclear deal would continue and perhaps expand. Rivalry and occasional tension between the UN system and regional or subregional organizations would continue to occur, but would not become entangled in the politics of a polarized UN Security Council.

Governance diplomacy cuts against the grain of today's nationalism and populism. We have included it because political tides can change; there could be a backlash against competitive/instrumentalist and "stabilization diplomacy." This could happen after further experience with the high costs of strongman rule and polarized proxy confrontations. It could happen in the wake of popular revulsion against the actions of a regional ally such as Saudi Arabia, or after experiencing more migrant drownings in the Mediterranean. The benefits of short-term stabilization could become sullied by the reputational and strategic costs of being sucked into the manipulations of regional friends in the Middle East or of counterterrorism allies in Africa. Moreover, as Daniel Benjamin points out in chapter 16, it is uncertain "how effectively Western nations can wall themselves off from developments in these more volatile parts of the world."

At a deeper level, the conflicts of tomorrow seem likely to be more complex, involving a greater range of internal and regional conflict parties whose political, commercial, security, and criminal interests shape the violence.

As Guéhenno notes, peace may not necessarily serve their interests. The German scholar Hanns Maull argues that state fragility and international disorder flow from the gap between the demand for, and supply of, global governance. Accordingly, "functioning national orders are an indispensable precondition for effective order beyond the state" (Maull 2019). If so, the time may come when major states once again recognize the importance of "governance diplomacy." Ana Palacio reminds us in chapter 5 that "governance diplomacy" is the form of statecraft most aligned with the culture and attributes of the European Union.

SCENARIO 3: LIMITED COOPERATION TO ACHIEVE PRAGMATIC GOALS

Scenario 3 explores prospects for a "concert of great powers," a far less liberal and less rules-based variant of scenario 2. In such a concert, states with different ideologies, values, and domestic systems nonetheless find it possible to cooperate on specific fields of common interest, with the general goal of upholding the balance of power and maintaining global order—rather than opportunistically exploiting potential opportunities within them. The multipolarity in this scenario is complex because states may align with distinct partners on different issues, and in doing so may pursue agendas that differ from others in the partnership arrangement. These informal alliances may be a means of increasing advantages for some while serving as a way to provide regional stability and harmony for others. The attitude of various states toward peace and conflict diplomacy will be defined by concrete challenges, specific regional situations, and their own national objectives rather than the promotion of universal governance norms. The effective pursuit of *stabilization diplomacy* is key to maintaining global order and stability because major powers are willing to curb—or disguise—their ambitions (unlike in scenario 1). As Dimitri Trenin makes clear in chapter 6, this scenario—based on cold calculations of national interest—may best suit Russia's interests, history, and geopolitical situation. It is possible that China may come to a similar conclusion after experiencing the reaction from the United States and others to its military muscle-flexing and expansive initiatives in trade, infrastructure, and cyber technology. In chapter 15, Stacie Hoffmann, Samantha Bradshaw, and Emily Taylor capture the type of challenge that could build toward confrontation, possibly inducing major states to define new rules of the road in 5G technology.

Modest rules of the road, rather than ambitious governance standards, are the essence of a concert system. Initiatives to act in concert are often improvised and reflect a "muddling through" approach, as discussed in chapter 2. Such rules can emerge as a result of hard experience with difficult problems, such as costly wars, pandemics, nuclear proliferation, climate crisis, and terrorism. Shared practices could evolve on issues related to peacekeeping in weak states, migration crises, naval confrontation in busy waterways, or hybrid warfare. Rules can emerge when states eschew "grandiose aspirations in favor of functional, practical, and actionable cooperative activities" that support confidence building and conflict prevention, as See Seng Tan notes in chapter 11, on Southeast Asia. He cites actions taken within the ASEAN Defense Ministers Meeting–Plus format in seven practical but sensitive fields: maritime security, humanitarian assistance and disaster relief, counterterrorism, peacekeeping operations, military medicine, humanitarian demining, and cybersecurity.[2]

In addition to taming the fires of regional conflict, *stabilization diplomacy* would require some core principles of behavior to be accepted among states, especially powerful ones. Henry Kissinger underscored both points in an interview after the 2016 US election: "The world is in chaos. Fundamental upheavals are occurring in many parts of the world simultaneously, most of which are governed by disparate principles. We are therefore faced with two problems: first, how to reduce regional chaos; second, how to create a coherent world order based on agreed-upon principles that are necessary for the operation of the entire system" (Goldberg 2016b).

These principles, for the most part, are under strain or do not exist at all today. But they can be restored or created when statesmanship returns in enough places, possibly in the wake of much harder and more dangerous experiences than seen so far. Richard Haass (2019) correctly notes that the old orders of post-1945 and post-1989 cannot be resurrected, but some elements of them can still be strengthened and supplemented with new provisions to reflect changed power dynamics and newly emerging global challenges, such as health, cyber activity, and climate. Creating a new concert among the major states is, in this view, a long-term imperative. Before reflexively assuming that globalization has run its course, we may be better advised to take into account the other side of this coin: grasping that interdependence is here to stay, and that global shocks may impel a heightened measure of realistic global thinking rather than go-it-alone self-isolation (Cooley and Nexon 2020).

REGIONAL VARIATIONS

How do the three variations on peace and conflict diplomacy play out on the regional stage? The implications for key regions will depend in part on what regional states do, acting on a national or regional basis; and in part on the still-unknown decisions of major states and the UN system. The previously noted Southeast Asia example discussed by See Seng Tan is an encouraging one, suggesting the potential for largely unheralded concertation and confidence building. Writing about regional states and great powers in South Asia and the Indian Ocean, in chapter 10 Kanti Bajpai sees a future that is "more realist than either liberal or intermittently functional," and he notes the possibility that "balances of power, deterrence, and restraint and conflict management could maintain at least a cold peace." Yet he acknowledges that a realist order in this region can coexist with a variety of structures in other regions and issue areas, leading to a future global order that is likely to be "an undulating one, varying by the mix of realism, liberalism, and functionalism across space, time, and subject." If he is right, regional variations will continue to play a central role, but we do not yet know the extent to which precedents will "bleed" into each other, affecting norms and decisions more broadly.

In the case of the Middle East, Shadi Hamid argues in chapter 9 that Arab regimes use state authority and the soft power of state-sponsored religion to reify nationalism and the nation, warding off all ideological and/or political challengers. Solidly embracing a realist scenario, most Arab regimes resist democratization and serious reform, privileging the need for strong states in order both to maintain power and to prevent the sort of regional turmoil that can follow from domestic instability. In response, external powers appear generally content to play along. Stronger, more effective states seem better at resisting terrorism, undertaking economic reform, and maintaining a monopoly on the use of force. Yet this posture will only "strengthen and entrench the repressive capabilities of those same states." *Stabilization diplomacy* could turn out to be a relatively short-term affair, producing seeds of future crises and instability.

In sharp contrast, the post–Cold War African state system evolved toward models that placed far greater weight on governance standards and the rule of law under the elaborately conceived regional security framework described by Solomon Ayele Dersso in chapter 8. The African Peace and Security Architecture is explicitly inspired by the norms and policies of a liberal peace model, however much actual practice may differ from the model in specific cases. The problem, however, is that state sovereignty norms rather than liberal ones have been bleeding into the region, as a function of examples from elsewhere and of the substantially less liberal external environment that has emerged since the African Union's charter was adopted twenty years ago. In places as diverse as Mali, the Central African Republic, the Democratic Republic of Congo, Burundi, South Sudan, Uganda, and Cameroon, the breakdown of order is a predictable consequence of electoral theft and strongman rule—a pattern that undermines Africa's liberal security regime.

In chapter 7 Marcos Tourinho describes the evolution of South and Central America since the 1980s, finding that standards of national and regional governance have trended upward. Nearly all conflicts were brought to an end, and a range of regional institutions were created to embody regional and subregional approaches in the economic and political arenas, culminating in the creation of the Union of South American Nations and its Defense Council. After placing the region squarely in a liberal universe where *governance diplomacy* prevails, Tourinho identifies factors behind the downward drift in more recent years in the performance of regional governance institutions—notably the spillover effects of global geopolitics and UN Security Council division, the inability of regional states to agree on action to stem the Venezuela crisis, and a rise in authoritarian tendencies at the national level.

Perhaps the greatest unknown factors are the implications for peace and conflict diplomacy of the triangular relationships between the United States, Russia, and China. On one hand, Trenin paints a picture of Russian interest-based realism and tactical flexibility. The United States, as discussed by Binnendijk, has signaled (as of the time of writing) its decision to step back from its leadership roles in support of peace and conflict management. Writing on China-US relations, in chapter 12 Chas Freeman portrays a bilateral race to the bottom as each side scapegoats the other and Washington points accusing fingers at Beijing on trade, human rights in Xinjiang and Hong Kong, and the response to the SARS-CoV-2 pandemic. It is clear that two can play this game, exercising their domestic political reflexes. The chapter by Hoffmann and colleagues on 5G further illustrates the potential for confrontation. None of this bodes well for the practice of peace and conflict diplomacy by the major powers. But it is likely that their preferences for managing and ending conflicts will play a central role in defining the years ahead (Howard and Stark 2018).

SUMMING UP

In assessing the future of peace and conflict diplomacy, we find support for the argument that the liberal, rules-based order is on the defensive, and that scenario 1 looks increasingly familiar, at least in the short term. But this is only a partial answer to the questions we must consider. Today's conflict arenas do not lend themselves to hierarchy and top-down conflict management—by powerful states, singly or in combination, under UN auspices. In chapter 3 Jean-Marie Guéhenno describes a "pervasive sense of loss of control" by major actors over regional states and local actors, making it less likely that either the

UN or regional organizations will have the coherence or the resources to do top-down peace and conflict diplomacy.

The ultimate paradox is that the return of geopolitics and the rise of nationalism and populism are not pointed in the direction of expeditionary or ambitious initiatives by major states to solve world security problems. As Hans Binnendijk observes in discussing US policy trends, there is a trend toward a diplomacy of restraint and disengagement. So we return to the questions raised above. Can *stabilization diplomacy* be squared with today's widely recognized era of strategic retrenchment (Walt 2019; Cohen 2019)? If the major power centers are content to work with whichever potentates and strongmen seize or cling to power in places like Egypt, Venezuela, North Korea, Saudi Arabia, Uganda, or Turkey, will such "stability" endure or will it lay the seeds of future revolt and trigger future conflicts? If it does, we can expect to see more *competitive/instrumentalist diplomacy* as major actors scramble to exploit the openings created by state fragility and civil war.

An alternative conclusion is that retrenchment by the major powers will reduce barriers to entry for innovative forms of peace and conflict diplomacy. These would need to address the "loss of control" challenge by engaging in new ways—where this is possible—at various levels of regional, national, and subnational authority. If the space for action is left open by the major powers, nonofficial and small and medium-sized state initiatives will remain as available options for peace and conflict diplomacy (Whitfield 2019). The UN system also retains a residual potential to offer a forum and platform for concerted diplomatic action, as it has in the past. These are big "ifs," but as the chapters in this book underscore, the evolution of the international order is not foreordained.

With concerted leadership, the instruments and institutions of both *stabilization and governance diplomacy* can help to avert violent conflict, even as new global shocks impel governments to see the merit of pragmatic collaboration. In many ways, *stabilization and governance diplomacy* are complementary assets or tools, for the simple reason that we have a foot in each of the three scenarios or "worlds" that animate the analyses in this book. The world is a much more complicated place than deterministic theories of international relations allow for, and human agency in the form of effective and well-executed diplomacy still has a vital role to play in managing and resolving conflict between, among, and within nations.

NOTES

1. Our conception of *governance diplomacy* differs from former national security adviser Susan Rice's use of the term of "transformational diplomacy," which was a distinctive US-led foreign policy objective of the Obama administration directed at promoting human

rights and democracy, particularly in the countries of the Middle East. We believe that efforts to promote pluralism and more inclusive forms of governance, which fall short of these more ambitious democracy-building goals, should also be included in the definition as well as the recognition that transformative governance can be an objective of nonstate and intergovernmental actors as well other states in the international system, i.e., it does not have to be entirely led by the United States. See US Department of State (2006).

2. The ADMM-Plus format includes the ten ASEAN states and eight of its dialogue partners: Australia, China, India, Japan, New Zealand, Russia, South Korea, and the United States.

REFERENCES

"新型冠状病毒感染的肺炎疫情知识问答." 2020. Wuhan Municipal Health Commission, http://wjw.wuhan.gov.cn/xwzx_28/gsgg/202004/t20200430_1199594.shtml.

Aall, Pamela, and Chester A. Crocker. 2018. "Minding the Gap: African Conflict Management in a Time of Change." Centre for International Governance Innovation.

Abbate, Janet. 1999. *Inventing the Internet*. Cambridge, MA: MIT Press.

Abi-Habib, Maria. 2018. "Pakistan's Military Has Quietly Reached Out to India for Talks." *New York Times*, September 4. www.nytimes.com/2018/09/04/world/asia/pakistan -india-talks.html.

Abi-Habib, Maria, and Austin Ramzy. 2019. "Indian Jets Strike in Pakistan in Revenge for Kashmir Attack." *New York Times*, February 25. www.nytimes.com/2019/02/25/world /asia/india-pakistan-kashmir-jets.html.

Acharya, Amitav. 1994. "Preventive Diplomacy: Issues and Institutions in the Asia Pacific Region." Eighth Asia-Pacific Roundtable, Kuala Lumpur, June 6–8. www.amitavacharya .com/sites/default/files/Preventive%20Diplomacy.pdf.

———. 1997. "Ideas, Identity, and Institution-Building: From the 'ASEAN Way' to the 'Asia-Pacific Way.'" *Pacific Review* 10, no. 3: 319–46. https://doi.org/10.1080/09512749 70819226.

———. 2004. "How Ideas Spread: Whose Norms Matter? Norm Localization and Institutional Change in Asian Regionalism." *International Organization* 58, no. 2 (Spring): 239–75. https://doi.org/10.1017/S0020818304582024.

"Address by President Vladmir Putin." 2004. Organization for Security and Co-operation in Europe, September 6. www.osce.org/what/military-reform/36479?download=true.

Adler, Emanuel. 1997. "Imagined (Security) Communities: Cognitive Regions in International Relations." *Millennium: Journal of International Studies* 26, no. 2 (June): 249–27.

———. 2004. *Communitarian International Relations: The Epistemic Foundations of International Relations*. London: Routledge.

Adler, Emanuel, and Michael N. Barnett. 1998. *Security Communities*. Cambridge: Cambridge University Press.

AHA Centre. 2017. *AJDRP: ASEAN Joint Disaster Response Plan*. Jakarta: AHA Centre.

Akkad, Dania. "Saudi Dissidents in US Warned by FBI After Khashoggi Killing." 2019. *Middle East Eye*, July 12. www.middleeasteye.net/news/exclusive-saudi-dissidents-us-warned-fbi -after-khashoggi-killing.

Alaoui, Sarah. 2019. "Morocco, Commander of the (African) Faithful?" Brookings Institution, April 8. www.brookings.edu/blog/order-from-chaos/2019/04/08/morocco-commander -of-the-african-faithful/.

Albert, Eleanor. 2020. "Trump Quietly Signs Legislation Strengthening Ties to Taiwan." *The Diplomat*, April 3. https://thediplomat.com/2020/04/trump-quietly-signs-legislation -strengthening-ties-to-taiwan/.

Alemu, Tekeda. 2019. "The Conundrum of Present Ethiopian Foreign Policy: In Search of a Roadmap for Ethiopia's Foreign and National Security Policy and Strategy." CDRC Ethiopia. www.cdrcethiopia.org/index.php/resorces/publications/download/2-cdrc-digest /25-cdrc-digest-january-2019.

Allard, Tom. 2017. "Southeast Asian States Launch Intelligence Pact to Counter Islamist Threat." Reuters, January 25. www.reuters.com/article/us-asia-intelligence/southeast-asian -states-launch-intelligence-pact-to-counter-islamist-threat-idUSKBN1FE163.

Allen, John R., Hady Amr, Daniel L. Byman, Banda Felbab-Brown, Jeffrey Feltman, Alice Friend, Jason Fritz, Adel Abdel Ghafar, Bruce Jones, Mara Karlin, Karim Mizran, Michael E. O'Hanlon, Federica Saini Fasanotti, Landry Signe, Arturo Varvelli, Frederic Wehrey, and Tarik M. Yousef. 2019. "Empowered Decentralization: A City-Based Strategy for Rebuilding Libya." Washington, DC: Brookings Institution Press. www.brookings .edu/research/empowered-decentralization-a-city-based-strategy-for-rebuilding-libya/.

Allison, Christine Rothmayr, and Denis Saint-Martin. 2011. "Half a Century of 'Muddling': Are We There Yet?" Policy and Society 30 (1): 1–8.

Allison, Graham. 2012. "Thucydides's Trap Has Been Sprung in the Pacific." Financial Times, August 21. www.ft.com/content/5d695b5a-ead3-11e1-984b-00144feab49a.

———. 2017. Destined for War: Can America and China Escape Thucydides's Trap? Boston: Houghton Mifflin Harcourt.

———. 2018. "The Myth of the Liberal Order: From Historical Accident to Conventional Wisdom." Foreign Affairs, July–August. www.foreignaffairs.com/articles/2018-06-14/myth -liberal-order.

Amorim, Celso. 2010. "Speech at the International Institute for Strategic Studies (IISS)." Ministry of Foreign Affairs, September 11. www.itamaraty.gov.br/en/speeches-articles -and-interviews/8080-sistemas-e-instituicoes-de-seguranca-perspectivas-regionais-8 -conferencia-anual-do-international-institute-for-strategic-studies-genebra-11-09-2010.

Andrew, Christopher, and Vasili Mitrokhin. 1999. The Sword and the Shield: The Mitrokhin Archive and the Secret History of the KGB. New York: Basic Books.

Aneme, Girmachew Alemu. 2011. A Study of the African Union's Right of Intervention against Genocide, Crimes against Humanity and War Crimes. Oisterwijk, NL: Wolf Legal.

Aning, Kwesi, and Mustepha Abdala. 2016. "Confronting Hybrid Threats in Africa: Improving Multidimensional Responses." In The Future of African Peace Operations: From the Janjaweed to Boko Haram, edited by Cedric de Coning, Linnea Gelot, and John Karlsrud. Chicago: University of Chicago Press.

Archibugi, Daniele. 2008. The Global Commonwealth of Citizens: Toward Cosmopolitan Democracy. Princeton, NJ: Princeton University Press.

Arms Control Association. 2019. "Nuclear Weapons: Who Has What at a Glance." www.arms control.org/factsheets/Nuclearweaponswhohaswhat.

"Army Chief Bipin Rawat Warns Pakistan: Misadventure Will Be Repelled with Punitive Response." 2019. Indian Express, July 13. https://indianexpress.com/article/india/india -pakistan-china-tension-kargil-war-anniversary-bipin-rawat-5827601/.

Art, Robert J. 2013. A Grand Strategy for America. Ithaca, NY: Cornell University Press.

Article 19. 2017. "Privacy: Yes! But Not at the ITU." Article 19, October 16. www.article19.org /resources/privacy-yes-but-not-at-the-itu/.

ASEAN (Association of Southeast Asian Nations). 2007. "ADMM-Plus Concept Paper." November 14. www.aseansec.org/21216.pdf.

————. 2009. Concept Paper on ASEAN Defense Ministers' Meeting-Plus (ADMM-Plus): Principles for Membership." February 26. www.aseansec.org/18471-e.pdf.

————. 2016. *ASEAN Political-Security Community Blueprint 2025*. Jakarta: ASEAN Secretariat.

————. 2017. "ASEAN Defense Ministers Launch Hotline for Quick Response." Xinhua, October 24. www.xinhuanet.com/english/2017-10/24/c_136703047.htm.

————. 2020. "Asian Americans Report Rise in Racist Attacks Amid Pandemic." PBS, April 1. www.pbs.org/newshour/show/what-anti-asian-attacks-say-about-american-culture-during-crisis.

Autesserre, Severine. 2014. *Peaceland: Conflict Resolution and the Everyday Politics of International Intervention*. Cambridge: Cambridge University Press.

Bah, Alhaji, Elizabeth Choge-Nyangoro, Solomon Dersso, Brenda Mofya, and Tim Murithi. 2014. *The African Peace and Security Architecture: A Handbook*. Bonn: Friedrich-Ebert-Stiftung.

Bajpai, Kanti. 2013. "India's Regional Disputes." In *Shaping the Emerging World Order: India and Multilateralism*, edited by WPS Sidhu, Pratap Bhanu Mehta, and Bruce Jones, 115–30. Washington, DC: Brookings Institution Press.

————. 2017. "Narendra Modi's Pakistan and China Policy: Assertive Bilateral Diplomacy, Active Coalition Diplomacy." *International Affairs* 93, no. 1: 69–91. https://doi.org/10.1093/ia/iiw003.

Baldino, David, and Andrew Carr. 2016. "Defence Diplomacy and the Australian Defence Force: Smokescreen or Strategy?" *Australian Journal of International Affairs* 70, no. 2: 139–58. https://doi.org/10.1080/10357718.2015.1113229.

Banim, Guy. 2014. *The EU in Myanmar: Preventive Diplomacy in Action?* ISS Brief 24/2014. Paris: EU Institute for Security Studies.

Banim, Guy, and Eva Pejsova, eds. 2017. *Prevention Better Than Cure: The EU's Quiet Diplomacy in Asia*. Paris: EU Institute for Security Studies.

Barnes-Darcey, Julien. 2019. "The Geopolitics Of Reconstruction: Who Will Rebuild Syria?" European Council on Foreign Relations, September 16. www.ecfr.eu/article/commentary_the_geopolitics_of_reconstruction_who_will_rebuild_syria.

Barnett, Michael N., and Martha Finnemore. 1999. "The Politics, Power, and Pathologies of International Organizations." *International Organization* 53, no. 4 (Autumn): 699–732. https://doi.org/10.1162/002081899551048.

————. 2004. *Rules for the World: International Organizations in Global Politics*. Ithaca, NY: Cornell University Press.

Barwise, Patrick. 2018. "Why Tech Markets Are Winner-Take-All." Media Policy Project, June 14. https://blogs.lse.ac.uk/mediapolicyproject/2018/06/14/why-tech-markets-are-winner-take-all/.

Basu, Nayanima. 2020. "India Lodges Protest with Pakistan After Ceasefire Violation Kills Youth in Poonch." *The Print*, May 01. https://theprint.in/diplomacy/india-lodges-protest-with-pakistan-after-ceasefire-violation-kills-youth-in-poonch/412918/.

Baweja, Harinder. 2019. "Let Pakistan Army Chief Come Through Government for Talks: Gen Bipin Rawat." *Hindustan Times*, July 28. www.hindustantimes.com/india-news/let-pakistan-army-chief-come-through-government-for-talks-gen-bipin-rawat/story-Rb590Rcth1UoUbDJiCzoLJ.html.

Beardsley, Kyle. 2011. "Peacekeeping and the Contagion of Armed Conflict." *Journal of Politics* 73, no. 4 (October): 1051–64. https://doi.org/10.1017/S0022381611000764.

Beardsley, Kyle, and Kristian Skrede Gleditsch. 2015. "Peacekeeping as Conflict Containment." *International Studies Review* 17, no. 1 (March): 67–89. https://doi.org/10.1111/misr.12205.

Becker, Jasper. 2004. "China Fights UN Sanctions on Sudan to Safeguard Oil." *The Independent*, October 15. www.independent.co.uk/news/world/africa/china-fights-un-sanctions-on-sudan-to-safeguard-oil-543801.html.

"Beijing Hits Back at Trump Call to Block US Pension Fund Investment in China." 2020. *Financial Times*, May 13. www.ft.com/content/a0da73e0-33c2-4ac5-a635-fb5fd9160293.

Bellamy, Alex J., Paul D. Williams, and Stuart Griffin. 2010. *Understanding Peacekeeping*, 2nd ed. Cambridge: Polity Press.

"Best of Today: Today." 2019. *BBC Sounds*, January 31. www.bbc.co.uk/sounds/play/p06zkjpt.

Betigeri, Aarti. 2019. "The Remarkable Political Influence of the Indian Diaspora in the US." *The Interpreter*, Lowy Institute, April 16. www.lowyinstitute.org/the-interpreter/remarkable-political-influence-indian-diaspora-us.

Bhattacharya, Kallol. 2020. "Pakistan's Contribution Triggers Debate Over SAARC COVID-19 Emergency Fund." *The Hindu*, April 10. www.thehindu.com/news/national/pakistans-contribution-triggers-debate-over-saarc-covid-19-emergency-fund/article31303918.ece.

Bialik, Kristen. 2018. "How the World Views the US and Its President in 2018 in 9 Charts." Pew Research Center, October 09. www.pewresearch.org/fact-tank/2018/10/09/how-the-world-views-the-u-s-and-its-president-in-9-charts/.

Bimal, Samridhi. 2014. "Investment in Pakistan: Prospects and Challenges for India." *Ideas for India*, July 21. www.ideasforindia.in/topics/macroeconomics/investment-in-pakistan-prospects-and-challenges-for-india.html.

Binnendijk, Hans. 2016. *Friends, Foes, and Future Directions: US Partnerships in a Turbulent World*. Santa Monica, CA: RAND Corporation. www.rand.org/pubs/research_reports/RR1210.html.

Blair, Robert. 2020. *Peacekeeping, Policing and the Rule of Law after Civil War*. Cambridge: Cambridge University Press.

Blatchford, Andy. 2019. "The Bank of Canada Is Very Worried About the US-China Trade War Getting Worse, Wilkins Says." *Financial Post*, May 30. https://business.financialpost.com/news/economy/trade-war-escalation-major-preoccupation-for-bank-of-canada-top-official.

Bloomfield, Lincoln P. 1959. "The Tools of Diplomacy: The Relationship Between Means and Ends Is the Central Problem in Foreign Policy." *Worldview Magazine* (Carnegie Council) 2, no. 5 (May).

Boutros-Ghali, Boutros. 1992. *An Agenda for Peace: Preventive Diplomacy, Peace-Making and Peace-Keeping*. New York: United Nations.

———. 1993. "An Agenda for Peace: One Year Later." *Orbis* 37, no. 3 (Summer): 323–32. https://doi.org/10.1016/0030-4387(93)90148-6.

Bove, Vincent, and Andrea Ruggeri. 2016. "Kinds of Blue: Diversity in UN Peacekeeping Missions and Civilian Protection." *British Journal of Political Science* 46, no. 3: 681–700.

Bradshaw, Samantha, and Laura DeNardis. 2018. "The Politicization of the Internet's Domain Name System: Implications for Internet Security, Universality, and Freedom." *New Media & Society* 20 (1): 332–50. https://doi.org/10.1177/1461444816662932.

Brands, Hal. 2017. *American Grand Strategy in the Age of Trump*. Washington, DC: Brookings Institution Press.

Britton-Purdy, Jedediah. 2018. "Normcore." *Dissent*, Summer. www.dissentmagazine.org/article/normcore-trump-resistance-books-crisis-of-democracy.

Broad, William J., David Sanger, and Raymond Bonner. 2004. "A Tale of Nuclear Proliferation: How Pakistni Built His Network." *New York Times*, February 12. www.nytimes.com/2004 /02/12/world/a-tale-of-nuclear-proliferation-how-pakistani-built-his-network.html.

Brockmeier, Sarah, Oliver Stuenkel, and Marcos Tourinho. 2016. "The Impact of the Libya Intervention Debates on Norms of Protection." *Global Society* 30, no. 1: 113–33. https:// doi.org/10.1080/13600826.2015.1094029.

Broder, John M., and Jim Mann. 1994. "Clinton Reverses His Policy, Renews China Trade Status : Commerce: President 'De-Links' Most-Favored-Nation Privilege from Human Rights. He Admits Failure of Earlier Course and Says Broader Strategic Interests Justify Switch." *Los Angeles Times*, May 27. http://articles.latimes.com/1994-05-27/news/mn -62877_1_human-rights.

"Brussels Summit Declaration: Issued by the Heads And Government Participating in the Meeting of the North Atlantic Council in Brussels, 11–12 July 2018." 2018. North Atlantic Treaty Organization, July 12. www.nato.int/cps/en/natohq/official_texts_156624 .htm?selectedLocale=en.

Bryan-Low, Cassell, Colin Packham, David Lague, Steve Stecklow, and Jack Stubbs. 2019. "Special Report: Hobbling Huawei—Inside the US War on China's Tech Giant." Reuters, May 21. https://ca.reuters.com/article/technologyNews/idINKCN1SR1EV.

Bull, Benedicte. 1999. "'New Regionalism' in Central America." *Third World Quarterly* 20, no. 5 (October): 957–70. www.jstor.org/stable/3993606.

Bull, Hedley. 1977. *The Anarchical Society: A Study of Order in World Politics*. London: Macmillan.

Byler, Darren. 2019. "China's Hi-Tech War on Its Muslim Minority." *Guardian*, April 11. www .theguardian.com/news/2019/apr/11/china-hi-tech-war-on-muslim-minority-xinjiang -uighurs-surveillance-face-recognition.

Byman, Daniel. 2005. *Deadly Connections: States That Sponsor Terrorism*. Cambridge: Cambridge University Press.

Caballero-Anthony, Mely, and Alistair Cook, eds. 2013. *Non-Traditional Security in Asia: Issues, Challenges and Framework for Action*. Singapore: ISEAS Yusof Ishak Institute.

Cabestan, Jean-Pierre. 2018. "China's Evolving Role as a UN Peacekeeper in Mali." US Institute of Peace Special Report. www.usip.org/publications/2018/09/chinas-evolving-role -un-peacekeeper-mali.

"The Cabinet Committee on Security Reviews Operationalization of India's Nuclear Doctrine." 2003. Ministry of External Affairs, January 4. https://mea.gov.in/press-releases .htm?dtl/20131/The_Cabinet_Committee_on_Security_Reviews_perationalization _of_Indias_Nuclear_Doctrine+Report+of+National+Security+Advisory+Board+on +Indian+Nuclear+Doctrine.

Cahill, Kevin M. 1996. *Preventive Diplomacy: Stopping Wars Before They Start*. New York: Basic Books.

Calahan, Alexander B. 1995. "Countering Terrorism: The Israeli Response to the 1972 Munich Olympic Massacre and the Development of Independent Covert Action Teams." Master's thesis, April. https://fas.org/irp/eprint/calahan.htm.

Calamur, Krishnadev. 2018. "Africa Is the New Front in the US-China Influence War." *Atlantic*. www.theatlantic.com/international/archive/2018/12/trump-national-security-adviser -unveils-new-africa-strategy/578140/.

Campbell, Susanna. 2018. *Global Governance and Local Peace*. Cambridge: Cambridge University Press.

Caplan, Richard. 2005. *International Governance of War-Torn Territories: Rule and Reconstruction*. Oxford: Oxford University Press.

Carnegie, Allison, and Christoph Mikulaschek. 2016. "The Promise of Peacekeeping: Protecting Civilians in Civil Wars." www.peio.me/wp-content/uploads/PEIO9/102_80_1443668392515_CarnegieMikulaschek30092015.pdf.

Cartwright, Jan. 2009. "India's Regional and International Support for Democracy: Rhetoric or Reality?" *Asian Survey* 49, no. 3 (May): 403–28. https://doi.org/10.1525/as.2009.49.3.403.

Carver, Fred. 2018. "Peacekeeping Budget Approval and Cuts Leave Fundamental Questions Unaddressed." Global Observatory. https://theglobalobservatory.org/2018/09/peacekeeping-budget-approval-cuts-questions-unaddressed/.

CBS News. 2018. "Saudi Crown Prince: If Iran Develops Nuclear Bomb, So Will We." March 15. www.cbsnews.com/news/saudi-crown-prince-mohammed-bin-salman-iran-nuclear-bomb-saudi-arabia/.

Cerulus, Laurens. 2017. "China's Ghost in Europe's Telecom Machine." *Politico*, December 11. www.politico.eu/article/huawei-china-ghost-in-europe-telecom-machine/.

Chandler, Ainslie. 2020. "China Suspends Meat Imports from Four Australian Abattoirs." MSN, May 11. www.msn.com/en-us/news/world/china-suspends-meat-imports-from-four-australian-abattoirs/ar-BB13SYAB.

Chang, Jun Yan, and Alan Chong. 2016. "Security Competition by Proxy: Asia Pacific Interstate Rivalry in the Aftermath of the MH370 Incident." *Global Change, Peace & Security* 28 (1): 75–98. https://doi.org/10.1080/14781158.2016.1115756.

"Chapter Ten: Rising Military Expenditure in Asia: Towards Greater Strategic Autonomy?" 2018. In *Asia-Pacific Regional Security Assessment 2018*, 149–64. London: International Institute for Strategic Studies.

Chen, Stephen. 2018. "China's Brightest Children Are being Recruited to Develop AI 'Killer Bots.'" *South China Morning Post*, November 8. www.scmp.com/news/china/science/article/2172141/chinas-brightest-children-are-being-recruited-develop-ai-killer.

Cheng, Guangjin. 2010. "Chinese Combat Troops 'Can Join UN Peacekeeping.'" *China Daily*, July 7. www.chinadaily.com.cn/china/2010-07/07/content_10073171.htm.

Chergui, Ismail. 2019. "Statement by Ambassador Smail Chergui, AU Commissioner for Peace and Security on Security Threats and Challenges Faced by Africa at the First China-Africa Peace and Security Forum, 14 July 2019 in Beijing, China." African Union Peace and Security, July 15. www.peaceau.org/en/article/statement-by-ambassador-smail-chergui-au-commissioner-for-peace-and-security-on-security-threats-and-challenges-faced-by-africa-at-the-first-china-africa-peace-and-security-forum-14-july-2019-in-beijing-china.

Cheung, Tai Ming. 2018. "The Rise of China as a Cybersecurity Industrial Power: Balancing National Security, Geopolitical, and Development Priorities." *Journal of Cyber Policy* 3, no. 3: 306–26. https://doi.org/10.1080/23738871.2018.1557234.

"China Registers 8,000 Standby Peacekeepers at the UN." 2017. Xinhua, September 28. www.xinhuanet.com/english/2017-09/28/c_136645953.htm.

China's Role in UN Peacekeeping. 2018. Stockholm: Institute for Security and Development Policy.

"Chinese General to Lead UN Peacekeeping Force." 2011. *Straits Times*, January 14.

Chirgwin, Richard. 2012. "Huawei Banned from Australia's NBN: Reports." *The Register*, March 25. www.theregister.co.uk/2012/03/25/huawei_nbn_ban/.

Choong, William. 2017. "Trump and the Asia-Pacific: Managing Contradictions." *Survival* 59, no. 1: 181–87. https://doi.org/10.1080/00396338.2017.1282672.

Christensen, Jen, and Michael Nedelman. 2018. "Climate Change Will Shrink US Economy and Kill Thousands, Government Report Warms." CNN, November 26. www.cnn.com /2018/11/23/health/climate-change-report-bn/index.html.

Christensen, Thomas J. 1996. *Useful Adversaries: Grand Strategy, Domestic Mobilization, and Sino-American Conflict, 1947–1958*. Princeton, NJ: Princeton University Press.

"CJCS Admiral Mullen's January 17 Meeting with President Uribe." 2008. Wikileaks Cable 08BOGOTA337, US Embassy in Bogotá.

Clinton, Bill. 2019. "Dayton Accords." *Encyclopedia Britannica,* November 14. www.britannica .com/event/Dayton-Accords.

Clover, Charles. 2017. *Black Wind, White Snow: The Rise of Russia's New Nationalism*. New Haven, CT: Yale University Press.

Cockayne, James. 2020. *Hidden Power: The Strategic Logic of Organized Crime*. Oxford: Oxford University Press.

Coe, Andrew J., and Jane Vaynman. 2015. "Collusion and the Nuclear Nonproliferation Regime." *Journal of Politics* 77 (4): 983–97. https://doi.org/10.1086/682080.

Cohen, Eliot A. 2019. "America's Long Goodbye: The Real Crisis of the Trump Era." *Foreign Affairs,* January–February. www.foreignaffairs.com/articles/united-states/long-term-disaster -trump-foreign-policy.

Coll, Steve. 2009. "The Back Channel: India and Pakistan's Secret Kashmir Talks." *New Yorker,* February 23. www.newyorker.com/magazine/2009/03/02/the-back-channel.

"Commentary: Xi Demonstrates China's Role as Responsible Country in New Year Address." 2018. Xinhua, January 1. www.xinhuanet.com/english/2018-01/01/c_136865307.htm.

Communist Party of China. 2012. "Communiqué on the Current State of the Ideological Sphere." Document No. 9.

Cooley, Alexander, and Daniel Nexon. 2020. "Trump Announced the US Will Suspend WHO Funding. That Could Leave Another Global Initiative Under China's Influence." *Washington Post,* April 14.

Cooper, Andrew F. 2017. "The Organization of American States." In *Handbook of South American Governance,* edited by Pia Riggirozzi and Christopher Wylde. London: Routledge.

Corfield, Gareth. 2019. "Huawei's Half-Arsed Router Patching Left Kit Open to Botnets: Chinese Giant Was Warned Years Ago—Then Bungled It." *The Register,* March 28. www .theregister.co.uk/2019/03/28/huawei_mirai_router_vulnerability/.

"COVID-19 and China: A Chronology of Events (December 2019–January 2020)." 2020. Congressional Research Service, May 13. https://crsreports.congress.gov/product/pdf /download/R/R46354/R46354.pdf/.

Crawford, Susan. 2018. *Fiber*. New Haven, CT: Yale University Press.

Crocker, Chester A. 2019a. "African Governance: Challenges and Their Implications, Governance in an Emerging New World Order." Hoover Institution, January 14. www.hoover .org/research/african-governance-challenges-and-their-implications.

———. 2019b. "The Diplomacy of Engagement: Ending Civil Wars in Transitional Middle Eastern States." In *Escaping The Conflict Trap: Civil Wars in the Middle East,* edited by Ross Harrison and Paul Salem. Washington, DC: Middle East Institute.

Crocker, Chester A., Fen Osler Hampson, and Pamela Aall. 2011a. "Collective Conflict Management: A New Formula for Global Peace and Global Security Cooperation?" *International Affairs* 87, no. 1 (January): 39–58. www.jstor.org/stable/20869610.

———, eds. 2011b. *Rewiring Regional Security in a Fragmented World*. Washington, DC: US Institute of Peace.

————. 2013. *Managing Conflict in a World Adrift*. Washington, D.C.: United States Institute of Peace Press.

————. 2021. *Diplomacy and the Future of World Order*. Washington, DC: Georgetown University Press.

Cruz, Carlos Alberto dos Santos, William R. Phillips, and Salvator Cusimano. 2017. "Improving Security of United Nations Peacekeepers: We Need to Change the Way We Are Doing Business." UN Peacekeeping, December 19. https://peacekeeping.un.org/sites/default/files/improving_security_of_united_nations_peacekeepers_report.pdf.

Cunliffe, Philip. 2013. *Legions of Peace: UN Peacekeepers from the Global South*. London: Hurst.

Cunningham, David. 2016. "Preventing Civil War: How the Potential for International Intervention Can Deter Conflict Onset." *World Politics* 68, no. 2 (April): 307–40. https://doi.org/10.1017/S0043887115000404.

Curtis, Devon. 2012. "The Contested Politics of Peacebuilding in Africa." In *Peacebuilding, Power And Politics in Africa*, edited by Curtis Devon and Gwinyan A. Dzinesa. Athens: Ohio University Press.

Daalder, Ivo, and James Lindsay. 2007. "Democracies of the World, Unite." *The American Interest* 2, no. 3. www.the-american-interest.com/2007/01/01/democracies-of-the-world-unite/.

Dallas, Mary Elizabeth. 2020. "Global COVID-19 Cases Top 4.2 Million." ShareCare, May 12. www.sharecare.com/health/coronavirus/article/what-know-about-wuhan-coronavirus.

Dalton, Toby. 2019. "Signaling and Catalysis in Future Nuclear Crises in South Asia: Two Questions after the Balakot Episode." Nuclear Crisis Group and Carnegie Endowment for International Peace. https://carnegieendowment.org/2019/06/25/signaling-and-catalysis-in-future-nuclear-crises-in-south-asia-two-questions-after-balakot-episode-pub-79373.

Dalton, Toby, Wyatt Hoffman, Ariel (Eli) Levite, Li Bin, George Perkovich, and Tong Zhao. 2017. "Toward a Nuclear Firewall: Bridging the NPT's Three Pillars." Carnegie Endowment for International Peace, March 20. https://carnegieendowment.org/2017/03/20/toward-nuclear-firewall-bridging-npt-s-three-pillars-pub-68300.

Dalton, Toby, and Michael Krepon. 2015. "A Normal Nuclear Pakistan." Stimson Center and Carnegie Endowment for International Peace. https://carnegieendowment.org/files/NormalNuclearPakistan.pdf.

Dalton, Toby, Byun Sunggee, and Lee Sang Tae. 2016. "South Korea Debates Nuclear Options." Carnegie Endowment for International Peace. https://carnegieendowment.org/2016/04/27/south-korea-debates-nuclear-options-pub-63455.

Darkwa, Linda. 2016. "The Strategic Relationship between the African Union and Its Partners." In *The Future of African Peace Operations: From the Janjaweed to Boko Haram*, edited by Cedric de Coning. Linnea Gelot, and John Karlsrud. Chicago: University of Chicago Press.

Dasgupta, Sumona. 2015. "Kashmir and the India-Pakistan Composite Dialogue Process." RSIS Working Paper 291. www.rsis.edu.sg/wp-content/uploads/2015/05/WP291.pdf.

Davis, Mark. 2015. "How World War II Shaped Modern Russia." *Euro News*, May 4. www.euronews.com/2015/05/04/how-world-war-ii-shaped-modern-russia.

Day, Jeff, Roger Shepherd, Paul Kearney, and Richard Storer. 2018. "Secure Design Best Practice Guide." IoT Security Foundation.

De Carvalho, Gustavo. 2017. "Looking for a Home: Mediation and the AU." Institute for Security Studies Africa Report. https://issafrica.s3.amazonaws.com/site/uploads/ar-1.pdf.

Delfs, Arne. 2018. "Germany Toughens Stance and Blocks China Deal." Bloomberg, August 1. www.bloomberg.com/news/articles/2018-08-01/germany-said-to-block-company-purchase-by-chinese-for-first-time.

Della-Giacoma, Jim. 2011. "Preventive Diplomacy in Southeast Asia: Redefining the ASEAN Way." International Crisis Group, December 31. www.crisisgroup.org/asia/south-east-asia /preventive-diplomacy-southeast-asia-redefining-asean-way.

Deltenre, Damien, and Michel Liégeois. 2016. "Filling a Leaking Bathtub? Peace-Keeping in Africa and the Challenge of Transnational Armed Rebellions." *African Security* 9, no. 1: 1–20. https://doi.org/10.1080/19392206.2016.1132902.

Deng, Yong. 2008. *China's Struggle for Status: The Realignment of International Relations.* Cambridge: Cambridge University Press.

De Oliveira, Ricardo Soares, and Harry Verhoeven. 2018. "Taming Intervention: Sovereignty, Statehood and Political Order in Africa." *Survival* 60, no. 2: 7–32. https://doi.org/10 .1080/00396338.2018.1448558.

Dersso, Solomon A. 2012. "The Quest for Pax Africana: The Case of AU's Peace and Security Regime." *African Journal of Conflict Resolution* 12, no. 2: 11–47.

———. 2013a. "The African Peace and Security Architecture." In *Handbook of Africa's International Relations,* edited by Timothy Murithi. London: Taylor & Francis.

———. 2013b. "The African Union." In *An Institutional Approach to the Responsibility to Protect,* edited by Gentian Zyberi. Cambridge: Cambridge University Press.

———. 2016. "To Intervene or Not to Intervene? An Inside View of the AU's Decision-Making on Article 4(H) and Burundi." World Peace Foundation, March 1. https://sites .tufts.edu/reinventingpeace/2016/03/01/to-intervene-or-not-to-intervene-an-inside -view-of-the-aus-decision-making-on-article-4h-and-burundi/.

———. 2017. "Defending Constitutional Rule as a Peacemaking Enterprise: The Case of the AU's Ban of Unconstitutional Changes of Government." *International Peacekeeping* 24, no. 4: 639–60. https://doi.org/10.1080/1353312.2017.1345314.

———. 2019. "If You Think AU's Action on Sudan Does Not Matter, Think Again." Solomondersso, June 6. https://solomondersso.wordpress.com/2019/06/06/if-you-think -aus-action-on-sudan-does-not-matter-think-again/.

De Spiegeleire, Stephan, Clarissa Skinner, and Tim Sweijs. 2017. *The Rise of Populist Sovereignism.* The Hague: Centre for Strategic Studies.

Deudney, Daniel, and G. John Ikenberry. 1999. "The Nature and Sources of Liberal International Order." *Review of International Studies* 25, no. 2 (April): 179–96. www.jstor.org /stable/20097589.

———. 2018. "Liberal World: The Resilient Order." *Foreign Affairs,* July–August, 16–24.

Deutsch, Karl W. 1957. *Political Community and the North Atlantic Area: International Organization in the Light of Historical Experience.* Princeton, NJ: Princeton University Press.

De Waal, Thomas. 2016. "Russia, Turkey, and a Multipolar World." Carnegie Europe, August 30. https://carnegieeurope.eu/strategiceurope/64421.

"Diplomatic Relations Between the United States and the People's Republic of China: Remarks at a White House Briefing, Following the Address to the Nation." 1978. *Jimmy Carter: The American Presidency Project,* December 15. www.presidency.ucsb.edu/documents /diplomatic-relations-between-the-united-states-and-the-peoples-republic-china-remarks.

Di Salvatore, Jessica. 2020. "Obstacle to Peace? Ethnic Geography and Effectiveness of Peacekeeping." *British Journal of Political Science* 50, no. 3: 1089–1109.

Donaldson, Kitty. 2018. "Spy Boss Says UK Must Decide If Huawei Suitable for 5G Network." Bloomberg, December 3. www.bloomberg.com/news/articles/2018-12-03/spy-boss-says -u-k-must-decide-if-huawei-suitable-for-5g-network.

Doran, Charles F. 2012. "Power Cycle Theory and the Ascendance of China: Peaceful or Stormy?" *SAIS Review* 32, no. 1: 73–87. https://doi.org/10.1353/sais.2012.0016.

Doyle, Michael W. 1983. "Kant, Liberal Legacies, and Foreign Affairs." *Philosophy and Public Affairs* 12, no. 3. (July): 205–35. www.jstor.org/stable/2265298.

Doyle, Michael W., and Nicholas Sambanis. 2006. *Making War and Building Peace: United Nations Peace Operations*. Princeton, NJ: Princeton University Press.

Drake, Bruce. 2014. "More Americans Say US Failed to Achieve Its Goals in Iraq." Pew Research Center, June 12. www.pewresearch.org/fact-tank/2014/06/12/more-americans-say-us -failed-to-achieve-its-goals-in-iraq/.

Drezner, Daniel. 2019. "This Time Is Different: Why US Foreign Policy Will Never Recover." *Foreign Affairs*, May–June. www.foreignaffairs.com/articles/2019-04-16/time-different.

Drozdiak, William. 2017. *Fractured Continent: Europe's Crises and the Fate of the West*. New York: W. W. Norton.

Drucker, Peter F. 1963. "Managing for Business Effectiveness." *Harvard Business Review*, May. https://hbr.org/1963/05/managing-for-business-effectiveness.

Dunn, Lewis A. 2010. "A World of Nuclear Powers: A *Gedanken* Experiment." In *Forecasting Nuclear Weapons in the 21st Century*, Vol. 1, edited by William C. Potter and Gaukhar Mukhatzhanova, 193–230. Stanford, CA: Stanford University Press.

Eck, Kristine, and Lisa Hultman. 2007. "One-Sided Violence against Civilians in War: Insights from New Fatality Data." *Journal of Peace Research* 44, no. 2: 233–246.

Eckel, Mike, and Carl Schreck. 2019. "Washington Autopsy Files Reveal Lesin Sustained Broken Bone in Neck." RadioFreeEurope, March 16. www.rferl.org/a/lesin-autopsy-record /29824566.html.

"The *Economist* Explains: What Are The Minsk Agreements?" 2016. *The Economist*, September 14. www.economist.com/the-economist-explains/2016/09/13/what-are-the-minsk -agreements.

Elders. 2019. "The Elders Call on Egypt's al-Sisi to Uphold AU Commitments on Sudan Transition." https://theelders.org/news/elders-call-egypt-s-al-sisi-uphold-au-commitments -sudan-transition.

El Gamal, Rania, and Katie Paul. 2017. "Saudi Arabia Hopes to Start Nuke Pact Talks with US in Weeks—Minister." Reuters, December 20. www.reuters.com/article/us-saudi-energy -nuclear/saudi-arabia-hopes-to-start-nuclear-pact-talks-with-u-s-in-weeks-minister -idUSKBN1EE2PJ.

"Emergency Hotline Set Up for ASEAN Defense Ministers." 2015. *Straits Times*, November 1–3. www.straitstimes.com/asia/se-asia/emergency-hotline-set-up-for-asean-defence-ministers.

"Emergency Session (of the AU Peace and Security Council) on the Situation in Sudan, Insights on the Peace and Security Council." 2019. Amani Africa. www.amaniafrica-et.org /images/Reports/EmergencysessiononontheSituationinSudan.pdf.

Emmers, Ralf. 2009a. *Geopolitics and Maritime Territorial Disputes in East Asia*. London: Routledge.

———. 2009b. "Comprehensive Security and Resilience in Southeast Asia: ASEAN's Approach to Terrorism." *Pacific Review* 22, no. 2: 159–77. https://doi.org/10.1080/0951 2740902815300.

Emmers, Ralf, and See Seng Tan. 2010. "The ASEAN Regional Forum and Preventive Diplomacy: Built to Fail?" *Asian Security* 7, no. 1: 44–60. https://doi.org/10.1080/14799855 .2011.548211.

Emmerson, Donald K. 2012. "Beyond the Six Points: How Far Will Indonesia Go?" *East Asia Forum*, July 29. www.eastasiaforum.org/2012/07/29/beyond-the-six-points-how-far -will-indonesia-go/.

Engel, Ulf, and João Gomes Porto. 2010. "Africa's New Peace and Security Architecture: Promoting Norms and Institutionalizing Solutions." *African Security* 2, no. 2: 82–96.

Epstein, Susan B., Cory R. Gill, and Marian L. Lawson. 2019. "Department of State, Foreign Operations and Related Programs: FY 2019 Budget and Appropriations." Congressional Research Service, March 12. https://fas.org/sgp/crs/row/R45168.pdf.

"Eradicating 'Ideological Viruses': China's Campaign of Repression Against Xinjiang's Muslims." 2018. Human Rights Watch. www.hrw.org/report/2018/09/09/eradicating -ideological-viruses/chinas-campaign-repression-against-xinjiangs.

Esquirol, Jorge L. 2012. "Latin America." In *The Oxford Handbook of the History of International Law*, edited by Bardo Fassbender and Anne Peters. Oxford: Oxford University Press.

ETSI (European Telecommunications Standards Institute). No date. "Why Do We Need 5G?" www.etsi.org/technologies/5g.

"EU-Turkey Joint Action Plan." 2015. European Commission, October 15. https://ec.europa .eu/commission/presscorner/detail/en/MEMO_15_5860.

"FCC Proposes to Protect National Security Through FCC Programs." 2018. Federal Communications Commission, April 18. www.fcc.gov/document/fcc-proposes-protect -national-security-through-fcc-programs-0.

Felbab-Brown, Vanda, Harold Trinkunas, and Shadi Hamid. 2017. *Militants, Criminals, and Warlords: The Challenge of Local Governance in an Age of Disorder.* Washington, DC: Brookings Institution Press.

Fidler, Mailyn. 2018. "African Union Bugged by China: Cyber Espionage as Evidence of Strategic Shifts." Council on Foreign Relations, March 7. www.cfr.org/blog/african-union -bugged-china-cyber-espionage-evidence-strategic-shifts.

Fifield, Mitch, and Scott Morrison. 2018. "The Government Provides 5G Security Guidance for Australian Carriers." Press release, Government of Australia.

Financial Times. 2018. "America's Scrambled Approach to Africa." December 17. www.ft.com /content/d9fd28cc-ff94-11e8-aebf-99e208d3e521.

"Finding the Right Role for the G5 Sahel Joint Force." 2017. International Crisis Group, Africa Report 258, December 12. www.crisisgroup.org/africa/west-africa/burkina-faso/258 -force-du-g5-sahel-trouver-sa-place-dans-lembouteillage-securitaire.

"First Agreement of Principles Governing the Normalisation of Relations." 2013. Serbia-Kosovo Agreement. Brussels, April 19.

Fitzpatrick, Mark. 2016. "Asia's Latent Nuclear Powers: Japan, South Korea, and Taiwan." International Institute for Strategic Studies, February.

Fjelde, Hanne, Lisa Hultman, and Desiree Nilsson. 2019. "Protection through Presence: UN Peacekeeping and the Costs of Targeting Civilians." *International Organization* 73, no. 1: 103–31. https://doi.org/10.1017/S0020818318000346.

Fletcher, Tom. 2016. *The Naked Diplomat: Understanding Power and Politics in the Digital Age.* London: HarperCollins UK.

Foot, Rosemary. 2014. "Doing Some Things in the Xi Jinping Era: The United Nations as China's Venue of Choice." *International Affairs* 90, no. 5: 1085–1100. https://doi.org/10 .1111/1468-2346.12158.

Fonte, Giuseppe, and Francesca Piscioneri. 2019. "Italy to Extend Golden Share Powers to 5G Technologies: League Party." Reuters, March 20. https://uk.reuters.com/article/us -china-italy-5g-idUKKCN1R10X8.

Forrell, Joseph, and Gareth Solaner. 1986. *Competition, Compatability and Standards: The Economics of Horses, Penguins and Lemmings.* Berkeley University of California Press.

Fortna, Virginia Page. 2004. "Interstate Peacekeeping: Causal Mechanisms and Empirical Effects." *World Politics* 56, no. 4 (July): 481–519. https://doi.org/10.1353/wp.2005.0004.

———. 2008. *Does Peacekeeping Work? Shaping Belligerents' Choices after Civil War.* Princeton, NJ: Princeton University Press.

Fortna, Virginia Page, and Reyko Huang. 2012. "Democratization after Civil War: A Brush-Clearing Exercise." *International Studies Quarterly* 56, no. 4 (December): 801–8. www.jstor.org/stable/41804834.

"Fragility, Conflict & Violence." 2020. World Bank, March 5. www.worldbank.org/en/topic/fragilityconflictviolence/overview.

Franco, Joseph Raymond Silva. 2013. "Malaysia: Unsung Hero of the Philippine Peace Process." *Asian Security* 9, no. 3: 211–30. https://doi.org/10.1080/14799855.2013.832210.

Freedom House. 2018. "Freedom in the World 2018: Democracy in Crisis." https://freedom house.org/report/freedom-world/freedom-world-2018.

Friedberg, Aaron L. 2012. *A Contest for Supremacy: China, America, and the Struggle for Mastery in Asia.* New York: W. W. Norton.

Fuhrmann, Matthew, and Benjamin Tkach. 2015. "Almost Nuclear: Introducing the Nuclear Latency Dataset." *Conflict Management and Peace Science* 32, no. 4: 443–61. https://doi.org/10.1177/0738894214559672.

Fung, Courtney J. 2016. "What Explains China's Deployment to UN Peacekeeping Operations?" *International Relations of the Asia Pacific* 16, no. 3: 409–41. https://doi.org/10.1093/irap/lcv020.

———. 2019. *China and Intervention at the UN Security Council: Reconciling Status.* Oxford: Oxford University Press.

"Future Thinking: Alissa Cooper on the Technical Impact of Internet Consolidation." 2019. Internet Society, February 12. www.internetsociety.org/blog/2019/02/future-thinking-alissa-cooper-technical-impact-internet-consolidation/.

Gajanan, Mahita. 2017. "Elon Musk Believes This Will Be the Most Likely Cause of World War III." *Fortune*, September 4. http://fortune.com/2017/09/04/elon-musk-ai-world-war-three/.

Ganguly, Sumit. 1995. "Discord and Cooperation in India-Pakistan Relations." In *Interpreting World Politics: Essays for A. P. Rana*, edited by Kanti P. Bajpai and Harish C. Shukul, 400–412. New Delhi: Sage.

Ganguly, Sumit, and S. Paul Kapur. 2012. *India, Pakistan, and the Bomb: Debating Nuclear Stability in South Asia.* New York: Columbia University Press.

George, Alexander L. 2000. "Strategies for Preventive Diplomacy and Conflict Resolution: Scholarship for Policymaking." *PS: Political Science and Politics* 33, no. 1: 15–19. https://doi.org/10.2307/420771.

Gewirtz, David. 2018. "Volume, Velocity, And Variety: Understanding the Three Vs of Big Data." *ZDNet*, March 21. www.zdnet.com/article/volume-velocity-and-variety-understanding-the-three-vs-of-big-data/.

Ghosh, Shona. 2019. "Huawei Says US Has 'No Evidence, Nothing' of Chinese Spying." *Business Insider*, February 26. www.businessinsider.com/huawei-says-us-has-no-evidence-nothing-of-chinese-spying-2019-2?r=US&IR=T.

Giarda, Raffaele, Antonio Lattanzio, and Jacopo Liotta. 2019. "Italy Tightens Foreign Investment Scrutiny over 5G Technology." Lexology. www.lexology.com/library/detail.aspx?g=ef072174-4897-4f52-8506-64fac69187ff.

Gill, Bates, and Chin-Hao Huang. 2009. "China's Expanding Role in Peacekeeping: Prospects and Policy Implications." Stockholm International Peace Research Institute policy paper.

Gilligan, Michael, and Ernest J. Sergenti. 2008. "Do UN Interventions Cause Peace? Using Matching to Improve Causal Inference." *Quarterly Journal of Political Science* 3, no. 1: 89–122. https://doi.org/10.1561/100.00007051.

Gilpin, Robert. 1981. *War and Change in World Politics.* Cambridge: Cambridge University Press.

Gilsinian, Kathy. 2019. "How the US Could Lose a War with China." *Atlantic*, July 25. www.theatlantic.com/politics/archive/2019/07/china-us-war/594793/.

Gladstone, Rick. 2018. "China and Russia Move to Cut Human Rights Jobs in UN Peace-keeping." *New York Times*, June 28. www.nytimes.com/2018/06/27/world/africa/china-russia-un-human-rights-cuts.html.

Glaser, Charles L. 2010. *Rational Theory of International Politics: The Logic of Competition and Cooperation.* Princeton, NJ: Princeton University Press.

———. 2011. "Will China's Rise Lead to War?" *Foreign Affairs*, March–April. www.foreignaffairs.com/articles/asia/2011-03-01/will-chinas-rise-lead-war.

Global Commission on Internet Governance. 2016. "One Internet: Centre for International Governance Innovation." www.cigionline.org/publications/one-internet.

Global Forum on Cyber Expertise. 2018. "The Cybersecurity Tech Accord Supports The GFCE's Call for Industry-Wide Adoption of Transparent Policies for Coordinated Vulnerability Disclosure (CVD)." Cybersecurity Tech Accord, September 10. https://cybertechaccord.org/supports-gfce-call-for-cvd/.

Goh, Evelyn. 2011. "Institutions and the Great Power Bargain in East Asia: ASEAN's Limited 'Brokerage' Role." *International Relations of the Asia-Pacific* 11, no. 3: 373–401. https://doi.org/10.1093/irap/lcr014.

Goldberg, Jeffrey. 2016a. "The Obama Doctrine," *Atlantic*, April. www.theatlantic.com/magazine/archive/2016/04/the-obama-doctrine/471525/.

———. 2016b. "The Lessons of Henry Kissinger." *Atlantic*, December. www.theatlantic.com/magazine/archive/2016/12/the-lessons-of-henry-kissinger/505868/.

Goldsmith, Jack, and Tim Wu. 2006. *Who Controls the Internet? Illusions of a Borderless World.* Oxford: Oxford University Press.

Gompert, David C., and Hans Binnendijk. 2016. "The Power to Coerce: Countering Adversaries Without Going to War." RAND Corporation. www.rand.org/pubs/research_reports/RR1000.html.

Gonzalez, Elisabeth. 2018. "Explainer: Latin American Countries' Rising Trade with China." Americas Society/Council of the Americas, November. www.as-coa.org/articles/explainer-latin-american-countries-rising-trade-china.

Gowan, Richard. 2018. "China Fills a Trump-Sized Vacuum at the UN." *Politico*, September 24. www.politico.com/magazine/story/2018/09/24/china-trump-united-nations-220529.

———. 2019. "A Decade After Failing to Stop Massacres in Sri Lanka, What Has the UN Learned?" *World Politics Review*, March 19. www.worldpoliticsreview.com/articles/27664/a-decade-after-failing-to-stop-massacres-in-sri-lanka-what-has-the-u-n-learned.

Gray, Noah. 2017. "Trump Compliments Egyptian President's Shoes." CNN, May 21. https://edition.cnn.com/2017/05/21/politics/trump-abdel-fattah-al-sisi-shoes/index.html.

Greene, Megan, and Daniel P. Kelemen. 2016. "Europe's Failed Refugee Policy." *Foreign Affairs*, June 28. www.foreignaffairs.com/articles/europe/2016-06-28/europes-failed-refugee-policy.

Gries, Peter Hays. 2005. *China's New Nationalism.* Berkeley: University of California Press.

GSMA (Global System for Mobile Communications Association). 2018. "Migration from Physical to Virtual Network Functions: Best Practices and Lessons Learned." October 12.

www.gsma.com/futurenetworks/5g/migration-from-physical-to-virtual-network
-functions-best-practices-and-lessons-learned/.

———. 2019. "5G Spectrum Positions Offer a Roadmap for Regulators." July 26. www.gsma
.com/spectrum/resources/5g-spectrum-positions/.

———. No date. "Fraud and Security Group." www.gsma.com/aboutus/workinggroups
/fraud-security-group.

Guardian. 2018. "New Zealand Blocks Huawei Imports Over 'Significant Security Risk.'" www
.theguardian.com/business/2018/nov/28/new-zealand-blocks-huawei-5g-equipment
-on-security-concerns.

———. 2019. "Huawei: China Calls US Charges 'Immoral' as Markets Slide." www.the
guardian.com/technology/2019/jan/28/huawei-china-telecoms-charged-us-trade
-secrets-fraud.

Guéhenno, Jean-Marie. 2015. *The Fog of Peace: A Memoir of International Peacekeeping in the
21st Century*. Washington, DC: Brookings Institution Press.

Gupta, Shishir. 2020. "Pak Launches Terror's New Face in Kashmir, Imran Khan Follows Up on Twitter." *Hindustan Times*, May 8. www.hindustantimes.com/india-news
/pak-launches-terror-s-new-face-in-kashmir-imran-khan-follows-up-on-twitter/story
-vDmvByzkeowrW8OKruhS3M.html.

Gupta, Sisir. 1966. *Kashmir: A Study in India-Pakistan Relations*. New Delhi: Asia Publishers.

Gurses, Mehmet, and T. David Mason. 2008. "Democracy Out of Anarchy: The Prospects for
Post-Civil-War Democracy." *Social Science Quarterly* 89, no. 2 (June): 315–36. www.jstor
.org/stable/42956316.

Haass, Richard. 2019. "How a World Order Ends, and What Comes in Its Wake." *Foreign Affairs*,
January–February. www.foreignaffairs.com/articles/2018-12-11/how-world-order-ends.

Hachigian, Nina, and David Shorr. 2013. "The Responsibility Doctrine." *Washington Quarterly*
36, no. 1 (February): 73–91. https://doi.org/10.1080/0163660X.2013.751652.

Hamid, Shadi, and Peter Mandaville. 2013. "Bringing the United States Back into the Middle
East." *Washington Quarterly* 36, no. 4 (Fall): 95–105. https://doi.org/10.1080/0163660X
.2013.861716.

Hampson, Fen Osler, and Paul Heinbecker. 2013. "Leadership in a Turbulent Age." *CIGI
Papers* 11, January 22. www.cigionline.org/publications/leadership-turbulent-age.

Hancock, Simon. 2019. "Panorama: Can We Trust Huawei?" BBC One. www.bbc.co.uk/iplayer
/episode/m0004cgm/panorama-can-we-trust-huawei.

Hanemann, Thilo, Daniel H. Rosen, Cassie Gao, and Adam Lysenko. 2020. "Two-Way Street:
US-China Investment Trends—2020 Update." Rhodium Group, May 11. https://rhg
.com/research/two-way-street-us-china-investment-trends-2020-update/.

Harris, Gardiner. 2018. "Pompeo Questions the Value of International Groups Like UN
and EU." *New York Times*, December 4. www.nytimes.com/2018/12/04/world/europe
/pompeo-brussels-speech.html.

Hartzell Caroline, Hoddie Matthew, and Rothchild Donald. 2001. "Stabilizing the Peace after
Civil War: An Investigation of Some Key Variables." *International Organization* 55, no. 1:
183–208.

Hashim, Ahmed. 2017. "State and Non-State Hybrid Warfare." Oxford Research Group,
March 30. www.oxfordresearchgroup.org.uk/Blog/state-and-non-state-hybrid-warfare.

Hassan, Hassan. 2018. "ISIS Is Poised to Make a Comeback in Syria." *Atlantic*, September 18.
www.theatlantic.com/ideas/archive/2018/09/isis-is-poised-to-make-a-comeback-in
-syria/569986/.

Hathaway, Oona A., and Scott J. Shapiro. 2017. *The Internationalists: How a Radical Plan to Outlaw War Remade the World*. New York: Simon & Schuster.

Hayden, Michael. 2016. *Playing to the Edge: American Intelligence in the Age of Terror*. New York: Penguin.

Heisbourg, François. 2018. "War and Peace after the Age of Liberal Globalisation." *Survival* 60, no. 1 (February–March): 211–28. https://doi.org/10.1080/00396338.2018.1427378.

Hemmings, John. 2018. "To Ban or to Banbury?" RUSI, December 7. https://rusi.org /commentary/ban-or-banbury.

Hersey, Frank. 2018. "Lenovo Founder in Public Backlash for 'Unpatriotic 5G Standards Vote.'" *TechNode*, May 16. https://technode.com/2018/05/16/lenovo-huawei-5g/.

Herz, Monica. 2008. "Does the Organisation of American States Matter?" Crisis States Working Paper 2, April.

High Commission of India. 2019. "Important Agreements." October 31. www.india.org.pk /pages.php?id=17.

"High-Technology Exports (Current US$)." No date. World Bank. https://data.worldbank .org/indicator/TX.VAL.TECH.CD?locations=CN.

Hirono, Miwa, and Marc Lanteigne. 2011. "Introduction: China and UN Peacekeeping." *International Peacekeeping* 18, no. 3: 243–56. https://doi.org/10.1080/13533312.2011 .563070.

Hitchens, Theresa, and Nancy W. Gallagher. 2019. "Building Confidence in the Cybersphere: A Path to Multilateral Progress." *Journal of Cyber Policy* 4, no. 1: 4–21. https://doi.org /1080/23738871.2019.1599032.

Hobbes, Thomas. 2010. *Leviathan: Or the Matter, Forme, & Power of a Common-Wealth Ecclesiasticall and Civil*, edited by Ian Shapiro. New Haven, CT: Yale University Press.

Hoffman, Samantha, and Elsa Kania. 2018. "Huawei and the Ambiguity of China's Intelligence and Counter-Espionage Laws." *Strategist*, September 13. www.aspistrategist.org.au /huawei-and-the-ambiguity-of-chinas-intelligence-and-counter-espionage-laws/.

Holland, Steve, and Jeff Mason. 2014. "Obama, in Dig at Putin, Calls Russia 'Regional Power.'" Reuters, March 25. www.reuters.com/article/us-ukraine-crisis-russia-weakness/obama -in-dig-at-putin-calls-russia-regional-power-idUSBREA2O19J20140325.

Holmes, Steven. 1993. "Africa from Cold War to Cold Shoulders." *New York Times*, March 7. www.nytimes.com/1993/03/07/weekinreview/the-world-africa-from-the-cold-war-to -cold-shoulders.html.

Horowitz, Michael. 2018. "Artificial Intelligence, International Competition, and the Balance of Power." *Texas National Security Review* 1, no. 3: 36–57. https://doi.org/10.15781 .T2639KP49.

Houvenaeghel, Joeffrey. 2015. *The European Contribution to the Mindanao Peace Process*, EAIS Briefing Paper 2015/1. Brussels: European Institute of Asian Studies.

Howard, Lise Morjé. 2008. *UN Peacekeeping in Civil Wars*. Cambridge: Cambridge University Press.

———. 2019. *Power in Peacekeeping*. Cambridge: Cambridge University Press.

Howard, Lise Morjé, and Anjali Kaushlesh Dayal. 2018. "The Use of Force in UN Peacekeeping." *International Organization* 72, no. 1 (Winter): 71–103. https://doi.org/10.1017 /S0020818317000431.

Howard, Lise Morjé, and Alexandra Stark. 2018. "How Civil Wars End: The International System, Norms, and the Role of External Actors." *International Security* 42, no. 3 (Winter): 127–71. https://doi.org/10.1162/ISEC_a_00305.

Huan, Amanda, and Ralf Emmers. 2016. "What Explains the Success of Preventive Diplomacy in Southeast Asia?" *Global Change, Peace & Security* 28, no. 5: 1–17. https://doi.org/10.1080/14781158.2016.1259214.

Huawei. 2018. "Huawei First to Complete IMT-2020 (5G) Promotion Group's Core Network Test for 5G Non-Standalone." Huawei Press Center, April 12. www.huawei.com/en/press-events/news/2018/4/IMT-2020-5G-Group-Core-Network-Test.

Huawei Cyber Security Oversight Board. 2019. "Huawei Cyber Security Evaluation Centre Oversight Board: Annual Report 2019." UK Government, March 28. www.gov.uk/government/publications/huawei-cyber-security-evaluation-centre-oversight-board-annual-report-2019.

"Huawei Is at the Centre of Political Controversy." 2019. *The Economist*, April 27. www.economist.com/briefing/2019/04/27/huawei-is-at-the-centre-of-political-controversy.

Hultman, Lisa, Jacob Kathman, and Megan Shannon. 2013. "United Nations Peacekeeping and Civilian Protection in Civil War." *American Journal of Political Science* 57, no. 4 (October): 875–91. https://doi.org/10.1111/ajps.12036.

———. 2014. "Beyond Keeping Peace: United Nations Effectiveness in the Midst of Fighting." *American Political Science Review* 108, no. 4 (November): 737–53. https://doi.org/10.1017/S0003055414000446.

Human Rights Watch. 2019. "World Report 2019." www.hrw.org/world-report/2019.

Huntington, Samuel P. 1991. *The Third Wave: Democratization in the Late Twentieth Century.* Norman: University of Oklahoma Press.

Hurel, Louise M., and Luisa Cruz Lobato. 2018. "Unpacking Cyber Norms: Private Companies As Norm Entrepreneurs." *Journal of Cyber Policy* 3, no. 1: 61–76. https://doi.org/10.1080/23738871.2018.1467942.

Hurley, John, Scott Morris, and Gailyn Portelance. 2018. "Examining the Debt Implications of the Belt and Road Initiative from a Policy Perspective." Center for Global Development, Policy Paper 121. www.cgdev.org/sites/default/files/examining-debt-implications-belt-and-road-initiative-policy-perspective.pdf.

Hurrell, Andrew. 1998a. "'An Emerging Security Community in South America?'" In *Security Communities*, edited by Emanuel Adler and Michael N Barnett, 264–88. Cambridge: Cambridge University Press.

———. 1998b. "Security in Latin America." *International Affairs* 74, no. 3 (July): 529–46. www.jstor.org/stable/2624967.

Ignatius, David. 2020. "Think We Have Military Primacy Over China? Think Again." *Washington Post*, May 12. www.washingtonpost.com/opinions/global-opinions/think-we-have-military-primacy-over-china-think-again/2020/05/12/268e1bba-948b-11ea-9f5e-56d8239bf9ad_story.html?utm_campaign=wp_post_most&utm_medium=email&utm_source=newsletter&wpisrc=nl_most.

Ikenberry, G. John. 2009. "Liberal Internationalism 3.0: America and the Dilemmas of Liberal World Order." *Perspectives on Politics* 7, no. 1 (March): 71–87. https://doi.org/10.1017/S153759270909112.

———. 2018. "The End of the Liberal International Order?" *International Affairs* 94, no. 1 (January): 7–23. https://doi.org/10.1093/ia/iix241.

Ikenberry, G. John, and Anne-Marie Slaughter. 2006. "Forging a World Under Liberty and Law: US National Security in the 21st Century." Princeton Project Papers, Woodrow Wilson School of International Affairs, Princeton University, September 27.

"India, Pakistan Can Take Two-Way Trade to $30 Billion, Says Indian Envoy." 2018. *Business Today,* March 31. www.businesstoday.in/current/economy-politics/india-pakistan-trade -30-billion-ajay-bisaria-indian-envoy-to-pak/story/273749.html.

"India to Dethrone China as World's Most Populated Country in Seven Years, UN Says." 2017. *South China Morning Post,* June 22. www.scmp.com/news/asia/east-asia/article /2099453/india-dethrone-china-worlds-most-populated-country-seven-years.

Inman, Phillip. 2018. "World Economy at Risk of Another Financial Crash, Says IMF." *Guardian,* October 3. www.theguardian.com/business/2018/oct/03/world-economy-at-risk -of-another-financial-crash-says-imf.

Intelligence and Security Committee, Great Britain, and Parliament. 2013. "Foreign Involvement in the Critical National Infrastructure: The Implications for National Security." London: Stationery Office.

International Atomic Energy Agency. 2016. "IAEA Sees Global Nuclear Power Capacity Growing Through 2030." September 23. www.iaea.org/newscenter/pressreleases/iaea -sees-global-nuclear-power-capacity-growing-through-2030.

———. 2019. "IPI Peacekeeping Database Graphs: Providing for Peacekeeping." www .providingforpeacekeeping.org/peacekeeping-data-graphs/.

International Crisis Group. 2016. "The African Union and the Burundi Crisis: Ambition versus Reality." Briefing 122. www.crisisgroup.org/africa/central-africa/burundi/african-union -and-burundi-crisis-ambition-versus-reality.

———. 2019. "A Tale of Two Councils: Strengthening AU-UN Cooperation." Africa Report 279.

IoT Security Foundation. 2017. "Vulnerability Disclosure Best Practice Guidelines." December. www.iotsecurityfoundation.org/best-practice-guidelines/.

"ISAF's Mission In Afghanistan (2001–2014) (Archived)." 2015. North Atlantic Treaty Organization, September 1. www.nato.int/cps/en/natohq/topics_69366.htm.

"Is China Contributing to the United Nations' Mission?" 2016. China Power Team, Center for Strategic and International Studies, March 7. https://chinapower.csis.org/china-un-mission/.

Jacob, Happymon. 2019. *Line on Fire: Ceasefire Violations and India-Pakistan Escalation Dynamics.* New Delhi: Oxford University Press.

Jervis, Robert L. 1976. *Perception and Misperception in International Politics.* Princeton, NJ: Princeton University Press.

———. 1978. "Cooperation under the Security Dilemma." *World Politics* 30, no. 2 (January): 167–214. https://doi.org/10.2307/2009958.

"John McCain: Russia Is a 'Gas Station Masquerading as a Country.'" 2014. *The Week,* March 16. https://theweek.com/speedreads/456437/john-mccain-russia-gas-station -masquerading-country.

Johnson, Clete. 2019. "Mitigating Security Risks to Emerging 5G Networks." Center for Strategic and International Studies, February 6. www.csis.org/events/mitigating-security -risks-emerging-5g-networks.

Johnston, A. I. 2008. *Social States: China in International Institutions, 1980–2000.* Princeton, NJ: Princeton University Press.

"Joint Communication to the European Parliament and the Council: Towards A Comprehensive Strategy with Africa." 2020. European Commission, March 9.

"Joint Comprehensive Plan of Action." No date. US Department of State Archive. https:// 2009-2017.state.gov/e/eb/tfs/spi/iran/jcpoa//index.htm.

"Joint Statement by the ADMM-Plus Defence Ministers on Practical Confidence-Building Measures." 2018. Singapore Ministry of Defence, October 20. www.mindef.gov.sg /web/portal/mindef/news-and-events/latest-releases/article-detail/2018/october /20oct18_fs.

Jones, Lee. 2010. "ASEAN's Unchanged Melody? The Theory and Practice of Nonintervention in Southeast Asia." *Pacific Review* 23, no. 3: 479–502.

Joshi, Madhav. 2013. "United Nations Peacekeeping, Democratic Process, and the Durability of Peace after Civil Wars." *International Studies Perspectives* 14, no. 3: 362–82. https://doi .org/10.1111/j.1528-3585.2012.00499.x.

Judis, John B. 2016. *The Populist Explosion: How the Great Recession Transformed American and European Politics.* New York: Columbia Global Reports.

"The Juncker Commission: A Strong and Experienced Team Standing for Change." 2014. European Commission, September 10. https://ec.europa.eu/commission/presscorner /detail/en/IP_14_984.

Kacowicz, Arie M. 1998. *Zones of Peace in the Third World: South America and West Africa in Comparative Perspective.* Albany: State University of New York Press.

Kagan, Robert. 2008. "The Case for a League of Democracies." *Financial Times,* May 13. www .ft.com/content/f62a02ce-20eb-11dd-a0e6-000077b07658.

———. 2018. "The World America Made and Trump Wants to Unmake." *Politico,* September 28. www.politico.com/magazine/story/2018/09/28/donald-trump-unga-liberal-world -order-220738.

———. 2019. "The Strongmen Strike Back." *Washington Post,* March 14. www.washingtonpost .com/news/opinions/wp/2019/03/14/feature/the-strongmen-strike-back/?utm_term =.f3836a4feb2e.

Kang, David. 2009. *China Rising: Peace, Power, and Order in East Asia.* New York: Columbia University Press.

Kant, Immanuel. 2016. *Perpetual Peace: A Philosophical Essay.* Translated by Mary C. Smith. Salt Lake City: Project Gutenberg.

Kaplan, Robert D. 2012. "Why John J. Mearsheimer Is Right (About Some Things)." *Atlantic,* January–February. www.theatlantic.com/magazine/archive/2012/01/why-john-j -mearsheimer-is-right-about-some-things/308839/.

———. 2019. "A New Cold War Has Begun." *Foreign Policy,* January 7. https://foreignpolicy .com/2019/01/07/a-new-cold-war-has-begun/.

Kapoor, Nivedita. 2019. "Russia-Pakistan Relations and Its Impact on India." Observer Research Foundation, July 3. www.orfonline.org/expert-speak/russia-pakistan-relations-impact-india -52715/.

Kapur, S. Paul, and Diane Wueger. 2018. "Nuclear Weapons and Sino-Indian Security Relations." In *Defence Primer: An Indian Military in Transformation?,* edited by Pushan Das and Harsh V. Pant, 92–100. New Delhi: Observer Research Foundation. www.orfonline.org /wp-content/uploads/2018/04/Defence_Primer_2018.pdf.

Karlin, Mara, and Tamara Cofman Wittes. 2019. "Ending America's Middle East Purgatory: The Case for Doing Less." *Foreign Affairs,* January–February. www.foreignaffairs.com /articles/middle-east/2018-12-11/americas-middle-east-purgatory.

Karpukhin, Sergei. 2017. "Putin: Leader in Artificial Intelligence Will Rule World." CNBC, September 4. www.cnbc.com/2017/09/04/putin-leader-in-artificial-intelligence-will-rule -world.html.

Kaspersen, Anja. 2015. "8 Emerging Technologies Transforming International Security." World Economic Forum, September 8. www.weforum.org/agenda/2015/09/8-technologies -transforming-international-security/.

Kathman, Jacob D., and Reed M. Wood. 2016. "Stopping the Killing During the 'Peace': Peacekeeping and the Severity of Postconflict Civilian Victimization." *Foreign Policy Analysis* 12, no. 2: 149–69. https://doi.org/10.1111/fpa.12041.

Katwala, Amit. 2019. "Here's How GCHQ Scours Huawei Hardware for Malicious Code." *Wired UK*, February 22. www.wired.co.uk/article/huawei-gchq-security-evaluation-uk.

Kelion, Leo. 2019. "Huawei's 'Shoddy' Work Prompts Talks of a Westminster Ban." BBC, April 8.

Kennedy, Scott. 2017. "The Fat Tech Dragon: Benchmarking China's Innovation Drive." Center for Strategic and International Studies, August.

Kent, Ann. 1999. *China, the United Nations, and Human Rights: The Limits of Compliance.* Philadelphia: University of Pennsylvania Press.

Khamooshi, Arash. 2016. "Breaking Down Apple's iPhone Fight with the US Government." *New York Times*, March 3. www.nytimes.com/interactive/2016/03/03/technology /apple-iphone-fbi-fight-explained.html.

Khan, Nyla Ali. 2018. "Sh Abdullah's Letter to Ayub Khan." *Daily Times*, April 18. https:// dailytimes.com.pk/229456/sh-abdullahs-letter-to-ayub-khan/.

Kioko, Ben. 2003. "The Right of Intervention under the African Union's Constitutive Act: From Non-Interference to Non-Intervention." *International Review of the Red Cross* 85, no. 852: 807–25.

Kirişci, Kemal, and Philippe Le Corre. 2018. "The New Geopolitics of Central Asia: China Vies for Influence in Russia's Backyard—What Will It Mean for Kazakhstan?" Brookings Institution, New Geopolitics of Asia Series.

Kissinger, Henry. 1984. *The Necessity for Choice.* Santa Barbara, CA: Greenwood Press.

Kühn, Ulrich, Tristan Volpe, and Bert Thompson. 2018. "Tracking the German Nuclear Debate." Carnegie Endowment for International Peace, August 15. https://carnegie endowment.org/2018/08/15/tracking-german-nuclear-debate-pub-72884.

Kuwali, Dan, and Frans Viljoen. 2015. "Africa and the Responsibility to Protect: Article 4(h) of the African Union Constitutive Act" *Journal of Conflict and Security Law* 20, no. 2: 323–28. https://doi.org/10.1093/jcsl/krv011.

Lacey, Robert. 2010. *Inside the Kingdom: Kings, Clerics, Modernists, Terrorists and the Struggle for Saudi Arabia.* London: Arrow Books.

Ladwig, Walter C. 2008. "A Cold Start for Hot Wars? The Indian Army's New Limited War Doctrine." *International Security* 32, no. 3 (Winter): 158–90. www.jstor.org/stable /30130521.

Lague, David, and Benjamin Kang Lim. 2019. "China's Vast Fleet Is Tipping the Balance in the Pacific." Reuters, April 16. www.reuters.com/investigates/special-report/china-army -navy/.

Lam, Lana, and Stephen Chen. 2013. "Exclusive: Snowden Reveals More US Cyberspying Details." *South China Morning Post*, June 22. www.scmp.com/news/hong-kong/article /1266777/exclusive-snowden-safe-hong-kong-more-us-cyberspying-details-revealed.

Landler, Mark, and Edward Wong. 2018. "Bolton Outlines a Strategy for Africa That's Really About Countering China." www.nytimes.com/2018/12/13/us/politics/john-bolton-africa -china.html.

Lanteigne, Marc. 2005. *China and International Institutions: Alternative Paths to Global Power*. London: Routledge.

———. 2018. "The Role of UN Peacekeeping in China's Expanding Strategic Interests." US Institute of Peace, November 6. www.usip.org/publications/2018/09/role-un-peace keeping-chinas-expanding-strategic-interests.

Larmer, Brook. 2018. "A Malaysian Insta-City Becomes a Flash Point for Chinese Colonialism—and Capital Flight." *New York Times*, March 13. www.nytimes.com/2018/03/13 /magazine/a-malaysian-insta-city-becomes-a-flash-point-for-chinese-colonialism-and -capital-flight.html.

Larson, Deborah Welch, and Alexei Shevchenko. 2010. "Status Seekers: Chinese And Russian Responses to US Primacy." *International Security* 34, no. 4 (Spring): 63–95.

Lawfare. 2018a. "Geoeconomics: The Chinese Strategy of Technological Advancement and Cybersecurity." December 3. www.lawfareblog.com/geoeconomics-chinese-strategy -technological-advancement-and-cybersecurity.

———. 2018b. "Geoeconomics: The US Strategy of Technological Protection and Economic Security." December 11. www.lawfareblog.com/geoeconomics-us-strategy-technological -protection-and-economic-security.

Layne, Christopher. 1997. "From Preponderance to Offshore Balancing: America's Future Grand Strategy." *International Security* 22, no. 1 (Summer): 86–124. https://doi.org/10 .2307/2539331.

———. 2006a. *The Peace of Illusions: American Grand Strategy from 1940 to the Present*. Ithaca, NY: Cornell University Press.

———. 2006b. "The Unipolar Illusion Revisited: The Coming End of the United States' Unipolar Moment." *International Security* 31, no. 2 (Fall): 7–41. https://doi.org/10.1162 /isec.2006.31.2.7.

Lazanski, Dominique. 2019a. "Governance in International Technical Standards Making: A Tripartite Model." *Journal of Cyber Policy* 4, issue 3.

———. 2019b. "China, Huawei and 5G Standards in the UK." *Forbes*, April 27. www.forbes .com/sites/dominiquelazanski/2019/04/27/china-huawei-and-5g-standards-in-the-uk/ #208c57f82fbd.

Lebow, Richard Ned. 2003. *The Tragic Vision of Politics*. New York: Cambridge University Press.

Lecher, Colin. 2019. "US Tells Germany to Stop Using Huawei Equipment or Lose Some Intelligence Access." *The Verge*, March 11. www.theverge.com/2019/3/11/18260344/us -germany-huawei-5g-letter-security.

Lee, Christine. 2020. "It's Not Just the WHO: How China Is Moving on the Whole UN." *Politico*, April 15. www.politico.com/news/magazine/2020/04/15/its-not-just-the-who -how-china-is-moving-on-the-whole-un-189029.

Lee, Kai-Fu. 2018. *AI Superpowers: China, Silicon Valley, and the New World Order*. New York: Houghton Mifflin Harcourt.

Lego, Jera. 2017. "Why ASEAN Can't Ignore the Rohingya Crisis." *The Diplomat*, May 17. https://thediplomat.com/2017/05/why-asean-cant-ignore-the-rohingya-crisis/.

Leifer, Michael. 1996. *The ASEAN Regional Forum: Extending ASEAN's Model of Security*, Adelphi Paper 302. London: Oxford University Press for International Institute for Strategic Studies.

———. 1999. "The ASEAN Peace Process: A Category Mistake." *Pacific Review* 12, no. 1: 25–38. https://doi.org/10.1080/09512749908719276.

Leon, Melissa. 2019. "White House Slams China's 'Highly Dubious' Infrastructure Project as Bolton Warns Ukraine." Fox News, August 28. www.foxnews.com/politics/white-house-china-dubious-infrastructure-project-bolton-ukraine.

Lessig, Lawrence. 2006. *Code: And Other Laws of Cyberspace, Version 2.0.* 2nd ed. New York: Basic Books.

Levite, Ariel. 2003. "Never Say Never Again: Nuclear Reversal Revisited." *International Security* 27, no. 3 (Winter): 59–88. www.jstor.org/stable/3092114.

Levite, Ariel, and Toby Dalton. 2017. "Leveling Up the Nuclear Trade Playing Field." Carnegie Endowment for International Peace, September 7. https://carnegieendowment.org/2017/09/07/leveling-up-nuclear-trade-playing-field-pub-73038.

Levitt, Barry S. 2006. "A Desultory Defense of Democracy: OAS Resolution 1080 and the Inter-American Democratic Charter." *Latin American Politics and Society* 48, no. 3 (Autumn): 93–123. www.jstor.org/stable/4490479.

Levy, Ian. 2019. "Security, Complexity and Huawei; Protecting the UK's Telecoms Networks." National Cyber Security Centre, February 22. www.ncsc.gov.uk/blog-post/security-complexity-and-huawei-protecting-uks-telecoms-networks.

Lewis, Jeffrey. 2018. *The 2020 Commission Report on the North Korean Nuclear Attacks Against the United States: A Speculative Novel.* New York. Houghton Mifflin Harcourt.

Lewis, John, and Xue Litai. 2016. "China's Security Agenda Transcends the South China Sea." *Bulletin of the Atomic Scientists* 16, no. 4 (June 16): 212–21. https://doi.org/10.1080/00963402.2016.1194056.

Li, Chien-Pin. 2011. "Norm Entrepreneur Or Interest Maximiser? China's Participation in UN Peacekeeping Operations, 2001–2010." *China: An International Journal* 9, no. 2: 313–27. https://doi.org/10.1142/S0219747211000185.

Li, Xiaojun. 2010. "Social Rewards And Socialization Effects: An Alternative Explanation to the Motivation Behind China's Participation in International Institutions." *Chinese Journal of International Politics* 3, no. 3: 347–77. https://doi.org/10.1093/cjip/poq011.

Liang, Fan, Vishnupriya Das, Nadiya Kostyuk, and Muzammil M. Hussain. 2018. "Constructing a Data-Driven Society: China's Social Credit System as a State Surveillance Infrastructure." *Policy & Internet* 10, no. 4: 415–53. https://doi.org/10.1002/poi3.183.

Lin, Herb. 2019. "Huawei and Managing 5G Risk." *Lawfare*, April 3. www.lawfareblog.com/huawei-and-managing-5g-risk .

Lindblom, Charles E. 1959. "The Science of Muddling Through." *Public Administration Review* 19, no. 2 (Spring): 79–88. https://doi.org/10.2307/973677.

———. 1979. "Still Muddling, Not Yet Through." *Public Administration Review* 39, no. 6 (November–December): 517–26. https://doi.org/10.2307/976178.

Loh, Dylan Ming Hui. 2016. "ASEAN's Norm Adherence and Its Unintended Consequences in HADR and SAR Operations." *Pacific Review* 29, no. 4: 549–72. https://doi.org/10.1080/09512748.2015.1022589.

Lotze, Walter. 2013. "Strengthening African Peace Support Operations: Nine Lessons for the Future of the African Standby Force." *ZIF*, December 17.

Luce, Edward. 2017. *The Retreat of Western Liberalism.* New York: Atlantic Monthly Press.

Lund, Michael S. 1995. "Underrating Preventive Diplomacy." *Foreign Affairs*, July–August. www.foreignaffairs.com/articles/1995-07-01/underrating-preventive-diplomacy.

———. 1996. *Preventing Violent Conflict: A Strategy for Preventive Diplomacy.* Washington, DC: US Institute for Peace.

Lundgren, Magnus. 2016. "Which Type of International Organizations Can Settle Civil Wars?" *Review of International Organizations* 12, no. 4: 613–41.

Lu-YueYang, Maggie. 2012. "Australia Blocks China's Huawei from Broadband Tender." Reuters, March 26. www.reuters.com/article/us-australia-huawei-nbn-idUSBRE82 P0GA20120326.

Lynch, Colum. 2016. "China Eyes Ending Western Grip on Top UN Jobs with Greater Control over Blue Helmets." *Foreign Policy*, October 2. https://foreignpolicy.com/2016/10 /02/china-eyes-ending-western-grip-on-top-u-n-jobs-with-greater-control-over-blue -helmets/.

———. 2018a. "At the UN, China and Russia Score Win in War on Human Rights." *Foreign Policy*, March 26. https://foreignpolicy.com/2018/03/26/at-the-u-n-china-and-russia -score-win-in-war-on-human-rights/.

———. 2018b. "Trump's War on the World Order." *Foreign Policy*, December 27. https:// foreignpolicy.com/2018/12/27/trumps-war-on-the-world-order/.

Maasho, Aaron. 2018. "South Sudan's President, Rebel Leader Sign Peace Deal." Reuters, September 12. www.reuters.com/article/us-southsudan-unrest/south-sudans-president -rebel-leader-sign-peace-deal-idUSKCN1LS2PW.

Mabon, Simon. 2018. *Saudi Arabia, Iran and the Struggle to Shape the Middle East.* London: Foreign Policy Centre.

MacKinnon, Mark, and Geoffrey York. 2017. "'America First,' from Ukraine to Africa: How Trumpism Threatens Democracy." *Globe and Mail*, March 12. www.theglobeandmail.com /news/world/trump-foreign-policy-from-ukraine-to-africa/article34238394/.

Madan, Tanvi. 2020. "How Is the Coronavirus Outbreak Affecting China's Relations with India?" Brookings Institution, April 30. www.brookings.edu/blog/order-from-chaos /2020/04/30/how-is-the-coronavirus-outbreak-affecting-chinas-relations-with-india/.

Magliveras, Konstantinos D., and Gino J. Naldi. 2002. "The African Union: A New Dawn For Africa?" *International and Comparative Law Quarterly* 51, no. 2 (April): 415–25. https:// doi.org/10.1093/iclq/51.2.415.

Malamud, Andrés, and Philippe C. Schmitter. 2011. "The Experience of European Integration and the Potential for Integration in South America." In *New Regionalism and the European Union: Dialogues, Comparisons and New Research Directions,* edited by Alex Warleigh-Lack, Nick Robinson, and Ben Rosamond. New York: Routledge.

Malamud, Carlos. 2008. "La Cumbre de Unasur en Santiago de Chile y El Conflicto en Bolivia." *Boletín Elcano* 107.

Malley, Robert. 2018. "Ten Crises to Watch in 2019." *Foreign Policy*, December 28. https:// foreignpolicy.com/2018/12/28/10-conflicts-to-watch-in-2019-yemen-syria-afghanistan -south-sudan-venezuela-ukraine-nigeria-cameroon-iran-israel-saudi-arabia-united-states -china-kurds-ypg/.

Maluwa, Tiyanjana. 2012. "The Transition from the Organization of African Unity to the African Union." In *The African Union: Legal and Institutional Framework: A Manual on the Pan-African Organization,* edited by A. A. Yusuf and F. Ouguergouz, 25–52. Leiden: Brill/ Nijhoff.

Mandaville, Peter, and Shadi Hamid. 2018. "Islam as Statecraft: How Governments Use Religion in Foreign Policy." Washington, DC: Brookings Institution. www.brookings.edu /research/islam-as-statecraft-how-governments-use-religion-in-foreign-policy/.

Manuel, Anja. 2017. "China Is Quietly Reshaping the World." *Atlantic*, October 17. www .theatlantic.com/international/archive/2017/10/china-belt-and-road/542667/.

Marks, Joseph. 2019. "The Cybersecurity 202: Huawei's Access to 5G Could Expand China's Surveillance State, Cyber Diplomat Warns." *Washington Post*, February 7. www.washington post.com/news/powerpost/paloma/the-cybersecurity-202/2019/02/07/the-cyber security-202-huawei-s-access-to-5g-could-expand-china-s-surveillance-state-cyber -diplomat-warns/5c5b26fc1b326b66eb09863b/.

Marks, Monica. 2017. "Tunisia." In *Rethinking Political Islam*, edited by Shadi Hamid and Will McCants. New York: Oxford University Press.

Marr, Bernard. 2019. "Chinese Social Credit Score: Utopian Big Data Bliss or Black Mirror On Steroids?" *Forbes*, January 21. www.forbes.com/sites/bernardmarr/2019/01/21/chinese -social-credit-score-utopian-big-data-bliss-or-black-mirror-on-steroids/#64519a5348b8.

Maull, Hanns W. 2019. "The Once and Future Liberal Order." *Survival: Global Politics and Strategy* 61, no. 2 (April–May): 7–32. https://doi.org/10.1080/00396338.2019.1589076.

Mavrakis, D. 2018. "Opinion: Is Europe's 5G Spectrum Strategy Falling Behind?" *Mobile Europe*, December 3. www.mobileeurope.co.uk/press-wire/opinion-is-europe-s-5g -spectrum-strategy-falling-behind.

Mbeki, Thabo. 2012. "Architecture of Post–Cold War Africa: Between Internal Reform and External Intervention." Address at Makerere University Institute of Social Research Conference, January 19. www.unisa.ac.za/static/corporate_web/Content/tmali/speeches /2012/Address%20at%20the%20Makerere%20University%20Institute%20of%20Social %20Research%20Conference.pdf.

McBride, James, and Andrew Chatzky. 2019. "Is 'Made in China 2025' a Threat to Global Trade?" Council on Foreign Relations, March 7. www.cfr.org/backgrounder/made-china -2025-threat-global-trade.

McGregor, Janyce. 2019. "As If Canada's Huawei Decision Isn't Tricky Enough: A 5G Ban Risks a Lawsuit." CBC News, February 17. www.cbc.ca/news/politics/huawei-canada -china-fipa-1.5021033.

Mearsheimer, John J. 2014. *The Tragedy of Great Power Politics*. New York: W. W. Norton.

Meerts, Paul. 2015. "Diplomatic Negotiation: Essence and Evolution." Clingendael Institute 2.

Mehta, Aaron. 2018. "AI Makes Mattis Question 'Fundamental' Beliefs about War." *Defense News*, February 17. www.defensenews.com/intel-geoint/2018/02/17/ai-makes-mattis -question-fundamental-beliefs-about-war/.

Melander, Erik. 2009. "Selected to Go Where Murderers Lurk? The Preventive Effect of Peacekeeping on Mass Killings of Civilians." *Conflict Management and Peace Science* 26, no. 4: 389–406. www.jstor.org/stable/26275090.

Mello, Eduardo, and Matias Spektor. 2018. "Brazil: The Costs of Multiparty Presidentialism." *Journal of Democracy* 29, no. 2 (April): 113–27. https://doi.org/10.1353/jod.2018.0031.

Meyer, Josh. 2019. "The CIA Sent Warnings to at Least 3 Khashoggi Associates About New Threats from Saudi Arabia." *Time*, May 9. http://time.com/5585281/cia-warned-jamal -khashoggi-associates/.

Meyer, Paul. 2009. "Breakthrough and Breakdown at the Conference on Disarmament: Assessing the Prospects for an FM(C)T." *Arms Control Today*, September. www.armscontrol.org /act/2009_09/Meyer.

———. 2017. "The Nuclear Nonproliferation Treaty: Fin de Regime?" *Arms Control Today*, April. www.armscontrol.org/act/2017-04/features/nuclear-nonproliferation-treaty-fin -de-regime.

Microsoft. 2003. "Microsoft Announces Government Security Program." January 14. https:// news.microsoft.com/2003/01/14/microsoft-announces-government-security-program/.

Miglani, Sanjeev. 2017. "Indian Navy the Odd Man Out in Asia's 'Quad' Alliance." Reuters, November 22. www.reuters.com/article/us-india-usa-quad/indian-navy-the-odd-man -out-in-asias-quad-alliance-idUSKBN1DM0UB.

Miglani, Sanjeev, and Drazen Jorgic. 2019. "India, Pakistan Threatened to Unleash Missiles at Each Other: Sources," Reuters, March 17. www.reuters.com/article/us-india-kashmir -crisis-insight/india-pakistan-threatened-to-unleash-missiles-at-each-other-sources -idUSKCN1QY03T.

Miles, Tom. 2019a. "Huawei Allegations Driven by Politics Not Evidence: UN Telecoms Chief." Reuters, April 5. www.reuters.com/article/us-usa-china-huawei-tech-un -idUSKCN1RH1KN.

———. 2019b. "China Warns Australia at WTO about 5G Restriction." Reuters, April 12. huawei-australia-china-wto-idUSKCN1RO20H.

———. 2019c. "China Pulls WTO Suit Over Claim to Be a Market Economy." Reuters. www.reuters.com/article/us-usa-china-wto-eu/china-pulls-wto-suit-over-claim-to-be-a -market- economy-idUSKCN1TI10A.

Miller, Steven E. 2019. "The Rise and Decline of Global Nuclear Order?" In *Nuclear Weapons in a Changing Global Order*. Cambridge, MA: American Academy of Arts and Sciences. www.amacad.org/publication/nuclear-weapons-changing-global-order.

Ministry of External Affairs. 2003. *The Cabinet Committee on Security Reviews Operationalization of India's Nuclear Doctrine*. New Delhi: Government of India. https://mea.gov .in/press-releases.htm?dtl/20131/The_Cabinet_Committee_on_Security_Reviews _perationalization_of_Indias_Nuclear_Doctrine+Report+of+National+Security +Advisory+Board+on+Indian+Nuclear+Doctrine.

Mironova, Vera, and Whitt, Sam. 2017. "International Peacekeeping and Positive Peace: Evidence from Kosovo." *Journal of Conflict Resolution* 61, no. 10: 2074–2104.

Mitra, Devirupa. 2018. "SCO Is New but Indian, Pak Troops Are Old Partners in Multilateral Missions." *The Wire*, April 30. https://thewire.in/security/india-pakistan-troops-sco -multilateral-missions.

Mitton, Roger. 2012. "Nargis Is the Turning Point." *Myanmar Times*, February 13–19. www .mmtimes.com/2012/news/614/news 61404.html.

Mitzen, Jennifer. 2013. *Power in Concert: The Nineteenth-Century Origins of Global Governance*. Chicago: University of Chicago Press.

Modi, Narendra. 2018. "Prime Minister's Keynote Address at Shangri La Dialogue (June 1, 2018)." Ministry of External Affairs, Government of India, June 1. www.mea.gov .in/Speeches-Statements.htm?dtl/29943/Prime+Ministers+Keynote+Address+at +Shangri+La+Dialogue+June+01+2018.

Monnet, Jean. *Memoirs*. 1979. New York: Doubleday.

Morgenthau, Hans. 1951. *In Defense of the National Interest*. New York: Alfred A. Knopf.

Morphet, Sally. 2000. "China as a Permanent Member of the Security Council: October 1971–December 1999." *Security Dialogue* 31, no. 2: 151–66. https://doi.org/10.1177 /0967010600031002002.

Morris, Iain. 2018. "Orange Rules Out Huawei for 5G in France." *Light Reading*, December 13. www.lightreading.com/mobile/5g/orange-rules-out-huawei-for-5g-in-france/d/d-id /748274.

Motwani, Nishank. 2018. "Be Prepared for an India-Pakistan Limited War." *The Diplomat*, October 5. https://thediplomat.com/2018/10/be-prepared-for-an-india-pakistan-limited-war/.

Muller, Robert. 2018. "Czech President's Aides Travel to China to Look into CEFC Chief Reports." Reuters, March 15. www.reuters.com/article/us-china-cefc-czech -idUSKCN1GR3C5.

Muncaster, Phil. 2013. "US Bill Prohibits State Use Of Tech Linked yo Chinese Government." Register, March 28. www.theregister.co.uk/2013/03/28/us_government_crackdown _china_it_firms/.

Mvukiyehe, Eric. 2018. "Promoting Political Participation in War-Torn Countries: Microlevel Evidence from Postwar Liberia." Journal of Conflict Resolution 62, no. 8: 1686–1726. https://doi.org/10.1177/0022002717698019.

Nair, Deepak. 2009. "Regionalism in the Asia Pacific / East Asia: A Frustrated Regionalism?" Contemporary Southeast Asia 31, no. 1 (April): 110–42. www.jstor.org/stable/41288791.

Nathan, Laurie. 2006. "Domestic Instability and Security Communities." European Journal of International Relations 12, no. 2 (June): 275–99. https://doi.org/10.1177/1354066 106064510.

Naughton, John. 2016. "The Evolution of the Internet: From Military Experiment to General Purpose Technology." Journal of Cyber Policy 1, no. 1: 5–28. https://doi.org/10.1080 /23738871.2016.1157619.

Neethling, Theo. 2017. "What the Djibouti Military Base Tells Us about China's Growing Role in Africa." The Conversation, August 2. https://theconversation.com/what-the -djibouti-military-base-tells-us-about-chinas-growing-role-in-africa-81783.

Newport, Frank. 2014. "More Americans Now View Afghanistan War as a Mistake." Gallup, February 19. https://news.gallup.com/poll/167471/americans-view-afghanistan-war -mistake.aspx.

Nichols, Michelle. 2018. "Congo's Kabila Delays UN Chief's Visit, Refuses to See US Envoy Haley." Reuters, July 9. https://af.reuters.com/article/topNews/idAFKBN1K00RR -OZATP.

Nichols, Michelle, and Saad Sayeed. 2019. "UN Blacklists Founder of Pakistan-Based Militant Group Jaish-e-Mohammed." Reuters, May 1. www.reuters.com/article/us-india-kashmir -pakistan-un/un-panel-blacklists-founder-of-pakistan-based-militant-group-jaish-e -mohammed-diplomats-idUSKCN1S73XN.

Nkrumah, Kwame. 1963. Africa Must Unite. New York: Praeger.

Nuclear Suppliers Group. No date. www.nuclearsuppliersgroup.org/en/.

"Number of Fatalities Due to Terrorist Attacks Worldwide Between 2006–2008." No date. Statista. www.statista.com/statistics/202871/number-of-fatalities-by-terrorist-attacks -worldwide/.

Nye, Joseph S., Jr. 2014. "The Regime Complex for Managing Global Cyber Activities." Global Commission on Internet Governance, Paper 1. www.cigionline.org/sites/default/files /gcig_paper_no1.pdf.

———. 2017. "Will the Liberal Order Survive?" Foreign Affairs, January–February, 10–16. www.foreignaffairs.com/articles/2016-12-12/will-liberal-order-survive.

Obiodu, Emeka, and Mark Giles. 2017. "The 5G Era: Age of Boundless Connectivity and Intelligent Automation." GSMA Intelligence. www.gsmaintelligence.com/research/?file= 0efdd9e7b6eb1c4ad9aa5d4c0c971e62&download.

O'Hara, Kieron, and Wendy Hall. 2018. "Four Internets: The Geopolitics of Digital Governance." CIGI Online, Paper 206. www.cigionline.org/publications/four-internets-geopolitics-digital -governance.

Okano-Heijmans, Maaike, Frans-Paul van der Putten, and Louise van Schaik. 2018. "A United Nations with Chinese Characteristics?" Clingendael, December 18. www.clingendael.org /publication/united-nations-chinese-characteristics.

Oliker, Olga. 2017. "Be Careful What You Wish For: Legacies, Realignments, and Russia's Evolving Role in South Asia." *War on the Rocks*, December 27. https://warontherocks .com/2017/12/careful-wish-legacies-realignments-russias-evolving-role-south-asia/.

Oliveira, Eliane, and Marina Gonçalves. 2019. "Governo Bolsonaro Enterra Unasul Criada Por Lula e Adere a Novo Organismo Regional." *O Globo*, March 7. https://oglobo.globo .com/mundo/governo-bolsonaro-enterra-unasul-criada-por-lula-adere-novo-organismo -regional-23505468.

Opongo, Elias Omondi. 2013. "The Africa Union and a Liberal Peace Agenda to Conflict." In *Handbook of Africa's International Relations*, edited by Timothy Murithi, 94–102. London: Taylor & Francis.

Oprysko, Caitlin. 2020. "'I Don't Take Responsibility at All': Trump Deflects Blame for Coronavirus Testing Fumble." *Politico*, March 13. www.politico.com/news/2020/03/13 /trump-coronavirus-testing-128971.

"The Oslo Accords and the Arab-Israeli Peace Process." No date. Office of the Historian, Foreign Service Institute, US Department of State. https://history.state.gov/milestones /1993-2000/oslo.

"Our Current Priorities." No date. European Defence Agency. www.eda.europa.eu/what-we -do/our-current-priorities.

Panda, Ankit. 2018. "Pentagon: Chinese Warship in 'Unsafe' Encounter with US Destroyer during Freedom of Navigation Operation." *The Diplomat*, October 2. https://thediplomat .com/2018/10/pentagon-chinese-warship-in-unsafe-encounter-with-us-destroyer -during-freedom-of-navigation-operation/.

Parameswaran, Prashanth. 2018. "What's Next for the New ASEAN 'Our Eyes' Intelligence Initiative?" *The Diplomat*, January 27. https://thediplomat.com/2018/01/asean -launches-new-our-eyes-intelligence-initiative/.

Pardo, Ramon Pacheco, and Jeffrey Reeves, eds. 2015. *Non-Traditional Security in East Asia: A Regime Approach*. Singapore: World Scientific.

Park, Yuni. 2017. "US-China Counter-terrorism Co-operation and Its Perspective on Human Rights." IRIS France, Asia Focus 56–Asia Program. www.iris-france.org/wp-content /uploads/2017/12/Asia-focus-56.pdf.

Parthasarathy, G. 2018. "How Not to Engage with Pakistan." *Hindu Business Line*, October 3. www.thehindubusinessline.com/opinion/columns/g-parthasarathy/how-not-to-engage -with-pakistan/article25114505.ece.

Parton, Charles. 2019. "China–UK Relations: Where to Draw the Border Between Influence and Interference?" RUSI, February. https://rusi.org/publication/occasional-papers/china -uk-relations-where-draw-border-between-influence-and-interference/.

Pasha-Robinson, Lucy. 2018. "The Long History of Russian Deaths in the UK Under Mysterious Circumstances." *The Independent*, March 6. www.independent.co.uk/news/uk /home-news/russian-deaths-uk-history-spies-murder-sergei-skripal-alexander-litvinenko -a8242061.html.

Patton, Dominique, and Rod Nickel. 2019. "China Blocks Some Canada Canola Shipments, Ottawa Expresses Concern." Reuters, March 5. www.reuters.com/article/us-china-canada -canola-trade-idUSKCN1QM0P8.

Paul, T. V. 2003. "Chinese-Pakistani Nuclear/Missile Ties and the Balance of Power." *Nonproliferation Review*, Summer, 1–9.

———. 2005. "Soft Balancing in the Age of US Primacy." *International Security* 30, no. 1 (Summer): 46–71. https://doi.org/10.1162/0162288054894652.

———. 2006. "Why Has the India-Pakistan Rivalry Been So Enduring? Power Asymmetry and an Intractable Conflict." *Security Studies* 15, no. 4: 600–630. https://doi.org/10.1080/09636410601184595.

———, ed. 2018. *The China-India Rivalry in the Globalization Era*. Washington, DC: Georgetown University Press.

Pauley, Logan. 2018. "China Takes the Lead in UN Peacekeeping." *The Diplomat*, April 17. https://thediplomat.com/2018/04/china-takes-the-lead-in-un-peacekeeping/.

Pejsova, Eva. 2017. "Introduction." In *Prevention Better Than Cure: The EU's Quiet Diplomacy in Asia*, edited by Guy Banim and Eva Pejsova, 3–5. Paris: EU Institute for Security Studies.

Piccone, Ted. 2018. "China's Long Game on Human Rights at the United Nations." Brookings Institution, October 9. www.brookings.edu/research/chinas-long-game-on-human-rights-at-the-united-nations/.

Pickering, Jeffrey, and Mark Peceny. 2006. "Forging Democracy at Gunpoint." *International Studies Quarterly* 50, no. 3 (September): 539–59. www.jstor.com/stable/4092792.

Pillsbury, Michael. 2015. *The Hundred-Year Marathon: China's Secret Strategy to Replace America as the Global Superpower*. New York: Henry Holt.

Piris, Jean-Claude. 2011. *The Future of Europe: Towards a Two-Speed EU?* Cambridge: Cambridge University Press.

"Plenary Session of St. Petersburg International Economic Forum." 2019. President of Russia, June 7. http://en.kremlin.ru/events/president/news/60707.

Pohlmann, Tim. 2018. "Who Is Leading the 5G Patent Race?" Lexology, December 12. www.lexology.com/library/detail.aspx?g=64ea84d0-f9ce-4c2b-939b-dec5c2560e06.

"Poland Calls for 'Joint' EU-NATO Stance on Huawei After Spying Arrest." 2019. *Guardian*, January 13. www.theguardian.com/world/2019/jan/12/huawei-sacks-chinese-worker-accused-of-spying-in-poland-wang-weijing.

Pollack, Kenneth M. 2016. "Security and Public Order." Brookings Institution and Atlantic Council. www.atlanticcouncil.org/images/publications/SecurityandPublicOrderReport.pdf.

Porter, Patrick. 2018. "A World Imagined: Nostalgia and Liberal Order." CATO Institute, June 5. www.cato.org/publications/policy-analysis/world-imagined-nostalgia-liberal-order.

Postelnicescu, Claudia. 2016. "Europe's New Identity: The Refugee Crisis and the Rise of Nationalism." *Europe's Journal of Psychology* 12, no. 2 (May): 203–9. doi:10.5964/ejop.v12i2.1191.

Press Trust of India. 2018a. "India-China Bilateral Trade Hits Historic High of $84.44 Billion." *Times of India*, March 7. https://timesofindia.indiatimes.com/india/india-china-bilateral-trade-hits-historic-high-of-84-44-billion-in-2017/articleshow/63202401.cms.

———. 2018b. "Indian Navy Aiming at 200-Ship Fleet by 2027." *Economic Times*, July 14. https://economictimes.indiatimes.com/news/defence/indian-navy-aiming-at-200-ship-fleet-by-2027/articleshow/48072917.cms.

———. 2019a. "If India Attacks Pakistan, We Will Retaliate: Imran Khan." *Hindu Business Line*, February 19. www.thehindubusinessline.com/news/world/if-india-thinks-it-will-attack-pakistan-then-we-will-retaliate-pakistan-pm-imran-khan-on-pulwama-terror-attack/article26313086.ece.

———. 2019b. "Indo-Pak Bilateral Trade Grows 5% in Last 7 Months Despite Tensions: Report." *Business Standard*, February 24. www.business-standard.com/article/pti-stories /indo-pak-bilateral-trade-posted-growth-despite-tensions-report-119022400294_1 .html.

———. 2019c. "Indian Envoy Rules Out Talks with Pakistan Unless It Stops Supporting Terror." *Economic Times*, May 24. https://economictimes.indiatimes.com/news/defence /indian-envoy-rules-out-talks-with-pakistan-unless-it-stops-supporting-terror/articleshow /69478191.cms.

Pretorius, Joelien, and Tom Sauer. 2019. "Is It Time to Ditch the NPT?" *Bulletin of the Atomic Scientists*, September 6. https://thebulletin.org/2019/09/is-it-time-to-ditch-the-npt/.

Price, Rob, and Shona Ghosh. 2018. "All the Times Russia Allegedly Carried Out Assassinations on British Soil." *Business Insider*, March 6. www.businessinsider.com/list-alleged -russian-assassinations-in-britain-litvinenko-2018-3.

Providing for Peacekeeping. 2019. "IPI Peacekeeping Database Graphs." www.providingfor peacekeeping.org/peacekeeping-data-graphs/.

Psaledakis, Daphne. 2019. "FBI Wishes It Had Acted Quicker as China Stole Intellectual Property." Reuters, November 19. www.reuters.com/article/us-usa-china-research -idUSKBN1XT2SJ.

Raja Mohan, C. 2007. "Balancing Interests and Values: India's Struggle with Democracy Promotion." *Washington Quarterly* 30, no. 3: 99–115. https://doi.org/10.1162/wash .2007.30.3.99.

———. 2011. "India, Libya and the Principle of Non-Intervention." *ISAS Insights* 122, April 13. www.files.ethz.ch/isn/128706/ISAS_Insights_122_-_Email_-_India,_Libya_and_the _Princple_of_Non-Intervention_19042011144243.pdf.

Rajagopalan, Rajeshwari Pillai. 2018. "What's Next for the India-Russia Strategic Partnership?" *The Diplomat*, June 16. https://thediplomat.com/2018/06/whats-next-for-the -india-russia-strategic-partnership/.

Rasmussen, Nicholas J. 2015. "Current Terrorist Threat to the United States." Hearing Before the US Senate Select Committee on Intelligence, February 12. www.dni.gov/files/NCTC /documents/news_documents/Current_Terrorist_Threat_to_the_United_States.pdf.

Redden, Elizabeth. 2019. "Closing Confucius Institutes." *Inside Higher Ed*, January 9. www .insidehighered.com/news/2019/01/09/colleges-move-close-chinese-government -funded-confucius-institutes-amid-increasing.

Reed, Matthew. 2018. "5G in the Middle East and Africa." Ovum. https://ovum.informa.com /~/media/informa-shop-window/tmt/whitepapers-and-pr/5g-in-the-middle-east-and -africa-pdf.pdf.

Reisner, Jon, Gennaro D'Angelo, Eunmo Koo, Wesley Even, Michael Hecht, Darin Comeau, Randell Bos, and James Cooley. 2018. "Climate Impact of a Regional Nuclear Weapons Exchange: An Assessment Based on Detailed Source Calculations." *Journal of Geophysical Research: Atmospheres* 123, no. 5: 2752–72. https://doi.org/10.1002/2017JD027331.

"Report on the Secretary General's High-Level Panel on Digital Cooperation." 2019. Digital Cooperation. https://digitalcooperation.org/.

"Research & Development—About Huawei." 2017. Huawei. www.huawei.com/en/about -huawei/corporate-information/research-development.

Reuters. 2019. "Poland Calls for 'joint' EU-NATO Stance on Huawei After Spying Arrest." *Guardian*. www.theguardian.com/world/2019/jan/12/huawei-sacks-chinese-worker -accused-of-spying-in-poland-wang-weijing.

Richardson, Courtney J. 2011. "A Responsible Power? China and the UN Peacekeeping Regime." *International Peacekeeping* 18, no. 3: 286–97. https://doi.org/10.1080/13533312.2011.563082.

Richmond, Oliver. 2012. *A Post-Liberal Peace*. London: Routledge.

Riedel, Bruce. 2015. "Lessons from 1963 for India-Pakistan Relations." Brookings Institution, December 14. www.brookings.edu/opinions/lessons-from-1963-for-india-pakistan-relations/.

Robertson, Adi. 2013. "Lenovo Reportedly Banned by MI6, CIA, and Other Spy Agencies over Fear of Chinese Hacking (Update)." *The Verge*, July 30. www.theverge.com/2013/7/30/4570780/lenovo-reportedly-banned-by-mi6-cia-over-chinese-hacking-fears.

Roche, Elizabeth. 2019a. "Azhar Designated Global Terrorist by UN in Diplomatic Coup for India." *LiveMint*, May 2. www.livemint.com/news/india/jaish-chief-masood-azhar-designated-as-global-terrorist-by-un-1556715605454.html.

———. 2019b. "Trump's Offer to Mediate in Kashmir Row Triggers Uproar." *LiveMint*, July 24. www.livemint.com/news/india/diplomatic-furore-erupts-in-india-over-donald-trump-s-kashmir-mediation-remarks-1563885480526.html.

Rogers, Mike, and Dutch Ruppersberger. 2012. "Investigative Report on the US National Security Issues Posed by Chinese Telecommunications Companies Huawei and ZTE." US House of Representatives, October 8. https://stacks.stanford.edu/file/druid:rm226yb7473/Huawei-ZTE%20Investigative%20Report%20%28FINAL%29.pdf.

Rogin, Josh. 2018. "Trump's Only Foreign Policy Doctrine Is Trumpism." *Washington Post*, October 25. www.washingtonpost.com/opinions/global-opinions/trumps-only-foreign-policy-doctrine-is-trumpism/2018/10/25/c2df8190-d892-11e8-83a2-d1c3da28d6b6_story.html.

Rolland, Nadège. 2017. *China's Eurasian Century? Political and Strategic Implications of the Belt and Road Initiative*. Seattle: National Bureau of Asian Research.

Rosen, Daniel. H., and Scott Kennedy. 2019. "Building a Better Deal with China." Center for Strategic and International Studies, January 28. www.csis.org/analysis/building-better-deal-china.

Rosenberg, Scott. 2020. "Huawei's Trial by 'What If.'" Axios, January 30. www.axios.com/huawei-china-security-britain-5g-evidence-d2a86be0-f8d0-4baa-a138-0be790599c50.html.

Roser, Max. 2013. "Democracy." *Our World in Data*. https://ourworldindata.org/democracy.

———. 2020. "Democracy." *Our World in Data*. https://ourworldindata.org/democracy.

Ruggeri, Andrea, Han Dorussen, and Theodora-Ismene Gizelis. 2013. "Managing Mistrust: An Analysis of Cooperation with UN Peacekeeping in Africa." *Journal of Conflict Resolution* 57, no. 3 (June): 387–409. www.jstor.org/stable/23414720.

———. 2017. "Winning the Peace Locally: UN Peacekeeping and Local Conflict." *International Organization* 71, no. 1 (Winter): 163–85. https://doi.org/10.1017/S0020818316000333.

Ruggie, John Gerard. 1993. "Wandering in the Void: Charting the UN's New Strategic Role." *Foreign Affairs* 72, no. 5: 26–31.

Rüland, Jürgen. 2012. "The Rise of 'Diminished Multilateralism': East Asian and European Forum Shopping in Global Governance." *Asia Europe Journal* 9: 255–70. https://doi.org/10.1007/s10308-012-0311-9.

Rushe, Dominic. 2018. "Qualcomm Deal Over as Trump Blocks Singaporean Chip Maker's Bid." *Guardian*, March 13. www.theguardian.com/business/2018/mar/12/qualcomm-broadcom-deal-trump.

Russon, Mary-Ann. 2019. "Huawei: 'We Stand Naked in Front of the World.'" BBC, June 10.

Sacks, Samm. 2018. "Disruptors, Innovators, and Thieves: Assessing Innovation in China's Digital Economy." Center for Strategic and International Studies, January 8.

Sagan, Scott D. 1997. "Why Do States Build Nuclear Weapons? Three Models in Search of a Bomb." *International Security* 21, no. 3 (Winter): 54–86. https://doi.org/10.1162/isec .21.3.54.

Sahgal, Arun. 2018. "Indian Military in Transformation: Potential and Military Capabilities vis-à-vis China." In *Defence Primer: An Indian Military in Transformation?* edited by Pushan Das and Harsh V. Pant, 55–71. New Delhi: Observer Research Foundation. www .orfonline.org/wp-content/uploads/2018/04/Defence_Primer_2018.pdf.

Sahu, Ambuj. 2019. "Analysing the Trends in China-Pakistan Arms Transfer." Observer Research Foundation, June 14. www.orfonline.org/expert-speak/analysing-trends-arms -transfer-china-pakistan/.

Saifi, Sophia, and Helen Regan. 2019. "India Demands Pakistan Take Action and 'Stop Misleading' on Kashmir Attack." CNN, February 19. https://edition.cnn.com/2019/02/19 /asia/imran-khan-kashmir-attack-intl/index.html.

Salik, Naeem Ahmad. 2010. "Confidence Building Measures Between India and Pakistan." *NDU Journal*, 47–84. www.ndu.edu.pk/issra/issra_pub/articles/ndu-journal/NDU -Journal-2010/03-CBM.pdf.

Santoro, David. 2012. "ASEAN's WMD Scorecard: The Association of Southeast Asian Nations in the Global Safety, Security and Non-proliferation Regimes." *Issues & Insights* 12, no. 3. www.files.ethz.ch/isn/145153/issuesinsights_v12n03.pdf.

Saradzhyan, Simon. 2017. "Russia: Counterterrorism Partner or Fanning the Flames." Testimony at House Committee on Foreign Affairs, US Congress, November 7. https:// docs.house.gov/meetings/FA/FA18/20171107/106596/HHRG-115-FA18-Wstate -SaradzhyanS-20171107.pdf.

Saran, Shyam. 2017. *How India Sees the World: Kautilya to the 21st Century*. New Delhi: Juggernaut.

Sceats, Sonya, and Shaun Breslin. 2012. "China and the International Human Rights System." Chatham House: Royal Institute of International Affairs, October.

Scharre, Paul. 2018. *The Army of None: Autonomous Weapons and the Future of War*. New York: W. W. Norton.

Schelling, Thomas C. 1966. *Arms and Influence*. New Haven, CT: Yale University Press.

Schmitt, Eric. 2019. "Where Terrorism Is Rising in Africa and the US Is Leaving," *New York Times*, March 1. www.nytimes.com/2019/03/01/world/africa/africa-terror-attacks.html.

Schneier, Bruce. 2018. "Supply-Chain Security." *Schneier on Security*, May 10. www.schneier .com/blog/archives/2018/05/supply-chain_se.html .

Schomerus, Mareike. 2017. "The UN Wants to Focus on People—But Is More 'Peace Diplomacy' the Answer?" Overseas Development Institute, September 19. www.odi .org/comment/10549-un-wants-focus-people-more-peace-diplomacy-answer.

"The Schuman Declaration—9 May 1950." 1950. European Union. http://europa.eu/about -eu/basic-information/symbols/europe-day/schuman-declaration/index_en.htm.

Schweller, Randall L. 2006. *Unanswered Threats: Political Constraints on the Balance of Power*. Princeton, NJ: Princeton University Press.

———. 2018. "Three Cheers for Trump's Foreign Policy: What the Establishment Misses." *Foreign Affairs*, September–October.

Schwirtz, Michael. 2019. "Russia Ordered a Killing that Made No Sense. Then the Assassin Started Talking." *New York Times*, March 31.

Science and Technology Committee. 2019. "Oral Evidence: UK Telecommunications Infrastructure—10 Jun 2019." UK Parliament, June 10. http://data.parliament.uk /writtenevidence/committeeevidence.svc/evidencedocument/science-and-technology -committee/uk-telecommunications-infrastructure/oral/102931.html.

Scott, Mark. 2018. "Telcogeopolitics: West vs. China in 5G Race." *Politico*, July 1. www .politico.eu/article/5g-telecommunications-infrastructure-china-us-eu-qualcomm-nokia -ericsson-huawei/.

"Secret Meeting of Indian and Pakistani Security Advisers Spells Hope: Dawn." 2018. *Straits Times*, January 2. www.straitstimes.com/asia/south-asia/secret-meeting-of-indian-and -pakistani-security-advisers-spells-hope-dawn.

Seligman, Lara. 2019. "Fears Rise of an ISIS Comeback." *Foreign Policy*, July 2. https:// foreignpolicy.com/2019/07/02/fears-rise-of-an-isis-comeback/.

Sengupta, Somini. 2015. "Three Peacekeepers Accused of Rape in Central African Republic." *New York Times*, August 19. www.nytimes.com/2015/08/20/world/africa/3-peacekeepers -accused-of-rape-in-central-african-republic.html.

Shahzad, Tanvir, and Shamil Shams. 2012. "India Allows Direct Investments from Pakistan." DW, August 2. www.dw.com/en/india-allows-direct-investments-from-pakistan /a-16139411.

Shambaugh, David. 2013. *China Goes Global: The Partial Power*. Oxford: Oxford University Press.

Sharma, Manoj, and Mudit Kapoor. 2019. "Economically Ruined Pakistan's Decision to Suspend Trade Makes No Dent on India; Here's Why." *Business Today*, August 9. www .businesstoday.in/current/economy-politics/pakistan-suspend-trade-with-india-370 -35a-modi-imran-khan/story/371213.html.

Sheline, Annelle. 2019. "Declaration Proliferation: The International Politics of Religious Tolerance." Berkley Forum (blog), Georgetown University Berkley Center–Brookings Institution Geopolitics of Religious Soft Power Project, July 11. https://berkleycenter .georgetown.edu/posts/declaration-proliferation-the-international-politics-of-religious -tolerance.

Shifter, Michael. 2012. "Plan Colombia: A Retrospective." *Americas Quarterly*, July 18. www .americasquarterly.org/fulltextarticle/plan-colombia-a-retrospective/.

Shoji, Tomotaka. 2013. "ASEAN Defense Ministers' Meeting (ADMM) and ADMM Plus: A Japanese Perspective." *NIDS Journal of Defense and Security* 14 (December): 3–17.

Shulze, Kirsten E. 2007. *Mission Not So Impossible: The AMM and the Transition from Conflict to Peace in Aceh, 2005–2006*. RSIS Working Paper 131. Singapore: S. Rajaratnam School of International Studies, Nanyang Technological University.

Sirilal, Ranga. 2018. "Chinese Firm Pays $584 Million in Sri Lanka Port Debt-to-Equity Deal." Reuters, June 20. www.reuters.com/article/us-sri-lanka-china-ports/chinese-firm-pays -584-million-in-sri-lanka-port-debt-to-equity-deal-idUSKBN1JG2Z6.

Slim, Hugo. 2019. "Humanitarian Diplomacy: The ICRC's Neutral and Impartial Advocacy in Armed Conflicts." *Ethics and International Affairs* 33, no. 1 (Spring): 67–77. https://doi .org/10.1017/S0892679418000904.

Small, Andrew. 2015. *The China-Pakistan Axis: Asia's New Geopolitics*. Oxford: Oxford University Press.

Smeltz, Dina, Ivo Daalder, Karl Friedhoff, Craig Kafura, and Lily Wojtowicz. 2018. "America Engaged." Chicago Council on Global Affairs. www.thechicagocouncil.org/sites/default /files/report_ccs18_america-engaged_181002.pdf.

Smith, Jeff. 2020. "Fistfighting in the Himalayas: India and China Go Another Round." *The Diplomat*, May 15. https://thediplomat.com/2020/05/fistfighting-in-the-himalayas-india-and -china-go-another-round/.

Smith Diwan, Kristin. 2018. "Saudi Nationalism Raises Hopes of Greater Shia Inclusion." Arab Gulf States in Washington, May 3. https://agsiw.org/saudi-nationalism-raises-hopes -greater-inclusion-shias/.

Sohn, Injoo. 2012. "After Renaissance: China's Multilateral Offensive in the Developing World." *European Journal of International Relations* 18, no. 1: 77–101. https://doi.org/10 .1177/1354066110392083.

Sood, Rakesh. 2019. "Does Balakot Define a New Normal?" Observer Research Foundation, March 22. www.orfonline.org/expert-speak/does-balakot-define-a-new-normal -49198/.

"Speech by Mario Draghi, President of the European Central Bank at the Global Investment Conference in London, 26 July 2012." 2012. European Central Bank, July 26. www.ecb .europa.eu/press/key/date/2012/html/sp120726.en.html.

Stähle, Stefan. 2008. "China's Shifting Attitude towards United Nations Peacekeeping Operations." *China Quarterly* 195 (September): 631–55. www.jstor.org/stable/20192238.

Standish, Reid. 2019. "She Fled China's Camps—But She's Still Not Free." *Foreign Policy Flash Points*, February 2. https://foreignpolicy.com/2019/02/06/she-fled-chinas-camps-but -shes-still-not-free/.

Stares, Paul B. 2018. "Preventive Priorities Survey 2019." Council on Foreign Relations, December 17. www.cfr.org/report/preventive-priorities-survey-2019.

———. 2019. *Preventive Engagement*. New York: Columbia University Press.

"Statement in Response to Report the FBI Is Urging Universities to Monitor Chinese Students and Scholars." 2019. Pen America, August 12. https://pen.org/fbi-universities -monitoring-chinese-students/

Steinbock, Dan. 2017. "The Global Economic Balance of Power Is Shifting." World Economic Forum, September 20. www.weforum.org/agenda/2017/09/the-global-economic-balance -of-power-is-shifting/.

Stott, Michael, and Gideon Long. 2020. "Venezuela: Refugee Crisis Tests Colombia's Stability." *Financial Times*, February 18. www.ft.com/content/bfede7a4-4f44-11ea-95a0 -43d18ec715f5.

Strange, Susan. 1992. "States, Firms and Diplomacy." *International Affairs* 68, no. 1 (January): 1–15. https://doi.org/10.2307/2620458.

Stuenkel, Oliver, and Andreas E Feldman. 2017. "The Unchecked Demise of Nicaraguan Democracy." Carnegie Endownment for International Peace, November 16. https:// carnegieendowment.org/2017/11/16/unchecked-demise-of-nicaraguan-democracy -pub-74761.

Sullivan, Jake. 2018. "The World After Trump." *Foreign Affairs*, March–April. www.foreignaffairs .com/articles/2018-03-05/world-after-trump.

"Summary of Commission Decision of 6 February 2019 Declaring a Concentration to Be Incompatible with the Internal Market and the Functioning of the EEA Agreement (Case M.8677-Siemens/Alstom)." 2019. European Commission, September 5.

"Summary of the 2018 National Defense Strategy of the United States of America." 2018. US Department of Defense. https://dod.defense.gov/Portals/1/Documents/pubs/2018 -National-Defense-Strategy-Summary.pdf.

Tan, See Seng. 2012. "'Talking Their Walk'? The Evolution of Defense Regionalism in Southeast Asia." *Asian Security* 8, no. 3: 232–50. https://doi.org/10.1080/14799855.2012.723919.

———. 2013. "Herding Cats: The Role of Persuasion in Political Change and Continuity in the Association of Southeast Asian Nations (ASEAN)." *International Relations of the Asia-Pacific* 13, no. 2: 233–65. https://doi.org/10.1093/irap/lcs020.

———. 2015. *Multilateral Asian Security Architecture: Non-ASEAN Stakeholders.* New York: Routledge.

———. 2017a. "Rethinking 'ASEAN Centrality' in the Regional Governance of East Asia." *Singapore Economic Review* 62, no. 3: 721–40. https://doi.org/10.1142/S02175908 18400076.

———. 2017b. "Can the ADMM-Plus Do 'CUES' in the South China Sea?" *PacNet* 78, October 30. www.pacforum.org/analysis/pacnet-78-can-admm-plus-do-%E2%80%9Ccues%E2 %80%9D-south-china-sea.

———. 2018. "Sending in the Cavalry: The Growing Militarization of Counterterrorism in Southeast Asia." *PRISM: The Journal of Complex Operations* 7, no. 4, November 8. https:// cco.ndu.edu/News/Article/1682045/sending-in-the-cavalry-the-growing-militarization -of-counterterrorism-in-southe/.

———. 2019. *The Responsibility to Provide in Southeast Asia.* Bristol: Bristol University Press..

———. 2020. "Is ASEAN Finally Getting Multilateralism Right? From ARF to ADMM+." *Asian Studies Review* 44, no. 1: 28–43. https://doi.org/10.1080/10357823.2019.1691502.

Tan, See Seng, and Hitoshi Nasu. 2016. "ASEAN and the Development of Counter-Terrorism Law and Policy in Southeast Asia." *UNSW Law Journal* 39, no. 3: 1219–38.

Tana Forum. 2018. "Reforming for Peace: The State of Peace and Security in Africa 2018."

Tang, Wenfang. 2018. "The 'Surprise' of Authoritarian Resilience in China." *American Affairs* 2, no. 1 (Spring). https://americanaffairsjournal.org/2018/02/surprise-authoritarian -resilience-china/.

Tannenwald, Nina. 2018. "The Great Unraveling: The Future of the Nuclear Normative Order." In *Emerging Risks and Declining Norms in the Age of Technological Innovation and Changing Nuclear Doctrines.* Cambridge, MA: American Academy of Arts and Sciences. www.amacad.org/publication/emerging-risks-declining-norms/section/3.

"Tashkent Declaration Signed by Prime Minister of India and President of Pakistan." 1966. Ministry of External Affairs, January 10. https://mea.gov.in/bilateral-documents.htm?dtl /5993/Tashkent+Declaration.

Tasleem, Sadia. 2016. "Pakistan's Nuclear Use Doctrine." Carnegie Endowment for International Peace, June 30. https://carnegieendowment.org/2016/06/30/pakistan-s-nuclear -use-doctrine-pub-63913.

Taylor, Adam. 2015. "Italy Ran An Operation That Saved Thousands of Migrants from Drowning in the Mediterranean, Why Did It Stop?" *Washington Post,* April 20. www .washingtonpost.com/news/worldviews/wp/2015/04/20/italy-ran-an-operation-that -save-thousands-of-migrants-from-drowning-in-the-mediterranean-why-did-it-stop/.

———. 2018. "The Pentagon Says China and Russia Are Bigger Problems for US Than Terrorists—American Voters May Not Agree." *Washington Post,* January 20. www .washingtonpost.com/news/worldviews/wp/2018/01/20/the-pentagon-says-china

-and-russia-are-bigger-problems-for-u-s-than-terrorists-american-voters-may-not-agree/
?noredirect=on.

Taylor, Brendan. 2018. *The Four Flashpoints: How Asia Goes to War*. Melbourne: La Trobe
University Press.

Teasdale, Anthony, and Timothy Bainbridge. 2012. *The Penguin Companion to European
Union*. 4th ed. London: Penguin Books.

Tellis, Ashley. 1997. "Stability in South Asia." RAND Corporation, March 27. www.rand.org
/content/dam/rand/pubs/documented_briefings/2005/DB185.pdf.

———. 2015. "US-India Relations: The Struggle for an Enduring Partnership." In *The Oxford
Handbook of Indian Foreign Policy*, edited by David M. Malone, C. Raja Mohan, and Sri-
nath Raghavan, 488–94. Oxford: Oxford University Press.

Tieku, Thomas Kwasi. 2004. "Explaining the Clash and Accommodation of Interests of Major
Actors in the Creation of the African Union." *African Affairs* 103, no. 411 (April): 249–
67. https://doi.org/10.1093/afraf/adh041.

———. 2009. "Multilateralization of Democracy Promotion and Defense in Africa." *Africa
Today* 56, no. 2 (Winter): 75–91.

"Time for Action: Statement in the European Parliament Plenary Session Ahead of the
Vote on the College." 2014. European Commission, October 22. https://ec.europa.eu
/commission/presscorner/detail/en/SPEECH_14_1525.

"Time to Reset African Union-European Union Relations." 2017. International Crisis Group,
Africa Report 255, October 17. www.crisisgroup.org/africa/255-time-reset-african
-union-european-union-relations.

Tong, Scott. 2019. "Here's Why There's No US Telecom Giant Like Huawei." Marketplace,
March 1. www.marketplace.org/2019/03/01/tech/heres-why-theres-no-us-telecom-giant
-huawei.

"Treaty Between the Federal Republic of Germany and the French Republic on Franco-
German Cooperation and Integration (Élysée Treaty)." 2019. Aachen, January 22.

"Treaty Between the French Republic and Federal Republic of Germany on Franco-German
Cooperation (Élysée Treaty)." 1963. Paris, January 22.

"Treaty Establishing the European Coal and Steel Community (ECSC Treaty)." 1951. Paris,
April 18.

"Treaty on European Union (TEU)." 1992. Maastricht, February 07.

"Treaty of Lisbon amending the Treaty on European Union and the Treaty establishing the
European Community (Lisbon Treaty)." 2007. Lisbon, December 13.

"Treaty on the Non-Proliferation of Nuclear Weapons." 1968. www.un.org/disarmament
/wmd/nuclear/npt/text.

Treviño, Rusty. 2013. "Is Iran an Offensives Realist or a Defensive Realist? A Theoretical
Reflection on Iranian Motives for Creating Instability." *Journal of Strategic Security* 6, no. 3
(Fall): 382–92. https://doi.org/10.5038/1944-0472.6.3S.33.

Triolo, Paul, Kevin Allison, and Clarise Brown. 2018. "The Geopolitics of 5G." Eurasia Group,
November 15. www.eurasiagroup.net/live-post/the-geopolitics-of-5g.

Trivedi, Atman. 2019. "One Year On, Should India Rethink Its Reset with China?" War on
the Rocks, April 17. https://warontherocks.com/2019/04/one-year-on-should-india
-rethink-its-reset-with-china/.

Trubowitz, Peter, and Peter Harris. 2019. "Will Dysfunctional Politics Finally End the American Century?" Chatham House, May 16. www.chathamhouse.org/expert/comment/will
-dysfunctional-politics-finally-end-american-century.

Trump, Donald J. 2018. "Remarks by President Trump to the 73rd Session of the United Nation General Assembly." New York, September 25. www.whitehouse.gov/briefings -statements/remarks-president-trump-73rd-session-united-nations-general-assembly -new-york-ny/.

Twagiramungu, Noel, Allard Duursma, Mulugeta Gebrehiwot Berhe, and Alex de Waal. 2019. "Re-Describing Transnational Conflict in Africa." *Journal of Modern African Studies* 57, no. 3: 377–91. https://doi.org/10.1017/S0022278X19000107.

UK Department for Digital, Culture, Media & Sport. 2018. "Telecoms Supply Chain Review Terms of Reference." www.gov.uk/government/publications/telecoms-supply-chain -review-terms-of-reference.

UN General Assembly. 2009. "Approved Resources For Peacekeeping Operations for the Period From 1 July 2009 to 30 June 2010." United Nations Digital Library.

———. 2018. "Approved Resources for Peacekeeping Operations for the Period from 1 July 2018 to 30 June 2019." United Nations Digital Library.

United Nations. 2004. "A More Secure World: Our Shared Responsibility." Report of the High Level Panel on Threats, Challenges, and Change. www.un.org/ruleoflaw/files/gaA .59.565_En.pdf.

United Nations Peacekeeping. 2020. "Peacekeeping Fact Sheet April 2020." https://peace keeping.un.org/en.

"Uniting Our Strengths for Peace: Politics, Partnership and People." 2015. UN High-Level Independent Panel on United Nations Peace Operations, June 16. www.refworld.org /docid/558bb0134.html.

"Uppsala Conflict Data Program." No date. Department of Peace and Conflict Research, Uppsala University. www.pcr.uu.se/research/ucdp/.

US Department of Defense. 2018a. "Nuclear Posture Review." Office of the Secretary of Defense, February. https://media.defense.gov/2018/feb/02/2001872886/-1/-1/1/2018 -nuclear-posture-review-final-report.pdf.

———. 2018b. "Summary of the 2018 National Defense Strategy of the United States of America." https://dod.defense.gov/Portals/1/Documents/pubs/2018-National-Defense -Strategy-Summary.pdf.

US Department of State. 2006. "Fact Sheet." Office of the Spokesman, January 18. https:// 2001-2009.state.gov/r/pa/prs/ps/2006/59339.htm.

"The US–North Korean Agreed Framework at a Glance." 2018. Arms Control Association. www.armscontrol.org/factsheets/agreedframework.

"US Pursuit of FONOPS in the South China Sea Irritates China." 2019. Navy Recogni-tion, February 13. http://navyrecognition.com/index.php/news/defence-news/2019 /february/6822-us-pursuit-of-fonops-in-the-south-china-sea-irritates-china.html.

Vaddi, Pranay. 2019. "Leaving the INF Treaty Won't Help Trump Counter China." Carnegie Endowment for International Peace, January 31. https://carnegieendowment.org/2019 /01/31/leaving-inf-treaty-won-t-help-trump-counter-china-pub-78262.

Valencia, Mark J. 2017. "A South China Sea Code of Conduct? Don't Get Your Hopes Up." *The Diplomat*, May 20. https://thediplomat.com/2017/05/a-south-china-sea-code-of -conduct-dont-get-your-hopes-up/.

Van Evera, Steven. 1999. *Causes of War: Power and the Roots of Conflict*. Ithaca, NY: Cornell University Press.

Vanderklippe, Nathan. 2019. "Two Canadians Detained in China for Four Months Prevented from Going Outside, Official Says." *Globe and Mail*, April 10. www.theglobeandmail

.com/world/article-two-canadians-detained-in-china-are-prevented-from-seeing-the -sun-or/.

Vertin, Zach. 2018. "A Poisoned Well: Lessons in Mediation from South Sudan's Troubled Peace Process." International Peace Institute, April.

Vidal, John, Allegra Stratton, and Suzanne Goldenberg. 2009. "Low Targets, Goals Dropped; Copenhagen Ends in Failure." Guardian, December 19. www.theguardian .com/environment/2009/dec/18/copenhagen-deal.

Vigevani, Tullo, and Haroldo Ramanzini Júnior. 2014. "Autonomia, Integração Regional e Política Externa Brasileira: Mercosul e Unasul." Dados 57, no. 2: 517–52. https://doi.org /10.1590/0011-5258201415.

Vines, Alex. 2013. "A Decade of African Peace and Security Architecture." International Affairs 89, no. 1: 89–109. https://doi.org/10.1111/1468-2346.12006.

Volpe, Tristan. 2017. "Atomic Leverage: Compellence with Nuclear Latency." Security Studies 26, no. 3: 517–44. https://doi.org/10.1080/09636412.2017.1306398.

———. 2019. "Dual-Use Distinguishability: How 3D-Printing Shapes the Security Dilemma for Nuclear Programs." Journal of Strategic Studies 42, no. 6: 814–40. https://doi.org/10 .1080/01402390.2019.1627210.

von Billerbeck, Sarah. 2017. Whose Peace? Local Ownership and United Nations Peacekeeping. Oxford: Oxford University Press.

"Vote on Draft Resolution on the Financing of AU Peace Support Operations." 2018. What's in Blue, December 18. www.whatsinblue.org/2018/12/vote-on-draft-resolution-on-the -financing-of-au-peace-support-operations.php#.

Waelchli, H., and D. Shah. 1994. "Crisis Negotiations Between Unequals: Lessons from a Classic Dialogue." Negotiation Journal 10, no. 2 (April): 129–46. https://doi.org/10.1111 /j.1571-9979.1994.tb00013.x.

Walker, Christopher. 2018. "What Is 'Sharp Power'?" Journal of Democracy 29, no. 3: 9–23.

Wallensteen, Peter. 2014. Regional Organizations and Peacemaking: Challengers to the UN? London: Routledge.

Walt, Stephen M. 2018. "Has Trump Become a Realist?" Foreign Policy, April 17. https:// foreignpolicy.com/2018/04/17/has-trump-become-a-realist/.

———. 2019. "The End of Hubris and the New Age of American Restraint." Foreign Affairs, May–June. www.foreignaffairs.com/articles/2019-04-16/end-hubris.

Walter, Barbara. 1997. "The Critical Barrier to Civil War Settlement." International Organization 51, no. 3: 335–64. www.jstor.com/stable/2703607.

———. 2002. Committing to Peace: The Successful Settlement of Civil Wars. Princeton, NJ: Princeton University Press.

Walter, Barbara, Lise Howard, and Virginia Page Fortna. 2021. "The Extraordinary Relationship between Peacekeeping and Peace." British Journal of Political Science. https://www .cambridge.org/core/journals/british-journal-of-political-science/article/abs/extra ordinary-relationship-between-peacekeeping-and-peace/D2D5D262B60315387B0B23 D1D4F79CC9

Watts, Stephen, Bryan Frederick, Jennifer Kavanagh, Angela O'Mahony, Thomas S. Szayna, Matthew Lane, Alexander Stephenson, and Clin P. Clarke. 2017. A More Peaceful World? Regional Conflict Trends and US Defense Planning. Santa Monica, CA: RAND Corporation.

Weisbrot, Mark, and Jake Johnston. 2010. "The Gains from Trade: South American Economic Integration and the Resolution of Conflict." Center for Economic and Policy Research, November.

Wessel, Michael. 2019. "Prepared Testimony of Commissioner Michael Wessel Before the Senate Commerce, Science & Transportation Committee." Senate Commerce, Science & Transformation Committee, February 6. www.commerce.senate.gov/public/_cache /files/3b1ad4d5-b73a-4b01-bf93-8e6695095ca8/7FA65EC59FA17F43EAE42CFF3 C13D808.02-01-2019wessel-testimony.pdf.

Westad, Odd Arne. 2005. *The Global Cold War: Third World Interventions and the Making of Our Times.* Cambridge: Cambridge University Press.

"What Was the Good Friday Agreement?" 2018. BBC UK, April 10. www.bbc.co.uk/news round/14118775.

Whitfield, Teresa. 2019. "Mediating in a Complex World." Background paper prepared for the Oslo Forum: Centre for Humanitarian Dialogue.

White House. 2017. "National Security Strategy of the United States of America." www .whitehouse.gov/wp-content/uploads/2017/12/NSS-Final-12-18-2017-0905.pdf.

———. 2019. "Executive Order on Securing the Information and Communications Technology and Services Supply Chain." www.whitehouse.gov/presidential-actions/executive -order-securing-information-communications-technology-services-supply-chain/.

Wijnen, Pieter. 2019. "Norway Not Naïve with Regards to Huawei." *Norway Today*, February 15. https://norwaytoday.info/news/norway-not-naive-with-regards-to-huawei/.

Williams, Paul D. 2007. "From Non-Intervention to Non-Indifference: The Origins and Development of the African Union's Security Culture." *African Affairs* 106, no. 423 (April): 253–79. https://doi.org/10.1093/afraf/adm001.

———. 2016. "Special Report, Part 2: The AU's Less Coercive Diplomacy on Burundi." Global Observatory, February 16. https://theglobalobservatory.org/2016/02/burundi -nkurunziza-african-union-maprobu/.

———. 2017a. "Continuity and Change in War and Conflict in Africa." *Prism* 6, no. 4: 33–48.

———. 2017b. "Global and Regional Peacekeepers: Trends, Opportunities, Risks and a Way Ahead." *Global Policy* 8, no. 1 (February): 124–29. https://doi.org/10.1111/1758-5899 .12393.

Williams, Paul, D., and Solomon A. Dersso. 2015. "Saving Strangers and Neighbors: Advancing UN-AU Cooperation on Peace Operations." International Peace Institute, February.

Winner, Langdon. 1980. "Do Artifacts Have Politics?" *Daedalus* 109, no. 1: 121–36. www.jstor .com/stable/20024652.

Withers, Tracy. 2019. "New Zealand Says China's Huawei Hasn't Been Ruled Out of 5G." Bloomberg, February 18. www.bloomberg.com/news/articles/2019-02-18/new-zealand -says-china-s-huawei-hasn-t-been-ruled-out-of-5g-role.

Wong, Edward. 2017. "China Approves Sweeping Security Law, Bolstering Communist Rule." *New York Times*, December 21. www.nytimes.com/2015/07/02/world/asia/china -approves-sweeping-security-law-bolstering-communist-rule.html.

"Working Together for Peace and Security in Africa: The Security Council and the AU Peace and Security Council." 2011. *Security Council Report* 2: 1–34. www.securitycouncilreport .org/atf/cf/%7B65BFCF9B-6D27-4E9C-8CD3-CF6E4FF96FF9%7D/Research %20Report%20Working%20Together%20for%20Peace%20and%20Security%20in %20Africa%2010%20May%202011.pdf.

World Bank. 2019. "Gross Domestic Product 2018." December 23. https://databank .worldbank.org/data/download/GDP.pdf.

———. No date. "High-Technology Exports (Current US$)." https://data.worldbank.org /indicator/TX.V AL.TECH.CD?locations=CN.

"World Inequality Report 2018." 2018. World Inequality Lab. https://wir2018.wid.world/.

WTO (World Trade Organization). No date–a. "Dispute Settlement: Disputes by Country/ Territory." www.wto.org/english/tratop_e/dispu_e/dispu_by_country_e.htm.

———. No date–b. "WTO Services: CBT—Basic Purpose and Concepts—Most-Favoured-Nation Treatment." www.wto.org/english/tratop_e/serv_e/cbt_course_e/c1s6p1_e.htm.

Wright, Robin. 2019. "All Swagger, Trump's Talks with North Korea Collapse." *New Yorker*, February 28. www.newyorker.com/news/our-columnists/after-all-the-swagger-trumps -talks-with-north-korea-collapse.

Wright, Thomas. 2018. "The Return to Great-Power Rivalry Was Inevitable." *Atlantic*, September 12. www.theatlantic.com/international/archive/2018/09/liberal-international-order -free-world-trump-authoritarianism/569881/.

Wuthnow, Joel, and Phillip C. Saunders. 2017. "Chinese Military Reforms in the Age of Xi Jinping: Drivers, Challenges, and Implications." China Strategic Perspectives 10. Washington, DC: National Defense University.

Xavier, Constantino. 2018. "The New Indian Realpolitik China Is Pushing India's Foreign Policy into Uncharted Waters." *Foreign Affairs*, December 20. www.foreignaffairs.com /articles/china/2018-12-20/new-indian-realpolitik.

Xi, Jinping. 2017. "A New Partnership of Mutual Benefit and a Community of Shared Future (Speech at the General Debate of the 70th Session of the UN General Assembly at the UN Headquarters in New York, 28 September 2015)," in *The Governance of China II*. Beijing: Foreign Languages Press.

Yee, Albert. 1996. "The Causal Effects of Ideas On Policies." *International Organization* 50, no. 1: 69–108. www.jstor.com/stable/2706999.

Yost, Casimir. 2018. "Grand Strategy and Strategic Surprise." Georgetown University Institute for the Study of Diplomacy.

Yusuf, Abdulqawi A. 2003. "The Right of Intervention by the African Union: A New Paradigm in Regional Enforcement Action?" *African Yearbook of International Law* 11, no. 1: 3–21. https://doi.org/10.1163/221161703X00016.

Yusuf, Moeed. 2018. "How the India-Pakistan Conflict Leaves Great Powers Powerless." *Foreign Policy*, December 10. https://foreignpolicy.com/2018/12/10/954587-india-pakistan -mumbai-terror/.

Yuzawa, Takeshi. 2006. "The Evolution of Preventive Diplomacy in the ASEAN Regional Forum: Problems and Prospects." *Asian Survey* 46, no. 5: 785–804. https://doi.org/10 .1525/as.2006.46.5.785.

Zangger Committee. No date. "Our Mission." www.zanggercommittee.org/our-mission.html.

Zarroli, Jim. 2019. "China's Close Government-Business Ties Are a Key Challenge in US Trade Talks." NPR, March 6. www.npr.org/2019/03/06/700474697/chinas-close -government-business-ties-are-a-key-challenge-in-u-s-trade-talks.

Zartman, I., William. 2015. *Preventing Deadly Conflict*. Cambridge: Polity Press.

Zhang, Feng. 2015. *Chinese Hegemony: Grand Strategy and International Institutions in East Asian History*. Stanford, CA: Stanford University Press.

Zhao, Tong. 2019. "China in a World with No US-Russia Treaty-Based Arms Control." Carnegie-Tsinghua Center for Global Policy, April 1. https://carnegietsinghua.org/2019 /04/01/china-in-world-with-no-u.s.-russia-treaty-based-arms-control-pub-78894.

Zhou, Bo. 2017. "How China Can Improve UN Peacekeeping." *Foreign Affairs*, November 15. www.foreignaffairs.com/articles/china/2017-11-15/how-china-can-improve-un-peace keeping.

Zhou, Laura. 2018. "Beijing Has Oversold Benefits of US$62 Billion China-Pakistan Economic Corridor, Expert Says." *South China Morning Post*, November 24. www.scmp.com /news/china/diplomacy/article/2174757/beijing-has-oversold-benefits-us62-billion -china-pakistan.

Zhuang, Pinghui. 2016. "Two Chinese UN Peacekeepers Killed, Two Seriously Injured in Attack in South Sudan." *South China Morning Post*, July 12. www.scmp.com/news /china/diplomacy-defence/article/1988348/two-chinese-un-peacekeepers-killed-two -seriously.

Zittrain, Jonathan. 2008. *The Future of the Internet: And How to Stop It*. New Haven, CT: Yale University Press.

Zoellick, Robert B. 2005. "Whither China: From Membership to Responsibility?" US Department of State–Archive, September 21. https://2001-2009.state.gov/s/d/former /zoellick/rem/53682.htm.

CONTRIBUTORS

PAMELA AALL is senior adviser for conflict prevention and management at the US Institute of Peace and an adjunct professor at American University. She serves on the board of Women in International Security and is a member of the World Refugee Council. She has coauthored and coedited articles and books in the field of conflict management with Chester Crocker and Fen Hampson. She has also written on nongovernmental organizations in conflict environments. Her forthcoming book (coedited with Dan Snodderly) is *Responding to Violent Conflicts and Humanitarian Crises: A Guide to Participants* (Palgrave Macmillan).

KANTI BAJPAI is Wilmar Professor of Asian Studies and director of the Centre on Asia and Globalisation at the Lee Kuan Yew School of Public Policy in the National University of Singapore. His most recent publication is *The Routledge Handbook of China-India Relations* (Routledge, 2020). He has also published on Narendra Modi's foreign policy in the journals *International Affairs* (2017) and *Pacific Affairs* (2018).

DANIEL BENJAMIN is the president of the American Academy in Berlin. He served as ambassador-at-large and coordinator for counterterrorism from 2009 to 2012 at the US Department of State. Earlier in his career, he was a special assistant to President Bill Clinton and director for transnational threats. He is the coauthor of *The Age of Sacred Terror*, which was awarded the Arthur Ross Prize by the Council of Foreign Relations. He has written articles that were published in the *New York Times*, *Wall Street Journal*, *Washington Post*, *Politico*, *Foreign Affairs*, and *The New York Review of Books*.

HANS BINNENDIJK is a distinguished fellow at the Atlantic Council. He has served in senior positions at the US Senate Foreign Relations Committee, the National Security Council, the US Department of State, and the National Defense University. In academia, he was director of Georgetown University's Institute for the Study of Diplomacy and director of studies for the International Institute for Strategic Studies in London. He is the author, coauthor, or editor of about twenty books and has written over two hundred articles, editorials, and reports. His most recent book is *Friends, Foes, and Future Directions* (RAND Corporation).

SAMANTHA BRADSHAW is a leading expert on technology and democracy. Her research is at the forefront of theoretical and methodological approaches for studying the complex relationship between social media and democracy, particularly the impact of technology on political expression and privacy. Her work has been featured by numerous media outlets, including the *Washington Post*, CNN, Bloomberg, and the *Financial Times*. She is completing her PhD at Oxford University.

WILLIAM J. BURNS has been nominated to the director of the CIA. He is president of the Carnegie Endowment for International Peace. He retired in 2014 from the US Foreign Service, where he served as deputy secretary of state, ambassador to Russia, assistant secretary of state for Near Eastern affairs, and ambassador to Jordan. He is the author of *The Back Channel: A Memoir of American Diplomacy and the Case for Its Renewal* (Random House) and is a contributing writer for *The Atlantic*.

CHESTER A. CROCKER is the James R. Schlesinger Professor of Strategic Studies at Georgetown University's School of Foreign Service, where his teaching focuses on international conflict management and mediation. His government career began at the National Security Council (1970–72), followed by service as assistant secretary of state for African affairs (1981–89). He served on the board of the US Institute of Peace for twenty years, through 2011, including twelve years as chairman. He has coauthored or coedited ten books on conflict management with the coeditors of this one, most recently *International Negotiation and Mediation in Violent Conflicts* (Georgetown University Press, 2018). He is a founding director of the Global Leadership Foundation.

TOBY DALTON is codirector of the Nuclear Policy Program and a senior fellow at the Carnegie Endowment for International Peace, where he works on issues of nonproliferation and regional security in East Asia and South Asia. He is the coauthor of *Not War, Not Peace? Motivating Pakistan to Prevent Cross-Border Terrorism* (Oxford University Press, 2016). Before joining the Carnegie Endowment, he served in senior policy positions at the US Department of Energy's National Nuclear Security Administration, including a posting as energy attaché to the US Embassy in Islamabad.

SOLOMON AYELE DERSSO teaches human rights law and African Union law as adjunct professor at the College of Law and Governance Studies of Addis Ababa University. He is the founding director of Amani Africa, an Ethiopia-based, pan-African policy research, training, and consulting think tank. He is a leading expert on the African Union Peace and Security Council, the highest-standing decision-making body on peace and security in Africa. He serves as the chairperson of the African Commission on Human and Peoples' Rights, the premier human rights body of the African Union. He also served as an expert member of the team that reviewed the Ethiopian foreign policy. He received a PhD from the University of the Witwatersrand. He is the author of four monographs on African peace and security issues, two edited books, and numerous peer-reviewed articles and book chapters on a wide range of issues related to international organizations, peace and security in Africa, the African Union's peace and security system, and international and transitional justice.

CHAS W. FREEMAN JR. is the author of five books on statecraft and the editor of the *Encyclopedia Britannica* article on "diplomacy." He is a former US assistant secretary of defense, ambassador to Saudi Arabia, principal deputy assistant secretary of state for African affairs, chargé d'affaires ad interim in Bangkok and Beijing, acting US commissioner for refugee affairs, and director of program coordination and development at the US Information Agency. He was the principal American interpreter during President Nixon's 1972 opening of US relations with China.

JEAN-MARIE GUÉHENNO is a member of the United Nations High-Level Advisory Board on Mediation. A French diplomat, for eight years (2000–2008) he was the UN undersecretary-general for peacekeeping. He has published several books, including a memoir of his years at the United Nations, *The Fog of Peace* (Brookings, 2015).

SHADI HAMID is a senior fellow at the Brookings Institution and the author of *Islamic Exceptionalism: How the Struggle Over Islam Is Reshaping the World*, which was short-listed for the 2017 Lionel Gelber Prize for best book on foreign affairs. He is also the coeditor of *Rethinking Political Islam*. His first book, *Temptations of Power: Islamists and Illiberal Democracy in a New Middle East*, was named a *Foreign Affairs* Best Book of 2014. He received his BS and MA from Georgetown University's School of Foreign Service and his PhD in political science from Oxford University.

FEN OSLER HAMPSON is Chancellor's Professor at Carleton University in Ottawa and president of the World Refugee & Migration Council. He was codirector of the Global Commission on Internet Governance and received his PhD and AM from Harvard University, an MSc (Econ) from the London School of Economics and Political Science, and a BA (Hon) from the University of Toronto. A fellow of the Royal Society of Canada, he is the author or coauthor of fourteen books and editor or coeditor of thirty other volumes. In addition, he has written more than a hundred articles and book chapters on international affairs, including *Master of Persuasion: Brian Mulroney's Global Legacy* (Penguin 2018). His newest book, *Braver Canada: Shaping Our Destiny in a Precarious World* (with Derek Burney; McGill–Queens University Press), was published in March 2020.

STACIE HOFFMANN is an Internet governance and cybersecurity expert at Oxford Information Labs. She works with industry, policymakers, and governments around the world to address a range of issues, from technical standards to policy development. In addition to researching, writing, and engagement, she provides expert comments to the media, publishes articles, and chairs panels. She has been featured on podcasts and broadcast news, including regional and national BBC radio.

LISE MORJÉ HOWARD is a professor of government at Georgetown University, and chair of the Academic Council on the UN System. She is the author of *Power in Peacekeeping* (Cambridge University Press, 2019).

ANA PALACIO is a lawyer specializing in international and European law and a visiting professor at the Georgetown University School of Foreign Service. She is a former foreign minister of Spain, senior vice president and general counsel of the World Bank Group, and member of the European Parliament.

SEE SENG TAN is president and CEO of International Students Inc., a faith-based nonprofit organization in the United States, and concurrently professor of international relations at the S. Rajaratnam School of International Studies of Nanyang Technological University in Singapore. His latest books include *The Responsibility to Provide in Southeast Asia: Towards an Ethical Explanation* (Bristol University Press, 2019) and *The Legal Authority of ASEAN as a Security Institution* (Cambridge University Press, 2019).

EMILY TAYLOR is CEO of Oxford Information Labs. She is an associate fellow of Chatham House, editor of the *Journal of Cyber Policy*, and a research associate at the Oxford Internet Institute. Her research interests include 5G, Internet governance, disinformation and social media platforms, privacy, and linguistic diversity online. A lawyer by training, she has worked in the Internet sector for nearly twenty years. She is a regular commentator on technology issues in news and broadcast media.

MARCOS TOURINHO is a fellow at the School of International Relations at Fundação Getulio Vargas in São Paulo. He received a PhD from the Graduate Institute of International and Development Studies in Geneva, and his recent publications include *The Co-Constitution of Order* (International Organization, forthcoming); *UN Targeted Sanctions Datasets, 1991–2013* (*Journal of Peace Research*, 2018); and *Targeted Sanctions: The Impacts and Effectiveness of United Nations Action* (Cambridge University Press, 2016).

DMITRI TRENIN has been director of the Carnegie Moscow Center since 2008. Before joining the Carnegie Endowment for International Peace in 1994, he served in the Russian military for twenty-one years. His assignments included Iraq (for a military assistance group); East Germany and West Berlin (as a liaison with Western allies); Geneva (for arms control talks); and Rome (the NATO Defense College).

INDEX

www.ingramcontent.com/pod-product-compliance
Lightning Source LLC
Chambersburg PA
CBHW030913270326
41929CB00008B/678